CALL OF DUTY®
BLACK OPS

SINGLE-PLAYER COVERAGE

MULTIPLAYER COVERAGE

INTRODUCTION

We hope you're ready for another exciting *Call of Duty* experience!

The *Call of Duty: Black Ops* single-player campaign offers a deep and complex storyline which takes place between the events of *World at War* and *Modern Warfare*. A direct sequel to *World at War*, the *Black Ops* story takes you across the globe as you fight with special operative teams in Cuba, Vietnam, and the Soviet Union.

Because *Call of Duty: Black Ops* features such an intense story, we've been extra careful to avoid any spoilers in either the training chapter or the campaign walkthrough. Feel free to use these chapters if you get stuck, need some tips, or want to track your Intel and game progress without spoiling your experience.

When you've completed your campaign, check out the Secrets chapter for full reveals of the plethora of unlockable extras available to you. The Secrets chapter *does* contain story spoilers, so save it for after you complete the single-player campaign in order to enjoy its compelling plot fully.

If this is your first *Call of Duty* game, we've got you covered. Start with the Specialized Training chapter, and we'll tell you everything you need to survive, even on the harder difficulties.

This section of the guide is spoiler-free, and it's primarily aimed at players new to the *Call of Duty* franchise, or players who want a refresher on game basics. Here we cover basic tactics that can help you survive any tactical scenario in the field.

THE BARE BASICS

Call of Duty: Black Ops, like all other *Call of Duty* games, is a first-person shooter (FPS). This means you play most of the game looking through the eyes of the main character as he fights his way through the campaign's many scenarios.

This section of the guide is for users new to first-person shooters, or those who haven't played an FPS in a few years.

Controls

Throughout the guide, we refer to the basic controls by the official name of the command (Fire, Aim Down Sight, Melee, Interact, etc.). To determine which controls are bound to which buttons on your system of choice, refer to your user manual or the game's Options Menu.

The game doesn't have an official tutorial, but the onscreen prompts found throughout should give you hints on how to handle any new situations.

Basic Loadout

In the *Call of Duty: Black Ops* campaign, you can carry two weapons (no matter how large the weapons are) and two grenade types. Within the campaign, you don't get to pick the types of grenades you carry, but the tactical grenades are tailored to each mission.

You also carry a knife that you can deploy at any time via the Melee button. Some campaign sequences introduce you to special weapons beyond the primary and secondary weapons in your loadout.

Firing from the Hip

When you equip a firearm in *Call of Duty: Black Ops*, a crosshair appears in the middle of the screen. This crosshair represents the spread of your weapon if you "fire from the hip," which means simply to shoot your gun without targeting it.

While firing from the hip is less accurate than aiming down the sights, and it's generally not the best way to kill enemies, it does have its purpose. Short-range guns like SMGs and shotguns actually work quite well firing from the hip. If an enemy surprises you at close range, it's much better to fire from the hip rather than carefully try to aim.

The only time you should never fire from the hip is when you are equipped with a sniper rifle or rifle. These weapons are completely inaccurate from the hip, and it's better to switch to your alternate weapon rather than try for a blind rifle shot.

Aim Down Sight

Most of the time, you should fire your weapon while holding the Aim Down Sight button. This gives you a realistic view of your weapon as your character's eye lines up with its sights.

As mentioned in the previous section, Aiming Down Sight is generally not necessary for short-range weapons, but doing so can increase the range and accuracy of SMGs and shotguns.

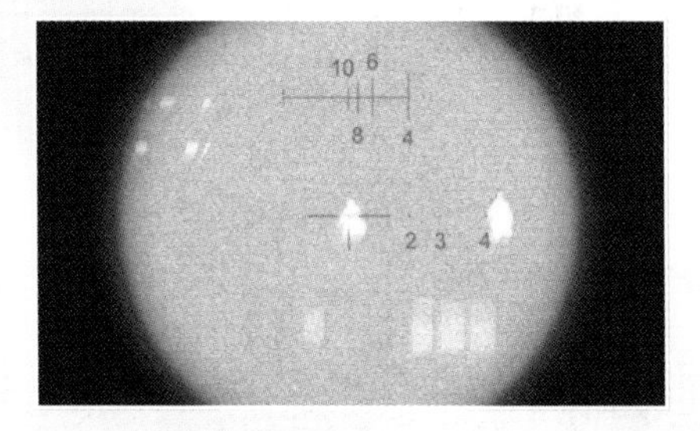

Aiming Down Sight automatically triggers sniper mode if you're using a weapon with a long-range sight, like a Dragunov sniper rifle.

Cover

Cover is a vital concept in *Call of Duty: Black Ops*, and we refer to finding cover frequently in the walkthrough. Cover is simply any obstacle that you can put between yourself and the enemies to get some level of protection from their incoming fire.

Whenever you encounter enemies, you should try to find and move to cover before returning fire on the enemies. Trying to take them down in the open frequently results in death on the harder difficulty settings.

Stances

There are three stances in *Call of Duty: Black Ops*: crouched, prone, and standing.

Standing:
This is your regular stance. It offers no increase to your firing accuracy, but it allows you to move quickly. You must be standing to Sprint.

Prone:
In the prone position, you are crawling on the ground. This makes you a difficult target for your enemy, and it dramatically increases your firing accuracy. When you get caught in bad situations, going prone is often a good tactic to reduce the visual target you present to the enemy. It is very difficult to move while you're prone; you move at an extremely slow speed.

Crouched:
Crouching is a happy medium between the standing and prone positions. We recommend crouching when you advance forward in an area with an enemy presence.

Health

Health in *Call of Duty: Black Ops* is represented by actual damage that you see onscreen.

Generally, if you take hits beyond a graze, you should find cover and wait a few seconds for your health to restore.

Light Hit

Heavy Hit

Get to Cover!

Melee Attacks

As long as your character is not in a vehicle, you always have access to melee attacks. Melee is extremely deadly and almost always delivers a one-hit kill. However, the enemy must be directly in front of you for the melee to actually hit him. Reserve melee for when you sneak up on an enemy from behind, or for desperate close-range combat situations.

Grenades

Grenades are your most common tactical tool in *Call of Duty: Black Ops*. There are two basic types of grenades: frag and tactical. While the primary use for frag grenades is to blow your enemies to pieces, they also have a tactical purpose.

When you throw a frag grenade at enemies behind cover, they run from the grenade and out from cover. While they may escape your grenade's blast, you can pick them off with your rifle.

When you throw a frag grenade, you should always "cook" it first. To do this, simply hold the Frag Grenade button until you see your crosshair pulse onscreen. Throw the grenade when you see roughly two or three pulses to reduce the amount of time between your release and the grenade detonating.

Most tactical grenades in the *Call of Duty: Black Ops* campaign are flashbangs. Flashbang grenades stun enemies in a large radius, causing them to stumble out of cover and making them completely helpless.

Be careful, though—it's easy to stun yourself with your own flashbang. Make sure you look behind cover whenever one of your own flashbangs detonates.

GRENADE INDICATORS

Grenades can be very hard to see, so *Call of Duty: Black Ops* puts a grenade icon on your screen to help you locate a live grenade on the battlefield. Whenever you see a grenade icon, you have to make a split-second decision:

Run Away:
If you aren't sure exactly where the grenade is based on the indicator, your best option is to run away. Press the Sprint button and dash to another area, but be careful about leaving cover.

Throw the Grenade Back:
If you find the grenade quickly enough, you can move toward it to make a special icon appear onscreen. When it does, hold the Grenade button to toss it back at the enemy. Be careful; sometimes enemies cooks their grenades, particularly on harder difficulties.

Sprint Jumping

You are required to Sprint Jump at different points in the campaign. To do this, hold the Sprint Button while you're moving. When you get to an edge, hold the Jump button to add extra distance to your jump. This also makes you a harder target to hit and is a decent evasive maneuver.

Sprint Diving

A new feature in *Call of Duty: Black Ops* is the ability to Sprint Dive. To Sprint Dive, Sprint as normal, and then *hold* the Crouch button. This causes you to dive forward, making you a very difficult target for your enemies.

Weapons

Weapons are the tools of your success in *Call of Duty: Black Ops*, and knowing how to handle them is vital.

Each weapon has its own specific attributes, including accuracy, penetration power, damage, rate of fire, reload time, and weight. Weapons within the same class tend to share similar attributes.

ASSAULT RIFLES

Assault rifles deliver high damage, they're highly accurate at mid to long range, and they generally have mid-sized clips. You can fire assault rifles from the hip (without pressing the Aim Down Sight button), but they are somewhat less effective in this role. Due to their versatility, assault rifles are often your primary weapon on campaign missions.

SUBMACHINE GUNS

Submachine guns, or SMGs, are close-range combat weapons. You can squeeze some extra range out of them with a decent sight, such as the Reflex, but they cannot replace an assault rifle. SMGs have extremely high rates of fire and very quick reload times.

You can also find dual SMGs on some missions of the single-player game. Fire the left SMG by holding the Aim Down Sight button. Dual SMGs cannot be modded.

RIFLES

Rifles are single-fire, long-range weapons. Rifles are practically useless fired from the hip, but they are deadly at long range.

Additionally, rifles can have sniper scopes attached to them. These scopes allow you to pick off enemies at incredible distances. This allows you to kill enemies before you get within their firing range, making rifles great tactical weapons for strategic players.

PISTOLS

Pistols aren't exactly the most effective weapons in *Call of Duty: Black Ops*. When you use a pistol, it's often your last option thanks to an event that prohibits your customary loadout. Don't discount them completely, though. The Python and other high-caliber weapons can be very effective at short range, ripping through your enemies with high-damage rounds.

SHOTGUNS

Shotguns are an old favorite. Each shotgun has its own personality, and you should try each one before you bring it into combat. Some shotguns, like the KS-23, have moderate range, but most are good only at short-range.

All shotguns in the single-player campaign have lengthy reload times, but that's a minor tradeoff for the extreme damage they inflict on enemies in tight spaces.

Weapon Mods

The weapons you find in the field during a campaign mission usually feature some type of modification, or mod. These mods give found weapons an added edge or enhancement to your combat style as you sift through the weapons of your fallen enemies.

Here are the types of mods you can find on your weapons and what they do:

Dual Mag:
This mod halves your weapon's reload speed.

Extended Mag:
This mod increases your weapon's clip size by about 25%.

Suppressor:
This mod makes your weapon silent.

ACOG Sight:
The ACOG sight is a medium- to long-range sight that allows you to pick off enemies from afar, but doesn't cut off your field of view. It's great in almost all tactical situations.

Reflex Sight:
The Reflex Sight is an optic that makes aiming your short- and medium-range weapons easier.

Red Dot Sight:
The Red Dot Sight is perfect for short- to medium-range weapons. It increases your weapon's accuracy by a moderate amount.

Infrared Scope:
The Infrared Scope displays a black-and-white image. Enemies (and friends) are outlined in white, making it easy to see targets in any combat condition: nighttime, in fog, through smoke, and so forth.

Masterkey:
The Masterkey is a shotgun attachment for assault rifles.

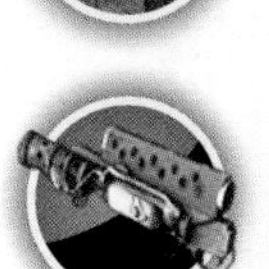

Flamethrower:
The Flamethrower attachment is available only for the AK-47 assault rifle.

Grenade Launcher:
Grenade Launcher attachments are available for most assault rifles, and they're fantastic for blowing enemies out of cover. If a grenade fired by a launcher is smothered, it may not explode.

Swimming

Swimming should come naturally if you've played other FPS games in the past. Use your Analog and Movement to move around in the water. You can freely move up and down while swimming.

You cannot use your weapons underwater in *Call of Duty: Black Ops.*

Breaching

Several points in the campaign require you to breach a doorway. When you breach, you temporarily yield control of your character's movement, allowing you to focus entirely on shooting your weapon.

When a breach event starts, the game enters slow motion, giving you more time to make a shot against an enemy in the next room.

Planting Explosives

Several points in the campaign require you to plant explosives. To do this, move to your objective marker and press the Interact button. Take a few steps back and trigger the activator switch to blow the explosives.

Guided Missiles

The Black Ops team in the campaign frequently employs player-controlled missiles. After you fire one of these special missiles (classified as TOW and Valkyrie), you control its movement in first-person mode.

Guide the missile into your targets to inflict massive damage.

GAME DIFFICULTY

When you first start your game, you can select the difficulty on which you want to play.

RECRUIT

If you are here for the story and cinematic experience, we recommend the Recruit difficulty. You run into only a few challenging situations during your playthrough.

REGULAR

The default difficulty is for the average player that wants some challenge, but doesn't want to run into anything too overwhelming. This is a good balance for a first playthrough.

HARDENED

This is the ideal difficulty for veterans of the FPS genre. You will be challenged throughout the game, and you'll have to use cover tactics to survive. The enemy AI is more dangerous and more likely to throw grenades.

VETERAN

This difficulty is reserved for masochists and achievement-hunters. The enemies are absolutely brutal, deadly accurate, and you have very little health. If you've completed Veteran playthroughs on previous *Call of Duty* games, you should find the enemies here a bit easier than *World at War* and about par with *Modern Warfare 2.*

This guide's walkthrough focuses on the Hardened difficulty setting. This doesn't affect the basic gameplay and strategy, but you may breeze through a section that we belabor if you're playing on an easier setting.

If you're playing on Veteran, you can still use our strategies, but you have to be extra patient and especially wary of enemy grenades.

LOWER DIFFICULTY OPTION

To get the most out of *Call of Duty: Black Ops*, we suggest you challenge yourself with at least the Regular difficulty. If you find yourself getting frustrated in a tough spot, remember that the game doesn't get progressively harder; some of the hardest spots are in the early levels. If you *really* get stuck, you can always use the Lower Difficulty option in the Pause Menu. This great feature allows you to soften the enemies without interrupting your playthrough.

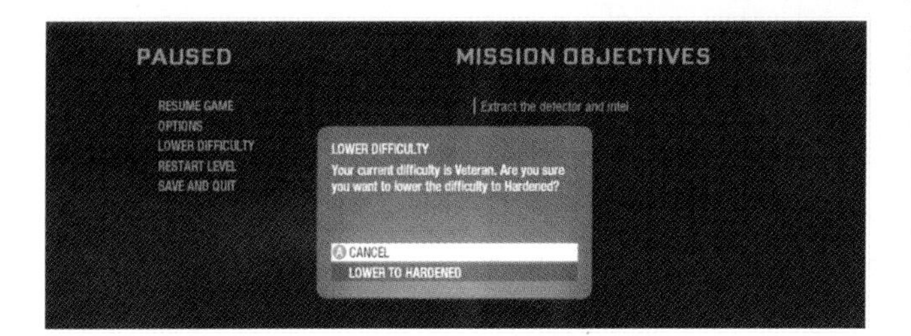

THE LOWER VIOLENCE SETTING

When you first start a new *Call of Duty: Black Ops* campaign, you are given the option to turn down the violence. *Call of Duty: Black Ops* is an extremely gory and violent game that features close-up kills, executions, and torture. If you are at all squeamish, we recommend you turn down the violence.

If you decide the game's violence is too much for you, you can always exit the campaign and toggle the setting in the game's Option Menu under the "Graphic Content" setting.

GENERAL TIPS

Subtitles

Consider turning on Subtitles via the Main Menu. This allows you to receive your commanding officer's orders even in the heat of an intense gunfight.

Reloading

Timing a reload is very important. If you get caught in the middle of a long reload, you can perish as the enemy pummels you with fire. Knowing when to reload is a crucial skill to learn for both single-player and multiplayer. Keep an eye on your ammo count in the bottom-right of your HUD. When your ammo counter is low, look around for cover to protect you from enemy fire.

The AI in *Call of Duty: Black Ops* tends to wait for you to reload before popping out of cover. This is especially true on harder difficulties. Sometimes an area you think is clear might have several enemies waiting for you to give them an opening. Be sure to find cover whenever you reload in a dangerous area.

Red Barrels

You frequently encounter red barrels in battle. These are filled with explosive materials that you can detonate by shooting the barrel. Whenever you see these barrels amongst a group of foes, detonate them to soften up enemy resistance. Oh, and don't take cover behind them.

Weapon Penetration

Most weapons, but particularly assault rifles, have good weapon penetration. This means you can fire your weapon through soft objects like wood crates and plaster walls and still hit the enemy. Use this tactic to your advantage when enemies are using cover.

Often, if you hit the very edge of a wall made of a hard substance, such as concrete or brick, you can use weapon penetration to kill or injure the enemy in cover.

Critical Shots

Always aim for an enemy's upper body. While headshots are ideal, they aren't always possible due to your foe's distance, whether it be unusually close or far.

Aim for the upper torso to score a critical hit and likely down the enemy with any weapon.

Short Bursts

Firing your weapons in short bursts is essential to maintain maximum accuracy. This has the added benefit of conserving your ammo, which can be a lifesaver on longer levels.

Downed (But Not Out) Enemies

Enemies in *Call of Duty: Black Ops* are a crafty lot. Just because a foe is knocked to the ground, it doesn't necessarily mean he's out of the fight. Enemies that are still up on one elbow can attack you with their sidearms.

Be sure to end their rally quickly by firing extra shots into them from a distance.

Sprinting and Melee Attacks Interrupt Your Reload

Some guns take a very long time to reload. Avoid interrupting the process with a Sprint or a melee attack while the reload plays out.

That's it for now—let's get to the action!

SINGLE-PLAYER WALKTHROUGH

OPERATION 40

0500 April 17, 1961
Undertake a daring assassination attempt during the Bay of Pigs invasion.

ALEX MASON

SUPPORT

TRANSMISSION# 15-18.
Designate: X-RAY
Location: Cayo Santa Maria, Cuba
Target: Fidel Castro

"WAKE UP... WAKE UP!"

The campaign takes place through an extended series of flashbacks as the main character, Mason, is interrogated by an unknown man.

The first memory takes you to a smoke-filled bar in Cuba, 1961.

IMPROVISED OUTFITTING

Black Ops specialists use the weapons they find in the battlefield, and rarely start a mission fully equipped.

"WE GOT COMPANY."

After the bartender outlines your route to your mission objective, your team is made by local security forces—your cover is blown. Check your aim, and take out the soldier with the jammed gun.

The M16, the weapon with which you start this mission, is incredibly versatile. It fires deadly rounds at medium to long range.

In a pinch, it can be used to "spray and pray" a close-up target, but you should start looking for a short-range weapon to replace your pistol as you escape the city.

WEAPON: M16

Clip Size	30
Range	Medium to Long Range
Weapon Type	Assault Rifle

The M16 is also equipped with a Grenade Launcher attachment, which you can activate by pressing left on the D-Pad. You also start with ten grenades, which is a lot—use them freely throughout the level.

Hitting targets accurately with the Grenade Launcher attachment takes some practice. Be aware that, unlike bullets, Grenades follow an arcing trajectory as they're lobbed from the muzzle. If you hit an enemy directly with one, the impact usually causes an instant kill, but it also prevents the grenade from exploding.

After the bartender tosses you an M16, move to the window and wait for the signal from Woods, your team leader.

OBJECTIVE Escape the Police

When the door opens, provide cover as Woods advances on the police car. Using the M16, fire into the front of the car to detonate it, taking out the nearby police.

Your team detonates a second car as it hurtles down the street. Stay behind Woods, move to a crouched position, and advance up the street.

In this section, it's important to use objects on the street for cover as hordes of police reinforcements respond to the locals' call for help.

Take your time as you advanced down the street. Be very careful not to get ahead of Woods—if you do, you're vulnerable to fire from multiple directions.

"GET TO THE ALLEY!"

About halfway up the street, two cars drive past your squad. Quickly turn to face these vehicles where they stop; fire a grenade to destroy them both.

As you move up the street, it isn't long before police completely overwhelm your team. A line of police cars forms a deadly roadblock at the end of the street.

OBJECTIVE Get Off the Streets

Follow Woods into the alley on the left to the running car. When you reach the car, move toward it to get into the driver's seat automatically. You don't have many options here—follow the onscreen instructions to back out of the alley and escape through the roadblock.

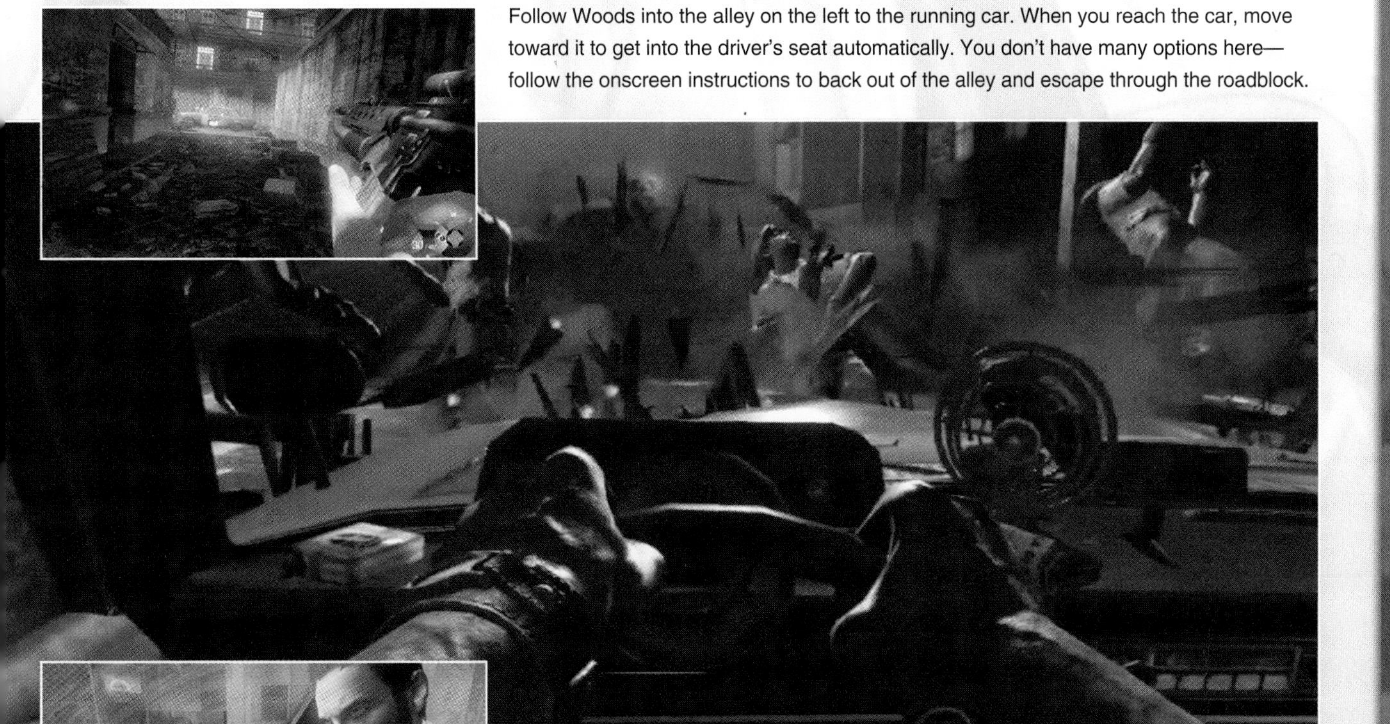

"THERE'S THE COMPOUND..."

After a brief return to the interrogation chair, you flash to a mountainside locale overlooking a large compound. This mission takes place shortly after the previous car escape, so your weapons—including your remaining Grenade Launcher ammo—carry over.

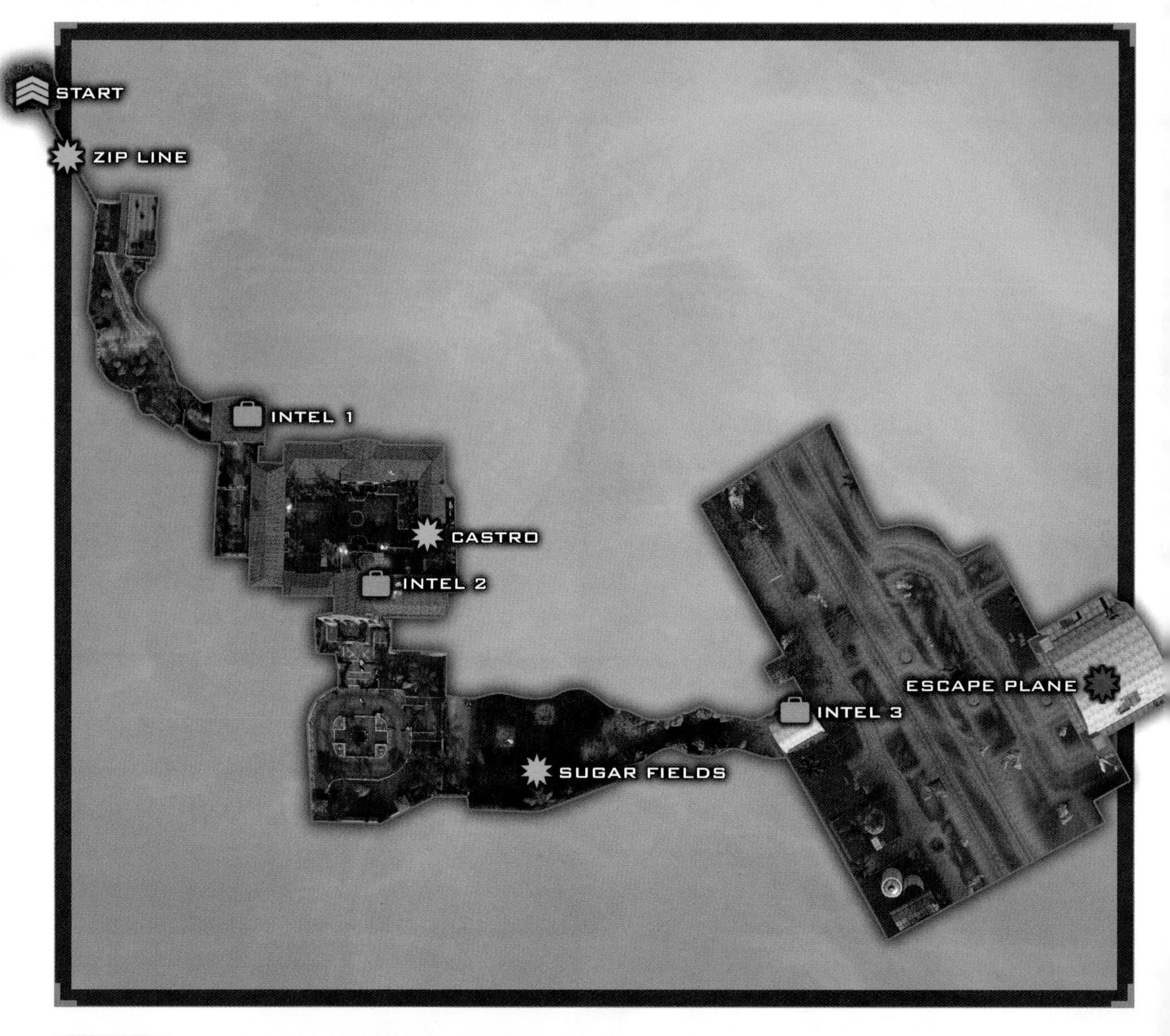

OBJECTIVE Use Zipline to Infiltrate Compound

After your advance team sets off a flare, follow Woods down the zipline by moving behind him and holding the Interact button.

OBJECTIVE Find and Kill Castro

All channels are go on your mission to kill Castro. Bowman and Woods have point as you begin your advance into Castro's compound.

The soldier that Woods lands on is carrying an FN FAL, which is an adequate weapon to switch out for your pistol temporarily.

Follow the team inside the nearby building, and move behind the soldier talking on the radio. Press the Melee button to kill the enemy silently.

"SIT TIGHT, DO NOT ENGAGE"

Your allies have created a major distraction on a nearby airfield, and the bulk of the compound's forces are headed that way. Wait with Woods as the enemies pass your location. If you fire on the troops or try to cross the street before Woods gives the order to cross, you fail the mission instantly.

When Woods gives the order, cross the street toward the next compound building.

Two soldiers emerge from a vehicle on your right; take them out, and more soldiers advance from the stairs above. Shoot them before you search the nearby building.

Before you follow your team up the stairs, you can search the building for a Skorpion with Supressor attachment, a Skorpion with Extended Mag, an FN FAL with ACOG Scope, and a RPK with ACOG scope. The soldiers are armed with more weapons, including a KS-23 Shotgun.

The Skorpion is a great close-range weapon and our recommended companion for your primary M16 weapon. Take the Extended Mag version, because the Suppressor is useless in this area. Alternatively, you can try out the KS-23 Shotgun if you're a fan of the weapon type.

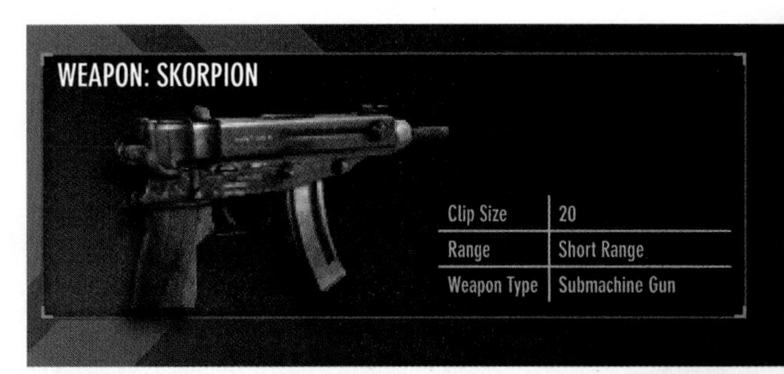

WEAPON: SKORPION

Clip Size	20
Range	Short Range
Weapon Type	Submachine Gun

It's best to use the Skorpion in close-quarters combat to riddle a nearby target with its tremendous rate of fire. Be warned—the Skorpion can empty a regular clip in less than five seconds, so it demands frequent reloading.

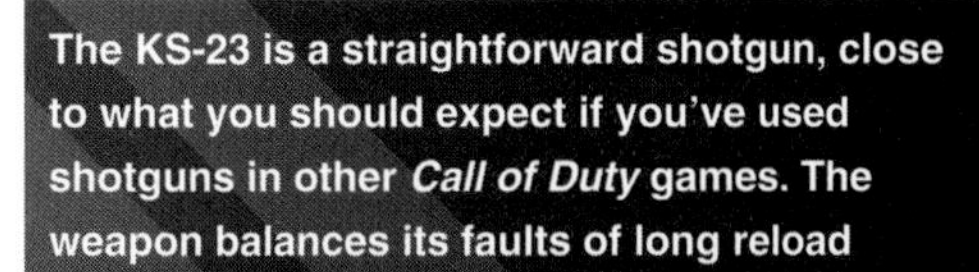

The KS-23 is a straightforward shotgun, close to what you should expect if you've used shotguns in other *Call of Duty* games. The weapon balances its faults of long reload time and slow firing rate with its virtue of extreme damage at close range. One well-placed shotgun blast can take out three soldiers at once!

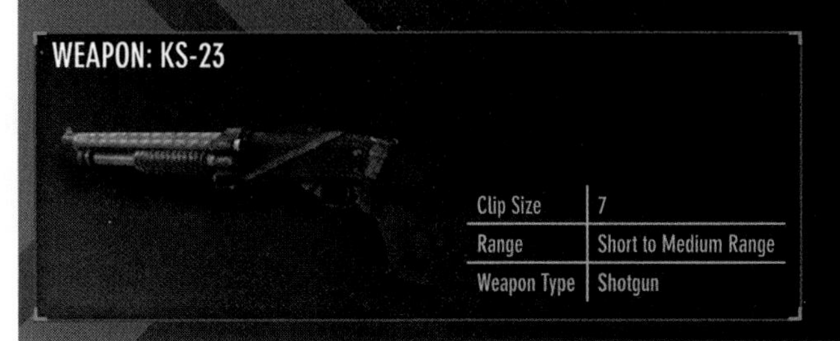

WEAPON: KS-23

Clip Size	7
Range	Short to Medium Range
Weapon Type	Shotgun

One of the KS-23's advantages is its extra range over most other shotguns. You can pick off enemies with it from a good 50 feet away if you take careful aim looking down the barrel.

"CASTRO'S PARANOID...WITH GOOD REASON."

At the top of the stairs, wait for Bowman and Woods to go through the door, but follow close behind. Provide fire support against the attacking enemies, and proceed out to the open area.

More soldiers attack your team through the stone archway ahead. Find cover behind a nearby concrete barrier, and use your M16 to take them out.

Just before the archway, more Grenade Launcher-enabled M16 assault rifles rest against some crates to your right. These guns do not possess the scope that your default M16 has.

INTEL

Look on the wall on the room's opposite side for your first piece of Intel. It's just above an RPG leaning against a crate.

"INSIDE, GO!"

Before you proceed inside to the next building, switch to your close-range weapon. As you move in, watch out for enemies on your right.

Now your job is to search the entire mansion until you find Castro. Unfortunately, the building is crawling with enemies, and a tough room-to-room fight awaits you.

Stay low and advance with Woods. Use your close-range weapon to kill enemies as they pop out from surrounding doorways and fixtures.

ALTERNATE ROUTE

Instead of advancing through the hallways with Woods, you can move through the door on your left. This allows you to flank some of the enemies defending the compound.

Castro has spared no expense decorating his manor, providing plenty of expensive objects to use for cover as you move through the villa. Remember that your M16 can shoot through penetrable objects such as furniture if enemies take cover behind them.

FRAG OUT

You should've picked up some grenades by this point. Toss some of these babies to clear out enemies holed up in entrenched firing positions.

"OKAY, STACK UP."

When you reach the large double doors at the end of the hallway, Woods readies for a breach. Move in behind him to activate your first breach event.

BREACH

Use any gun except the shotgun for this breach—the shotgun is too slow.

There are three enemies to worry about. Shoot the middle guy first, before he can dive behind the sofa. Follow up with the guy on the left, because he has a clear shot at you. You have a few moments before you need to worry about the advancing soldier to the right.

The room contains more FAL and RPK weapons. Now move behind Woods again to activate your second breach.

BREACH

This breach has you firing on Castro while he holds a hostage. It's imperative that you aim carefully with your pistol. If your shot hits the prostitute without also killing Castro, he will fire and kill you.

To end the breach, use your pistol to shoot Castro in the head or hand.

DEATH TO DICTATORS 

Score a headshot on Castro in this second breach to earn this Achievement/Trophy. You know you triggered it correctly if a slow-motion mini-cinema plays during the headshot.

"THEY GOT HALF THE CUBAN ARMY DOWN HERE."

OBJECTIVE Escape Compound

With your mission complete, you must now execute the escape plan. Unfortunately, most of the Cuban forces have moved to the airfield, and that's your primary route for escape.

Follow Woods into the next building to rendezvous with Bowman. This next area requires you to engage the enemy at medium range, so it's a good idea to switch to the M16. You should have some grenades left in the launcher, so feel free to use them here to soften up any enemies blocking your escape.

This is the first truly challenging part of the level. The enemies can be very hard to see through the debris, and they have deadly accuracy with their long-range weapons. Rather than advancing with Woods and Bowman, stay far back, behind cover, and use your M16 to pick off enemies from a distance by aiming down your sights.

Watch out for further reinforcements from the double doors at the other end of the room. Also, beware of some stragglers that may arrive late from the mansion entrance below.

INTEL

A bedroom is on the right side of this extended hallway (the side through which Bowman breaches). You can find the second Intel piece on the dresser. Be sure you grab this before you descend the master staircase.

Follow your squad down the stairs, but be careful of the additional enemies that may be defending the doorway outside.

"WE'RE PINNED DOWN HERE!"

Outside, a large number of Cuban forces have arrived on transport trucks. A .50cal heavy machinegun on one of the trucks tears into your position.

OBJECTIVE Get to the Airfield

An RPG is directly ahead, next to the left set of sandbags. Swap out your short-range weapon for the RPG. Use the RPG to blow up the truck on which the .50 cal is mounted. If you have extra rockets, use them to destroy other nearby trucks and several soldiers with them.

WEAPON: RPG

Clip Size	N/A
Range	Long Range
Weapon Type	Rocket Launcher

While the RPG is powerful, it is notoriously inaccurate. Successfully hitting your targets from a distance requires some practice. When you fire the RPG, try to aim lower than where you want the rocket to go.

When you run out of RPGs, switch back to the Grenade Launcher, using any leftover rounds to clear the courtyard of enemies.

Stay behind the first line of cover, crouch down, and use your M16 to pick off remaining Cuban soldiers. Shortly, your ally Carlos arrives at the east wall, unleashing rockets to devastate the nearby Cuban forces.

"YOU THINK I'D LET YOU DOWN, WOODS?!"

Woods orders you forward, but don't rush up quite yet—an enemy armored assault vehicle arrives on the left side of the battlefield. Wait for Carlos' troops to destroy the tank before you make your way past the fountain in the courtyard.

TAKING MATTERS INTO YOUR OWN HANDS

Instead of waiting for Carlos to blow the APC, you can use the RPG mentioned earlier to destroy the armored car upon its arrival.

Follow Woods and Bowman into the nearby sugar field. This field is enemy-free, but it soon leads back out over the airfield.

"BETTER GET DOWN THERE, HOOK UP."

OBJECTIVE Rappel Down into the Airfield

Hold the Interact button to rappel down to the airfield. Follow your team to the hangar ahead.

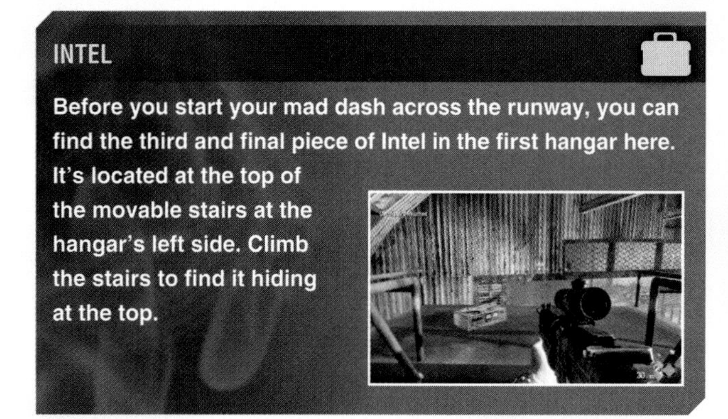

INTEL

Before you start your mad dash across the runway, you can find the third and final piece of Intel in the first hangar here. It's located at the top of the movable stairs at the hangar's left side. Climb the stairs to find it hiding at the top.

OBJECTIVE Get to the Plane

No time for complex strategy—use the Sprint button to keep up with Woods and Bowman as they dash across the field to reach your escape plane.

OBJECTIVE Protect the Plane from Damage

When you reach the plane, move to the rear to enter it automatically. You operate the plane's machine gun, and it's your job to defend the aircraft as it takes off.

"THEY'RE TRYING TO TAKE OUT OUR ENGINES!"

During this sequence, you get unlimited ammunition, and your gun can't overheat. Exploit this awesome power, aiming down your sight to direct fire onto the attacking enemies. Your primary targets should be any red barrels or nearby trucks you see. Both provide massive explosions that kill any surrounding soldiers.

When your plane turns up the runway to take off, a larger force of enemy weaponry lines the airfield. Prioritize the explosive fuel trucks and the enemy ZPUs.

ZPU

A ZPU is a soviet anti-aircraft gun. It fires rounds designed to take down vehicles. These are your biggest threat in this sequence.

Watch out for the RPG-wielders in the low airfield tower between the two ZPU positions.

If you make it to the end of the airfield, your teammates report that a line of vehicles has conspired to block the runway.

OBJECTIVE Use the ZPU to Clear the Runway

"MASON, ARE YOU CRAZY? THEY'LL CHEW YOU UP OUT THERE."

When you jump off the plane, sprint forward to the ZPU to mount it automatically. Fire on the gas trucks at the end of the runway to clear a path for your allies.

SACRIFICE

You automatically receive this Achievement/Trophy for completing this level.

VORKUTA

0600 October 6, 1963

ALEX MASON

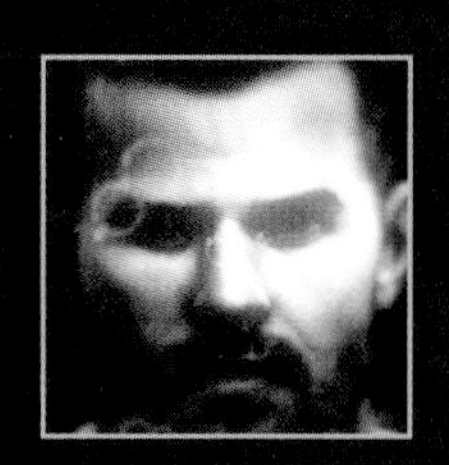

SUPPORT

TRANSMISSION# 9-19.

Designate: ROMEO
Location: Vorkuta Labor Camp, Komi Republic, U.S.S.R.
Objective: Escape Vorkuta!

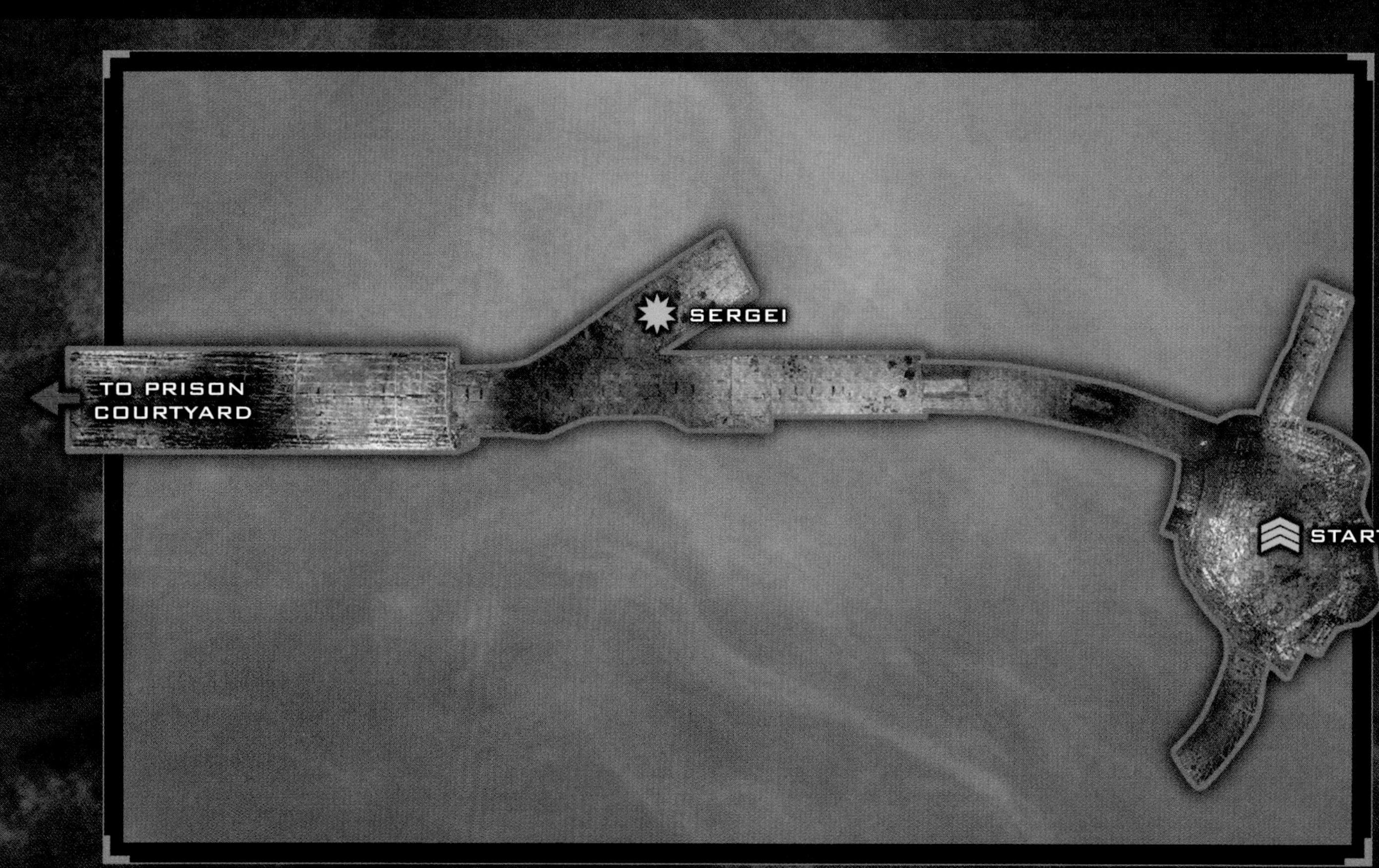

"YOU WILL BREAK, AMERICAN!"

This level starts with Mason in a brawl with a familiar face from *Call of Duty: World at War*.

The fight is a ruse. When you regain control of Mason, use the Melee button to crack the guard's head.

VIKTOR REZNOV

If you played *Call of Duty: World at War*, you may remember Reznov from the sniper level.

OBJECTIVE Step 1: Secure the Keys

ESCAPE

There are many steps to Reznov's escape plan, and each step is in a metaphorical code to prevent the guards from uncovering the plan before it's ready to hatch.

After Reznov's short speech, you are armed with an improvised knife (or "shiv"). Sprint after the other prisoners up the tunnel.

Follow Reznov and slice any guards that get in your way.

Soon you run into Sergei manhandling two prison guards. Wait for him to finish before you continue down the mining tunnel.

OBJECTIVE Step 2: Ascend from the Darkness

Join the prisoners on the tunnel elevator and listen in on Reznov's defense of your American citizenship.

After Sergei deals with a guard, look around for the Markov pistol on the ground before you proceed further into the mining complex. When the doors open, all chaos unleashes as the guards fire down onto the prisoners from above.

OBJECTIVE Step 3: Rain Fire

Wait for Reznov to sprint to the mine cart on the right. Follow closely and crouch behind the cart.

As Sergei and Reznov push the cart, use your pistol to fire on the enemies trying to flank your position on the left and right. At the end of the tracks, some prisoners use an improvised slingshot to blow up the guard tower and open the gate to the next section of the complex.

"NEVER LOSE FAITH, MY FRIENDS... NEVER!"

Follow Reznov up the path to the next door. It takes Sergei a while to tear down the metal door with his bare hands, so, in the meantime, follow Reznov up the guard tower's stairs.

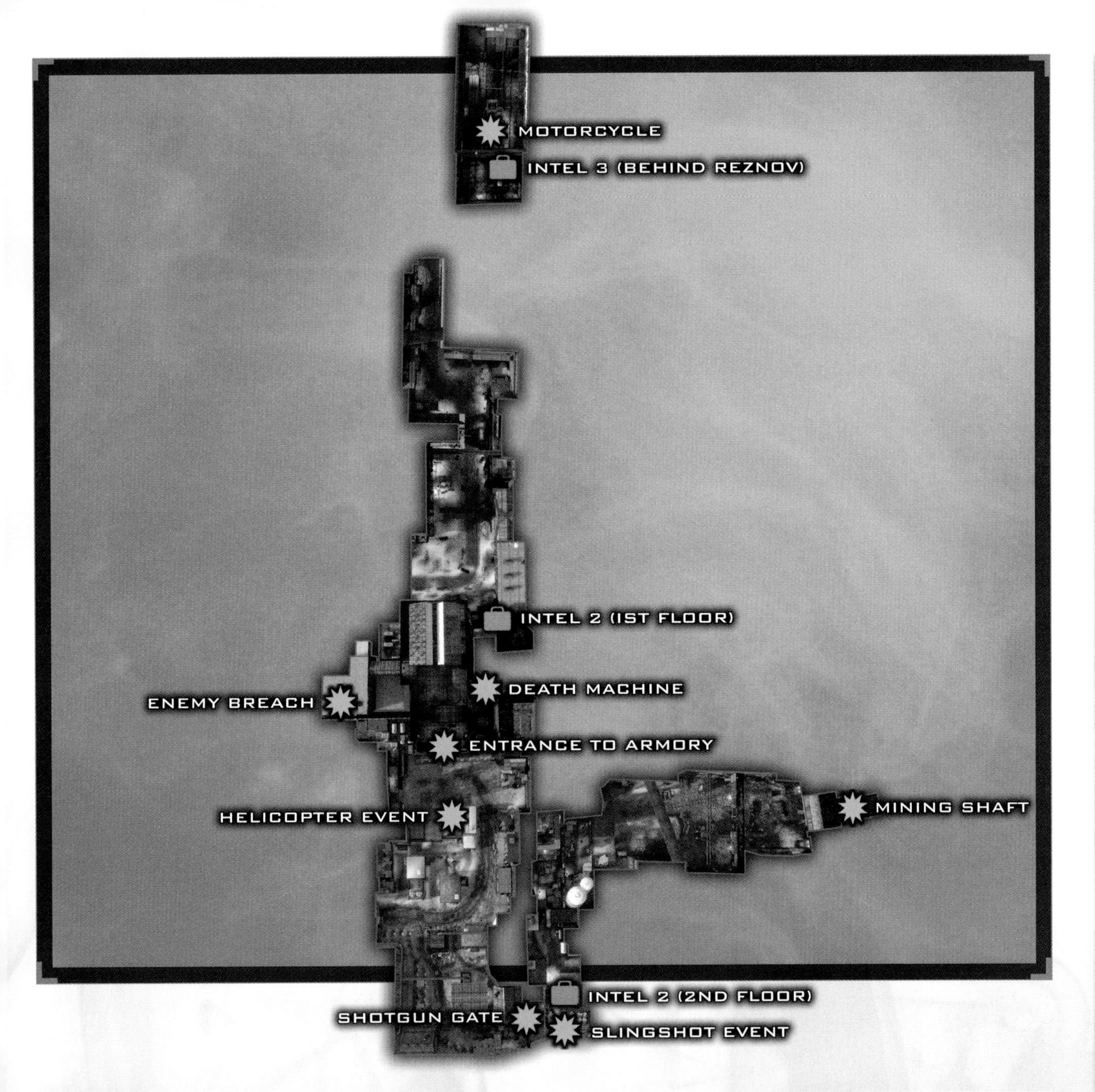

OBJECTIVE Step 4: Unleash the Horde

INTEL

When Reznov and Mason discuss Step 4 in the radio room, you can find the first piece of Intel sitting on a cabinet to the right of the radio.

After you discuss Step 4 with Reznov, proceed further up the tower. At the top, you find two prisoners armed with a makeshift slingshot. Your job is to fire flaming Molotovs into the surrounding buildings.

To fire the slingshot, pull back on the movement analog until you see the flaming cocktail at the bottom of the screen.

Aim just above the target you want to hit. Take out all three targets to complete your objective.

SLINGSHOT KID

To earn this Acheivement/Trophy, you must fire your slingshot perfectly: three bombs, three destroyed targets. The following screenshots depict exactly where you need to aim your bombs to hit their marks.

OBJECTIVE Get the Shotgun

Descend the stairs to discover Sergei has burst open the armament room. The shotguns on the ground here are the same kind you saw on the previous level in Cuba: the KS-23. Grab a shotgun and head back outside.

OBJECTIVE Shoot the Lock

Fire a shotgun shell into the lock to blow open the chain-link fence. Directly ahead, some guards emerge from the alley on the right. These guards carry AK-47s, which you should switch out for your pistol.

WEAPON: AK-47

Clip Size	30
Range	Medium to Long Range
Weapon Type	Assault Rifle

The AK-47 is the Soviet equivalent of the M16s you used in Cuba. It is an excellent medium- to long-range weapon and an ideal companion for the shotgun.

AK-47s can have Grenade Launcher attachments, and on some later levels, even a Flamethrower!

OBJECTIVE Step 5: Skewer the Winged Beast

Use your AK-47 to kill the guards defending the path to the compound's next area. As you round the first corner, an attack helicopter arrives. This is the "winged beast" in Reznov's code, and the task of taking it down falls to you.

For now, focus on the guards on the ground. Unload AK-47 ammunition into the truck sitting at the beginning of the next area until it explodes.

You can destroy another vehicle on the left to help clear out the enemies in that direction—blow it up the same way.

Be very careful of the helicopter flying overhead. If it starts to hit you, immediately return to cover.

When you've neutralized most of the enemies, sprint to the doorway marked by the objective marker. Reznov meets you inside; follow him up the stairs back outside.

"CHOOSE YOUR MOMENT."

The attack chopper is directly to your right. As you head outside, Mason automatically switches to his improvised harpoon gun. Carefully take aim at the chopper and fire to bring it down.

OBJECTIVE Get to the Armory

As you move into the armory, you pass through a crumbled wall. If you look around this area, you can find an AK-47 with a Grenade Launcher attachment. Switch to this weapon before you follow the other prisoners onward to the armory.

The enemies are holed up in here, so use your newfound Grenade Launcher to flush them out. Wait for Reznov to give the instructions to charge before you move forward behind him.

More enemies pour down the stairs. Stay behind cover and use your AK-47 to pick them off before they get too close.

Climb the stairs and switch back to the Grenade Launcher. Fire on the enemies trying to lock down the armory doors. Try to stay back, and use the staircase for cover. This keeps you out of the guards' weapon range.

Proceed forward when the enemies have stopped firing on you—hopefully before you exhaust your supply of grenades.

When you reach the end of the hall, you find Sergei holding open the closing armory door. Sprint to the door to slide underneath it automatically.

OBJECTIVE Deactivate the Security Door

As soon as the door closes behind you, sprint across the room to the glass-enclosed area. Crouch down and look for the button you must press to allow the rest of the prisoners into the room. Press the Interact button to complete the objective and get some relief from the fire overhead.

Wait for your fellow prisoners to enter the room and help clear it out. As you exit the enclosed area, watch for soldiers firing at you from above.

Follow Reznov upstairs, but keep an eye out for more enemies reinforcing the upper area.

OBJECTIVE Step 6: Wield a Fist of Iron

As you continue following Reznov, watch for more guards rappelling in from the glass ceiling above. Use your shotgun to dispose of them quickly before they get oriented and fire on you.

"THIS BLOWTORCH WILL SUIT OUR NEEDS."

As you continue through the armory, more soldiers arrive to breach the large garage door.

OBJECTIVE Protect Reznov

After the breach, a trio of heavily armored guards emerge from the smoke. Use your shotgun to debilitate them before they hurt you or Reznov.

When they're down, switch back to the AK-47 and fire at the soldiers on the rooftop behind you. More guards advance on you from the way you came. Kill them, and Reznov runs forward with his blowtorch.

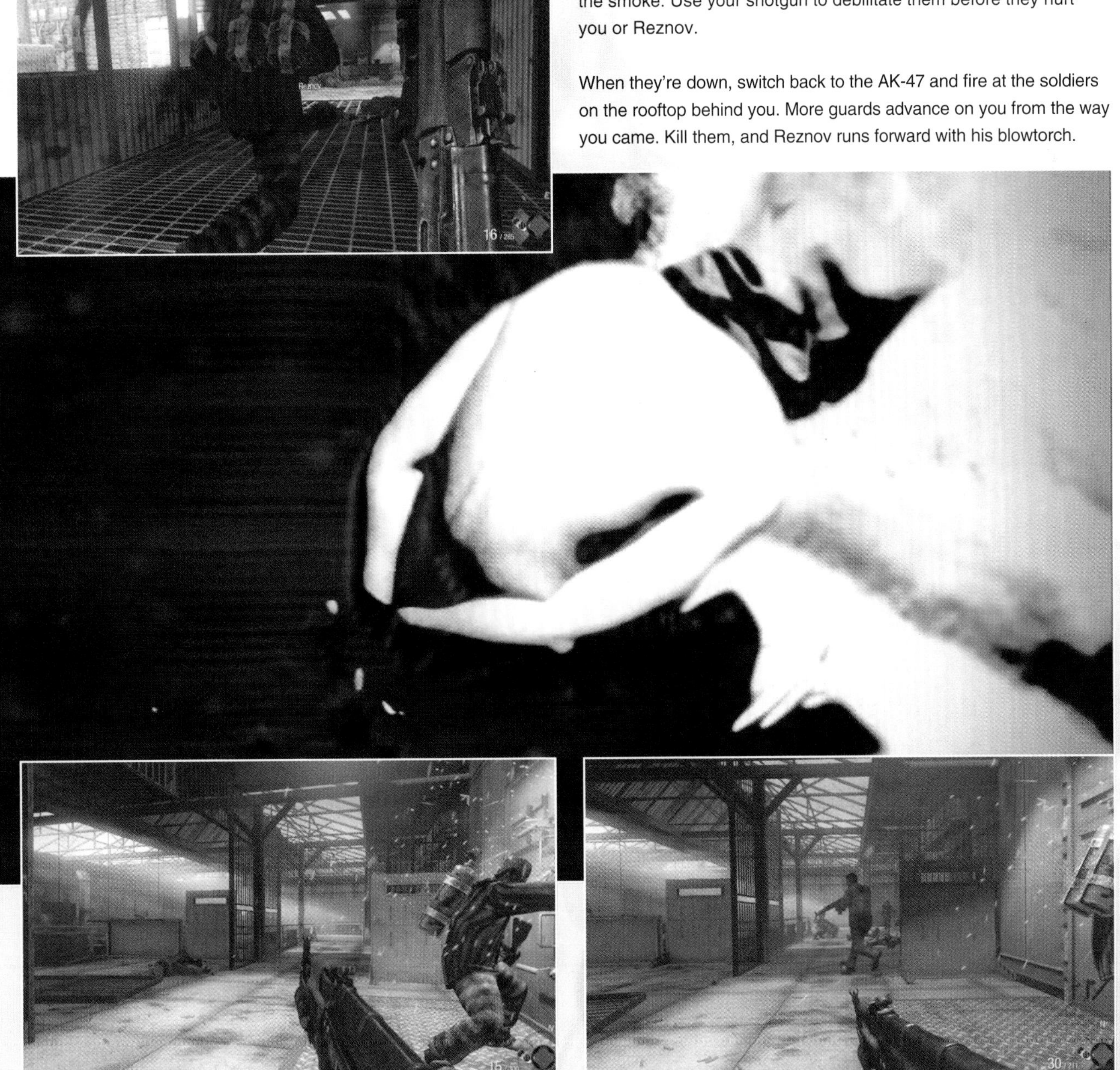

Watch Reznov's back as he uses the blowtorch to gain access to the armory. Guard reinforcements charge from the armory's lower area. Stay crouched behind Reznov and fire at them as they move up from below. After about a minute, Reznov finally breaks through the door.

OBJECTIVE Get Mingun

Head inside the armory and get the "Death Machine" sitting on a bench in the back.

OBJECTIVE Step 7: Raise Hell

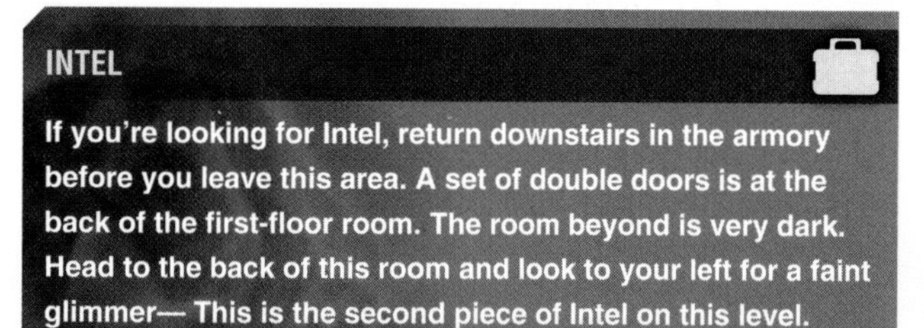

INTEL

If you're looking for Intel, return downstairs in the armory before you leave this area. A set of double doors is at the back of the first-floor room. The room beyond is very dark. Head to the back of this room and look to your left for a faint glimmer— This is the second piece of Intel on this level.

The Death Machine is a huge minigun with virtually unlimited ammo. It can kill enemies at any range and makes you virtually unstoppable.

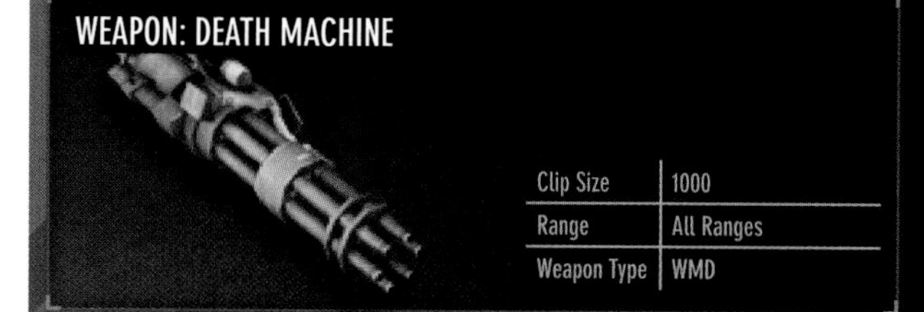

WEAPON: DEATH MACHINE

Clip Size	1000
Range	All Ranges
Weapon Type	WMD

While you move slowly and cannot sprint as you carry the weapon, you can quickly switch to your alternate weapon to increase your movement speed temporarily.

When you fire the minigun, there is a very slight delay while it spins up. You can circumvent this delay by holding the Aim Down Sight button, which keeps the gun's barrels spinning.

Your barrel can overheat if you fire the gun continuously. Avoid this by firing at enemies in bursts—this also conserves your ammo.

Follow the prisoners through the blown-out wall on the other side of the armory—Death Machine equipped. There may be some guards in the building still, so be careful as you move out; it's easy for them to get behind you.

Down below, several guards are near trucks. Use the minigun to demolish the trucks and their soldiers along with them.

Kill the guards emerging on the corrugated steel bridge above, and then lead your small army forward.

Watch for more enemies from both above and below as you move forward. Blow up the red barrels to decimate nearby enemies and stop any reinforcements from coming in that direction.

While you are extremely deadly with the minigun, you are not invincible. If enemies start to hit you, back up a bit and try to pinpoint their locations. Spin up the barrel and tap the Fire button a few times to kill them before you move forward.

As you turn the first corner, a transport truck arrives. Immediately blow it up by firing into the truck's engine.

Around the bend, more guards defend your last objective: the motorcycle warehouse. Kill them by detonating the trucks. Be sure to pick off any stragglers before you proceed down the corridor.

"THEY ARE USING TEAR GAS!"

As you walk down the corridor, a cloud of tear gas materializes, knocking you out.

INTEL

The last piece of Intel is hidden on a shelf behind Reznov in the warehouse. It is very hard to see in the darkness. If you have trouble finding it, you can turn up the brightness in the game or on your TV.

To find it, stand directly behind Reznov and walk forward. Halfway between Reznov and the yellow piece of machinery, turn left. The Intel is on the bottom shelf directly ahead.

When you awaken, move toward the motorcycle to mount it and begin your escape.

OBJECTIVE Step 8: Freedom

VEHICULAR SLAUGHTER

To earn the Vehicular Slaughter Achievement/Trophy, you must destroy all enemies on vehicles in this segment of the game. This is a tricky feat, and we've placed the details for earning it in the Achievements/Trophies chapter.

MOTORCYCLE HAVOC

Driving a motorcycle can be tricky at first, because you have to both drive and fire your weapon. Luckily, the shotgun you use in this segment has excellent range and a large burst radius.

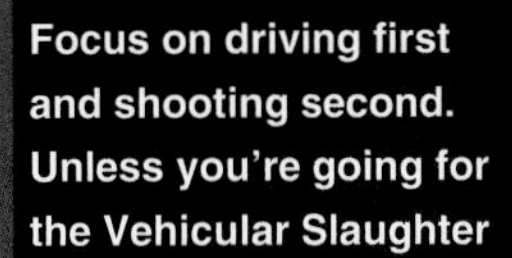

Focus on driving first and shooting second. Unless you're going for the Vehicular Slaughter Achievement/Trophy, only worry about enemies that get directly in front of you while you're driving.

To drive the motorcycle, hold the Fire button. There is no brake, but you can release the Fire button to slow down. Pressing the Aim Down Sight button fires the shotgun that Mason carries in his left hand.

"THEY'RE NOT LETTING US GO WITHOUT A FIGHT!"

When you get on the bike, accelerate to speed up the ramp and out of the warehouse. While enemies fire at you in this area, only the motorcycle-equipped ones are any threat, provided you keep moving.

No matter how fast you go, Reznov stays ahead of you, so it's a good idea to try to follow him as you speed to catch the train.

OBJECTIVE Jump on Truck

After you cross the riverbank, you get a flat tire. Drive into the transport truck ahead with the machinegun to board. Reznov takes care of the driver.

You know what to do once you're on the machine gun. Blow up the advancing troops and motorcycles as they approach your truck. Shortly, an opportunity to jump onto the train arises.

Successfully complete the jump to finish the level.

GIVE ME LIBERTY

You automatically receive this Achievement/Trophy for completing this level.

U.S.D.D.

1700 November 10, 1963

ALEX MASON

SUPPORT

TRANSMISSION# 0.

Designate:	ECHO
Location:	The Pentagon, Washington DC, USA
National Security Briefing:	Priority 1

"NOTHING LESS THAN OUR NATIONAL SECURITY IS AT STAKE."

U.S.D.D. is a briefing mission. While you can look around during the mission, you are not required to perform any actions.

To avoid spoiling some surprising revelations in the plot, we won't discuss the goings-on of this chapter.

VIP

You automatically earn this Achievement/Trophy at the end of this chapter on any difficulty setting.

U.S.D.D.

In case you're wondering, U.S.D.D. stands for United States Department of Defense, which is another name for the Pentagon.

EXECUTIVE ORDER

0700 November 17, 1963

ALEX MASON

SUPPORT

PRESIDENTIAL ORDER# 8-5.
Designate: ZULU
Location: Baikonur, Kazakhstan, U.S.S.R.
Intel confirms Dragovich and Ascension group on site.
Mission: Eliminate all threats with extreme prejudice.

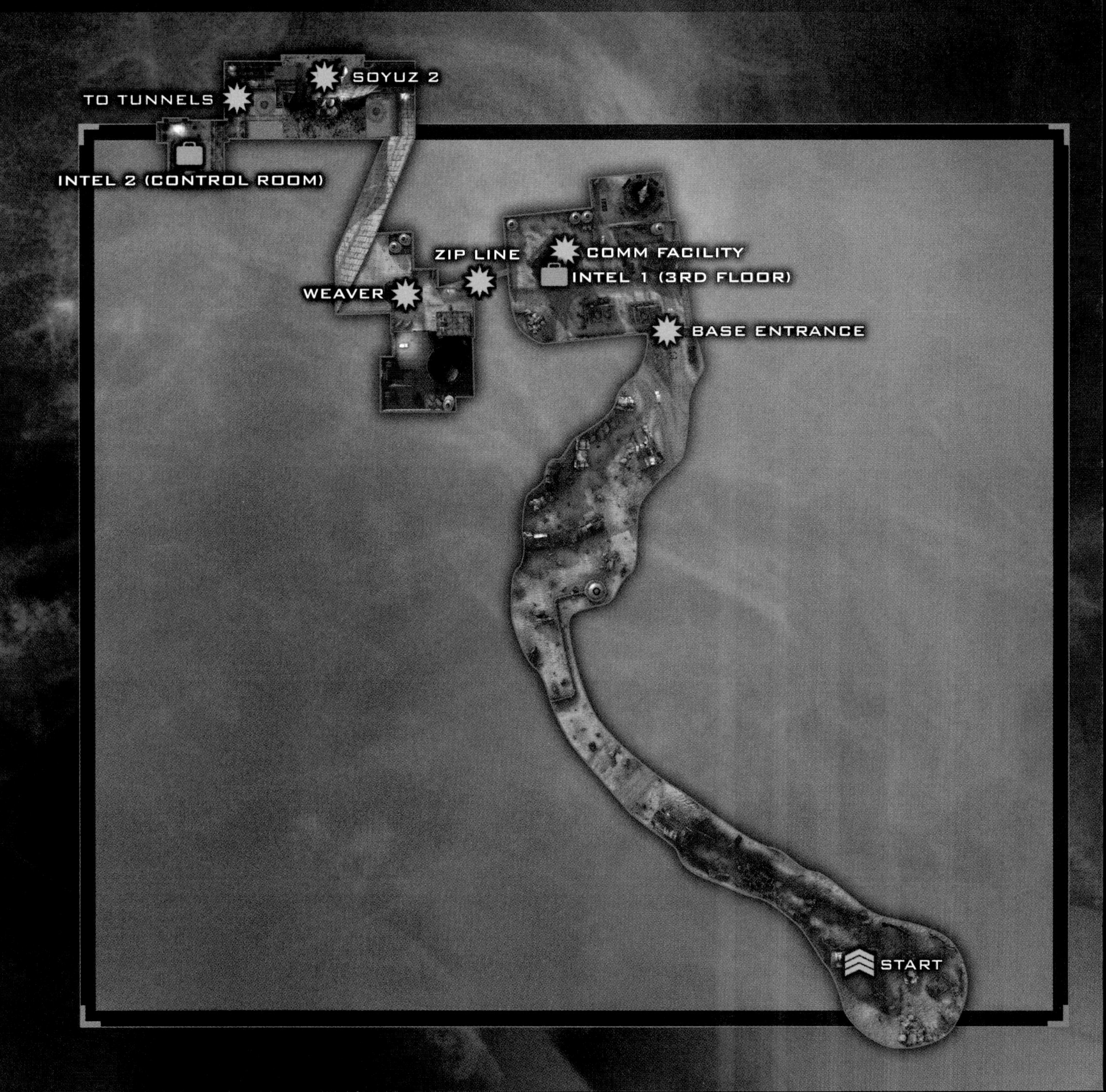

"STAY SHARP, MASON."

OBJECTIVE Infiltrate Baikonur Cosmodrome

In this mission, you have the same team you had in Cuba: Woods and Bowman. Your job is to demolish the Soviet rocket Soyuz 2 before it can take off.

The Colt Python .357 Magnum is an excellent sidearm, and it's your secondary starting weapon on this mission.

WEAPON: PYTHON

Clip Size	6
Range	Short to Medium
Weapon Type	Revolver

The revolver has only six shots, but it is extremely powerful, with a hit almost always resulting in a kill. While it isn't of much use early in the mission, when you go "weapons free" later on, it's a great backup weapon for medium- to short-range combat.

Start by following Woods through the rocket graveyard.

"THIS IS NOT GOOD."

At the top of the hill, a cinematic plays as Mason surveys the area.

After the cinematic, continue following Woods toward the rocket.

With the choppers overhead, you need to stay in cover. Run to the red pipe and listen closely to Woods' directions as he leads you through the area.

OBJECTIVE Stealth Kill Soldier

When Woods says you're good, follow him around the pipe and then hold the Jump button to hurdle the pipe, and follow him ahead. You need disguises; use your knife to sneak up on and kill the nearby enemies. Melee the guy on the left, and move the body to the nearby wreckage.

Now you are disguised as a Soviet soldier, which should make getting into the Cosmodrome a lot easier. Follow Woods' lead as he sneaks you past a couple of guards. When they're gone, sprint after him to rendezvous with Bowman.

Stay close to your teammates as you enter the base. When you get to the comms facility, let Brooks and Bowman subdue the guards.

"WE'VE BEEN MADE."

Because you had to use the AK-47 to complete your disguise, the better weapon here is your alternate Python pistol. Switch to the Python and get ready for Woods to open the door.

OBJECTIVE Clear Com Building

Unfortunately, you almost immediately blow your cover after the door opens. Get to work with your pistol, clearing out the few enemies on the bottom floor.

Watch for the additional reinforcements that come down from the staircase at the back of the room.

When you clear the area, move to crouching position and carefully climb the staircase. The second floor is filled with enemies ready for your advance. You can soften them up by tossing a grenade upward. Finish off any survivors with your Python or AK-47.

AN OLD FAVORITE

As in Vorkuta, the AK-47 with Grenade Launcher attachment is very useful on this level. You might find one on a guard if you search around. Attachments are random, so you don't always find the same loadouts on your enemies' weapons.

When the second floor is clear, continue up to the third. A few more enemies wait for you upstairs, but nothing worse than the second floor.

INTEL

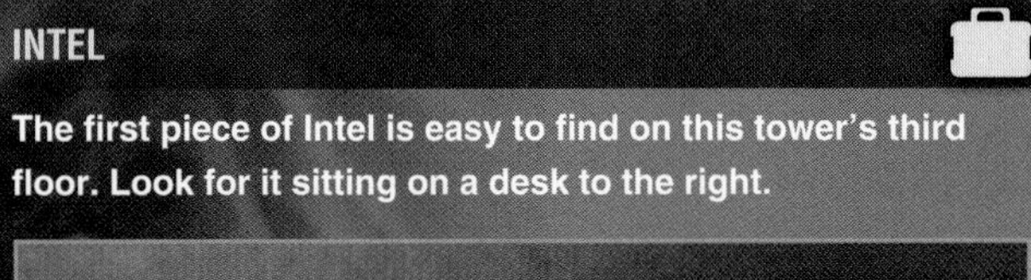

The first piece of Intel is easy to find on this tower's third floor. Look for it sitting on a desk to the right.

A ladder is on the other side of the room—climb it to reach the roof.

When you reach the top of the ladder, an enemy is directly ahead. Sprint forward and melee him before he spots you. Then turn to your right, picking off another soldier by the rail.

When the top floor is completely clear of enemies, you've completed your objective and can rest easy for a moment.

"CROSSBOW—EXPLOSIVE BOLTS. NOW!"

You can find Woods back where you climbed up the ladder. As you approach, he hands you a special Crossbow with Explosive Bolts.

OBJECTIVE Protect Bowman and Brooks

Directly below you, Bowman and Brooks are holed up next to a vehicle. Fire Explosive Bolts into approaching enemy vehicles to blow them up.

This special ops Crossbow with variable zoom comes equipped with several Explosive Bolts. These bolts give you deadly precision and can take out large groups of enemies.

When you fire an Explosive Bolt, a characteristic green light blinks where the projectile lands. The bolt then releases a massive explosion a moment later.

WEAPON: CROSSBOW

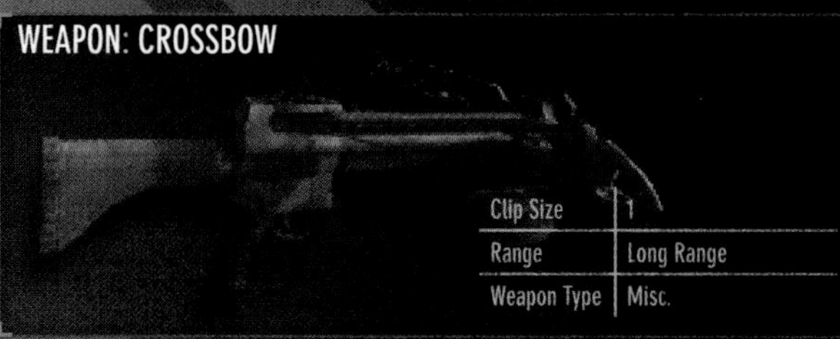

Clip Size	1
Range	Long Range
Weapon Type	Misc.

Firing these bolts into tight-knit groups of soldiers is very effective. Even more effective, however, is firing a bolt into an explosive object, such as a vehicle or a gas tank. This results in an immediate explosive payoff.

The regular bolts on the Crossbow are deadly one-hit kill rounds. While they aren't as exciting as the explosive variant, they still pack a punch. The Crossbow makes an excellent sniper weapon once the explosive rounds run out.

After both vehicles explode, your team moves up a bit further, but more enemies arrive. Use your Explosive Bolts to continue decimating their ranks.

You are safely out of the action, so you can take your time without worrying about getting shot. However, if you take *too* long, Bowman and Brooks eventually get killed, causing you to fail the mission.

OBJECTIVE Secure the Line

After you kill most of the enemies, you are tasked with firing a zipline above a window. Use the objective marker to figure out where you need to fire the line, and let loose to secure it. When the line is up, a breach event automatically triggers.

BREACH

You automatically switch to the MP5K as you descend the line. Fire through the glass to take out the front guy, and then concentrate on spraying the right side of the room to prevent Weaver's execution.

"I HAD TO KILL DRAGOVICH."

OBJECTIVE Abort the Launch at the Auxiliary Control Bunker.

After the brief intermission, you're back to your spec ops uniform and following Woods again. Jump over the ledge and follow him across the concrete bunker. Be careful to stay up top; going down below with Bowman results in a mission failure.

WEAPON: MP5K

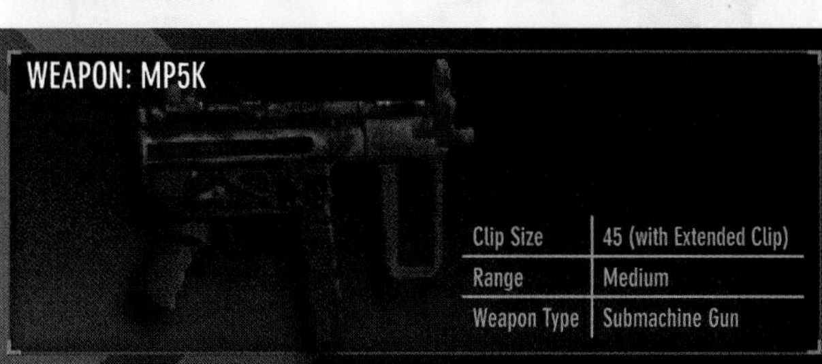

Clip Size	45 (with Extended Clip)
Range	Medium
Weapon Type	Submachine Gun

You start this level equipped with the new MP5K, a versatile medium-range weapon, but you don't get a chance to use it until the breach.

It's equipped with a Laser Sight and an Extended Clip. This is your go-to weapon for the rest of this level. It's best at medium range, but can still take out enemies from afar.

At short range, spray a rain of bullets from the hip, doing your best to keep the recoil from getting out of control.

Tons of enemies are on the ledge up and to your left. Switch back to the Explosive Bolts (Left on the D-Pad) and clear out the enemies before you follow Woods up the ladder.

With the enemies in the next area down, you can take point and proceed toward the objective marker. Move around the right side of the circular fence ahead. Use your MP5 to take down the few soldiers that arrive at the opposite end.

When you reach the other side, more Soviets are holed up in the area below. Fire down on them with your Crossbow to clear the area.

MORE EXPLOSIVES

If you run low on Explosive Bolts, you can switch out your Crossbow for another AK-47 with Grenade Launcher attachment. You should find one on the soldiers' bodies in this upper circular area.

Stay low as you move down into the next area, and watch for enemies hiding behind crates. As you reach the end of this corner area, more enemies wait for you behind the railing on your right, in the slightly raised area. Carefully peek around the corner and pick them off with your MP5K. Be very careful of more enemies charging your position from your left.

"MASON, BLOW A HOLE IN THAT ******* WALL!"

Continue down the path until you reach a dead end. Woods tells you what to do. Move near the C4 outline and hold the Interact button. Move back down the stairs and squeeze the Fire trigger to blow the wall.

INTEL

This level's second Intel is located in the room in which you blew a hole with the C4. It's on top of a computer bay on the opposite wall from the hole.

OBJECTIVE Destroy Soyuz 2

It's too late for your team to stop Soyuz 2 the planned way, so you must expedite things with a Valkyrie rocket. Head back outside to find the rocket launcher next to Woods.

The Soyuz 2 rocket is lifting off to your left. Look up and fire in the general vicinity of the Soyuz. This is a prototype user-guided rocket, so once you fire it, you control its path with your Movement analog.

This can be tricky the first time; you need to aim the rocket almost straight up into the air.

You get only one shot at this. But even if you fail, the most recent checkpoint only sets you back to just before you blow the wall with the C4.

"THAT'S A HELL OF A WAY TO TEST A PROTOTYPE."

Use the Sprint button to chase after Woods as he moves to evacuate the area. Use the Crouch button to duck under fallen rocket debris along the way. Ignore the flaming Soviets, and continue down the tunnel after Woods.

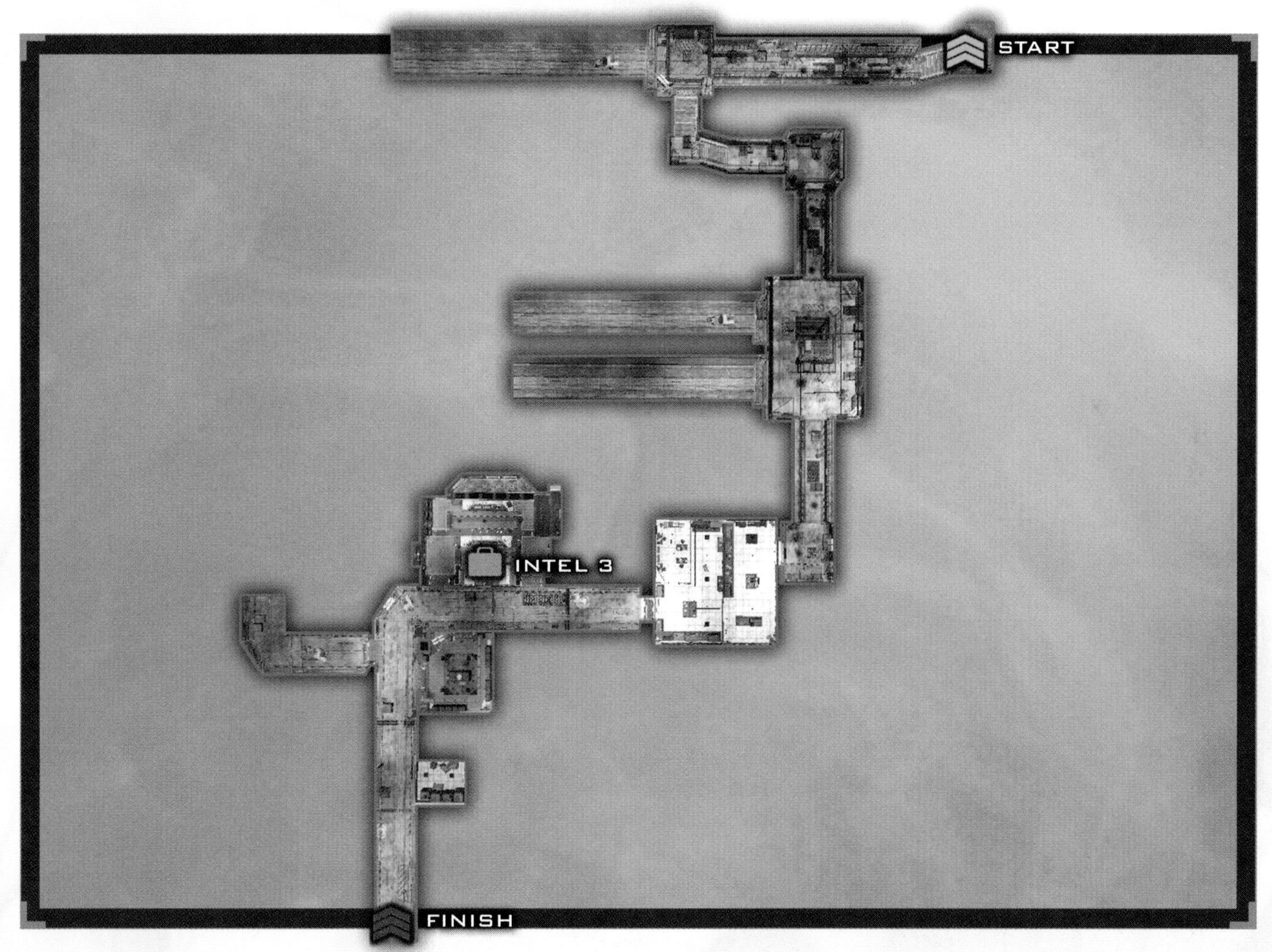

OBJECTIVE Find and Kill Dragovich

MORE OLD FAVORITES

Before you descend the stairs, you can find a stash of KS-23 shotguns and Dragunov sniper rifles on the tunnel's right side. The shotgun is useful for this last part of the level, so swapping out a longer-range weapon like the Crossbow in favor of the shotgun might be a good idea.

The Dragunov is useful for picking off enemies at the ends of tunnels. So, if you like using a sniper scope, feel free to switch out your MP5.

As you move downstairs, three enemies wait for you. Stay behind cover and pick them off. Wait for their reinforcements to arrive, and dispose of them before you move forward.

Stay close to Woods and provide him with fire cover as he advances through the tunnels. This is a fairly straightforward section. As long as you watch out for grenade indicators and stay behind Woods, you shouldn't have too much trouble advancing.

GRENADES

This is the first section of the game where the enemies use grenades effectively. Keep an eye on your HUD for a grenade indicator, and be sure to avoid or toss back any that land close to you. For more info on grenade counter-tactics, check the Training chapter.

When you reach the end of the tunnel, switch to your short-range weapon or your MP5. The first computer room is full of enemies. Use some grenades to soften them up, and then strafe out from the doorways to pick off the enemies one by one.

One or two enemies like to hide in this section; be patient and wait for them to pop their heads out. Or, if you're the daring type, charge in with your shotgun and blast them before they get a bead on you.

Another tunnel filled with Soviets awaits you on the other side of the room. Approach the tunnel entrance cautiously, and fire in with your medium- or long-range weapons.

This area is tricky because the enemies are very accurate from this range, and there are unlimited reinforcements. The only way to get through this section is to push forward continually, moving from cover to cover.

When you get halfway down the hallway, be very careful of the room on your right. Several more soldiers are in that room, and they can get a jump on you if you try to pass the room without engaging them.

AK-47 ACOG

The AK-47 ACOG has just the right range for this encounter. If you search around, you might be able to find one on the enemies you killed in the previous room. You also may find an AK-47 with Grenade Launcher, which is also a good option for this fight.

When you reach the room on your right, it's best to avoid moving into it directly. Move past the doorway and continue your advance down the hallway, using the crate directly ahead for cover.

When there's a pause in enemy fire at the crate, sprint ahead to the yellow vehicle at the corner of the hallway. This object gives you good cover, so you can clear out any lingering enemies in the locker room or down the hallway ahead. This method should also earn you a much-needed checkpoint.

INTEL

Once you safely earn a checkpoint, return to that dangerous room on your right. Check the top of the computer desk on your right, just below the window to find the last piece of Intel for this level.

A SAFER PLACE

You automatically receive this Achievement/Trophy for completing this level.

Clear the hallway and continue forward down this last hall. Watch out for three soldiers emerging from the smoke at the end of the hall. Find cover.

As soon as they appear, back up to return to cover behind the crates. When you finally take down the armored soldiers, it's safe to move to the end of the hall.

S.O.G.

0900 January 21, 1968

ALEX MASON

TRANSMISSION# 4-5-1-4.

Designate	NOVEMBER
Location	Khe Sanh Village, Quang Tri Province, Vietnam
Mission	Investigate Soviet involvement in Vietnam

You start the level reuniting with Woods several years after the previous mission. You automatically follow him onto a nearby vehicle, where he gives you the sitrep on Khe Sanh.

"LOOKS DON'T COUNT FOR **** IN THE JUNGLE. THIS IS 'NAM, BABY!"

S.O.G.

S.O.G. stands for Studies and Observations Group. This highly secretive, elite black ops unit performed anti-Communist intelligence gathering and classified missions throughout Southeast Asia in the 1960s and 1970s.

After the cinematic, carry Hudson down into the trench.

OBJECTIVE Get Hudson to the Bunker

Hudson recovers from the shellshock quickly. After you put him down, follow Woods through the trenches.

OBJECTIVE Defend Khe Sanh. Clear the Trenches.

A huge force of North Vietnamese Army (NVA) soldiers are approaching on your left. You can fire into the field for a few moments, but follow Woods as soon as he moves on.

As you move under a bridge, a soldier jumps down on you. Repeatedly tap the Interact button to turn the tables on the soldier.

You automatically start this level with the Masterkey variant of the M16. This one gun can cover all ranges. If you press Left on the D-Pad, the gun switches to a four-round shotgun mode, which is excellent in short-range combat. The Masterkey shotgun has extremely limited reach, so use it only at pointblank range. Otherwise, the gun operates exactly like other M16s you have used in previous levels. Unlike in MP, this M16 is fully automatic.

When you win the fight with the NVA soldier, move up to the crates. Use your M16 to clear out the attackers approaching down the trench and moving overhead. Staying behind these crates before you push forward will keep you safe.

You can either continue forward in this area or turn the next corner to follow Woods and Hudson. If you turn the corner, more enemies attack from above the trench, while another set bum-rushes Hudson. Don't worry about Hudson—he'll be fine—instead, focus your fire on the soldiers above you.

Follow Woods through the trenches and provide backup fire. When you see the flamethrower soldier, be sure to take care of him. More close-up battles await as you follow Woods and Hudson deeper into the conflict. When a tank falls in front of you, go prone and crawl underneath it.

"WE GOT A LINE OF NAPALM BARRELS TWENTY YARDS OUT."

Stay behind Woods as he assesses the area. Hundreds of infantry are advancing on your position from the north.

OBJECTIVE Hold the Line

Switch to your M60 and advance down the trenches. It's now your job to detonate the napalm barrels out in the field to try to stem the tide of advancing troops. As you move around the corner, fire your M60 at the approaching enemies, and continue moving toward your navigation marker.

When you get to the detonation switch, pick it up via the Interact button. Do not trigger the switch until Woods gives you the order.

After you blow the enemy line, switch back to your M60 and pick off any survivors. You must equip and use another detonator before you go for the LAW rockets at the end of the trench.

Don't let the "light" in "LMG" fool you; the M60 is a gigantic machinegun with extremely high damage and a tremendous clip size. However, the M60 is accurate only if you use Aim Down Sight while you are stationary. The M60 is one weapon you want to fire in brief bursts to ensure high accuracy and efficiency. The reload time is nearly ten seconds, so get the most out of each reload.

WEAPON: M60

Clip Size	100
Range	Medium Range
Weapon Type	Light Machinegun

You must now get to the end of the trench to reach the anti-tank LAW rockets... Easier said than done.

Fire at the advancing troops on your left with your M60. When you have an opening, stay crouched and move up to the newly opened hole in the sandbag wall to your right. Back down the hole toward Woods, cutting down any advancing enemies with your M60.

As you face the approaching enemy, a bunker building with a LAW rocket is on your left. You can switch out your M60 (which is likely empty by now) for the LAW. Now, quickly switch back to your M16 and watch the door for any late-arriving enemies.

If no one shows after a few seconds, it's safe to switch back to the LAW and pop your head up. Fire LAWs straight into the three tanks located in the area. When the three tanks are smoking, your air support arrives and cleans up the rest of the advancing enemies.

MORE LAW

More LAW rockets are located further up the hill. If you have trouble getting to the one described in the walkthrough, try rushing up the hill to the sandbag bunker. There, you can find an unlimited supply of rockets.

Continue following Woods up through the trenches. The area is relatively safe at this point, so you can search around for additional weapons. Among the weapons you can find are an M14 Grenade Launcher, a China Lake, a Stakeout Shotgun, more LAWs, and an M60 ACOG.

We recommend you switch your LAW out for an M60 ACOG.

INTEL

The first Intel piece is hidden amongst a large number of crates in this tank showdown area. You can find it directly across from the downed soldier holding the LAW halfway up the hill.

"WHAT'S YOUR STATUS?"

Follow Woods and Hudson down the ladder to a hill outside. The NVA are advancing on the hill. Stay behind cover and wait for Woods to move down. Use your M60 to pick off enemies as Woods moves forward. Clear out the enemies in the bunker section on your right, and then follow Woods.

Reload your M60 and move toward the arms bunker on your right. Clear out the NVA inside to give your marines access to the ammo stock.

Now your objective is to rush down the hill and kick over two of the napalm barrels to create a literal firewall against the advancing troops.

This is a challenging proposition, as the enemy has unlimited reinforcements coming up the hill. The best way to accomplish this is to focus your fire on the enemies near the barrels. As soon as you get an opening, switch to your lighter weapon and sprint down the hill to the barrels. Hold the Interact button to kick two barrels down the hill.

INTEL

The second Intel piece is a tricky find, located in one of the area's bunkers. To find it, move to the northeastern corner of the hill's base after you clear out all the enemies with the napalm. Turn 180 degrees around, and you should see a bunker room directly in front of you.

Enter the bunker to find the Intel sitting in the window on the right.

This should clear the hill and trigger a checkpoint. Stay in cover as your allies move up and pick off any stragglers.

OBJECTIVE Retake the Hill

"THOSE ARE OUR OWN MORTARS. DO THEY KNOW WE'RE HERE?"

When this area is safe, stay very close to Woods as he rushes to the next area. Use the fallen trees for cover, and fire at the enemies up the hill with your M60.

The enemies up the hill have excellent cover. Use primed grenades to flush them out. Wait for Woods to continue moving up the hill, and follow him, firing on any NVA you see. Watch for the flamethrower soldier up to the right as you advance—use your M60 to take him out from a safe distance.

"SHOVEL! TWO FIVE ACTUAL! CEASE FIRE! CEASE FIRE!"

The enemies don't stop coming at this point. To get past them, you must push up the hill as quickly as you can. The best route is up the right-hand path.

Kill any enemies perched at the end of the path. When it's clear, you have a few seconds to sprint up the hill. If you start taking shots from your left, immediately go prone and get ready to clear the enemies at the end of the path again.

When you make it to the top, turn back to your left and fire on the enemies until Woods and the marines make it up to your position.

When Woods gets ahead of you, cautiously follow him. A lot more NVA are further up the hill.

"KEEP PUSHING!"

Use cover and advance slowly. The only way to progress here is to continue your advance by moving from cover to cover. Continue moving toward the objective marker on your screen, and immediately go prone if you start taking shots.

If you get to the top of the mountain, a huge blast detonates near you. Don't give up—you still have a chance. Save Woods by scoring a shot on the NVA soldier standing over him.

Follow Woods through the destroyed bunker.

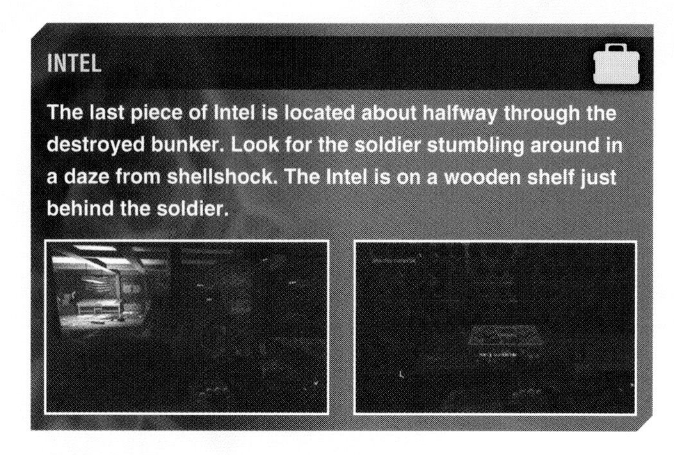

INTEL

The last piece of Intel is located about halfway through the destroyed bunker. Look for the soldier stumbling around in a daze from shellshock. The Intel is on a wooden shelf just behind the soldier.

OBJECTIVE Get in the Vehicle

Once you're back outside, join Woods and Hudson in the running vehicle. Your ride is equipped with a TOW rocket launcher and an M60 on the back, but you start out with a normal China Lake grenade launcher.

WEAPON: CHINA LAKE

Clip Size	4
Range	Long Range
Weapon Type	Grenade Launcher

The China Lake is a superbly accurate grenade launcher, and it's the best way to get grenades directly into your enemies' midst.

The China Lake fires in a much more direct arc than the assault rifle grenade launchers do, making it much easier to aim at enemies.

OBJECTIVE Destroy the Six T55 Tanks

Use your M60 and China Lake to keep the enemies around you at bay. TOW rockets are user-guided, requiring you to steer them into your target.

Each time you stop, you must blow a tank clearly highlighted with a red target. Some shots are easier than others are. Take your time and make sure you don't have to steer around any tough obstacles before you fire.

Controlling the rockets is identical to the Valkyrie rocket you used to blow up the Soyuz earlier. Use the Look Analog to steer your rockets straight into your target.

The first tank is a straight shot.

Destroy it, and Woods drives you to position two, where you must target two more tanks. Both of these tanks are easy shots; just be sure you stay high enough to avoid the ground.

The last three tanks are a bit trickier. Take them in order from left to right. Wait a few moments for the left tank to get into a better position, and then fire high, steering the TOW rocket down into it. Now fire straight shots as quickly as you can to the fifth and sixth tanks. If you wait too long, they can send a tank round into your vehicle.

TOUGH ECONOMY

TOW rockets are expensive. Save the U.S. government some money by using your TOWs efficiently to earn this award. Don't use more than six rockets to destroy all the tanks to accomplish this fiscally conservative goal.

Take your time and make sure you have a clear shot before you fire. Be very careful to avoid steering the rocket too close to the ground as you approach the tank—it can result in an early explosion. Also, be sure to avoid hitting boost or remote detonation if you're going for this achievement.

CAPT. MASON, A

RE-ASSIGNMEN

COORDINATE WITH S

investigate Soviet th

"THIS IS THE START OF SOMETHING ELSE... THEY'LL BE BACK."

LOOKS DON'T COUNT

You earn this Achievement/Trophy automatically for completing this level on any difficulty.

THE DEFECTOR

1900 February 2, 1968

ALEX MASON

SUPPORT

TRANSMISSION# 20-8-5-18-5.
Designate: OSCAR
Location: Huê City, Vietnam
Mission: Extract Soviet defector

"THIS IS WHERE IT REALLY STARTED TO UNRAVEL FOR YOU, MASON."

This level is another S.O.G. mission with Woods. After recovering, you are armed with a new weapon: the SPAS-12 shotgun.

The SPAS-12 is a semiautomatic shotgun that normally inflicts massive damage at short range, and it reloads significantly faster than other shotguns you've used earlier in the game.

WEAPON: SPAS-12

Clip Size	8
Range	Short to Medium
Weapon Type	Shotgun

With the incendiary rounds, the SPAS-12 becomes hell on earth for your enemies. It can instantly kill several enemies at once, lighting an entire room full of enemies aflame.

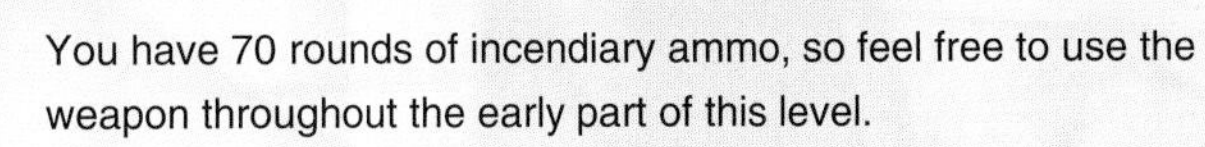

You have 70 rounds of incendiary ammo, so feel free to use the weapon throughout the early part of this level.

OBJECTIVE Extract the Defector and Intel

Proceed out the door and take point, killing any Vietnamese soldiers that get in your way. While several NVA soldiers are in this burning building, none of them stands a chance against your weapon. As you plow through their ranks, aim low to ensure you don't miss.

WATCH THE CIVILIANS

This is a normal business office, so, while it is filled with enemy soldiers, quite a few civilians also run around in the carnage. Be sure to shoot only people wearing uniforms—if you accidently kill a civilian, it's mission abort.

As you advance, you get some helicopter support. Hang back while the chopper's MG tears through the enemies ahead of you.

“THE WHOLE DAMN BUILDING’S OVERRUN!”

Advance further into the building, and Bowman rappels down in front of you. Give him support from behind the desks as you get an update on your mission sitrep.

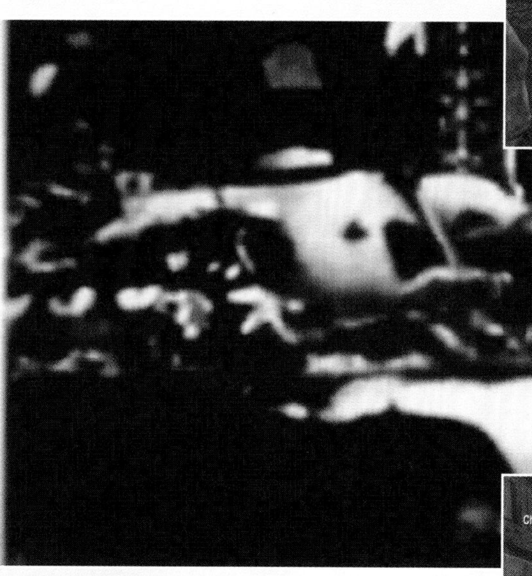

THE DRAGON WITHIN

If you stick to using your shotgun’s incendiary rounds on this level, this Achievement/Trophy will unlock in no time. It takes about ten confirmed kills for the award to trigger.

Continue through the office, but be warned: some civilians are held hostage in the room ahead. When you approach this room, you must avoid shooting the fleeing civilians in the foreground and take down the enemies in the back. You may want to switch to your Commando assault rifle for better precision.

When the room is clear, switch back to your SPAS and proceed to the next room. Shoot the two soldiers at the balcony on the left, hang back, and watch the enemy across the way throw a Molotov. Switch to your Commando rifle and pick off the enemies firing on your position from below. Several enemies hide in the flames, so be sure the area is clear before you move down the staircase. A grenade from your Commando can help clear the area.

The safe room is just downstairs, but the enemy has already breached it. Watch out for enemies from above, and help Woods and Bowman clear the room.

When you're finished clearing the room, move to the far door to activate a breach.

The next area is full of enemies. Stay low and use your SPAS to kill any enemies that get too close. When you get to the large war room, switch to the Commando and kill the enemies hiding behind cover on the opposite side.

BREACH

Your primary target on this breach is the shotgunner that charges through the door on the right. Shoot him with your SPAS, and then finish off the NVA at the desk.

MORE DRAGON'S BREATH

You can find more Dragon's Breath for your SPAS in the small, improvised armory on the right side of this large room's upper area.

A bunch of enemies defends the lower part of this area. Move up to the railing and rain fire down on them with your SPAS. If a couple survive, flush them out with a tossed grenade.

Follow Woods downstairs to the next breach door.

BREACH

Reznov does the heavy lifting on this breach.

"I AM HERE WITH A WARNING THAT YOUR GOVERNMENT WOULD DO WELL TO HEED."

Follow Reznov as he leads you outside to the streets.

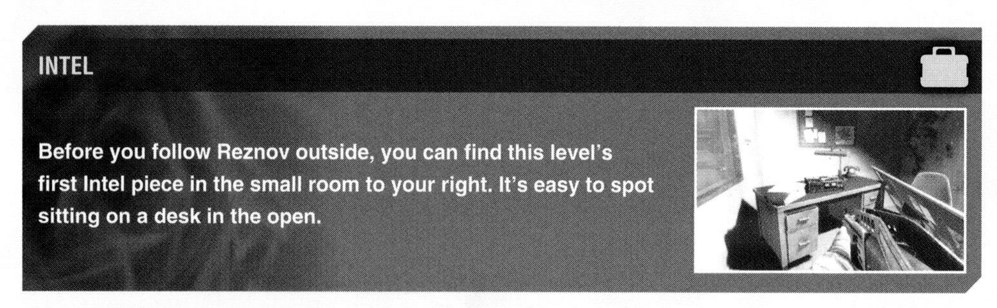

INTEL

Before you follow Reznov outside, you can find this level's first Intel piece in the small room to your right. It's easy to spot sitting on a desk in the open.

OBJECTIVE Get to the LZ

Outside, Woods and Bowman rendezvous with you. Follow them through the streets up to the soldier with the radio. Hold the Interact button to commandeer the radio from him. You now have the ability to call in Airstrikes.

AIRSTRIKES

You can now call Airstrikes for much of this level. To aim an Airstrike, look around to position the green cursor on your desired target area. Try to fire on large groups of soldiers.

When you find a good position, press the Fire button and a helicopter soon arrives to clear out the position with dual MGs.

Activate your first Airstrike on the building to your left.

Stay behind cover and wait for your squad to receive the move-out orders. Jump back down to street level, and remember that you can call more Airstrikes at anytime by pressing Right on the D-Pad.

RAINING PAIN

You can earn the special Raining Pain Achievement/Trophy in this part of the level by using helicopter strikes against the enemies here. Kill 20 enemies with your air support to receive the award.

Be sure to achieve this goal before you move off the streets. If you find a building filled with enemies, continual Airstrikes are a good option for racking up the required kills.

Call in a second Airstrike on the building at the end of the street, and follow the armored vehicle. Don't follow too close, as it explodes when it reaches roughly the halfway point down the next street.

An NVA tank will appear from an alley to the left. Tag the NVA tank with an Airstrike attack and take cover in a nearby building.

INTEL

While you take cover, you can grab the second piece of Intel. It's located in the building at the corner of the street, back the way you came.

Look for two cars—one blue, one white—parked in the street. The building directly behind these cars contains the Intel on a desk in the first-floor room.

After Texas blows the top off the tank, continue calling in Airstrikes on the surrounding buildings. When all the buildings are smoking, it's safe to advance. This is a good spot to try to earn the Raining Pain Achievement/Trophy.

Move to the building doorway on your right where Bowman is crouching. Switch to the Dragon's Breath and clear any enemies inside. Peek outside and unleash another Airstrike on the fortified enemies across the street.

Keep deploying Airstrikes until all the buildings in the area are smoking. Pick off any stragglers with your Commando, and move up to the metal rail. Wait for Woods to open the gate, and follow him onto the street. Anti-aircraft weaponry is spotted in the area, so your chopper support bails.

OBJECTIVE Destroy the ZSU Gun Emplacement

Follow Woods closely and help him open the door by quickly pressing the Interact button.

"STILL IN ONE PIECE, MY FRIEND?"

After you recover from the explosion, switch to your Dragon's Breath and move up the stairs. Kill the two soldiers at the top, and then blow out the window on your right. Kill the enemies behind the window, and then move out through the windowpane.

You're teamed up with Reznov again, just like at Vorkuta. Move outside and kill the five NVA that arrive to defend the ZSU. When the area is clear, move to the building below the ZSU. Look up to plant the C4, get out of the way, and blow out the floor.

"LOOKS LIKE WE GOTTA WAIT—EVERYONE LOAD UP, I WANT THIS LZ SECURE."

OBJECTIVE Setup Defenses to Defend the LZ

The chopper doesn't have enough room for everyone, so you have to set up defenses to hold the area until the chopper can make another run. Look near the MG in the middle of the area to find some Claymores. The NVA attack from the northeast, so quickly set up the Claymores in that direction—you have only a few seconds before the attack commences.

CLAYMORES

Claymores are special mines that explode when an enemy passes through the laser tripwire on one side.

It's important to place your Claymores facing toward the enemy, as they are more likely to detonate and inflict major damage.

You have very little time to place your Claymores here, so don't worry too much about placement—just put them down as quickly as you can.

INTEL

To get the last piece of Intel, you must sacrifice some of your setup time to explore the area. The Intel is located in a building at the square's northeast end. Look for a blown-out brick wall. Enter this building to find the Intel on a wooden stand in the open.

If you're playing on a lower difficulty, you can use the MG in the middle of the area to shoot down the enemies as they emerge from the smoke clouds. On harder difficulties, stay in cover off to the side and carefully pick off the enemies.

After roughly two minutes, the NVA pulls back to regroup. Move to the area's rearward, western end and find good cover in the blown-out area. A tank arrives to the northeast. Stay behind cover—none of your weapons can damage the tank.

GOOD HIDING SPOTS

You don't have to kill anyone for this last sequence. If you find a good enough hiding spot, you can just wait for the end of the level and rush out to the last checkpoint during a break in the gunfire. If you want to take the, uh, less...brazen...path, hide in the room where the third piece of Intel is located.

Stick to this building's southwest corner, facing the double windows. Use the Dragon's Breath to kill any enemies jumping through the windows.

When Bowman says, "They're pulling back," return to the main area.

Soon, the radio informs you that the Navy is on its way to rescue you. Call in an Airstrike on the tank, and then sprint for the level exit. You have only twenty seconds to make it out—no time to watch your Airstrike take down the tank.

SOG RULES

You automatically earn this Achievement/Trophy for completing this mission.

NUMBERS

1700 February 9, 1968

JASON HUDSON

SUPPORT

TRANSMISSION# 23-1-19 .
Designate: VICTOR
Location: Kowloon City, Hong Kong
Target: Dr. Daniel Clarke

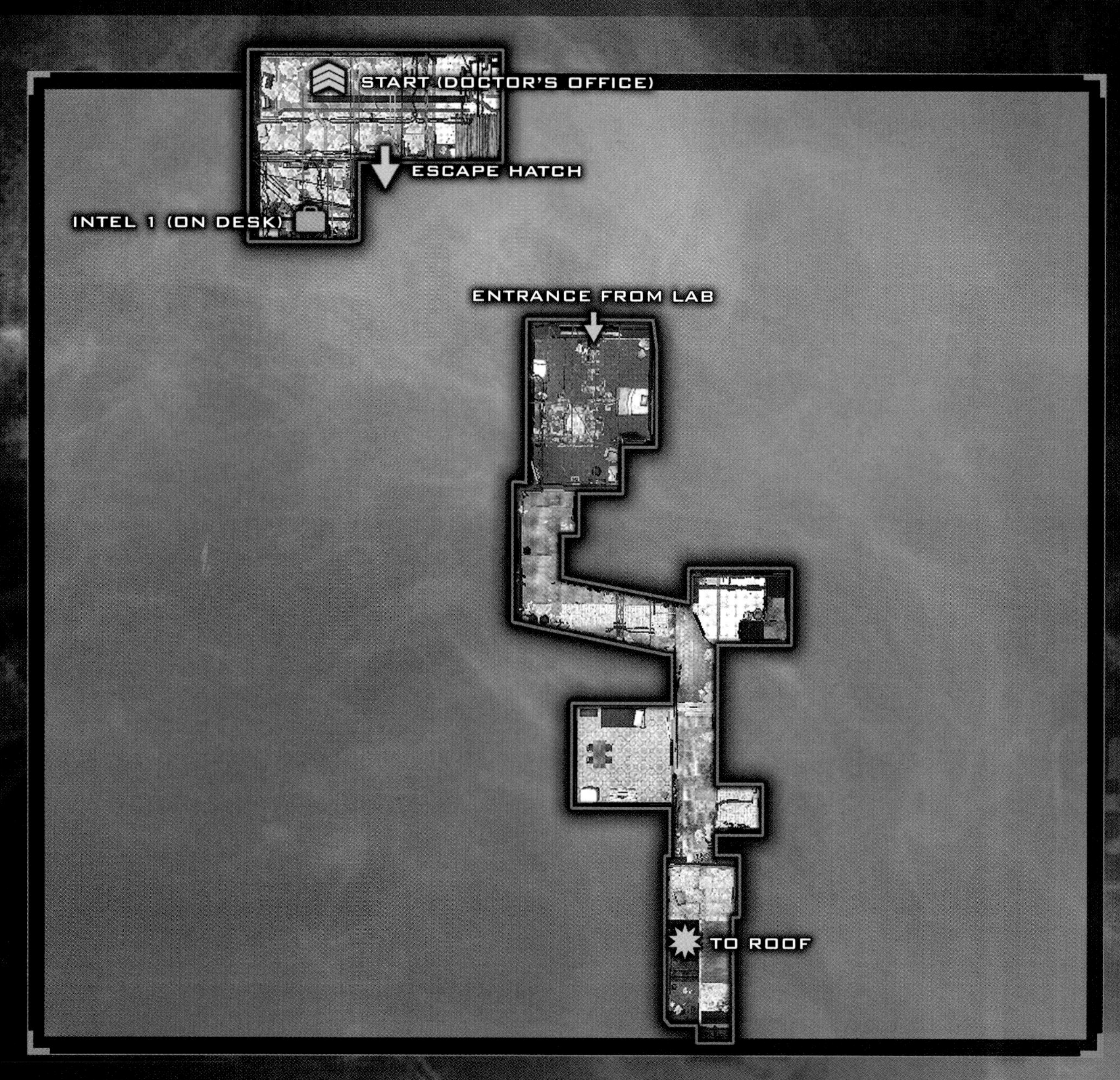

"YOU LED THEM RIGHT TO ME!"

Your interrogation is interrupted by people that want the doctor much more than you do. You need the information from the doctor, so it's your job to defend him.

Take cover behind the table with Weaver and fire on the enemies with your CZ75 pistols.

The CZ75 Dual Pistols are for desperate situations only. They are very hard to fire accurately, and they deliver low damage. The pistols' one advantage is their large clip size. Unless you are going for the Double Trouble Achievement, switch out these weapons as soon as possible.

To fire the left gun, squeeze the Aim Down Sight trigger.

WEAPON: CZ75 DUAL PISTOLS

Clip Size	20/20
Range	Short Range
Weapon Type	Pistol

Whatever you do, don't advance on the enemies—a canister of Nova 6 gas eventually blows up down the hall. Coming in contact with the gas means instant death.

DOUBLE TROUBLE

You need to use only dual-wielding weapons throughout this level to earn this Achievement/Trophy. That means you're stuck with the pistols for now. However, you get access to SMG upgrades early in the level.

You can complete this goal on any difficulty, so we recommend you try for it on the Recruit setting.

INTEL

Don't miss the first piece of Intel before you climb the ladder after the doctor. You can find it in this first room's back area, on a desk in the doctor's lab. It's next to his old-school personal computer.

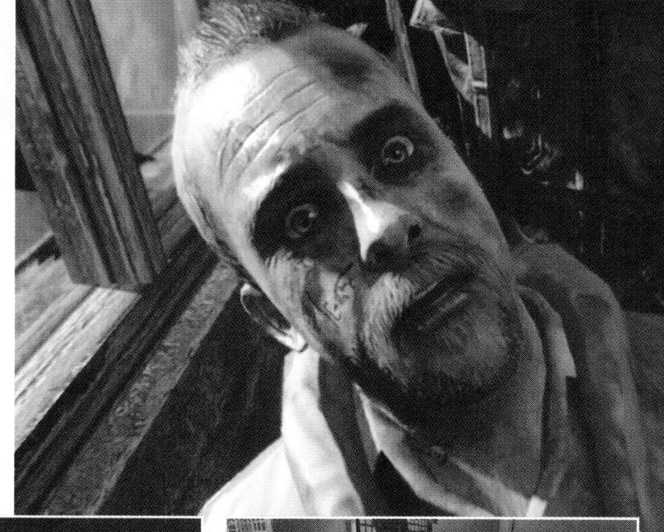

After the gas fills the corridor, follow the doctor up the hatch on your right.

OBJECTIVE Escape with Dr. Clarke

Upstairs, the doctor reveals that the Spetsnaz are the ones after him. Spetsnaz are Soviet special operatives, and they can mean serious trouble.

Around the first corner, a couple of civilians run by, so be careful you don't shoot them.

Use your pistols to finish the enemies at the end of the corridor. Cautiously approach and search the ground for some replacement weapons. You should be able to find a SPAS shotgun and a Kiparis SMG. Both guns are good choices for the upcoming section.

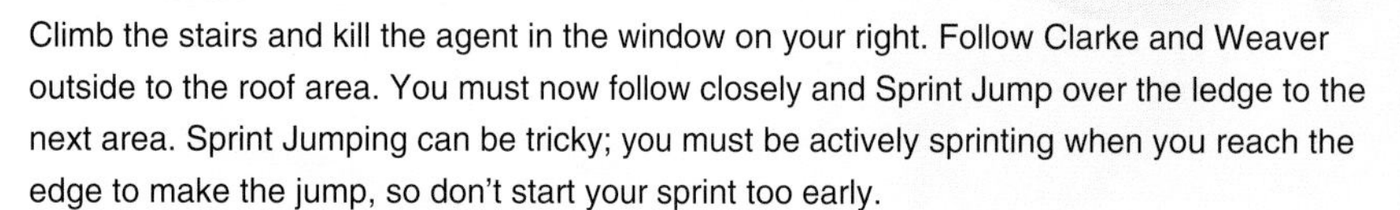

Climb the stairs and kill the agent in the window on your right. Follow Clarke and Weaver outside to the roof area. You must now follow closely and Sprint Jump over the ledge to the next area. Sprint Jumping can be tricky; you must be actively sprinting when you reach the edge to make the jump, so don't start your sprint too early.

DRAGUNOV

A sniper rifle can be handy on this level, and you can find the classic Russian rifle—the Dragunov—on the guards on this rooftop.

While you can get by with an assault rifle, the extra range that the Dragunov provides can be useful in some of the level's tougher parts up ahead.

"YOU'RE VERY WELL-PREPARED FOR A DEAD MAN."

After you make the jump, wait for Dr. Clarke to move the refrigerator, revealing his weapons stash. You can pretty much take your choice of weapons here—almost everything from this era is available.

The G11 and the China Lake are both good choices, but be sure you take long-range and short-range capable weapons. If you are going for the Double Trouble Achievement/Trophy, you can get a pair of dual-wielding Kiparis, which are a major upgrade to your pistols.

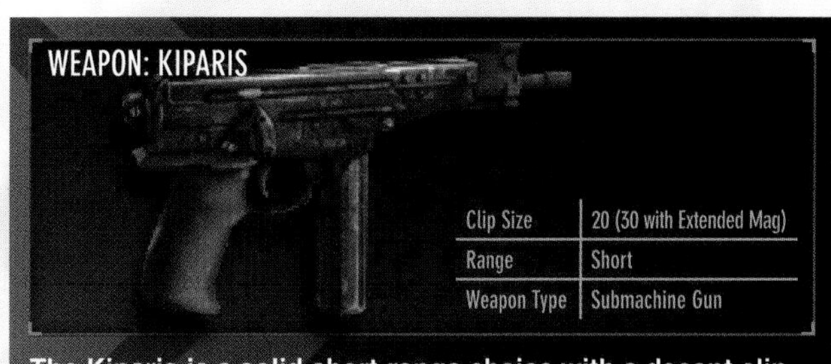

WEAPON: KIPARIS

Clip Size	20 (30 with Extended Mag)
Range	Short
Weapon Type	Submachine Gun

The Kiparis is a solid short-range choice with a decent clip size and excellent damage capability. Don't bother trying for headshots with the Kiparis; just spray the middle region of your target to take it down.

Switch to your short-range weapon and stack up behind Dr. Clarke. When he opens the door, clear out the enemies standing in the hallway. Take cover to avoid the incoming fire from reinforcements, and watch out for grenades.

Stay low and move down the hall with your short-range weapon. A flashbang is set about halfway down this hall. Fire blindly down the hallway to kill any enemies trying to take advantage.

Be wary of enemies jumping you at very short range from either side of the hall. When you come to the end, you should see a greenhouse-type deck. Watch for enemies on your right—blow them away with your short-range weapon.

The enemies here are dressed in full dark gear, which can make them difficult to see. Proceed forward carefully, using your shotgun or submachine guns to clear any enemies before you press forward.

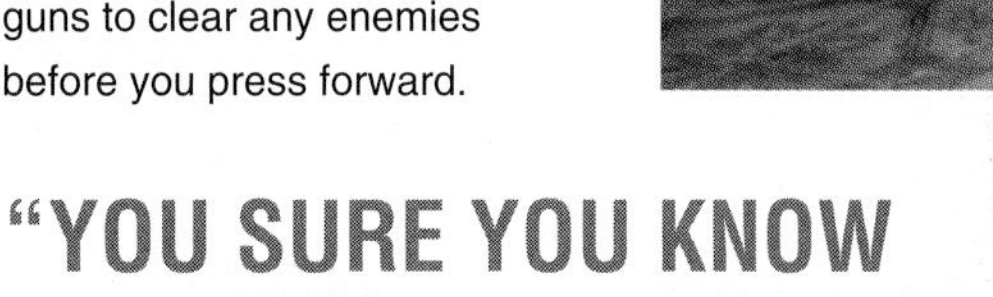

"YOU SURE YOU KNOW WHERE YOU'RE GOING?"

When you reach the end of the outer hallway, a set of enemies defends from the building opposite. Use your long-range weapon to shoot them through the thin, corrugated metal.

Some tricky-to-spot enemies are down below on your left. Be sure to pick them off before you stick your head out too far.

When you don't see any more enemies, you can safely jump down to the roof below.

This area is chaotic and completely covered by enemies. Whatever you do, don't rush forward. Instead, hang back and take cover behind an edge of the roof. Fire on the enemies advancing from the right, and be sure you kill all the enemies you can see before you proceed.

Weaver goes over the top of the building. Instead of following him, go around the roof's lower-left area. Use your short-range weapon to kill any enemies here, and peak around the corner to ensure there aren't any snipers in the buildings around you.

Move forward toward the objective point, watching for enemy heads popping up from the building opposite.

After you reach the objective, descend the stairs and move up to the next doorway. Several enemies are inside: three low, and two high toward the back.

Use your long-range weapon to clear the area. When the snipers in the back are down, you can safely move forward. Hudson automatically grabs a nearby pipe to slide down as you approach it.

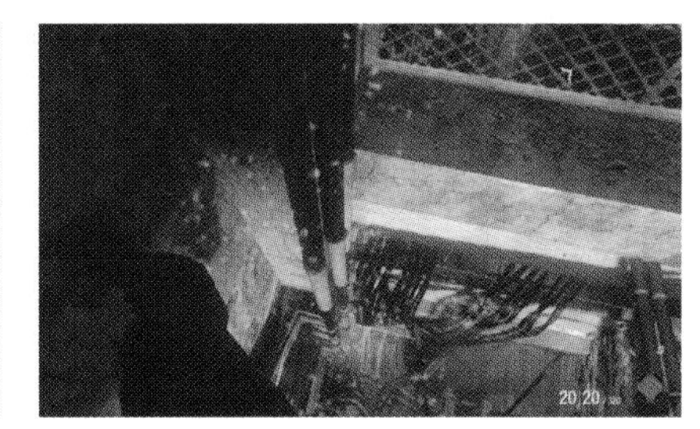

"DRAGOVICH IS GOING THROUGH A LOT OF TROUBLE TO SHUT YOU UP... WHAT ARE YOU NOT TELLING US?"

Crawl along the wires and stay quiet while the two enemies pass below. When they do, fire down on them with your short-range weapon, and continue along the rooftop.

Be very careful not to fall down the small gap between the two rooftops as you follow Dr. Clarke and Weaver. As you move forward along the rooftops, you automatically enter breach mode, sliding down a rooftop into a group of enemies.

BREACH

Before you slide down the roof, switch to a fully automatic weapon. You can make this breach a lot easier if you blow up the red barrel sitting conveniently amidst this area's enemies.

INTEL

This level's second Intel piece is located behind the corrugated metal in the area where you land after you slide. Grab it while you wait for the doctor to blow up his lab.

The doctor destroys his own lab to prevent the Nova 6 from falling into the wrong hands. A weapons stash is on a shelf in this lower area. Stock up on any ammo or weapons you need before you continue after Dr. Clarke.

The combat ahead is similar to the previous rooftop encounter, so equip your favorite weapons for this type of battle.

Before you jump down to the lower roof section, shoot the enemies defending from the deck and windows on the area's left side. Then turn your attention to the enemies in the right building. Be cautious of the enemy in the lower window—he's armed with an RPG.

Now, edge forward looking down. Many enemies swarm in below. Before you advance, kill them with your long-range weapon from behind cover. Once you dispatch most of the enemies, sprint straight ahead and down to the balcony designated with the objective marker.

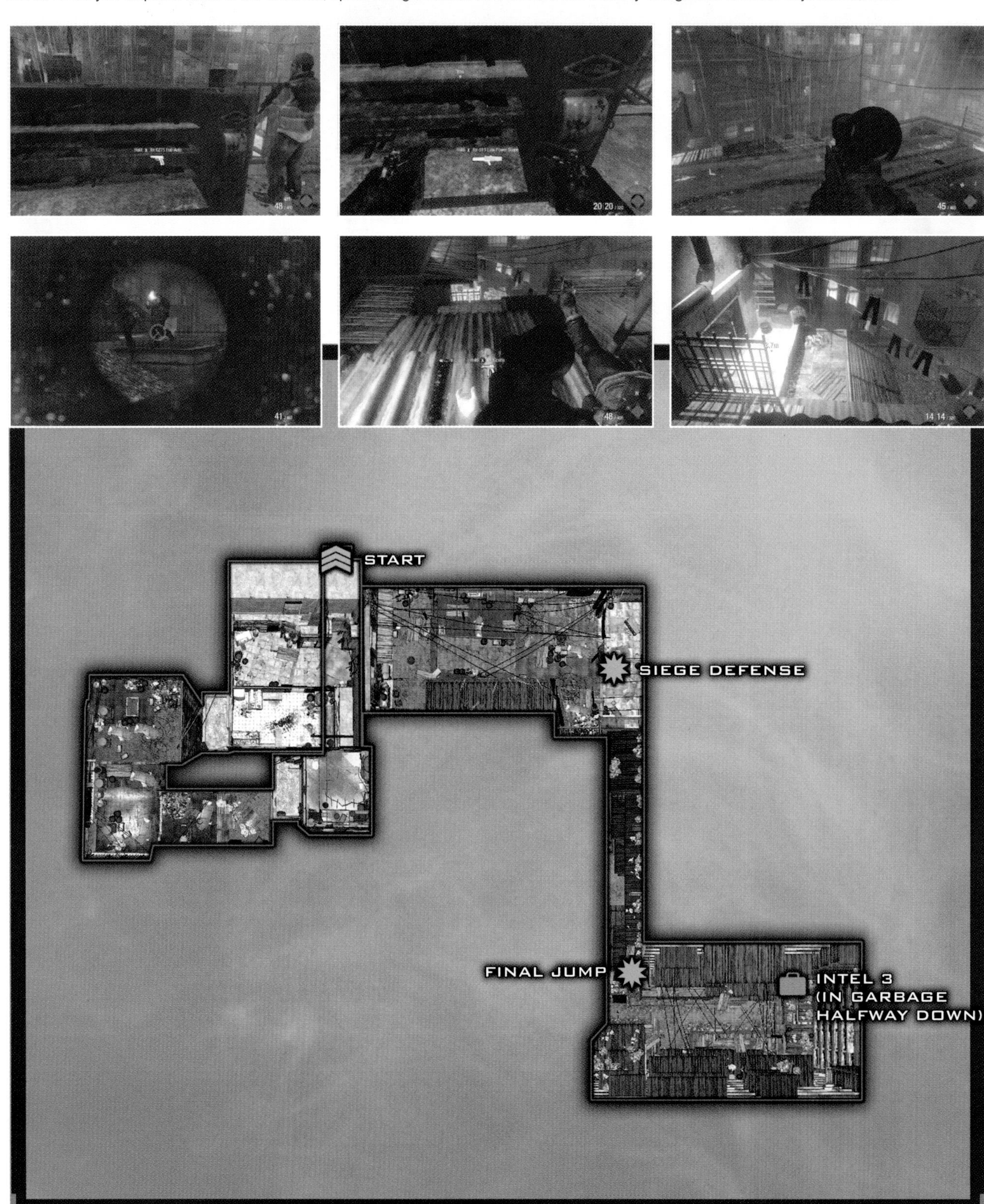

Equip your short-range weapon, crouch, and slowly advance into the apartment. As you get halfway in, an enemy breach occurs. Fire through the smoke with your short-range weapon to kill the breaching enemies.

Be careful—two more enemies are in the hallway beyond. Reload your weapon and proceed down the hall. Unload your weapon down the narrow hall to clear the way as soon as the enemies appear.

When you reach the end of the hall, the Spetsnaz breach from the floor above. Use your short-range weapon to kill the enemies that drop through, but watch out for the one operative who remains on top—he can be deadly with his SMG.

Follow the doctor's instructions and the objective markers to make your way down the balconies into another apartment. Stick with your short-range weapon as you move through this area; enemies attack in small numbers at close range.

"WEAPONS AND AMMUNITION—GRAB WHAT YOU NEED."

When you make it back outside, temporarily switch back to your long-range weapon and pick off the two enemies defending the blown-out building. You can find another weapons stock inside. This time, you must defend against advancing enemies; keep this in mind as you choose your weapons.

You can find a Grim Reaper rocket launcher in the area's front-middle section. While it's very cool, it's not very practical for defense. We recommend a shotgun and a submachine gun for defense.

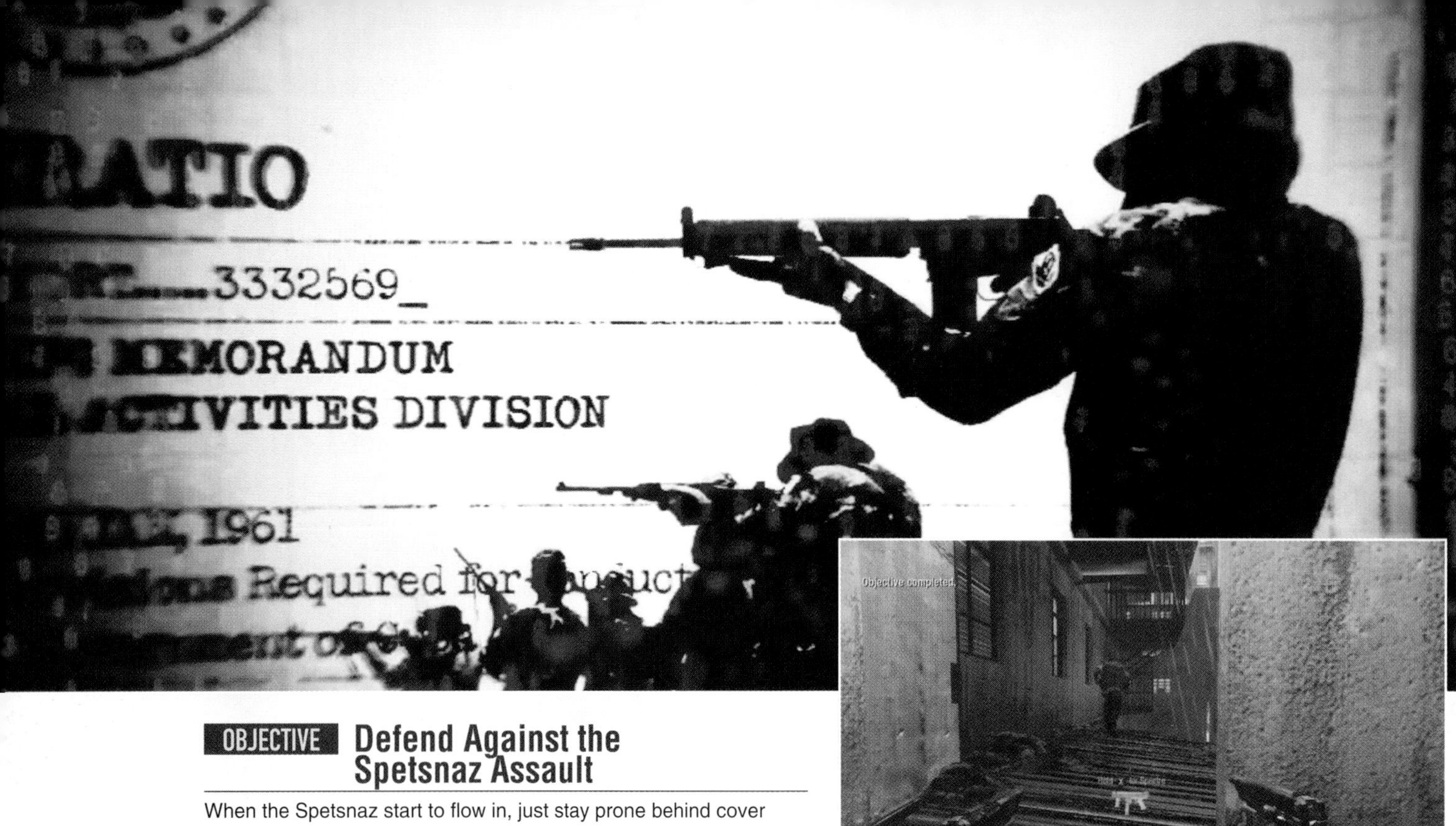

OBJECTIVE Defend Against the Spetsnaz Assault

When the Spetsnaz start to flow in, just stay prone behind cover and fire on any enemies that get close to your position. It takes the doctor only about 30 seconds to open the lock; when he does, follow him out the door.

"JUST ONE MORE LEAP OF FAITH."

Follow the doctor down. When you reach the last ledge, you have to Sprint Jump to make it across and save him. Now Weaver shows you a path down. Be careful to eliminate any Spetsnaz before you jump down to any rooftop.

INTEL

This level's last piece of Intel is a tricky find. Just before the final jump, you can turn around and find it covered in garbage. You'll know you're on the correct platform when you are looking at a yellow-lit wooden structure. When you see this, turn around and look for the Intel covered in trash.

When you reach the bottom of the rooftops, move forward to slide down the plank onto the awning. Unfortunately, there's no way to avoid losing your weapon here. Grab the nearby pistol and do your best to fend off the attacking enemies for a few moments until your extract arrives and takes care of any stragglers.

You land prone, so it can be very difficult to avoid taking damage. Focus on shooting the enemies in the back row, because they inflict the most damage and are armed with SMGs.

BROKEN ENGLISH

You automatically receive this Achievement/Trophy for completing this level.

PROJECT NOVA

1200 October 29, 1945

VIKTOR REZNOV

SUPPORT

TRANSMISSION# 23-8-15.

Designate: DELTA
Location: Arctic Circle
Target: Doctor Friedrich Steiner (BY ORDER OF RUSSIAN COMMAND: DO NOT KILL)

"DISOBEY... AND YOU WILL BE SHOT!"

You are now playing as Reznov in a post-WWII episode. When the level fades in, follow Petrenko down the hill to the troop transport truck.

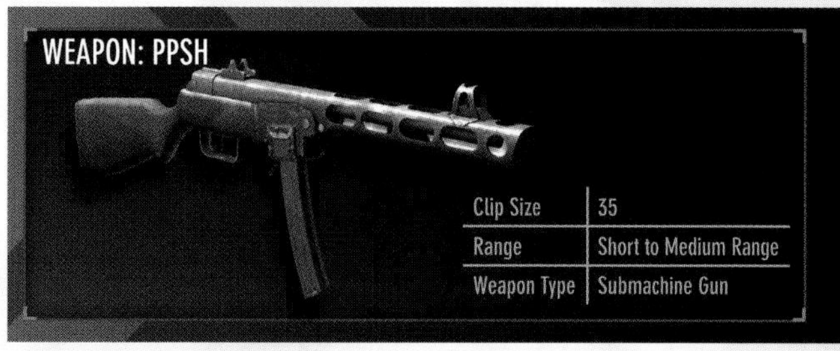

WEAPON: PPSH

Clip Size	35
Range	Short to Medium Range
Weapon Type	Submachine Gun

Reznov's primary weapon is the PPSH submachine gun. This is an excellent weapon to use throughout this level. The PPSH has an extremely high rate of fire and inflicts moderate damage.

"THESE MEN ARE NOT TO BE TRUSTED..."

This battle is against the last holdout of the Nazi resistance in a remote science base in the Arctic Circle.

OBJECTIVE Assault the German Base and Find Steiner

When you regain control of Reznov, pull out your Mosin Nagant rifle and move down the hill. The Nazi resistance is light, and it's easy to proceed forward. Pick off any outcroppings of enemies, but focus on advancing.

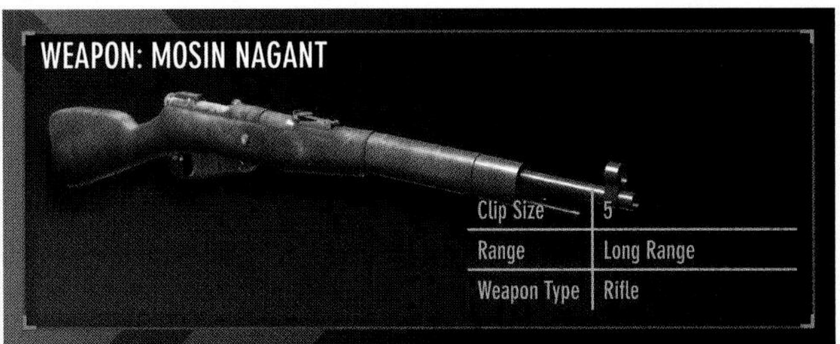

The default Russian rifle serves you well on this mission, and it's an ideal alternate weapon for the PPSH. If you like, you can switch it out for the STG44 that some of the Nazis use on the battlefield ahead. They both operate at the same range, but the STG44 is fully automatic.

As you march down the hill toward the objective point, watch out for German soldiers hiding in the building on your left. Spray the windows with your PPSH to kill them.

"THEY ARE TRYING TO SURRENDER..." "THEY HAVE TRIED BEFORE. DO NOT LET THEM."

When you reach the end of the hill, the next objective marker leads through a garage with a snow tank. From here, the Nazis start surrendering to you as you approach. This entire process is chaotic, and it's safest just to kill all the Germans because inevitably some of the Nazis stand and fight.

Take your time as you advance, and focus your fire on the Germans attacking you. The line of opposition leads you to a two-story building filled with Nazis. Clear out the enemies from cover, and then advance inside.

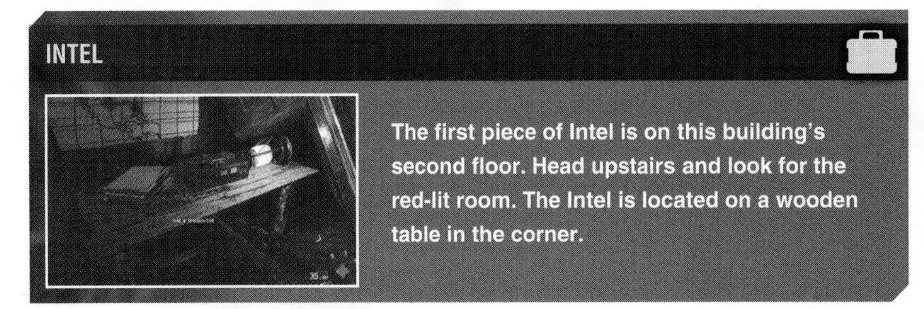

INTEL

The first piece of Intel is on this building's second floor. Head upstairs and look for the red-lit room. The Intel is located on a wooden table in the corner.

The next area is heavily fortified with Germans. These guys aren't as willing to surrender.

You are now equipped with special smoke grenades. Use these grenades to call in mortar strikes on enemy positions.

A machine gunner is on a bridge ahead. To advance your squad, you have to take out this bridge with your new mortar grenade. Sprint into the long building on your right, move to the door on the other end, and toss a smoke grenade at the bridge.

When you've destroyed the bridge, continue your advance to the next building. Switch to the PPSH and spray a clip into the building's doorway. Watch out for a German hiding behind an upturned table.

Clear out the building and proceed up the stairs. When you reach the top, toss a smoke grenade at the front of the hangar to kill the opposition pooled out front.

Carefully move toward the hangar, but be ready for more enemies to emerge. Toss another smoke grenade as soon as enemies emerge, and retreat to cover.

INTEL

The second piece of Intel is located in this hangar's back room. You can find it on a desk out in the open.

With the front of the hangar clear, it's safe to move inside. Enter the hangar and approach the metal door to proceed to the next area.

"AFTER THIS MISSION, DO YOU THINK WE WILL GO HOME?"

The last line of German resistance lies ahead. Take cover behind the snow bank and toss another mortar smoke grenade at the MG42 on the next hill. When you see bodies flying in the air, it's time to push forward.

Proceed to the left of the machinegun embankment and toss a grenade into the doorway. Clear out any survivors with your PPSH.

Peek your head out and toss the rest of your smoke grenades toward the Nazi resistance by the bridge. After the mortars land, move in with your PPSH and carefully advance toward the doorway marked by your objective target.

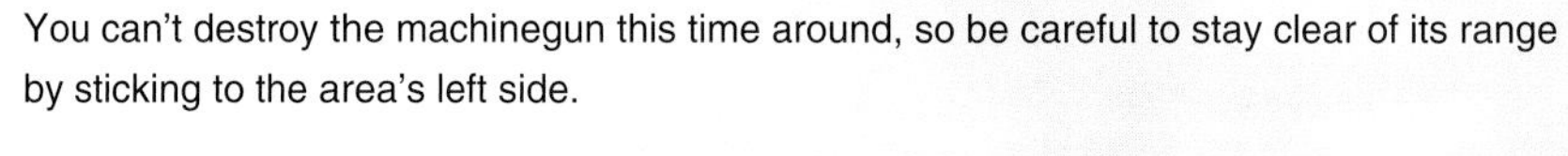

You can't destroy the machinegun this time around, so be careful to stay clear of its range by sticking to the area's left side.

One last building to clear. Head inside with your PPSH and spray the enemies as they move out of cover to confront you. When you reach the rooftop, use up your remaining frag grenades to kill the last line of defense before Steiner.

"...BUT I WAS A SOLDIER THEN. I STILL BELIEVED IN ORDERS."

After the brief interlude, follow your squad inside the ship.

OBJECTIVE Secure the German Weapons

When you're inside, follow the objective markers to the next area.

After the extended cinematic, you have to contend with a new enemy: British Special Forces.

OBJECTIVE Escape the Ship

"GO, FIGHT OUR WAY OUT!"

When you regain control of Reznov, the British fire explosives through the Nova 6 testing chamber and blow the doors off your cell.

When the way is clear, move up to the doorway. Reznov realizes he must destroy the Nova 6 WMD before he escapes the ship.

OBJECTIVE Rig the V2 Explosives

There's no need to rush yet, as British Operatives have entrenched themselves in the next room. Take your time and advance in a crouched position toward the large rocket room. More spec ops rappel down from the ceiling. Stay behind the crate and kill them as they arrive.

Once you eliminate all the enemies in the area, move in toward the rocket marked with the Objective indicator. Hold the Interact button to arm the dynamite. Once it's armed, you have three minutes to escape the ship before it explodes.

OBJECTIVE Escape the Ship before the Detonation

After you arm the bomb, you must shoot a glowing support beam on your left to knock down a nearby walkway that leads up to your escape. Sprint up the walkway and turn right when you reach the corridor. Watch out for the two special operatives at the end of the hall. Spray them with your PPSH and turn left when you get back outside.

LIGHT FOOT

To earn the Light Foot Achievement/Trophy, you must escape the ship in 45 seconds on Veteran difficulty. This leaves you practically no time to engage the enemy.

To complete this goal, practice the level a few times on lower difficulties to learn the path out. Avoid attacking enemies, and focus on sprinting from point to point.

If you aren't going for the Light Foot Achievement/Trophy, you can take your time as you fight your way to the front of the boat. Shoot the British operatives climbing the ship with their backs to you on your right. An explosive barrel there can make the job a lot easier.

When the British men are down, turn your attention to the traitorous Russian soldiers on the bow above. When the bow is clear, it's safe to sprint up to the top.

INTEL

Before you exit the ship, you can find the last Intel on the ground in the snow at the ship's bow.

When you reach the top, look for the rappelling line to hook up and conclude your escape.

SOME WOUNDS NEVER HEAL

You earn this Achievement/Trophy for completing this mission.

VICTOR CHARLIE

1200 February 9, 1968

ALEX MASON

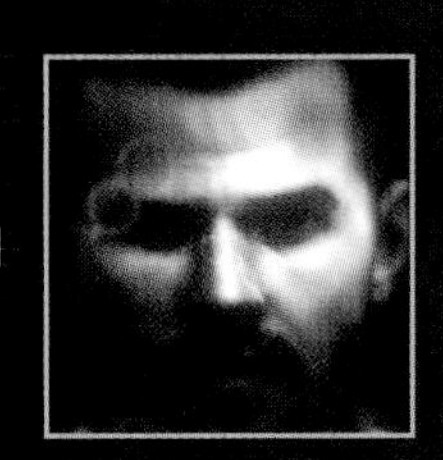

SUPPORT

TRANSMISSION# 14-15.
Designate: XRAY
Location: Knontum Province, Vietnam
Target: Soviet Colonel Kravchenko

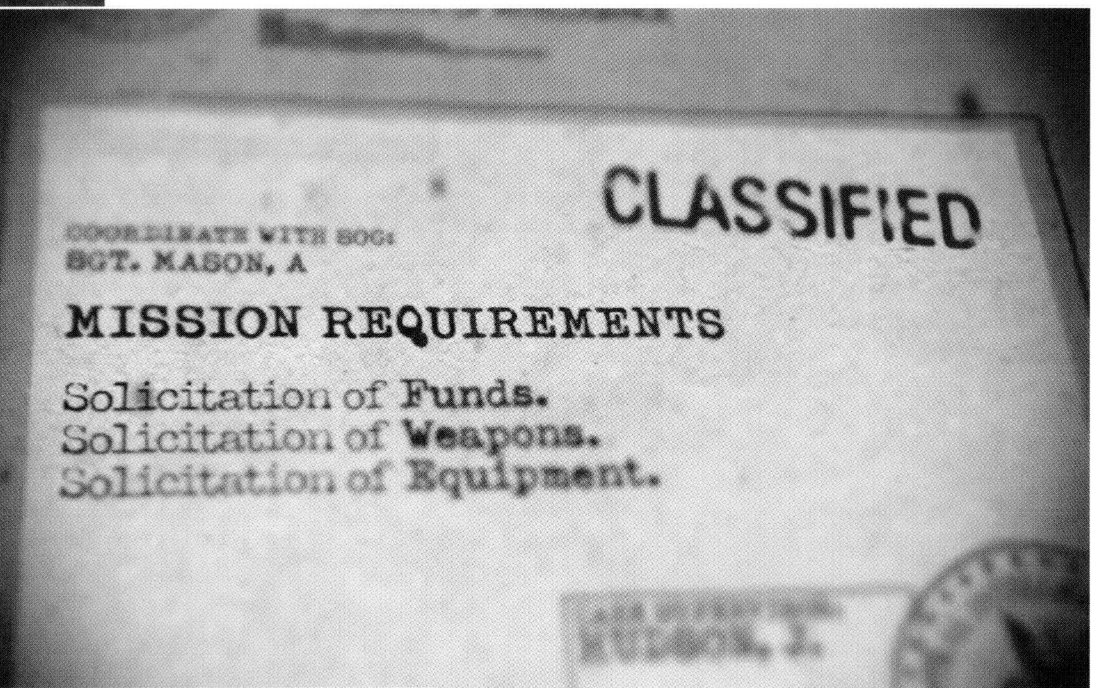

"I NEED SOME HELP HERE!"

You start this mission in a crashed helicopter. When you gain control of Mason, shoot the two NVA firing at you from the front of the helicopter. Rapidly press the Interact button to escape the helicopter.

VICTOR CHARLIE

"Victor Charlie" refers to the U.S. call sign for the enemy you face in this level: the Viet Cong. The Viet Cong are the guerilla forces entrenched in South Vietnam, and they're a major threat to U.S. and South Vietnamese forces alike.

After you're clear of the helicopter, swim forward to your objective marker. You automatically take control of the enemy on the boat. Use his weapon to fire into the enemies ahead and to the left.

Swim forward to the riverbank and kill the two soldiers on the cliff. Stay low and behind Woods, picking off enemies as they charge out of the jungle toward your position.

OBJECTIVE Rendezvous with Whiskey Team

Follow Woods up the river. Mason automatically switches to his knife. Swim toward the Viet Cong boat directly ahead. When you get about 15 meters away from the boat, dive below the surface and swim toward the boat underwater.

Be sure to stay underwater as you approach the boat; if you pop your head up, you fail the mission.

Underneath the boat, press the Melee button to finish off the V.C. onboard. Follow Woods off to the east.

When you get to the dock, you rendezvous with your old pal, Bowman.

"NEVER GETS OLD."

OBJECTIVE Destroy ZPU and Place C4

After Woods' briefing, dive back into the water and head for your first C4 placement spot, marked clearly by the objective indicator. After you place the C4, follow Woods back to the docks. Stay low and follow Woods closely past the sleeping guards. You must use your knife to take down the guard that's eating rice.

UP-CLOSE AND PERSONAL

To earn this Achievement/Trophy, you have to kill three soldiers with your knife. The first one was on the boat—you automatically kill him. The second is the sleeping guard here, and the third guard is resting near the radio a bit further ahead.

INTEL

The first piece of Intel is in the corner of the room just before you get to the enemy listening to the radio.

Stay close to Woods; when he tells you to split up, take a dive into the river via the nearby hole.

After you drop down, plant the Semtex explosive in the area indicated, and then continue upstream. Swim under the boats until you see the dead body. Climb up to get back with Woods.

"EXPLOSIVES ARE PRIMED AND READY."

OBJECTIVE Clear Village

When Mason pulls out the detonator, hold off on pulling the switch until Woods gives the order.

"LET'S SEE WHAT THIS SEMTEX CAN DO."

When you hear the order, pull the detonator. You've caught the Viet Cong completely by surprise. Stay in cover and pick them off from the tree line. Watch for the enemy with the RPG on the rooftop to your left.

WEAPON: WA2000

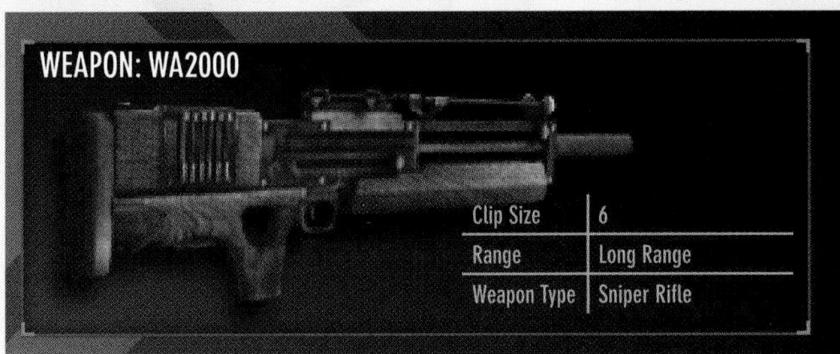

Clip Size	6
Range	Long Range
Weapon Type	Sniper Rifle

Your alternate weapon on this level is the WA2000, a decent sniper rifle. Like most weapons of its ilk, it almost always delivers an instant kill if you hit an enemy's chest area. Additionally, it allows you to stay far back from some of this level's deadlier action.

The small clip size and slow reload time really don't matter much, as this is the only sniper rifle you have access to at this point.

SWITCH OUT

If you aren't a fan of sniper rifles, you can switch out your average WA2000 for some of the cool weapons the Viet Cong employ. You can find variants like the AK-47 Masterkey and Commando ACOGs lying around.

When Bowman gives the go order, move up with your squad. Take cover behind a crate and wait for Woods to identify a spider hole nearby.

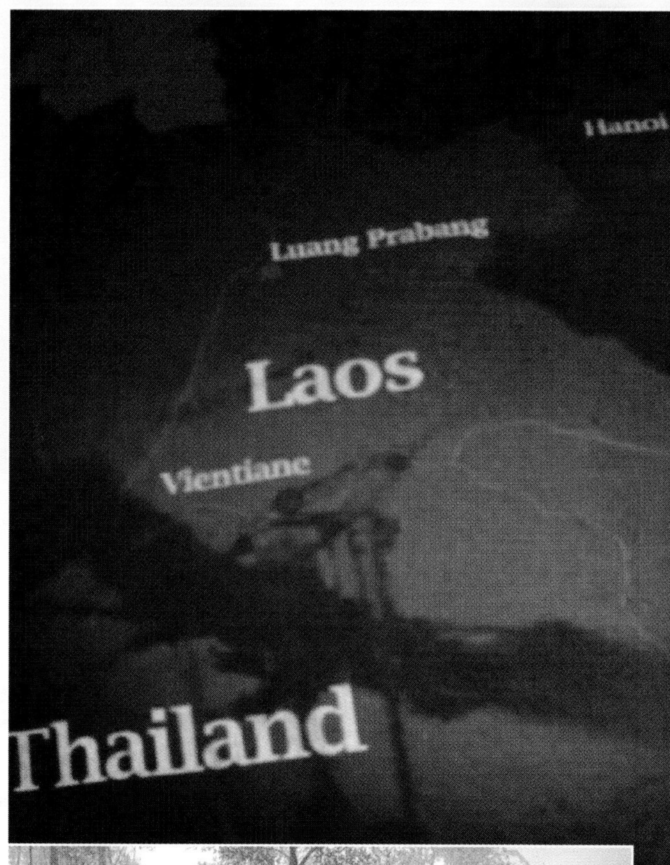

OBJECTIVE Destroy Rat Tunnel

Toss a grenade near the hole, and that's good enough to complete the objective.

INTEL

The second Intel piece is in the hut behind the rat tunnel. It's on the floor near the wooden bench.

Enter the hut and look to your left to see the wooden bench. Look at the floor behind the bench to find the Intel.

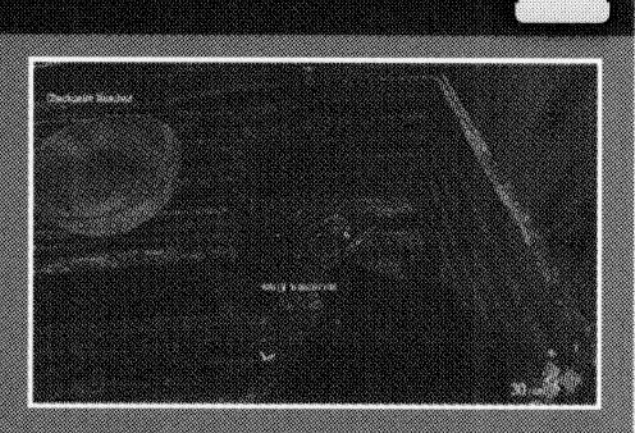

"MASON, MOVE IT, BROTHER."

More V.C. defend the village from the right. Use the wooden stairs for cover, and fire on them with your long-range weaponry. Move around the back of the house, and you come to your ZPU target. When you move toward the U.S. soldiers on the docks, one of them gets killed by incoming fire.

OBJECTIVE Pick Up the M202

The soldier has dropped a Grim Reaper rocket launcher. Move toward the soldier and pick up the rocket launcher. This is a dummy launcher, so you need to line up the shot before you fire.

Fire rockets into the ZPU position to neutralize the enemy and clear the way for your air support. Before you move on, be sure to switch out the Reaper for a more versatile weapon.

HEAVY HAND

If you want to earn the Heavy Hand Achievement/Trophy, you can hold onto the Grim Reaper after you destroy the ZPU. The next area has a MG that you can blow up with the Grim Reaper to earn the award.

More V.C. emerge from the building on your left: three stand on the deck on the building's right side, and one uses the large shutters for cover. Remember—wooden shutters don't provide much cover.

Watch out for the guys on the deck—they have serious RPG firepower. Either hang back and take them out from cover, or sprint past them to your next objective.

When you move up to the next house, stay inside and pick off the enemies outside, using the windows for cover. Watch out for the MG off to the right here; it can cut you down in seconds.

OBJECTIVE Clear North Village

Carefully peak out and use your longest-range weapon to fire at the body of the MG gunner—his head is well protected. When he goes down, Woods orders you onward. A few more enemies defend this last part of the village. They are no challenge for your squad. Take them down and proceed forward to the tunnels.

OBJECTIVE Find Kravchenko

Turn on your pistol's flashlight and follow Swift down the tunnel. Don't shoot Reznov when he leaps down from above.

"NO ONE FIGHTS ALONE."

There's no saving Swift as the V.C. plunges the knife into his chest. Save yourself and use your Python to kill the enemy before you continue down the tunnel.

Three V.C. guard the room at the tunnel's end. Use your Python to take them down, and wait for Reznov. Follow him deeper into the tunnels. When you take point, move forward carefully; more V.C. are ahead.

INTEL 

The third piece of Intel is down the left path when the tunnel splits during this section. Move down the left path, and you can't miss the Intel on the ground roughly halfway down the section.

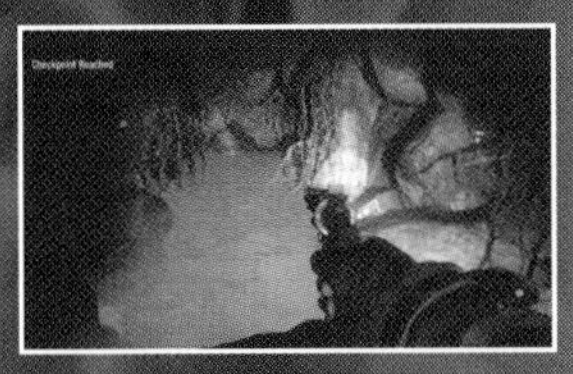

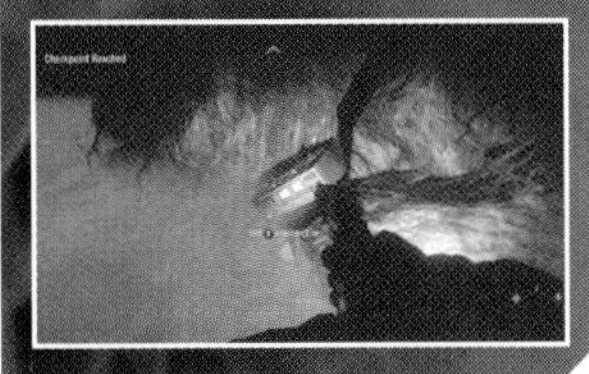

Continue forward, killing the enemies as they pop out in the tunnel ahead of you. There isn't much to this section—just be ready and beat the enemy to the shot. When you make it to Kravchenko's room, open the door and get ready to run.

KEEP YOUR GUN READY

After you kill each group of enemies, be sure to reload your Python; it can hold only six shots at once. You don't want to get caught a bullet short in these narrow tunnels.

"HURRY MASON! I DO NOT WISH THIS RAT HOLE TO BECOME MY GRAVE."

OBJECTIVE Escape

Fight your way out of the collapsing tunnel by pressing the Melee button to complete the level.

IT'S YOUR FUNERAL 

Earn this award for completing Numbers, Project Nova, and Victor Charlie on Veteran difficulty.

CRASH SITE

1300 February 11, 1968

ALEX MASON

SUPPORT

TRANSMISSION# 2-15-4-25.

Designate: INDIA
Location: Mekong River, Laos
Mission: Extract Intel from Crashed Soviet Plane

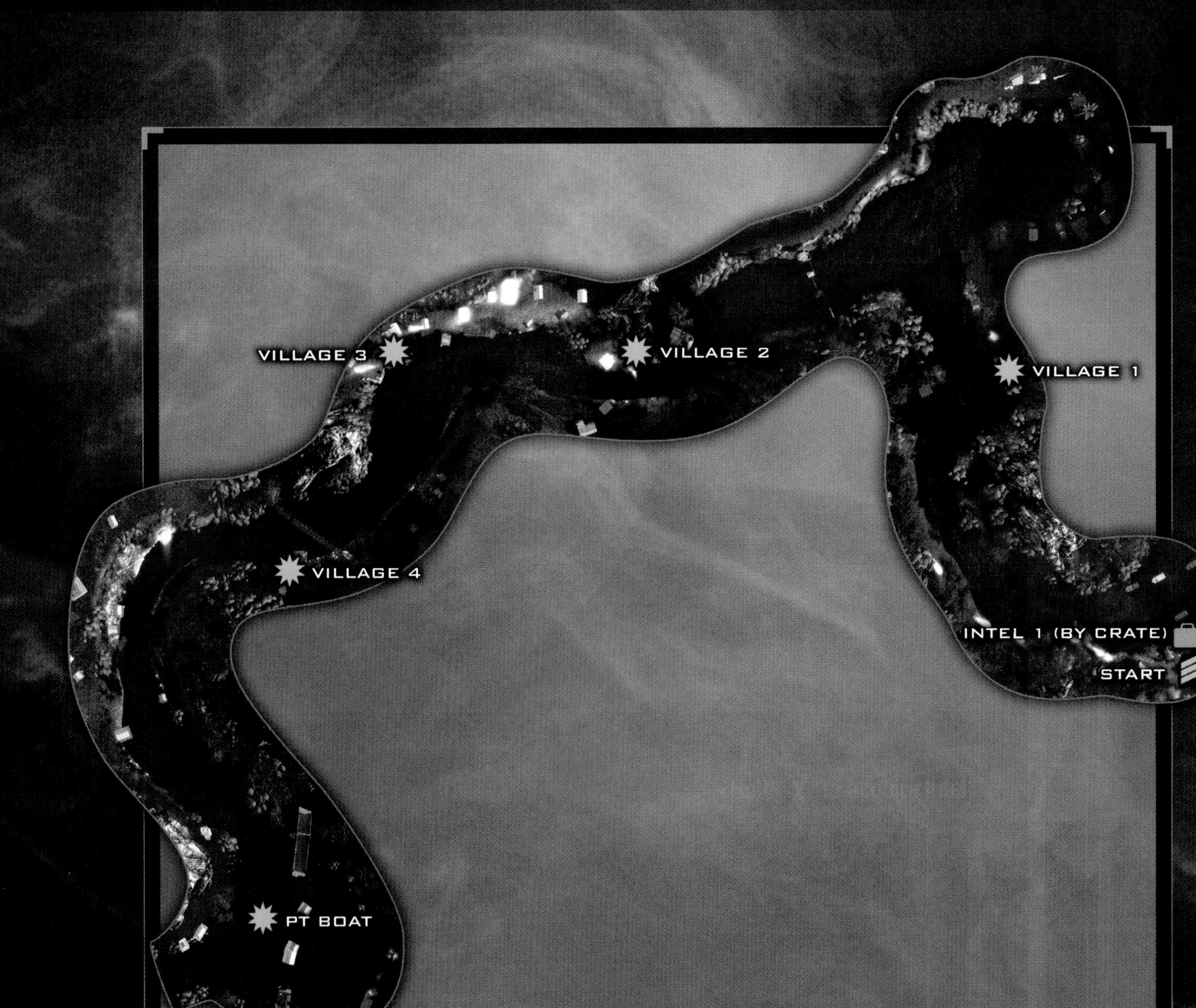

OBJECTIVE Regroup at Dock

When the level starts, move to the new objective marker to board the ship. Jump over the edge of the boat to board. Move to the steering wheel to take control.

INTEL 

This piece of Intel is directly ahead of your starting position and to the left, just before you get on the dock.

PBR

Patrol Boat, River, or PBRs, were armored war ships small enough to navigate rivers in Vietnam.

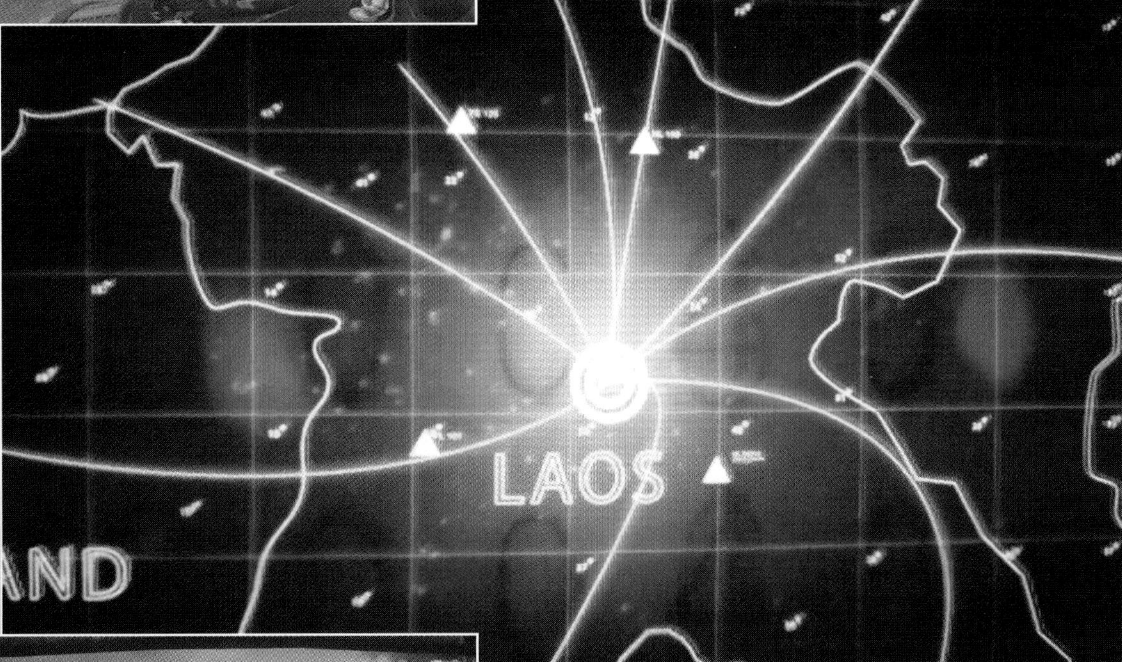

On this level, you primarily control the Swift Boat. Not only do you control where the boat goes, but you also aim and fire the missiles and the MG.

This can take some coordination, so until you get used to it, focus on firing your missiles first, and don't worry too much about driving around. There's no rush through this level. As long as you don't push forward too quickly, you can generally hang back and pick off the enemies with the boat's powerful weaponry.

The Aim Down Sight button fires missiles. Woods and Bowman fire the missiles for you from either side of the boat. When either runs out, it takes them a moment to reload their M202 rocket launchers.

"MAN THE GUN, DON'T GET KILLED."

The Fire button activates the extremely powerful MG. Don't underestimate the MG; it can generally do the same job as the missiles, but it just takes a bit longer. A meter below the MG icon on the screen's bottom-right indicates the gun's heat level.

You steer the boat with the Movement analog. Push forward and proceed up the river. When The Rolling Stones start playing, it's time to rock and roll.

OBJECTIVE Head Up River to Crash Site

LORD NELSON

This Achievement/Trophy is a tribute to the legendary Admiral Nelson who commanded an incredible victory against the French at the Battle of Trafalgar. To earn it, you must destroy every tower and vessel you encounter on this level.

This isn't too hard, as the level doesn't force you to rush at any point. Just be sure to fire rockets into any towers you see on the shorelines before you move to the next village. Also, don't forget to destroy all the towers in the final boss area.

Destroying the other vessels is part of the mission, so you should automatically fulfill that part of the requirement.

The award should pop after you kill the PT Boat at the end of the level's riverboat section.

As you approach the first village, light up the houses on your left. This should kill most of the enemies on that bank.

Now, turn your weaponry to the right shore. Hit the guard tower in the back with your missiles; use your MG to eliminate the RPG soldiers on the shore.

OBJECTIVE Destroy Missile Launchers

When you clear the first village, three targets light up on the ridge directly ahead. These are trucks carrying missile launchers. Hang back and take down each truck with your rockets.

When all the rocket trucks are destroyed, turn back and drive toward the dam.

OBJECTIVE Destroy Enemy Targets

The second village has another guard tower on the right. Focus on destroying the structures on the right side before you turn back to mop up any survivors on the bank's left side.

Up ahead, another missile truck fires from the road. Fire missiles at the objective indicator until you see the truck blow.

The third village has plenty more RPG-wielding V.C., but you can avoid them by hanging back and destroying the set of buildings closest to you on the right. Push forward a bit and use your rockets to take out the guard tower on the hill. Then turn your guns left to blow up the house on that side of the river bank.

Another missile-launching truck is just ahead on the left side of the road. Blow it to smithereens and continue along the river. If you take some damage in this section, wait a moment for the damage to clear before you push on.

When you approach the fourth village, focus your fire on the building on your left. Then fire your missiles at the large structure dead ahead. One last building is on the ridge above the large structure.

Turn your attention back to the river as some enemy boats attack you. It's hard to make out the boats because of their spotlights. Just unload into the spotlights with either of your weapons.

An MG-enabled truck sits up on the hill. Blow it with your missiles before you continue along the river.

Two more targets show up on your HUD. Before you move in to engage them, destroy the second wave of boats approaching on the river. Blow up the buildings on either side of the river to take care of any shoreline targets.

Now, fire your missiles into the target closest to you—this is another ZPU cannon. The second target is a stronghold, so use your missiles to tear it down.

"SOMETHING BIG IS ON ITS WAY..."

Proceed to the last checkpoint on the river, and a giant PT boat attacks you. To take down the PT boat, you have to fire into its rear. Move your boat to the left when the PT boat approaches; this should give you a clear shot at the ship's engines.

Follow the boat and unload with both of your weapons, and try to stay behind the PT boat as it moves around the area.

OBJECTIVE Head Up River to Crash Site

Move toward the next objective marker to trigger the end of this section of the level. When you regain control of the boat, follow the objective markers down the river. When you get off the boat, switch to the KS-23 shotgun and move up the trail.

INTEL

The second Intel piece is directly in the middle of the trail after you leave the boat behind—you can't miss it.

OBJECTIVE Investigate Crash Site

Several V.C. hide behind the rocks in the next area. Approach with caution and use the KS-23 to wipe them out when they attack. When the charging enemies are down, switch to your Commando and pick off the next two waves.

When the gunfire stops, crouch down and proceed a little further up the trail. There, more enemies emerge from the jungle. Use cover and pick them off from a distance.

Stay low and continue up the brook. When Woods warns you about snipers, find cover and look for the glint from the sniper's scope in the tree directly to your southeast. Finish off the soldiers advancing from the waterfall.

Continue along the path until you get a sniper warning. This shooter is in a tree to the northeast. Watch for his scope glass's glare to target him and pick him off before you move on.

An enemy helicopter arrives to drop off more soldiers in the area. Stay behind the rock overlooking the outcropping ahead. Use your flash grenades to stun the enemies out of cover, and pick them off with the ACOG scope on your Commando rifle.

"SNIPERS IN THE TREES!"

Turn up the hill to the west, but keep your eye on the palm tree to the right. A sniper appears there; when he does, pick him off with your Commando. As you move up the hill, more Spetsnaz helicopter into the area. Use your flash and frag grenades to flush them out.

"WE HAVE TO CLIMB THAT WING TO REACH THE FUSELAGE."

You've now made it to your main target: the crashed spy plane. Stay to the left as you climb the plane's wing to avoid getting knocked over the side when it shifts.

INTEL

On your way into the back of the plane, you can find this level's last piece of Intel. It's located on the ground along the main path, just after you jump off the plane's fuselage.

On the other side of the wing, jump down and enter the back of the plane. Woods and Bowman investigate the WMD crate—take the China Lake.

Wait for Bowman to remove the cargo netting, and move to the front of the plane.

OBJECTIVE Defend Crash Site

When you look out the front of the plane, you can see a lot of enemies crawling below. Fire into them with your China Lake. Be wary of the two enemy boats that arrive on the river. You can destroy them with your China Lake.

After about a minute, enemy choppers arrive and the level ends.

NEVER GET OFF THE BOAT

Earn this award for completing Crash Site.

WMD (PART 1)

0500 February 18, 1968

CAPTAIN MOSELY
JASON HUDSON

SUPPORT

TRANSMISSION# 9-19.
Designate: SIERRA
Location: Beale Air Force Base, California, USA
Mission: Assist Covert Team behind Enemy Lines

In the first part of this mission, you switch back and forth between CIA agent Jason Hudson on the ground and the SR-71 Blackbird pilot flying overhead.

Follow the onscreen instructions to get the jet off the ground.

When you're looking at the Blackbird's view screen, use the Movement analog and the Aim Down Sight and Fire buttons to adjust the view screen's crosshair.

PATHFINDER

To earn the Pathfinder Achievement/Trophy, you must get through the first part of the level without dying or restarting from a checkpoint. This isn't just while you're in the Blackbird—you also have to get through the first-person Hudson events to earn the award.

OBJECTIVE Locate Kilo One

Your first task is to locate your squad. They are the group of four soldiers just to the north of the camera starting position.

Zoom in on them to automatically highlight them on your screen. With your team highlighted, zoom out and instruct your squad to move east via the Jump button.

When your commander tells you that enemies are on their way, order your squad into the safe house to the north. Once in the safe house, you zoom down to control Hudson.

"ENEMY INFANTRY INCOMING... TAKE THEM OUT."

Hudson is crouched behind a desk. When you gain control of him, immediately face the wall behind you. Wait for the enemy's flashbang to go off, and then turn back to the room to kill any survivors.

Enemies attack from the east and south sides of the house. Use the desk for cover.

"KILO, YOU ARE CLEAR."

When you're back in the Blackbird, issue an order for the team to exit the rear of the house.

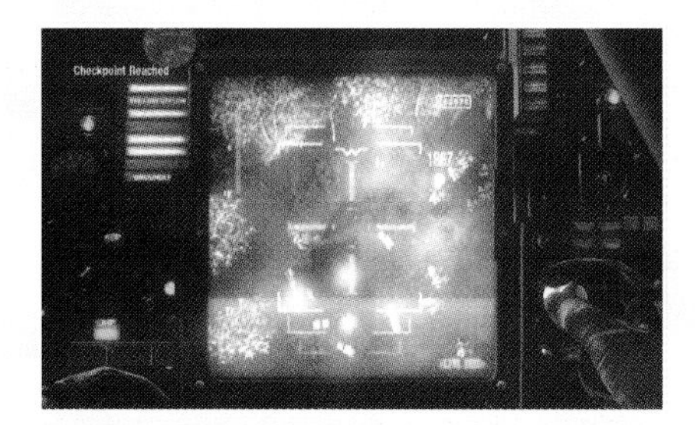

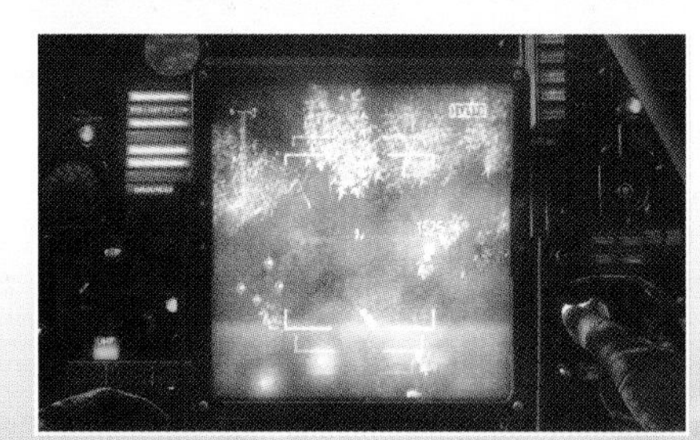

Just up the wood path, two soldiers are having a smoke. Issue a kill order on them by pressing the Jump button when the camera crosshairs are over them. Your squad automatically disposes of them. When they do, issue an order up to the next objective marker.

OBJECTIVE Regroup on the Ridge

When your squad gets halfway to the barracks, a surprise enemy patrol pops onscreen. Issue an order for your team to dig in immediately via the Melee button.

OBJECTIVE Clear Barracks and Destroy Com Link

Once the Major gives the all clear, order your troops on to the barracks.

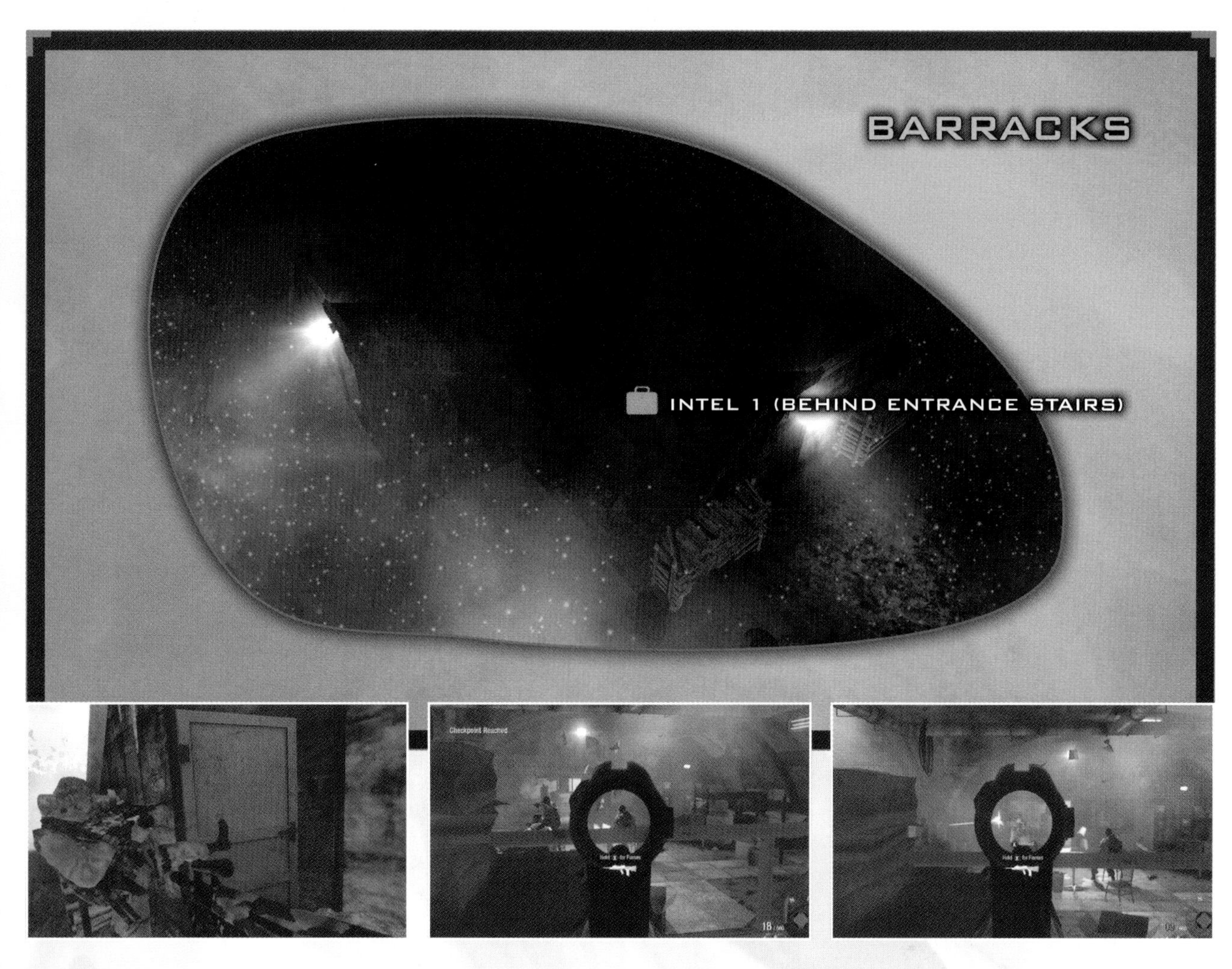

You once again control Hudson. This group of enemies is more challenging than the one you faced in the prior area. When you get through the door, immediately look for cover behind one of the metal crates in the entrance area.

Mind your squad as they breach on your left; you don't want to shoot them by accident. Focus your fire on the enemies directly ahead. They funnel in through the narrow doorway, and it's easy to mow them down. Feel free to use grenades to soften them up—you are weapons free in this area.

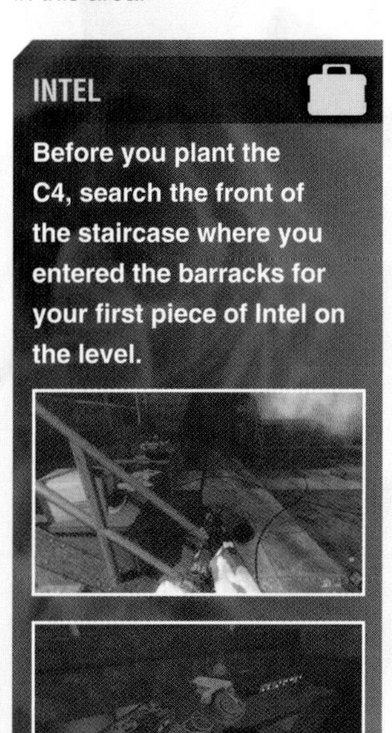

INTEL

Before you plant the C4, search the front of the staircase where you entered the barracks for your first piece of Intel on the level.

When the enemies are down, you hear the Major give you a green light. Look for the large wall breaker box and plant C4 on it. Step away and blow it to complete this part of the mission.

OBJECTIVE Guide Kilo One to the Insertion Point

When you return to the Blackbird, guide your team up to the last objective to set them up for phase two of the mission.

WMD (PART 2)

1700 February 18, 1968

CAPTAIN MOSELY

JASON HUDSON

SUPPORT

TRANSMISSION# 23-8-15.

Designate: DELTA

Location: Yamantau, Bashkortostan, USSR

Mission: Infiltrate and Destroy Nova 6 WMD Program

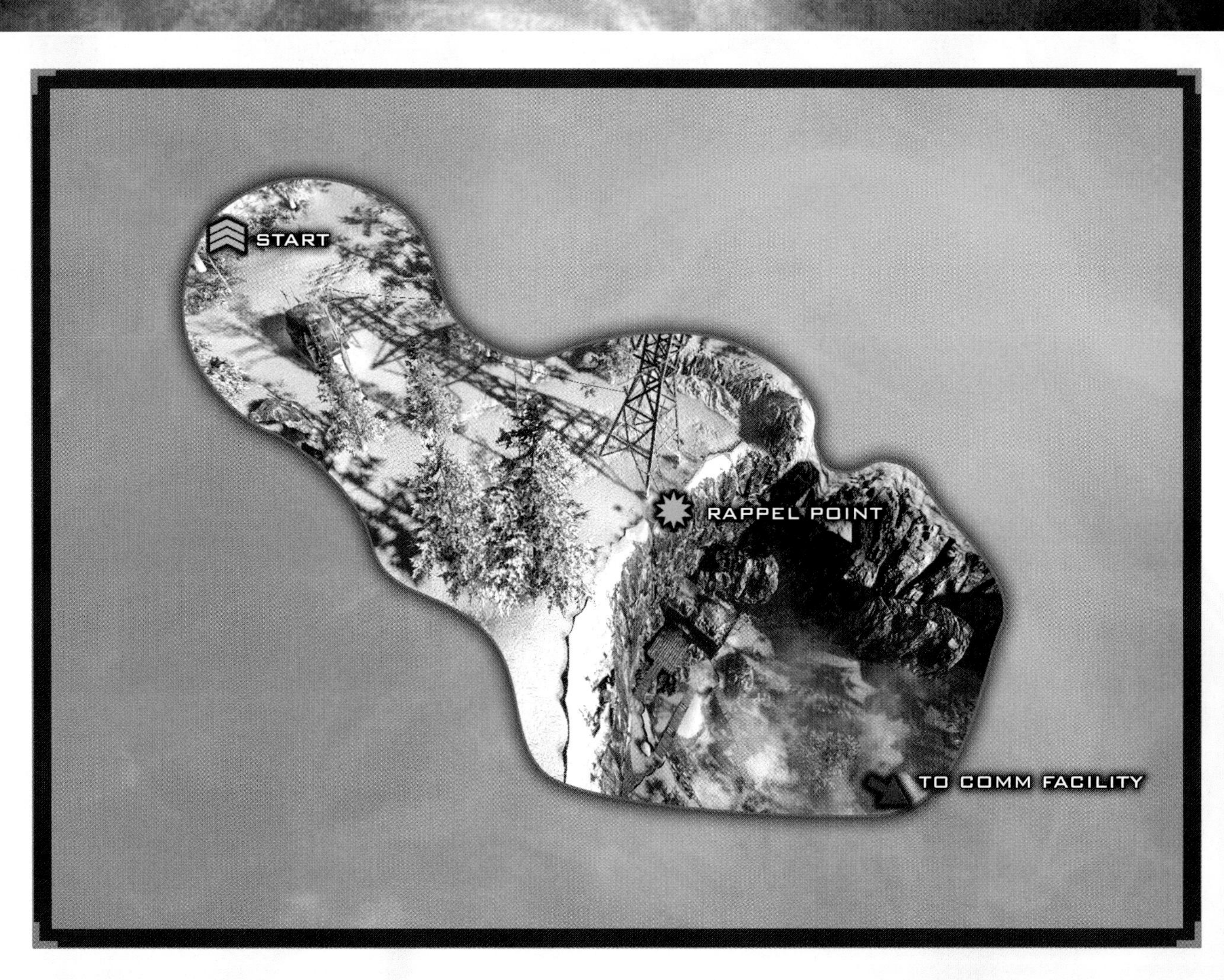

"STAY LOW."

MR. BLACK OP

There is another tricky Achievement/Trophy to earn on this level: get through to the relay station without getting spotted by the Soviets. This walkthrough covers the stealth path through the mission. If you blow your stealth, you can quickly restart at the most recent checkpoint by holding the Grenade button until it explodes in your hand...morbid but effective.

When you regain control of Hudson, follow Weaver ahead, but be ready to go prone at a moment's notice (hold the Crouch button). As soon as Hudson calls for it, go prone to avoid enemy detection.

OBJECTIVE Hook Up

Follow Weaver closely; when the area's clear, move up to the railing and use the Interact button to hook up your rappelling line. To Rappel safely, alternate pressing the Aim Down Sight and Fire buttons to release the rope and brake before you get too much speed. You should release for only a second or two before reapplying the brake.

The second time you hook up, it isn't actually a full-on rappel. Rather, it's a setup for a breach:

BREACH

Shoot the soldier manning the communications board directly in front of you. Next, fire at the guy directly behind him. Finally, take down the last man standing in the middle.

After the breach, follow your men out and down the metal stairs.

"KILO ONE APPROACHING THE OBJECTIVE."

When you see the two soldiers standing next to each other, switch to your crossbow and pick off either one—Weaver gets the other.

You must now handle a challenging series of encounters as you move toward your goal. We've broken down these encounters by target. When you encounter a target with more than one soldier, Weaver helps you by shooting the second target automatically.

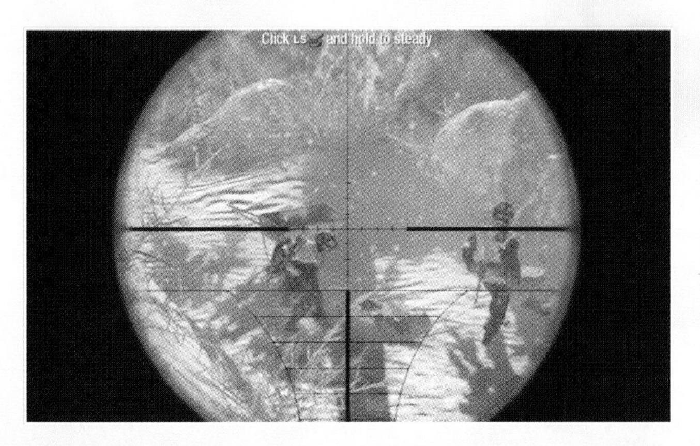

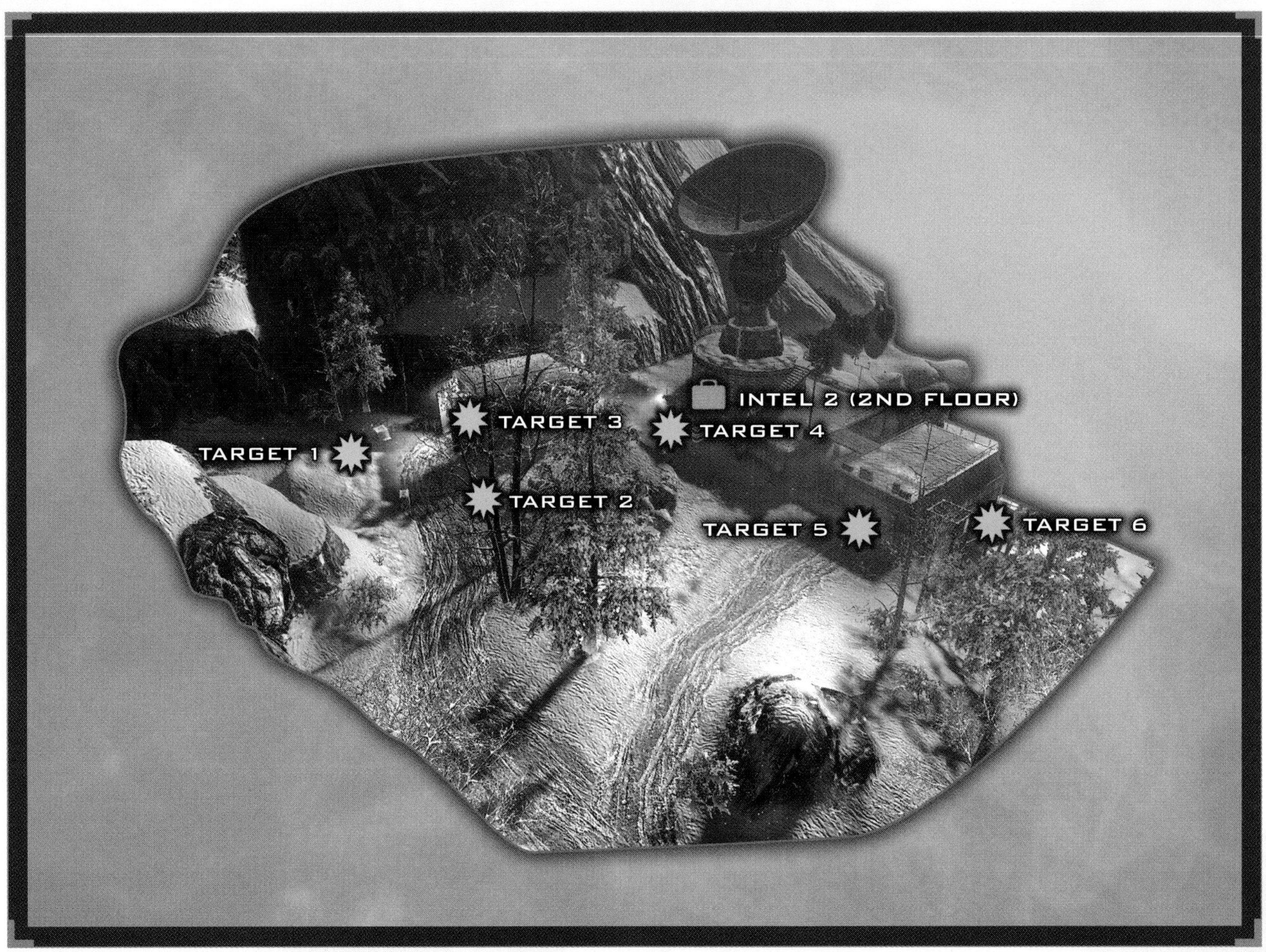

TARGET 1

The first target is the snow-covered soldier walking away from your squad on the left. You have to take him down before he reaches the soldiers working on the truck inside.

TARGET 2

The second target set is the two soldiers working on the truck to your right. Shoot either one with your crossbow.

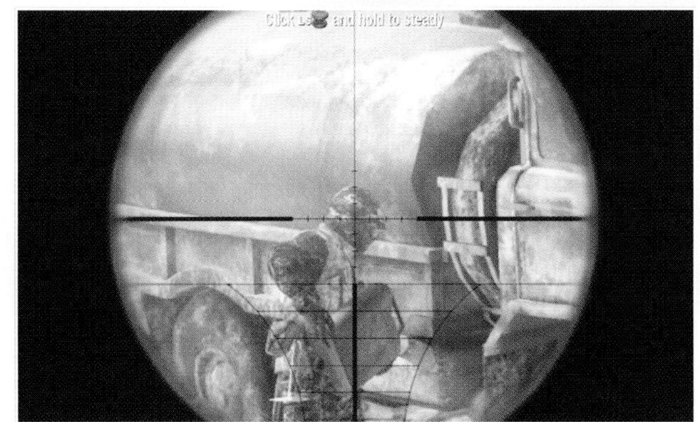

TARGET 3

Before you fire on target three, make sure Weaver is in position.

Target three is the pair of soldiers working on the truck to your left. Shoot the solider sitting on the barrel, and Weaver takes care of the guy in the back.

TARGET 4

To approach target four, move through the red garage that target three occupied. Two soldiers shovel snow directly ahead.

Wait until Weaver is in position (you can track him with the "Follow" indicator), and fire at the one on the left.

TARGET 5

Target five is the most difficult; there are three soldiers. One soldier is inside working on some machinery, one soldier is on the roof, and one soldier patrols in a circle.

You might want to circle back through the red shed to get a better vantage on the enemies. Wait until the patrol soldier is moving away from his two comrades, and then take out the soldier on the roof with your crossbow. Next up is the patrolling soldier. Make sure he's a good distance away from the soldier in the garage, and then take him out.

Finish off the soldier in the garage, and target five is clear.

TARGET 6

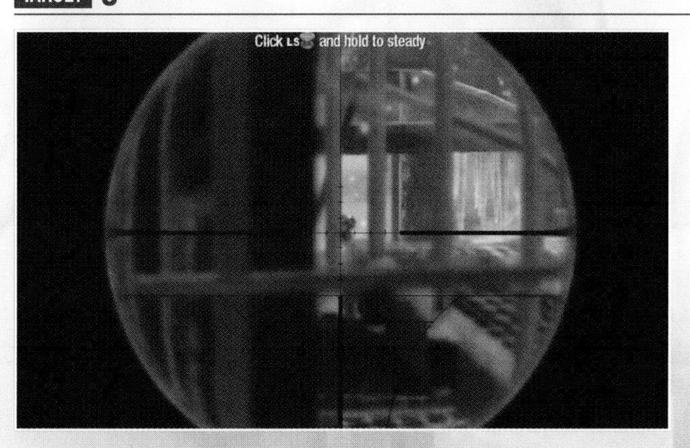

Target six is an enemy patrolling the staircase down to the next area. Use your silenced AUG assault rifle to kill him when his back is turned to your team. Move onto to the staircase slowly; it's easy to walk into his field of view as he patrols in a small circle.

With all six targets down, Weaver moves up to a door. Fire at the door's hinges with your AUG, and Weaver automatically takes down a soldier in the doorway.

Wait until your teammates say they are in position, and then open the door to enter the main communications facility.

OBJECTIVE Neutralize the Comstat Personnel

Many foes are in the downstairs area. Use grenades and your AUG to kill the enemies below. Wait until they are all dead before you proceed around the outside of the area.

CROSSBOW TIME!

You are now weapons free—time to use some more of those explosive bolts. Switch to your crossbow's explosive bolts by pressing Left on the D-Pad.

INTEL

The second Intel piece is located in a back room on this main communications area's second floor. Follow the upper railing around until you see an orange-lit room. Enter it to find the Intel on a nearby bench.

"KILO ONE, YOU HAVE MULTIPLE TARGETS INBOUND FOR THE COMSTAT."

Follow your team downstairs and provide them cover with your crossbow bolts. More soldiers attack from the upper railing where you entered. Shoot bolts into the walls behind the enemies to kill them regardless of whether they're behind cover.

OBJECTIVE Disable the Comstat

When your team has cleared the room, you must now disable the comm room satellite. Do so by moving toward the piece of electronics marked by your objective indicator. Head outside to trigger a special event.

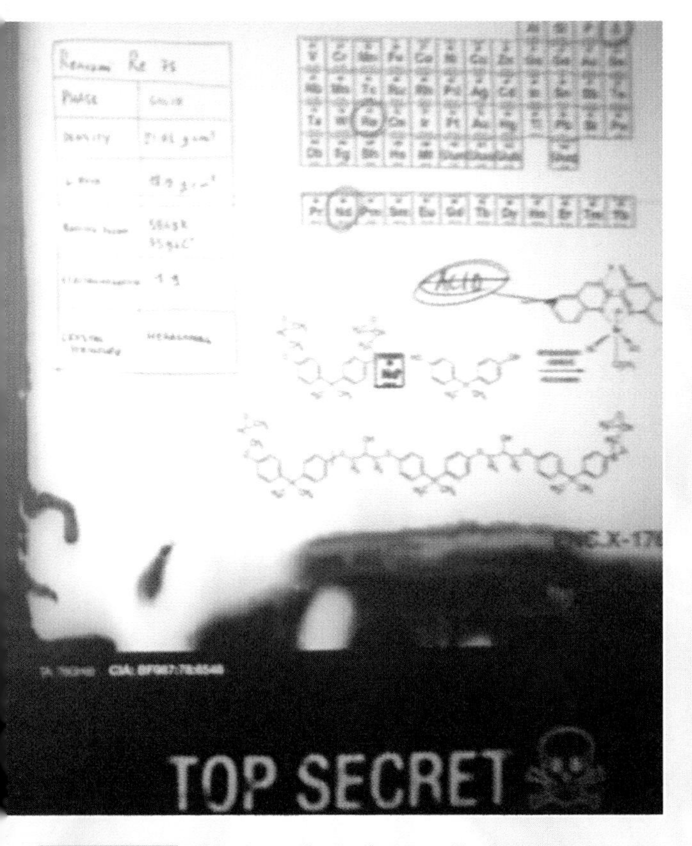

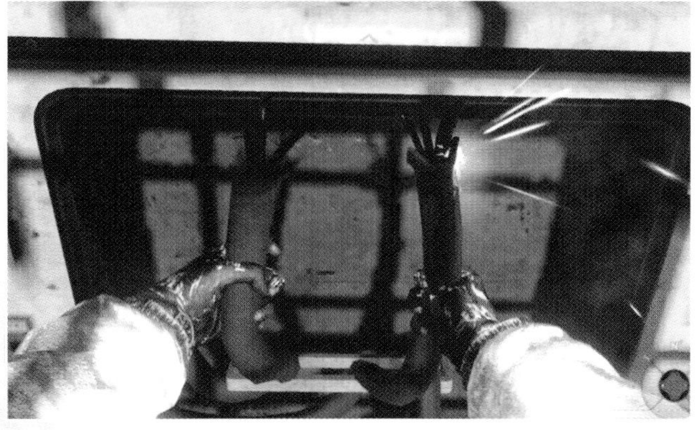

OBJECTIVE Proceed to Jump Point

To get across the bridge, you must Sprint Jump across. You should remember how to do this from the Numbers mission. The enemy rocket triggered an avalanche, so you must race to the ledge marked by your objective indicator to effect your escape. Hope you didn't forget your parachute.

"THEY'VE ALREADY STARTED CLEARING HOUSE—MOVE!"

After you land, you find a group of soldiers burning intelligence in some makeshift bonfires. Fire an explosive bolt into the truck at the rear, and clear out the rest with your Steyr AUG.

Stay behind cover and nail the troop transport that arrives on the scene with another explosive bolt. Advance through the area, sticking to cover. Watch out for the MG in a distant building; it explodes the truck at the intersection near your objective marker.

Head inside the building on the right to avoid the MG, and use your AUG to take down the enemies inside. Proceed around the corner, take cover, and toss stun grenades to soften up the resistance, making it easy to pick them off with your AUG. Follow Weaver when he advances into the next building.

Follow Weaver into Steiner's research lab.

INTEL

The building rigged with explosives contains your last piece of Intel on this level. Move to the middle of the area, and search the large tables for the Intel. It's located directly below two large, blue, explosive barrels.

OBJECTIVE Escape Yamantau Facility

After Steiner declares his bargain, he reopens the doors. You must escape the facility before it blows. Unfortunately, no one gave the nearby Soviet spec ops the news, so they do their best to keep you in the facility...even at the cost of their own lives.

Take cover behind the steel tables, and take down the agents as they advance on your team.

When the enemies inside are clear, move up behind cover and stick an explosive bolt on the machine gunner on the back of the truck outside. You can't destroy the truck because you need it to escape, so be sure to hit the gunner with the bolt.

With the outside relatively clear, move up to the truck to man the MG on the back.

Keep the enemies approaching from the truck's rear at bay while Weaver hotwires the ignition.

"COME ON—STUPID PIECE OF **** TRUCK!"

PAYBACK

1100 February 19, 1968

ALEX MASON

SUPPORT

TRANSMISSION# 14-15-20.
Designate: XRAY
Location: Somewhere in Vietnam...
Mission: Escape!

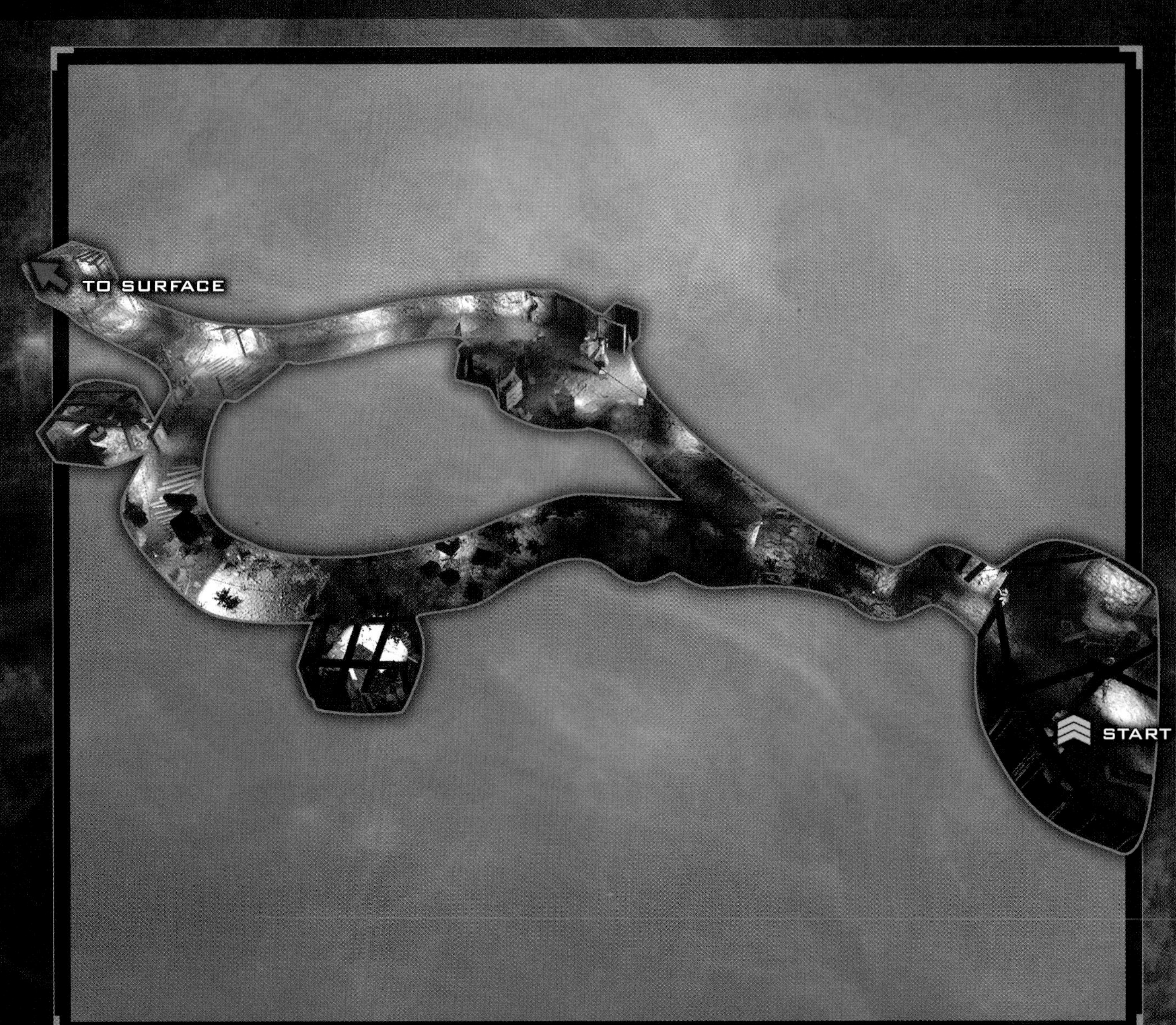

"DRAGOVICH HAD US LIKE RATS IN CAGES..."

TOP SECRET

MEMORANDUM TO: ██████████

FROM: Ryan Jackson, Chief Analyst

██████████ It is unknown what exactly transpired in the week after agents Mason, Woods, and Bowman were presumed Killed In Action during their mission in Laos. ██████████

What is clear is that the men were imprisoned and tortured by the Viet Cong. ██████████ Mason's debriefing indicated a vindictive and brutal enemy held them captive. ██████████

After the events that open the level, you regain control of Mason holding a V.C. hostage with a revolver. Use the enemy as a human shield and kill the two V.C. directly ahead.

OBJECTIVE Get the Soviet

Mason automatically loots and arms an AK-47 off the corpse of his hostage. Follow Woods down the tunnel ahead.

AK-47 MODS

Most of the enemies you kill on this level are armed with AK-47 rifles; each has a random mod. Mods you should look for are the ACOG scope and the Flamethrower attachment. Before you proceed after Woods, search the room for an upgrade to your vanilla AK.

Don't worry about keeping up with the Russian in this part. The V.C. is thick here, and you don't want to get killed by sprinting ahead too fast.

When the path splits, let Woods go right while you take the left path. Be ready for two enemies that drop into the tunnel directly ahead. Kill them and push forward.

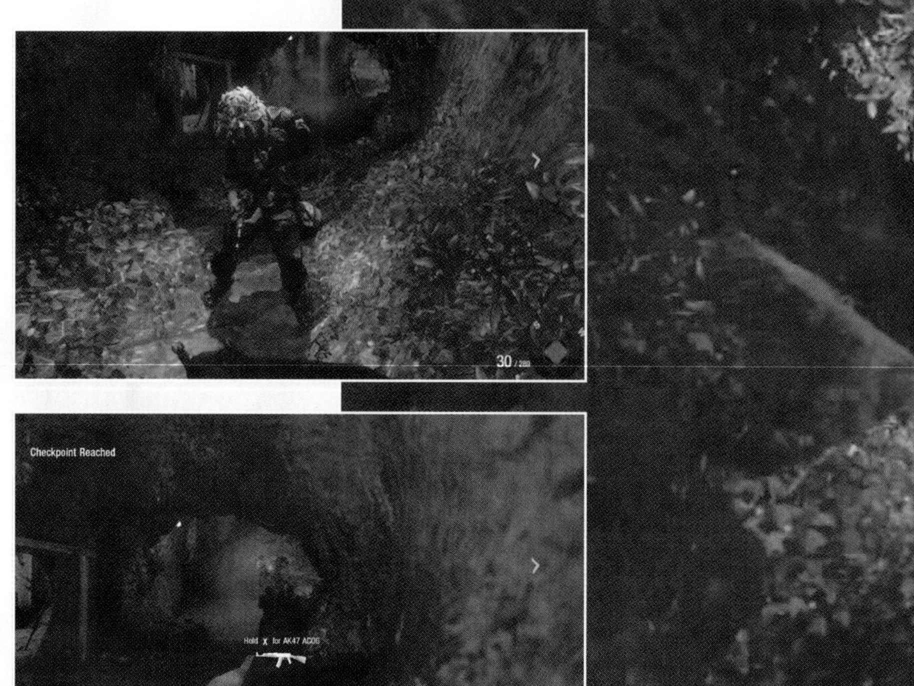

ARMORY ROOM

As you move down the left tunnel, you come across an ammo room to the left. Inside, you can find AK-47s with ACOG and Extended Mag mods, as well as a Galil rifle. There's also an RPG with two rockets.

Continue through the tunnel, and a small group of V.C. attack. Stay low and spray the tunnel with your AK to clear your path. Search the next room on your left for an Olympia shotgun, which makes a fine alternate weapon for your AK-47.

WEAPON: OLYMPIA

Clip Size	2
Range	Short Range
Weapon Type	Shotgun

The Olympia's biggest shortcoming is that it's only double-barreled. This means you have to reload every time you fire two shots.

However, a loaded Olympia is a great alternate weapon for your AK. Keep the Olympia loaded and ready to pull out in case an enemy gets the jump at you at short range.

AK-47 MODS

You can also find an AK-47 with Grenade Launcher attachment in the same room you find the Olympia shotgun.

Continue up the tunnel, killing the V.C. as they emerge. This is a straightforward shootout, so there isn't much strategy to employ beyond staying low and shooting anything that moves.

Remember that you have grenades and can use them to clear corners before you advance down each section of the tunnel.

Woods meets you at the intersection of the next tunnel. Press forward and kill the enemies at the upturned table. Move to the table and use it for cover to clear out the enemies in the next room. If you start taking shots, go prone and the enemies can't hit you.

Several enemies are in this room. Woods presses the attack, so you can hang back and pick off the enemies as they emerge. Use grenades to clear enemies behind cover.

INTEL

The first Intel piece is on a shelf directly to the right when you enter this room with the waterfall.

The Soviet is stuck on a locked gate at the end of the next tunnel. You know what to do.

OBJECTIVE Escape the Tunnels

Help Woods out of the tunnels, and you arrive on a helipad for a Hind helicopter.

OBJECTIVE Capture the Hind

Follow Woods and find some good cover. When Woods gives you the go, open up on the enemies. Start with a grenade, and use your AK to pick off the enemies in the chaos.

With the area clear, move up to the Hind.

INTEL

Before you board the Hind, you can grab the second Intel piece on a table in front of the green tent.

OBJECTIVE Fly to Kravcheno's Base

Like the patrol boat, you control all the weaponry and movement of the helicopter. Don't worry about crashing—the helicopter's altitude is controlled automatically as you move forward and back along the trail.

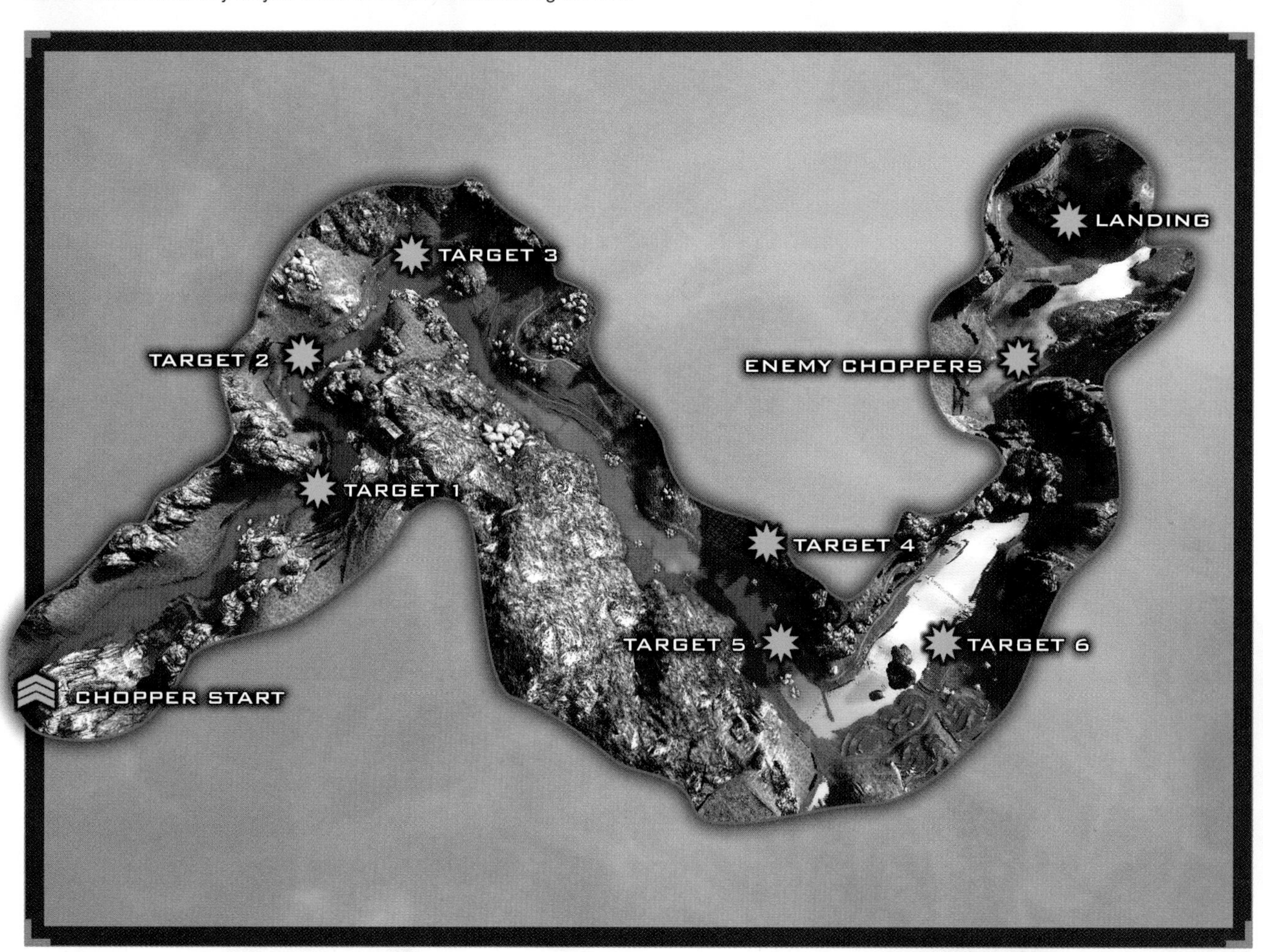

WITH EXTREME PREJUDICE

To earn this Achievement/Trophy, you need to use only the rockets equipped on the Hind, and completely avoid using the MG. Killing enemy choppers with only missiles is tricky on the harder difficulties, so we recommend trying it on Recruit difficulty. Keep your finger off the Fire button throughout this sequence to ensure you don't accidently fire the MG.

You receive this award when you successfully land the chopper at the end of your run.

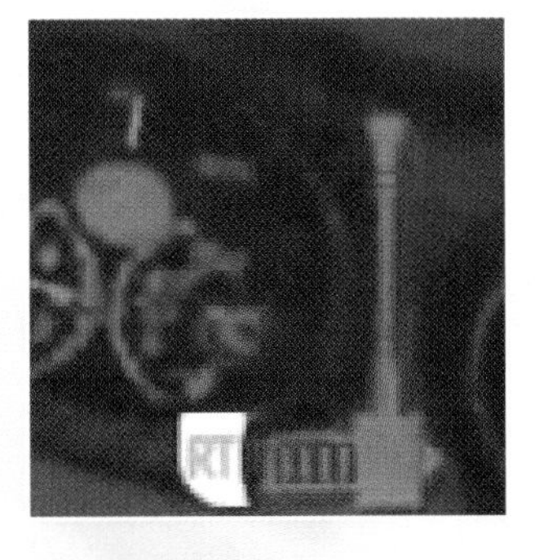

The helicopter has two weapons. The MG is simple to operate and similar to the one you had on the patrol boat, except that the gun cannot overheat. Hold the Fire button to activate it. Unless you're going for the special Achievement/Trophy, you should fire this gun almost the whole time.

The Hind's missiles work differently from other weapons you've used throughout the game. If you hold the Aim Down Sight button, the helicopter starts to ready the missiles for fire. If you hold the button for about five seconds, you can ready all eight missiles to be fired very quickly. This is a very effective tactic against tougher enemies, like helicopters.

One other note on the Hind's missiles is that they don't automatically reload unless you completely empty the payload. Press the Reload button to start the reload process just after you fire your rockets. When you feel like you have a good grasp of the Hind's control mechanisms, proceed forward along the river.

TARGET 1

"LOOKS LIKE A .50 CAL ON THAT BRIDGE."

Your first target is directly ahead: a wooden bridge mounted with AA weaponry. Position your helicopter above the bridge for a clear shot, and then unleash your missiles to destroy it.

TARGET 2

"CHARLIE'S HIGHWAY BELOW."

Next up is a large V.C. village. The village is full of ZPUs, RPG-wielding soldiers, and fuel trucks.

Destroy the base with missiles and MG fire from a safe distance. Watch out for the Vietnamese boats below.

TARGET 3

"THAT'S AN NVA SUPPLY STATION!"

A second base is just around the corner. Focus on the PT boat moving away in the front, and then start working on the enemies at the shoreline. Shortly, your first enemy helicopter arrives. When it does, shift focus to the helicopter. It's easier to hit the helicopter with the MG, but a full volley of missiles can take it down with one shot.

If this helicopter gives you some trouble, you can back down the river a ways to avoid getting hit by anti-aircraft fire from the village below.

TARGET 4

"RADAR LOCK!"

OBJECTIVE Destroy SAM Site

When you hear an alarm sound in the chopper's cabin, an enemy SAM (Surface to Air Missile) has a lock on you. Swerve to the right or left to avoid the incoming rockets, but push forward to your objective marker. If you wish, you can also shoot the incoming missiles.

As you approach, watch out for additional incoming missiles—swerve back and forth to shake the lock. Start firing rockets into the SAM cave when you get to about 300 meters.

TARGET 5

"CHARLIE'S BUILT A PIPELINE RIGHT ACROSS THE RIVER. TAKE IT DOWN AND HIT THE BRIDGE!"

Target five is an easy one—just nail the pipeline with one of your missiles.

TARGET 6

"WE'VE HIT THE MOTHER LODE! THAT'S THE HO CHI MINH TRAIL DOWN BELOW US.

Target six is a large base with five sub-targets to demolish before you can move further down the trail.

This section can be tricky, as ZPUs can cut into your helicopter if you get too close. We recommend you stay far and use your missiles to pick off each target from afar before you move up into the village. Some ZPUs are not marked by objective markers—one is directly in front of the radar tower. Watch out for these guys, as they can cut your ship to ribbons if you accidently fly over one.

The easiest target is the radar tower on your right. Fire a couple missiles into it to take it down. Next up, hit the ZPU hiding at the base of the cliff on your left. Now destroy the ZPU directly behind the tower. Two ZPUs are on the bridge crossing the river. Destroy both with your missiles before you continue downriver. One last ZPU is way off to the left. Destroy it to complete this objective.

OBJECTIVE Destroy Soviet Hinds

Your last objective in this level's helicopter section is to destroy the two Hinds that show up after you clear the base at Target Six. Use your MG and Missiles to attack the Hinds aggressively. Don't stop moving, as this allows the enemy to get a lock on your helicopter.

Remember to continue pressing your MG button, and wait to fire full missile volleys at the enemies when you have a clear shot. When both helicopters go down, Woods sets you down in a nearby clearing. Time to say hello to Kravchenko.

OBJECTIVE Kill Kravchenko

At the landing site, you find some new weapons, including an Uzi and a RPK with Drum Mag mod.

WEAPON: RPK

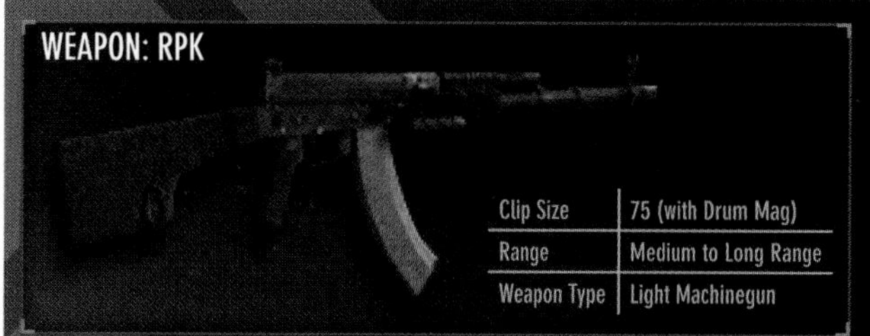

Clip Size	75 (with Drum Mag)
Range	Medium to Long Range
Weapon Type	Light Machinegun

While it has a tremendous clip size, the RPK isn't as versatile as the AK-47. The AK is more accurate, unleashes more damage, and has better mods available for it.

If you like, you can try out the RPK for the trek to Kravchenko's base, but switch back to the AK-47 with Flamethrower attachment when it becomes available.

WEAPON: UZI

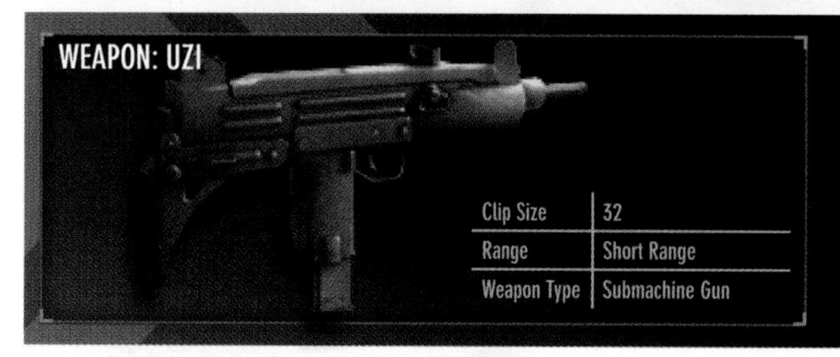

Clip Size	32
Range	Short Range
Weapon Type	Submachine Gun

Even if you aren't a big fan of submachine guns, the Uzi is an upgrade over the Olympia shotgun that you shouldn't overlook. The Uzi has a large clip size, moderate damage, and a very fast rate of fire.

Use the Uzi to spray enemies quickly if they get too close to you.

Follow Woods as he blazes up the trail to Kavchenko's base. Use the nearby rocks for cover, and fire at enemies with your long-range weapons. Use caution as you turn the first corner. A large number of enemies reinforce an MG truck at the base's entrance. Use the large rocks here for cover, and carefully pick off the enemies with your long-range weapons.

You can detonate some red barrels in the area to make the job a bit easier. An enemy with an RPG is just inside the cave. Make him your priority as you continue picking off the defenders from cover.

Wait for Woods to charge forward. When he does, cautiously follow—more enemies are just inside the cave entrance.

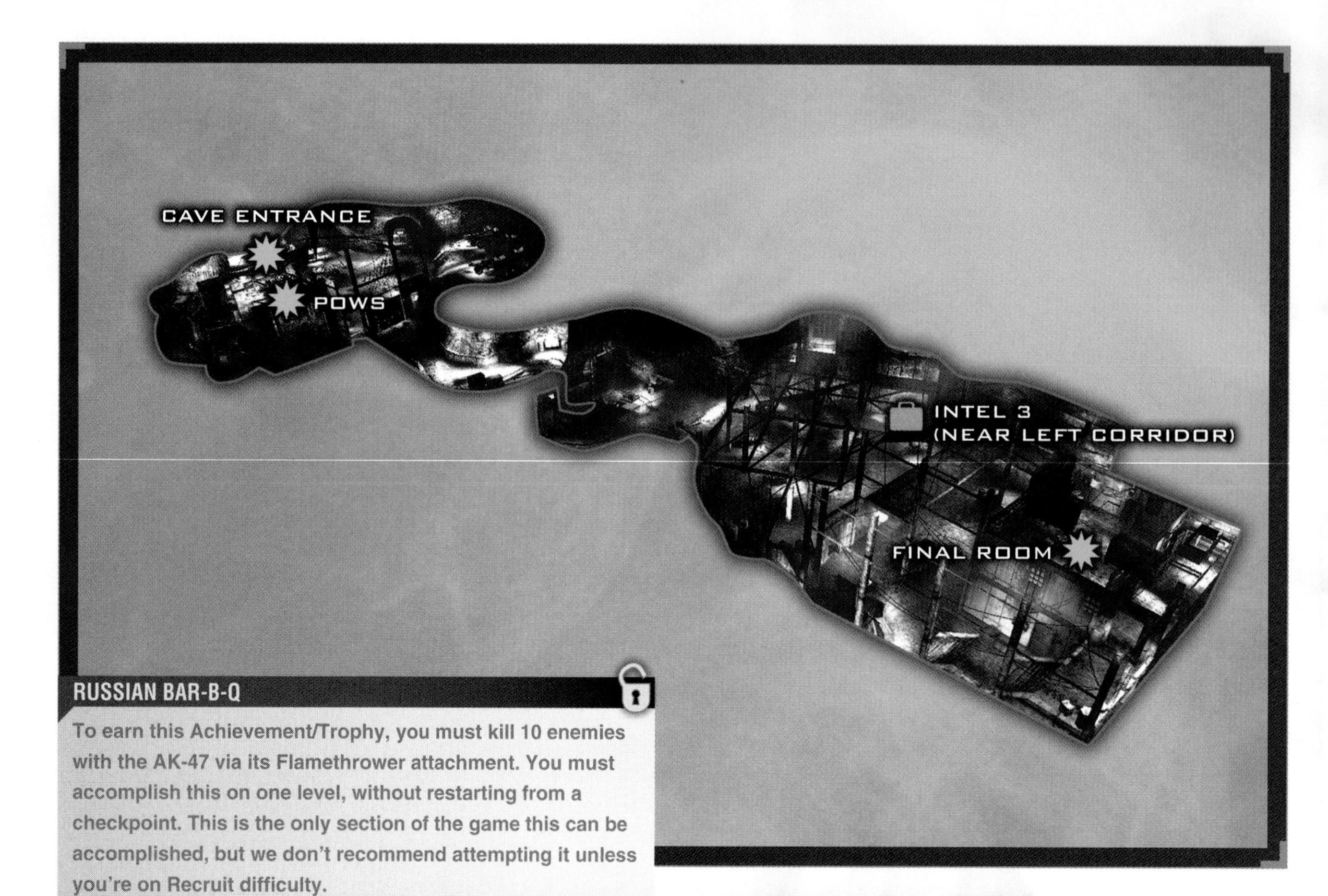

RUSSIAN BAR-B-Q

To earn this Achievement/Trophy, you must kill 10 enemies with the AK-47 via its Flamethrower attachment. You must accomplish this on one level, without restarting from a checkpoint. This is the only section of the game this can be accomplished, but we don't recommend attempting it unless you're on Recruit difficulty.

To kill an enemy with the Flamethrower, you need to get close, and this is extremely difficult on harder difficulties.

THE FLAMETHROWER

The Flamethrower is a special weapon that you can activate by pressing left on the D-Pad. Not only is the weapon cool, but it's extremely deadly at short range. Fire a burst directly into an enemy to take him out of the fight.

You can also lay down "firewalls" by spraying furniture and floors with the weapon. These prevent enemies from advancing to your position.

One of the enemies just inside has an AK-47 with Flamethrower attachment. Replace your long-range weapon with it as you continue forward.

OBJECTIVE Free POWs

When the room is clear, move up to the red button on the wall to free the POWs. Inside, you find an old friend.

Follow Reznov into the next set of caves.

This last room is overflowing with enemies. Stay back behind the crates, and pick off the front line with your AK-47. Use grenades liberally in this section to soften up the enemies and allow your squad to advance.

INTEL

This level's last Intel piece is on a crate to the left of the room. Wait until you clear it of enemies and search for the Intel in the dark corner by the corridor, along the east wall.

There are only about three waves of enemies, so patience gets you through this section. Stay behind cover and don't advance until your team does.

Cover Woods as he climbs the stairs up to Kravchenko's room. Open the door to complete the level.

NOT TODAY

To earn this award, complete Crash Site, WMD, and Payback on Veteran difficulty.

REBIRTH

2230 February 23, 1968

ALEX MASON

SUPPORT

TRANSMISSION# 8-5-19-1-25-19.
Designate: ECHO
Location: Vozrozhdeniye "Rebirth Island," Aral Sea, USSR
Mission: Kill Steiner

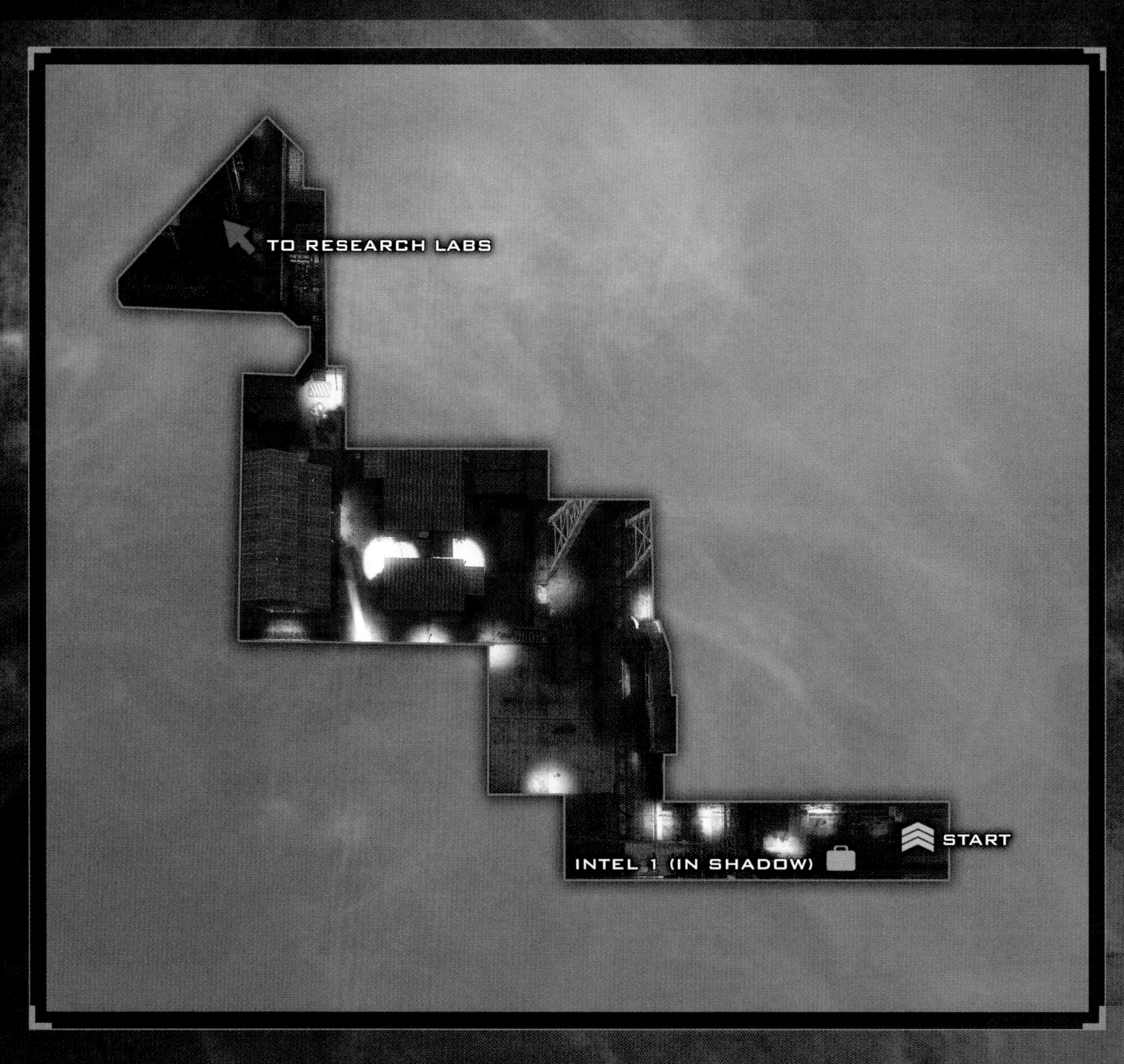

"FINALLY, STEINER WAS OURS..."

You start the level in a shipment crate with Reznov.

Open the door by holding the Interact button, and move in with the nearby hatchet to kill the mechanic.

OBJECTIVE Infiltrate the Soviet Lab and Confront Dr. Steiner

INTEL

The first Intel piece is on the ground to the left just outside the starting crate. Wait until after you kill the mechanic with the hatchet to look for it on the ground to the left.

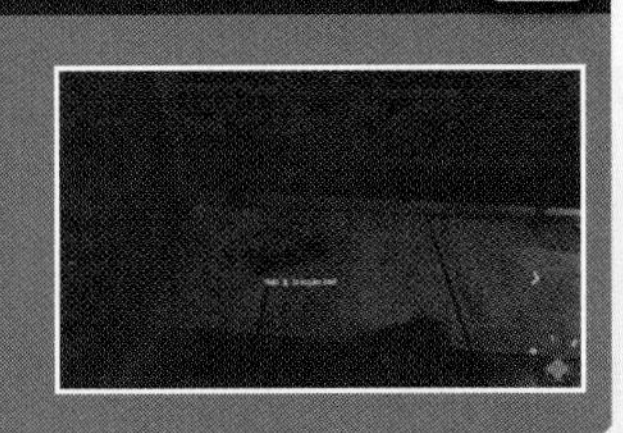

After you drag the body back to the crate, follow Reznov ahead.

Throughout this section, you have to avoid the spotlights of the helicopters flying overhead. Keep your eyes on the ground and stay out of the lights. If you're spotted, it's game over.

Stay behind Reznov as the helicopter moves overhead.

When Reznov signals, sprint across the long crate and hide in the shadow at the end.

Wait for Reznov's signal, and then follow him to the double set of buildings. Sprint forward and melee the soldier standing in the light between the buildings. Follow Reznov up to the next hiding place as the chopper comes back around.

Continue following Reznov up to the ladder. When he steps aside, climb the ladder and be ready to press the Melee button to take care of the soldier at the top.

Climb the second ladder to the facility's roof. Follow Reznov as he leads you through the facility.

When he opens the elevator hatch, switch to your KS-23 shotgun and kill the soldiers and scientists below.

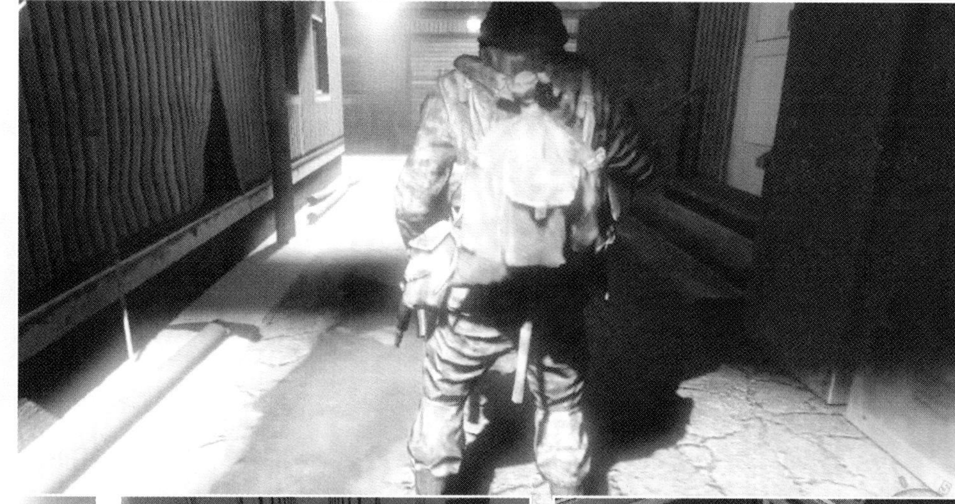

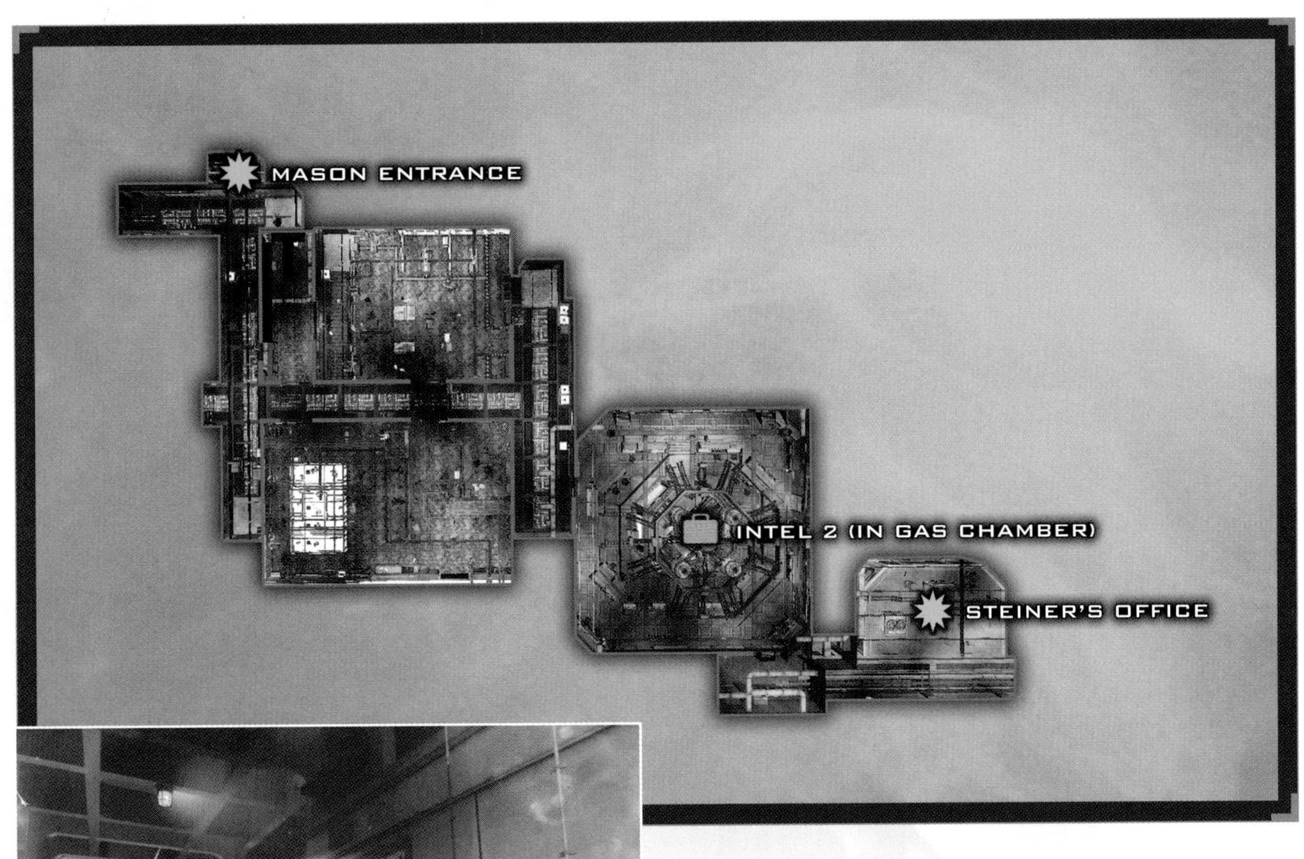

It's weapons free as the base is now aware of your presence.

This is a tough room-to-room battle until you get to Steiner's laboratory. Luckily, there's plenty of cover, which you must use to your advantage as you advance through the halls. At medium to long range, AK-47 or AK74u weapons are ideal. However, don't forget that the KS-23 shotgun has surprisingly long range for a shotgun.

Patience is key through this section. Wait until the enemy stops firing on you before you push forward through the labs. Use grenades to soften up resistance. Whatever you do, don't sprint forward, as the enemy will quickly overwhelm you, possibly triggering a checkpoint in a bad spot.

I HATE MONKEYS

Even if you don't hate monkeys, you still might want to try for this Achievement/Trophy as you make your way through the labs.

To earn it, you have to kill seven monkeys in ten seconds. It's best to do this by dropping multiple grenades near monkey cages.

A good spot is just before the flash chamber room. You should get a checkpoint, so if you fail, you can kill yourself and try again.

Toss a grenade into the corner of the cages, and then open up with your shotgun on the monkeys to the right.

INTEL

The second piece of Intel is one of the trickiest to collect in the game. It's located in the experiment chamber in the middle of the room with the observation deck. The chamber seals itself if the gas canisters in the center, above the monkey cages, are damaged.

First, clear all the enemies in the room. Be very careful not to use grenades or other explosives. Just stick to your long-range weapon and fire controlled bursts to clear out the room's defenders.

With the enemy presence down, kill the enemy inside the chamber. The Intel sits on top of a monkey cage.

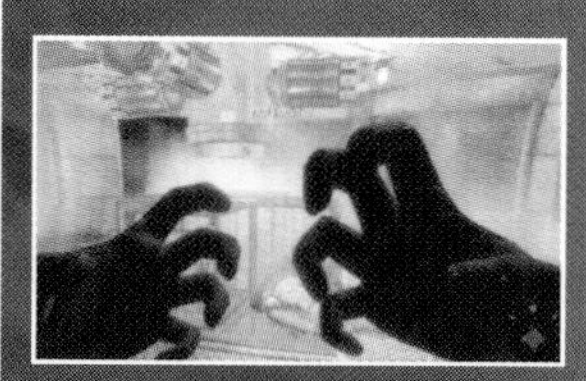

If you grab the Intel but are then killed by the Nova 6 gas, you still get to keep it after you respawn.

If you have trouble getting into this room, you might want to come back later and try it on an easier difficulty.

Clear the first set of three rooms, and move past the monkeys into the gas chamber room. More enemies attack from the observation area above. Use the doorway for cover to pick off the enemies before you enter.

When you step inside, be aware that there are probably more enemies on the other side of the gas chamber. Move around it and use grenades to break up their cover.

With the experiment room completely clear of enemies, move down the hall and open the door at the end.

"FRIEDRICH STEINER, THIS IS THE END."

Rebirth Island

REBIRTH (PART 2)

2200 February 23, 1968

JASON HUDSON

SUPPORT

TRANSMISSION# 8-5-19-1-25-19.
Designate: ALPHA
Location: Vozrozhdeniye "Rebirth Island," Aral Sea, USSR
Mission: Extract Steiner

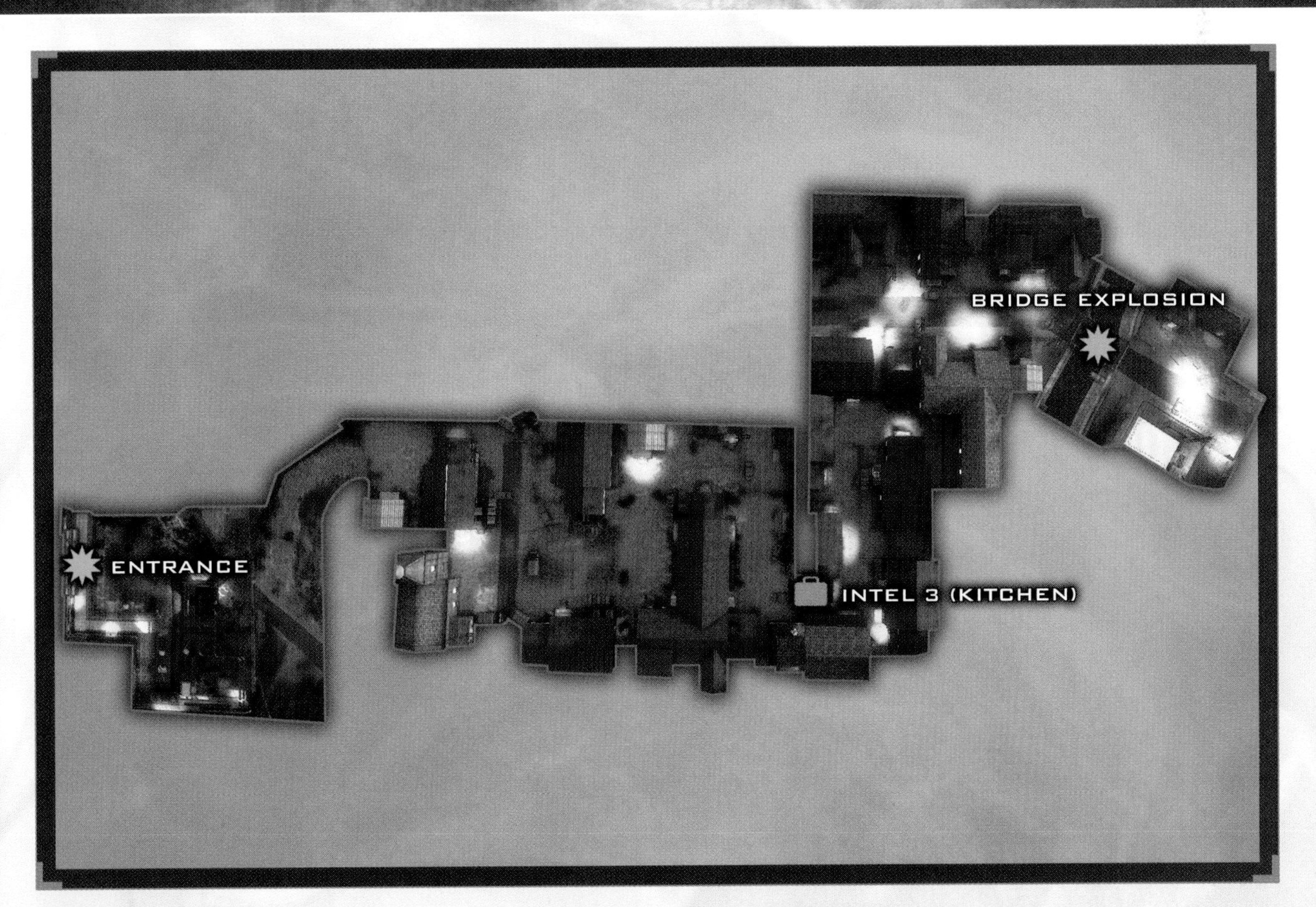

OBJECTIVE Infiltrate the Soviet Lab and capture Dr. Steiner

"THEY'VE ALREADY BEGUN TO EVACUATE."

You are now playing as Hudson on Rebirth island. You start the level on the back of an armored vehicle. Use the MG to blow up the cars blocking the road, and to kill the enemies firing RPGs from the roof above.

This vehicle also allows you to lob grenades at the enemy. Press either grenade button to fire them.

Focus your MG on the vehicles as your BTR moves down the street. Use burst fire to pick off enemies perched on the buildings' second floors as you traverse the area. When you get to the bridge, you can't avoid the helicopter's missiles.

You are now in a giant cloud of Nova 6, which means you are counting on your hazmat suit to keep you alive. This means you don't heal damage like you normally do in the game. Your suit can't repair itself if you take shots, so you must be extremely cautious as you move up the street.

NO LEAKS

To earn the No Leaks Achievement/Trophy, you have to make it all the way through this Nova 6 sequence without getting killed. This is an extremely difficult segment, and it's even challenging on Recruit difficulty.

If you are set on earning this award, consider lowering your difficulty via the in-game menu before you proceed.

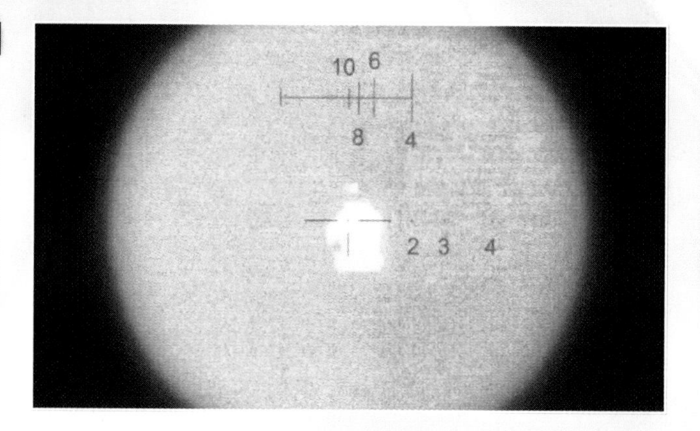

The scope on your Enfield allows you to see enemies through the clouds of poisonous gas.

THERMAL SCOPE

The Thermal Scope allows you to see tangos ahead, but it isn't easy to differentiate friend from foe. If you rest your scope on a target for a moment, and you don't see the friendly green text pop up, that means you're targeting an enemy—weapons free!

After you put on the hazmat suit, sprint forward to the jeep on your left. Use your scope to pick off the enemies as they advance up to your position. When you cleared out a few enemies, turn around and watch for any enemies approaching from the bridge behind you.

When you're sure the area is clear, carefully move up to the house. Stay in the house and fire on the foes outside. Enemies are on the second floor of the building ahead, and several more advance from the ground level.

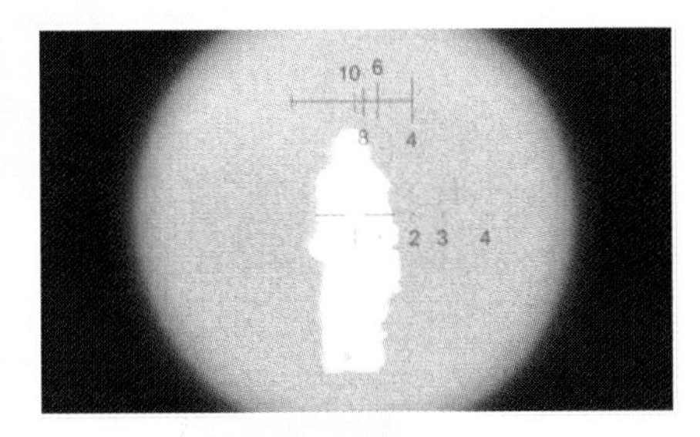

When the area is clear, carefully advance forward using the cords of wood and other objects in the courtyard for cover.

More enemies may pop out from windows in the buildings above you, so keep your weapon trained high.

TOP SECRET

CLASSIFIED

CLASSIFIED DOCUMENTATION

Paper - 2533/334 - PENT

Storage no. 998/347-3 -

Sensitive Information

relating to 87/1987/9

36 Hours

TO FIRST STRIKE – 36:00:00

> Key personnel prepare for attack <

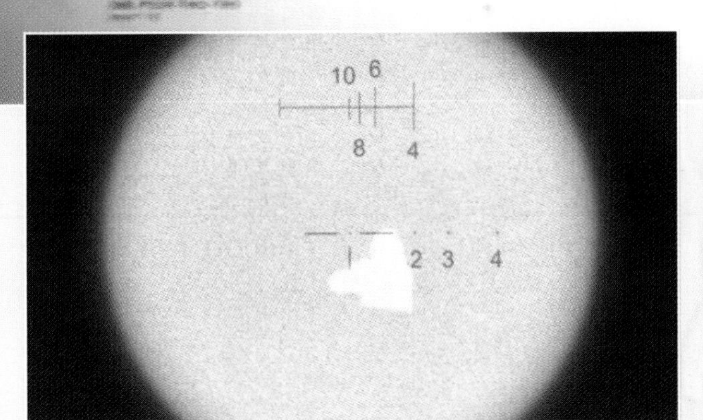

INTEL

The last house on the right contains your last piece of Intel for Rebirth Island. Move inside and search the kitchen counters for the Intel.

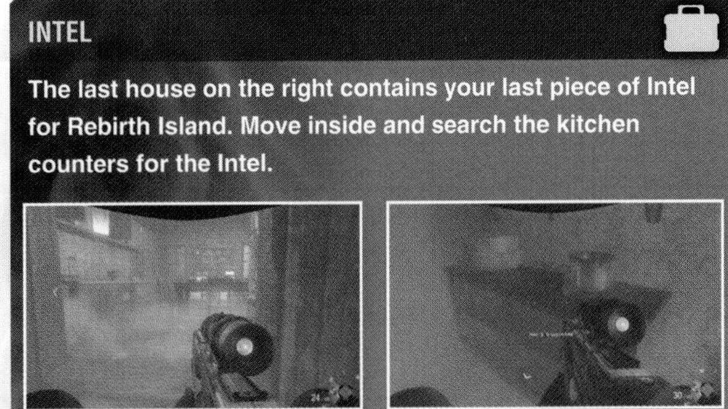

You earn a checkpoint when you enter the house at the end of the alley. Move up the staircase and use the doorway at the top for cover against the enemies advancing at your level. Now, look down to the courtyard below and pick off the enemies there. More foes are in the windows of the building directly across the way.

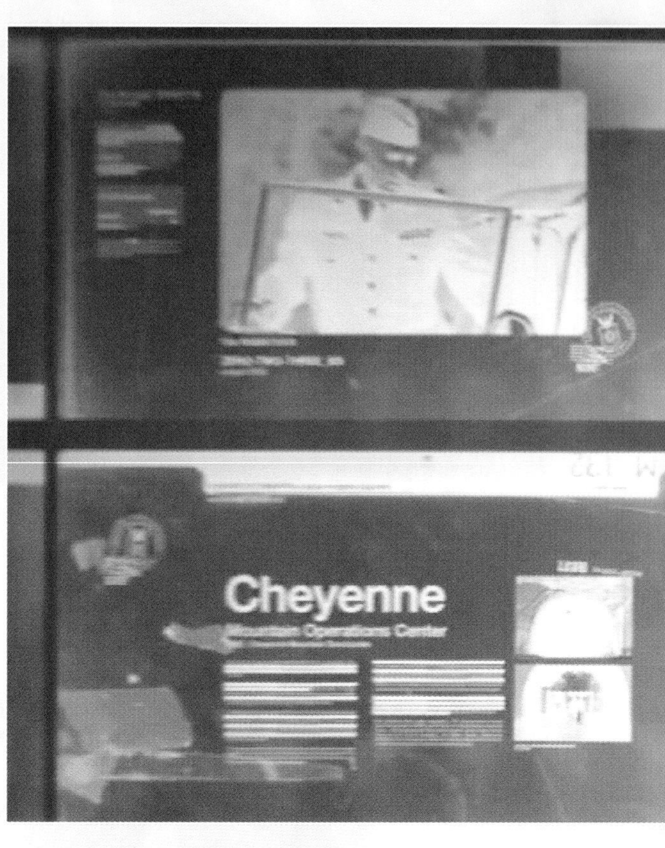

When you move outside, be careful to jump across the rooftop, and proceed through the next building down to the courtyard.

Pop your head out the door near your objective marker and shoot the enemies lined up on your left. Duck in and out of cover here until you kill them all.

OBJECTIVE Shoot Down the Enemy Helicopters

Off in the distance, a friendly helicopter gets shot down. Search the area for the Strela-3 Rocket Launcher.

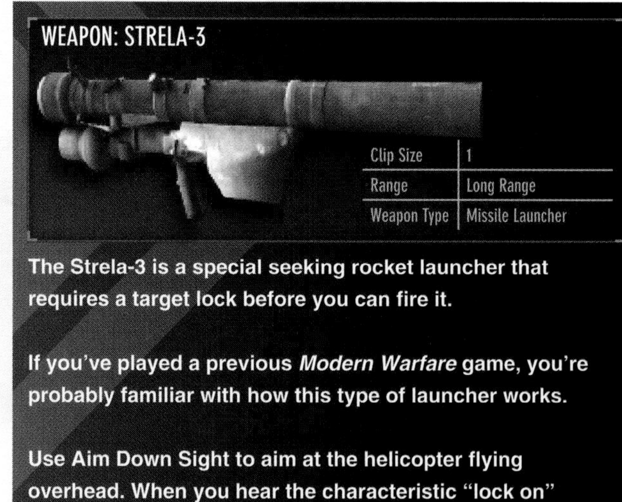

WEAPON: STRELA-3

Clip Size	1
Range	Long Range
Weapon Type	Missile Launcher

The Strela-3 is a special seeking rocket launcher that requires a target lock before you can fire it.

If you've played a previous *Modern Warfare* game, you're probably familiar with how this type of launcher works.

Use Aim Down Sight to aim at the helicopter flying overhead. When you hear the characteristic "lock on" sound, press the Fire button to let loose a rocket.

Use the Strela-3 to lock onto the two helicopters. If you take any damage, duck back under cover.

When both helicopters are down, push forward to escape the Nova 6 cloud. When you are clear, you can see the Nova 6 creation facility off to the right.

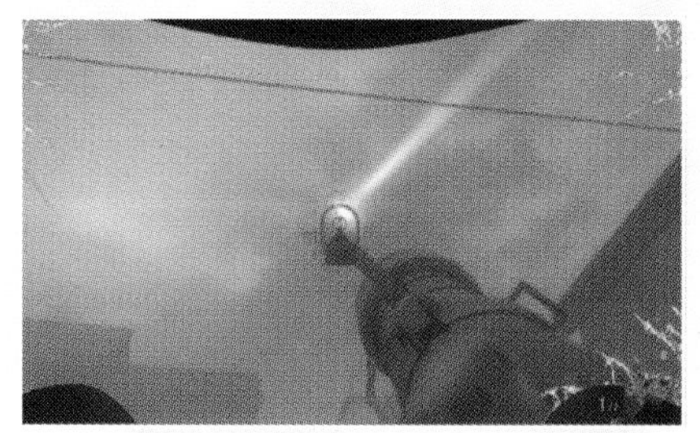

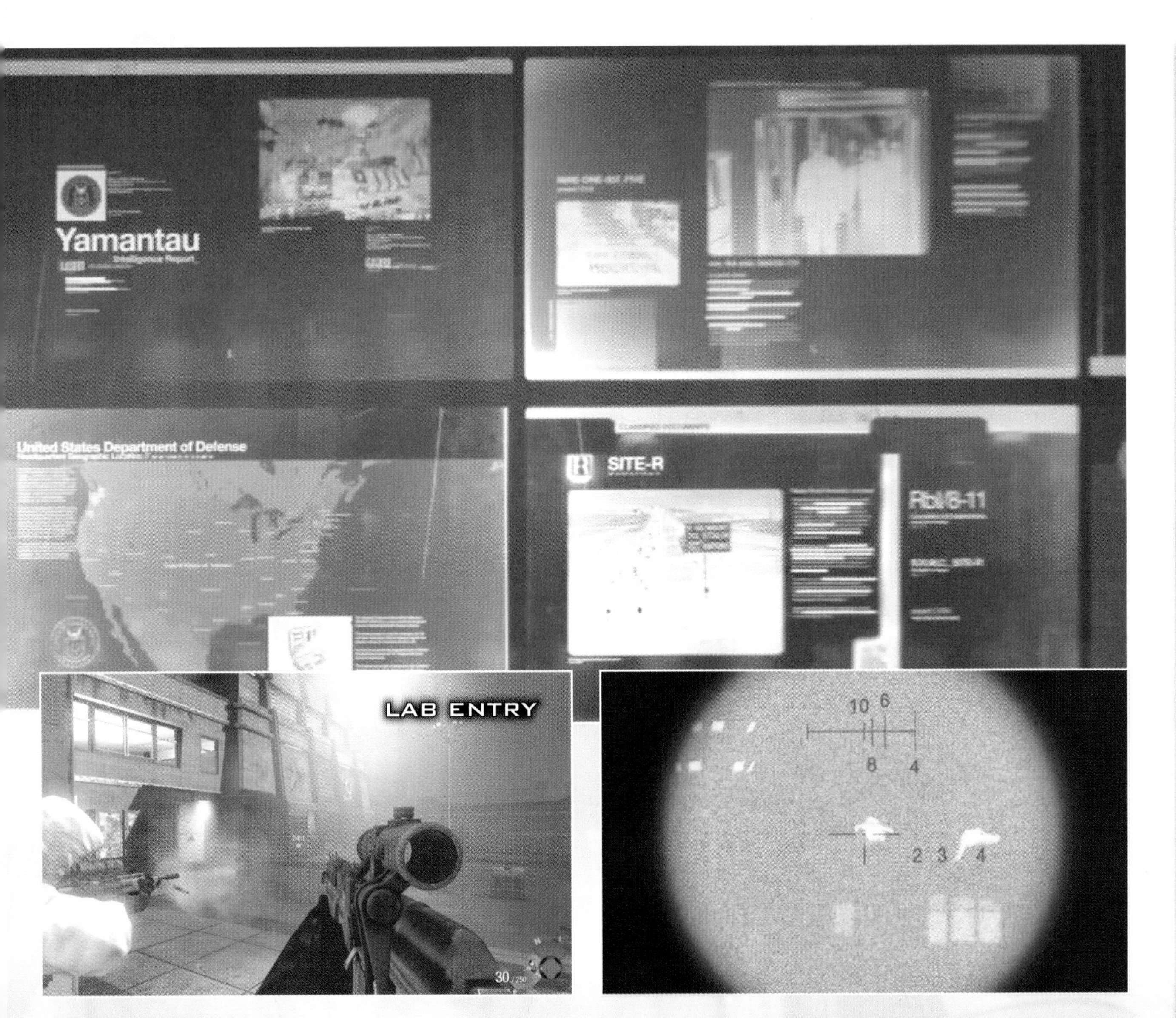

OUT OF AMMO?

If your Enfield runs low on ammo, feel free to switch it out for one of your enemy's AK74us. It doesn't have the Thermal Scope, but an ACOG scope will get the job done.

Shoot the enemies defending the gate below, and then turn your Enfield to the two RPG enemies on top of the building to your right.

When all the enemies in the area are eliminated, move about halfway down the hill, and a new enemy wave advances. Use the hillside's tactical advantage to pick off the foes from a distance with your Enfield.

Move through the gate and use the crates on your left for cover as you advance on the facility entrance. Keep an eye on the facility's roof; two more enemies emerge, and they can be a major threat if you don't take them down quickly.

Continue sticking to cover and slowly advance on the building. While a lot of soldiers are inside, it's not an unlimited number. Keep fighting until you manage to sneak up on the building's entrance.

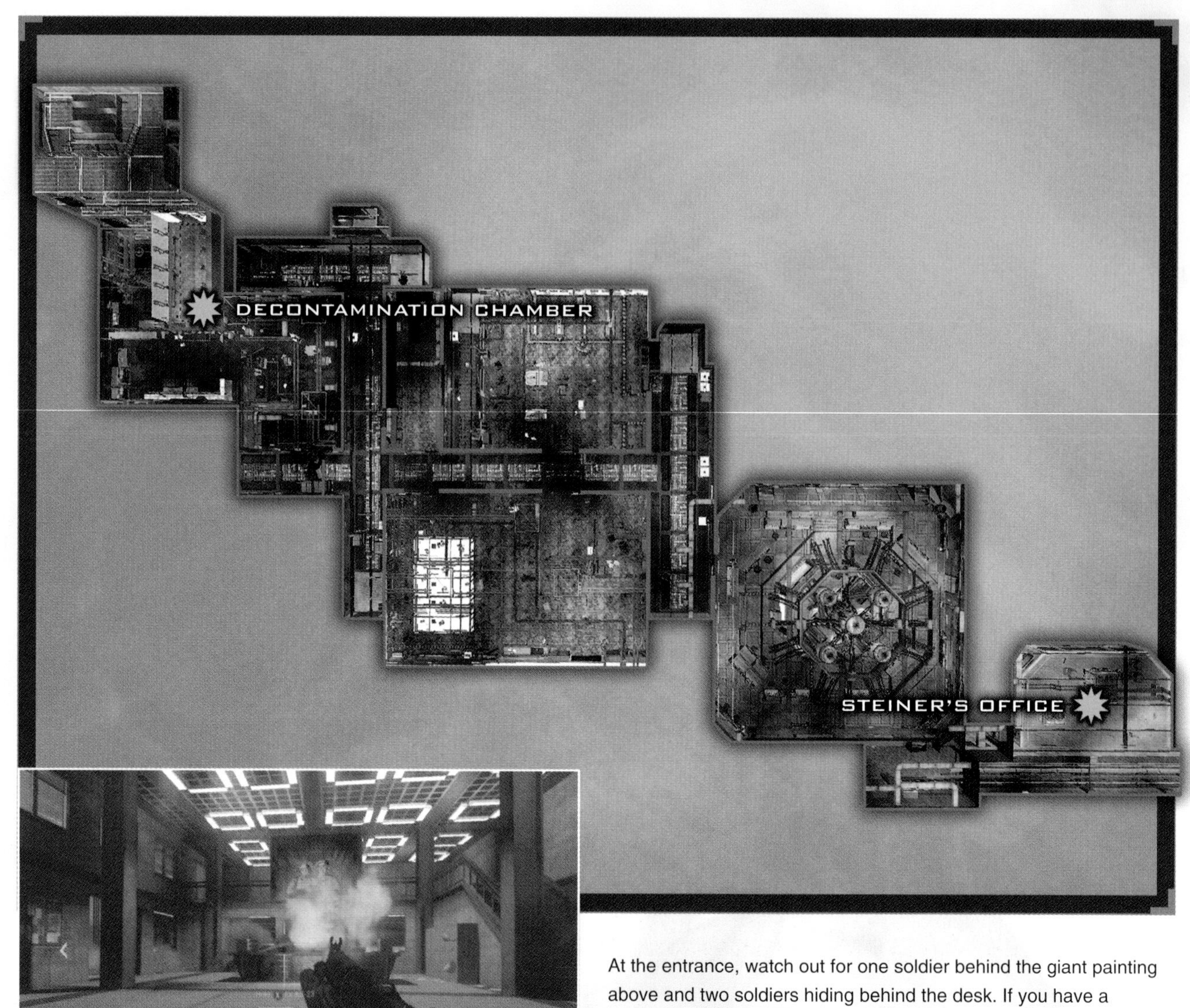

At the entrance, watch out for one soldier behind the giant painting above and two soldiers hiding behind the desk. If you have a grenade, use it on the desk.

"MASON, THIS IS HUDSON. WE KNOW YOU ARE ON REBIRTH ISLAND. TALK TO ME, MASON."

Watch out for more enemies guarding the corridor on your left. Follow Weaver up to the decontamination doorway.

Two foes climb the stairs on the other side of the decontamination chamber. Kill them and move with Weaver down the stairs. Continue through the facility and Mason's carnage. Some straggler enemies may be running around, so keep your shotgun ready as you follow the objective markers.

Eventually, you reach the hallway that leads to the experiment chamber you saw while playing as Mason. Watch out for the large group of foes approaching on the left. Kill them, and use the same tactics you used earlier to clear out the scientists defending this room.

This time, all the enemies are on the bottom floor. However, they defend the area more aggressively, making it more difficult to clear them out than it was previously.

When Weaver moves into the room, follow him to the steel door on the other side. Open it to complete the level.

REVELATIONS

2300 February 25, 1968

ALEX MASON

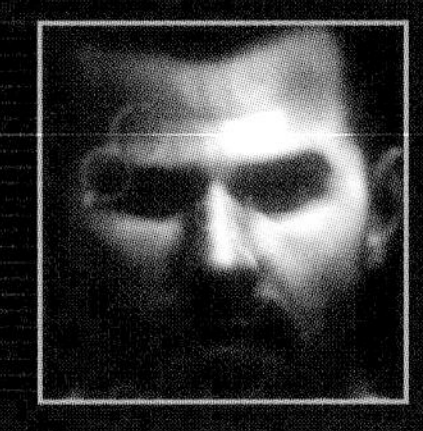

TRANSMISSION# 8-5.
Designate: DELTA
Location: ROOM 9
Mission: Unknown

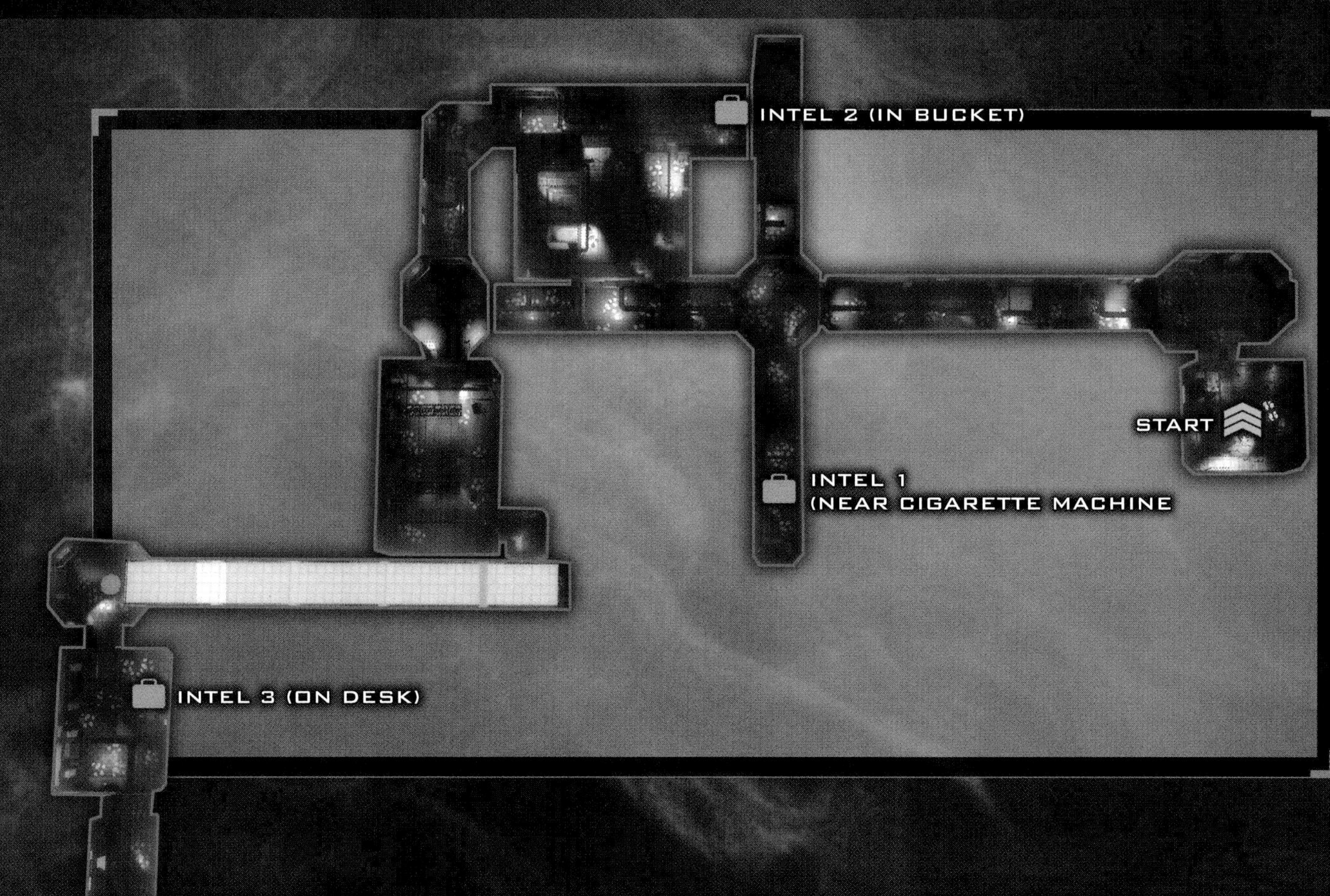

"NOT YET, I HAVE ONE MORE CARD TO PLAY."

OBJECTIVE **Ascension 9 18 8 23 8 3 8 22 15 21 17 6 16 1 7 8 19 10 22 19 23 14 17 14 22 0 12 8 8 10 7 1 1 22**

Revelations is a story level. It doesn't have any combat or require any strategy. We don't want to spoil the story, so we'll let you uncover the mysteries and answers the level holds for yourself.

There are three pieces of Intel to find on this level. We recommend you play through the level once so you can concentrate on the story. Come back for the Intel via the Mission Select menu.

OBJECTIVE **9 19 18 4 6 21 17 14 9 19 8 24 17 24 5 13 11 20 15 21 24 11 9 12 8 20 21 10 16 23 4 22 21 4 0 14**

OBJECTIVE **Ascension 1 23 9 12 3 13 5 9 22 21 0 21 10 15 5 17 12 21 18 8 5 13 22 10 2 11 5 11 8 9 19 23 2 14 17 10 7 15 7 12 21 25 16 25 0 23 12 23 13 22 8 9 25 4 20 19 11 14 24 17 9 21 0 2 16 16 1 22 1 20 22 22 25 0 15 1 1 22 17**

CLARITY

Complete this mission to earn this award.

INTEL 

After you stumble through the first set of double doors, go down the left hallway instead of moving directly toward your next objective marker.

The Intel sits on top of a cigarette machine.

INTEL 

When you leave the morgue area (after the cinematic where you are on the table), turn in the direction opposite the objective marker.

The Intel is located inside a small bucket.

INTEL 

After you see a rocket blast off in the hallway, you move through a CIA office. This office contains a couple of desks, some recording equipment, and a row of eight monitors. You can find the last piece of Intel in the outbox paper tray on the left desk.

REDEMPTION

0600 February 26, 1968

ALEX MASON

SUPPORT

WEAVER

TRANSMISSION# 9-19.
Designate: XRAY
Location: Gulf of Mexico
Target: Destroy the Secret Russian Sleeper Broadcast Base

"I THINK THEY WERE EXPECTING US!"

For the final mission, you once again pilot a helicopter. This time, you control a U.S. attack chopper.

OBJECTIVE Assault the Rusalka

Seven targets light up on your HUD. You must take down these anti-aircraft firing positions to clear the way for your forces.

The Fire button operates a high-powered MG that can overheat, so keep an eye on the heat meter just below the MG icon. The Aim Down Sight button fires your missiles. This chopper fires two missiles simultaneously. The missile launchers can launch two missiles per second with no need to reload.

Stay at a distance and use your helicopter's arsenal to destroy all seven targets. The biggest danger here is the missile launcher, which is directly in the middle. Focus your fire on that before you take out the secondary targets surrounding it.

When the first set of targets is down, a new set at midship pop on your HUD. Strafe your chopper to the right (but don't move up yet), and take down these targets as well.

Next, eight more targets appear at the ship's stern. You have to move in to get a good line of sight on these gunners and missile launchers.

If you stay at distance, the only thing you need to worry about is the rocket launcher at this portion of the ship's midsection. Dodge to avoid any rockets it sends your way.

OBJECTIVE Protect Squad

With your primary targets down, another helicopter lands a CIA team (including Weaver) on the back of the Rusalka. You must allow the team to advance up the ship by keeping the enemies on the deck at bay.

Hover your chopper over the boat's rear, and use your MG to cut down the soldiers as they pop out from the wreckage of the upper decks. The HUD highlights groups of enemies for you to kill.

More targets arrive middeck. Rotate your helicopter around the ship, and fire on the troops down below.

Follow your squad as they move up to the front of the ship. Many enemies are in the area, but Weaver and company are good at avoiding enemy fire.

OBJECTIVE Destroy Enemy Hind

When Weaver is clear, a Russian Hind helicopter arrives. This Hind isn't much of a challenge compared to the ones you fought on earlier levels. If you hear the missile lock alarm, focus on dodging its rockets. Otherwise, stay aggressive and cut into it with your MG and missiles.

02:27:0

Hours Until U.S. Strik

United States Nav

OBJECTIVE Land Helicopter

The chopper is down for the count. Maneuver it toward the nearby helipad marked with the objective symbol. Use your Look analog to stabilize the helicopter's back and forth movement.

"OUT OF THAT CHOPPER, JUMP! GO, GO, GO!"

After the ugly landing, wait for Hudson to recover, and then follow him up the ship.

OBJECTIVE Rendezvous with Weaver below Deck

Midship, you run into heavy resistance. There are plenty of crates around—use them for cover and carefully advance on the enemy. If you stay low and fire sharp, you can make steady progress.

OBJECTIVE Shoot Down Enemy Helicopters

INTEL

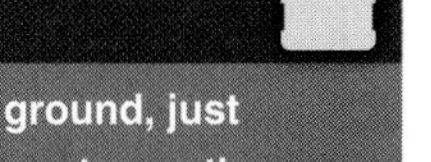

You can find the first piece of Intel on the ground, just outside the first large cargo crate you encounter on the deck. Look for a big, green crate with both doors open. The Intel is at the door located closest to the ship's bow—the direction you are currently headed.

Enemy helicopters arrive to provide defense against your assault. Luckily, some Valkyrie missiles lie on the deck nearby. You can see these highlighted by an objective marker. Sprint up to the missiles and switch them out for your Mac 11 alternate weapon.

Valkyrie missiles are the same type of guided arms you used to destroy the Soyuz 2 in the earlier mission, Executive Order.

DOUBLE WHAMMY

To earn this Achievement/Trophy, you have to take down both choppers with one Valkyrie guided missile. Wait behind cover for a moment when the choppers navigate very close to each other.

One advantage is that you get unlimited Valkyries. As long as you stay behind cover, you can continue making attempts. If you mess up and accidently take down one but not both, you can use a grenade to kill yourself and restart from the prior checkpoint (just before the helicopters arrive).

This Achievement/Trophy requires superb timing and accuracy. The two helicopters circle the area in a random manner, moving from one point to another. To get both with one rocket, you must wait until they are very close to each other. Fire a Valkyrie directly between them, and detonate the rocket early by pressing the Fire button.

The Valkyrie doesn't have a huge blast radius, so you have to be very close to both choppers when the rocket explodes.

Use the guided missiles to blow up both helicopters. These choppers aren't very aggressive, so don't worry too much about cover.

Use any remaining rockets to clear enemies up the deck, and then switch back to your FAMAS assault rifle. When most of the enemies are down, lead your forces further up the deck.

As you approach the area marked by your objective indicator, a number of enemy reinforcements arrive on the deck. Take cover behind a nearby crate, and pick them off with your FAMAS.

WATCH OUT FOR GRENADES!

The enemies in the upper deck area's last section really seem to like tossing grenades. Be ready for them, and toss them back as soon as they appear on your indicator.

The FAMAS is a formidable assault rifle, and it suits your combat needs throughout the mission. The FAMAS delivers damage equivalent to other assault rifles you've used in prior levels, but it has an extremely high rate of fire while maintaining adequate accuracy.

This FAMAS is equipped with the Dual Mag and Red Dot Sight attachments. The Dual Mag allows for significantly faster reloads.

WEAPON: FAMAS

Clip Size	30
Range	Medium to Long Range
Weapon Type	Assault Rifle

Wait for Hudson to move up here. When he does, follow him inside the ship.

"HUDSON, YOU NEED TO SEE THIS."

DOUBLE BACK

Before you head below deck, you might want to search for a short-range weapon. You engage the enemy at close range, and the FAMAS isn't as effective as some of the SMGs you can find top deck, such as the MAC11.

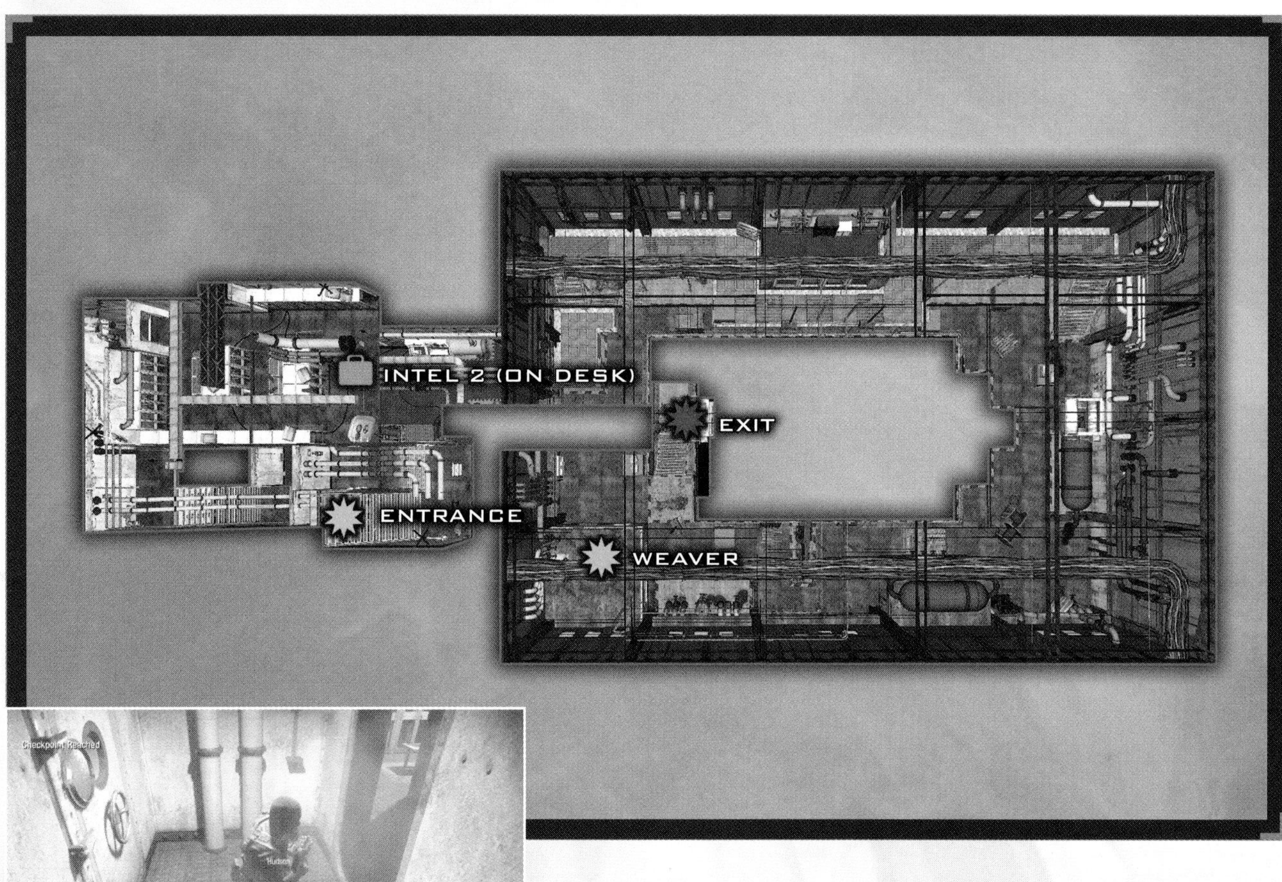

When Weaver lets you know he's pinned down, continue after Hudson. Be very careful when you approach the locker room. Toss a flash grenade inside, and ready your short-range weapon to pick off any enemies that pop out.

Three soldiers are in the locker room. Once you outmaneuver and dispose of them, continue further down the stairs.

OBJECTIVE Neutralize All Threats

HUDSON

Hudson is a great wingman on this level, and he's very aggressive. If you enter a tough spot, hang back behind him—he's invincible and will do much of the work for you.

Next up is a lightly defended control room. Use the doorway for cover and swat them out of your way.

INTEL

The second Intel piece is hidden very well under a desk in this control room. Search under the desk with the green boxes. The Intel is sandwiched between two boxes below.

When Hudson charges forward, follow him to the large room. Watch out for the enemy hiding behind the wooden planks immediately to your left.

This next area is a large machinery room with a pool in the middle. Use the steel railing for cover, and fire at foes with your FAMAS. Only about four are visible, so once you take them down, switch to your short-range weapon and advance forward.

Three enemies guard this next enclosed room. Mow them down with your short-range weapon and use the opposite doorway for cover.

Down below, many enemies have converged to defend against your assault toward Weaver. Poke your head out and use the limited railing cover to pick off the enemies one by one. Use up any frag grenades you have to help reduce their numbers.

In particular, focus your fire on the hatch across the hold. You know when you've cleared the area when a new objective pops onscreen.

"GET OUT OF HERE, WEAVER. WE'RE GONNA FINISH THIS."

OBJECTIVE Infiltrate the Numbers Station

When you regain control of Mason, swim toward your objective marker.

When you emerge from the pool, hang back behind your squad and find some good cover in the doorway to the next room.

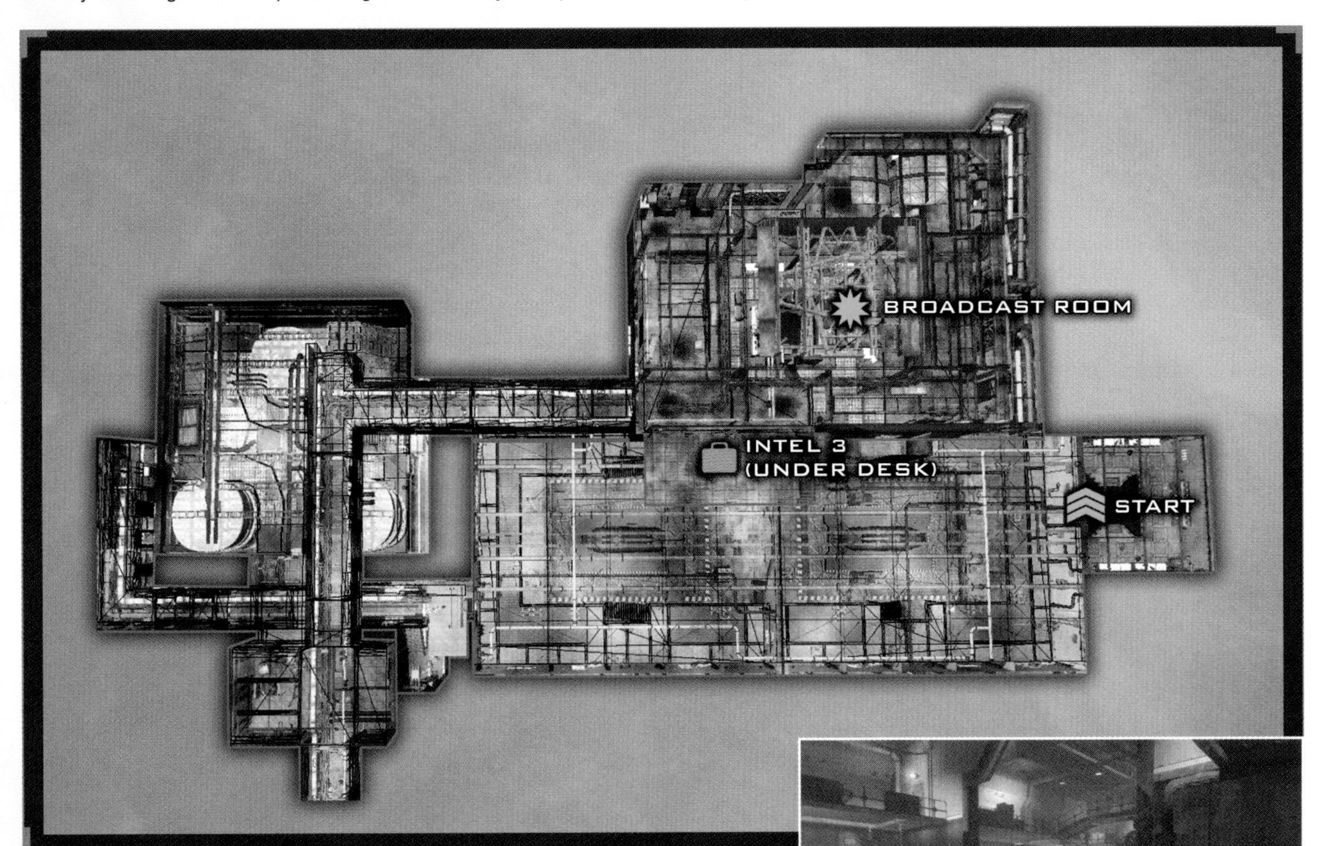

OBJECTIVE Find and Kill Dragovich

AK74U WITH GRENADE LAUNCHER

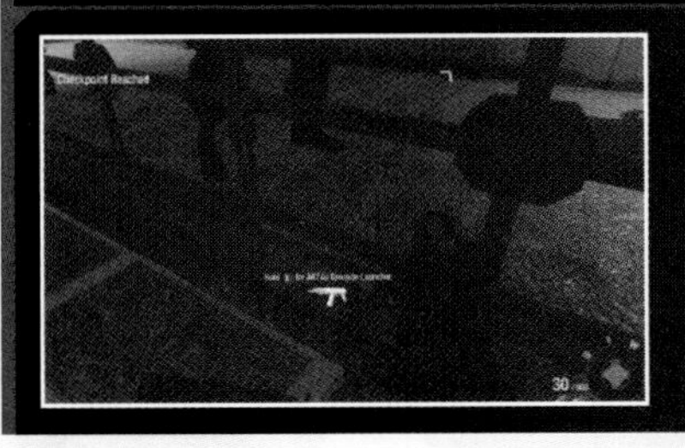

You can find an AK74u with Grenade Launcher attachment lying on a shelf in this room. Switch out your short-range weapon for it before you move on to engage the enemy.

The area is well defended. Use the doorway's cover to peek out with your FAMAS and pick off enemies. They can be hard to see, but the more patient you are, the easier it is to make your way to Dragovich.

"TOO LATE TO BACK OUT—SLAM IT IN."

When the Russians stop firing, carefully move forward to the second room. Keep your gun trained on the doorway at the opposite side of the room. More enemies emerge as you near the end of the third pool. A well-timed grenade can take care of the group in one blast.

Switch to your short-range weapon and move into the stairwell. Watch out for an enemy charging down the staircase. Two more enemies wait for you at the top of the stairs.

When you exit the stairwell, immediately look left, and move against the right wall for cover from the two Russian soldiers defending the narrow passage. Push forward to the next room, and you automatically trigger an explosion.

Press the Jump button to get out of the water.

After you escape the flooded area, you have to clear several narrow hallways filled with defending enemies. Stick to your short-range weapon and frag grenades to clear the halls.

It can be difficult to see through the water spraying into the hallways. Answer with your own spray, courtesy of your SMG—clear the enemies down each passage.

These passages eventually dump you into a large communications room. Three enemies defend the area. Use a frag grenade to flush them out, and use the doorway for cover.

As you move around the area's back end, three more soldiers arrive as reinforcements. Kill them, using the railings for cover, and then proceed up the stairs.

OBJECTIVE Stop the Transmission

Switch to your short-range weapon and ascend the stairway. At the top, two aggressive guards defend a small communications room. If you have any grenades left, use them; if not, spray them with your SMG.

Stay behind the doorway's cover and get ready for a heavily armored soldier to charge toward you. Spray for the head to bring him down before he can do too much damage to you.

The room ahead has one more armored soldier, and several engineers try to transmit the sleeper activation code. The engineers can be a threat if you get too close, so shoot them from the doorway. Step out and pick off the heavily armored soldier from across the railing.

Just a few more engineers stand between you and your final objective. Take them out and move to the objective marker.

One final sequence remains. Revenge is a dish best served cold, so we'll let you take care of Dragovich on your own.

Congratulations on beating *Call of Duty: Black Ops!*

INTEL

This last comms room contains your last piece of Intel. You can find it on the floor under the second desk.

STAND DOWN

Finish the campaign on any difficulty to receive this Achievement/Trophy.

BLACK OP MASTER

If you beat the game on Hardened or Veteran difficulty, we salute you! Treyarch provides their own special reward with this valuable Achievement/Trophy, which unlocks after the credits roll.

BURN NOTICE

Complete Rebirth and Redemption on Veteran difficulty to earn this award.

UNLOCKED SECRET MODES

Your *Black Ops* experience isn't over with the end of the campaign. There's still a ton more to do.
For more information on the secret game modes that unlock after you beat the game, check out our Secrets chapter.

ZOMBIES

Zombies is a special Call of Duty game mode that originated in Call of Duty: World at War as "Nazi Zombies." The mode was hugely popular and spawned several DLC mini-sequels, as well as iPhone and iPad versions of the game.

This time around, Zombies is immediately available with the level Kino der Toten when you first startup the game. You can also unlock a completely unique and separate level by completing the campaign. Details on these levels' special features appear in the Secrets chapter.

This chapter focuses on the basics of Zombies gameplay. We've avoided any spoilers in this section—that's why map-specific strategy appears in the Secrets chapter.

Survival in Zombies comes down to three things: knowledge, skill, and luck. We can help you with the knowledge part—that's what this guide is all about. But skill and luck come only with time. Zombies are unique and challenging enemies. They are pathetic on their own, but they can scare the pants off even the most hardcore FPS gamer when they attack in numbers.

Zombies gameplay can be frustrating due to its extreme difficulty—there are no separate difficulty levels. We hope the following tips and strategies help you on your path toward successful and memorable runs in this challenging game mode.

THE BASICS

In Zombies, you start with minimal equipment and earn money by repairing barricades and killing Zombies. You can use money to set traps, upgrade with Perks, activate special features on a map, and purchase weapons and ammo.

Zombies attack randomly through barricade points. You can rebuild these points at any time by pressing the Interact button while standing near them.

Zombies is an infinite game mode. The challenge isn't to get to the end. Rather, it's to develop strategies on each map to survive as long as possible.

The types of waves you face are randomly assigned, but they increase in difficulty exponentially the more you play. Additionally, Zombie health increases each round, making them harder and harder to kill.

Co-Op vs. Solo

Zombies is the most fun when played co-operatively with up to three friends, but you can also play it in solo mode. In Solo, the rules are slightly different. Specifically, significantly fewer monsters spawn each round, and the Quick Revive Perk functions differently (see below for more details).

You don't have to be online to play Zombies. The game mode supports two-player split-screen on one console (for Xbox 360 and PS3 only).

One big advantage to playing in Solo mode is that you can pause the game at any time. This is a great way to learn the maps via the strategies we provide in this guide.

THE GRITTY DETAILS

In many ways, Zombies is a numbers game. Your goal is to save up enough money to progress and eventually upgrade all your weapons. Getting the most points out of the Zombies is essential to long-term survival. In this section, we break down exactly how many points you get for each action you perform.

ZOMBIE KILLIN'

ACTION	POINTS EARNED
Any Zombie - Non-Lethal Hit	10 Points
Any Zombie - Lethal Hit	50-60 Points
Any Zombie - Lethal Headshot	100 Points
Any Zombie - Non-Lethal Melee	10 Points
Any Zombie - Lethal Melee	130 Points
Gas Zombie	Same as regular Zombie
Hellhound Hit	10 points
Hellhound Death	60-100 Points

While all regular Zombies pretty much look the same, they can have different speed and health attributes. Zombies you encounter in round one are slugs compared to the brain-eating machines you find in round five and later.

Gas Zombies crawl on the ground and start to spawn with the Zombie waves once you turn on the power on each map. These Zombies have a tendency to explode into a cloud of Nova 6 gas. This gas blurs your vision and makes it very difficult to see.

Hellhounds appear only on the Kino der Toten level, but they are generally not much of a threat. Use your machinegun to spray them as they approach you. If you have the extra health provided by Jugger-Nog, you can survive several hits from the dogs.

Rebuilding Structures

Getting bonus points for rebuilding barricades is a great way to get extra points between rounds. There is a cap to how many points you can earn from rebuilding Barricades each round though. This cap increases each round.

10 Points per Board
60 Points for a Fully Torn-Down Barricade

ROUND CAPS FOR REPAIRS

Round 1	40 Points
Round 2	90 Points
Round 3	140 Points
Round 4	140 Points

Getting Downed

If you take enough damage to go down from a Zombie, you are immediately put in "Last Stand" mode. This allows you to attack the Zombies from the ground with your knife and pistol.

When you get downed, you lose 10% of your points. However, if you are playing multiplayer, your partners gain back some percentage of the lost points when they revive you.

Perks

Each level contains Perks. Perks can be purchased in vending machines found dispersed throughout each level. You can find the exact Perk vending machine locations with the strategies for the specific maps.

These Perks work similarly to the way Perks work in Multiplayer. They provide an extra bonus to your character, making survival a little easier.

Here is a summary of the Perks, what they cost, and what they do:

QUICK REVIVE

Cost: 500 Solo
Cost: 1500 Co-Op.

Quick Revive is the cheapest Perk, and it's the most essential one in the Solo game.

It functions differently in Solo and Co-Op gameplay. In Solo mode, when you get downed by a Zombie and you have the Quick Revive Perk, you are brought back to life roughly ten seconds later…just enough time for the nearby Zombies to disperse. You should always have a Quick Revive active in Solo. You can buy three Quick Revives in one Solo game. After the third revive, the machine disappears.

In Co-Op multiplayer, Quick Revive allows you to revive a fallen comrade at about 3x speed.

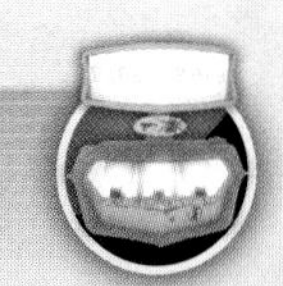

PACK-A-PUNCH

Cost: 5000

Pack-a-Punch is the ultimate upgrade—and it's usually hardest to access. Feed it a normal weapon, and it spits out a super-upgraded version of that weapon. The upgraded weapons have larger clip sizes, ammo, and damage…all things vital for making it into the double-digit rounds.

When you upgrade a wall weapon with Pack-a-Punch, getting more ammo for it from the wall for that weapon costs significantly more.

JUGGER-NOG

Cost: 2500

Based on the infamous multiplayer Juggernaut Perk, Jugger-Nog is vital for the Solo campaign. It allows you to rush past Zombies and still survive if they hit you a few times. It gives you just enough room for error to get out of most situations, and it's vital for surviving in the later rounds.

Jugger-Nog is also very useful against the Hellhounds, which tend to kill you through multiple damaging hits.

DOUBLE TAP ROOT BEER

Cost: 2000

Double Tap allows you to fire your gun at a significantly faster speed. This can be a great upgrade for slower firing weapons, like the M16, but it's not so great for high RoF weapons with small clips, such as the AK74u.

SPEED COLA

Cost: 3000

Speed Cola is the first upgrade you should really try to get after you turn on the power and get your first Pack-a-Punch upgrade. It halves your reload time, making it less likely for you to get caught between clips as you face down the undead hordes.

The Mystery Box

The Mystery Box is the key to getting the best weapons in the game. The wall weapons are supposed to be *just good enough* to get you to the mid-level rounds (8, 9). To go further, you have to pack a bigger punch. That punch comes from the Mystery Box.

Here's a complete list of weapons you can earn from the crate:

FN FAL	Crossbow (Explosive Bolt)	RPK
CZ75	Famas	HS10
Thunder Gun	Dargunov	Ray Gun
Cymbal Monkey	HK21	Freeze Ray ("Five" map only)
Spectre	China Lake	FN FAL
Python	Galil	CZ 75
G11	Ballistic Knife	M72 LAW
SPAS	Commando	AUG

Each use of the crate costs 950 points. You have a few seconds to grab the weapon after it's selected. If you wait too long, it fades away.

You can replenish ammo for weapons you get out of this crate only by grabbing a Max Ammo power-up (or by upgrading a weapon via the Pack-a-Punch).

After a random number of uses, you receive a teddy bear when you use the crate. This means the crate is exhausted, and will teleport to another location on the map shortly. The teddy bear does issue a refund for points spent on the crate.

Random Drops

If you kill a Zombie in the main play area, it has a small chance of dropping a special power-up. These power-ups aren't just bonuses—they are essential to your survival, particularly after round five.

When a power-up drops, it floats in the air and waits for a player to touch it to activate it. When a power-up starts blinking, it's about to go away. Sometimes waiting to use a power-up is good strategy, particularly in the early rounds when you don't want to waste easy kills.

NUKE

The Nuke kills all Zombies on the map. If not all of the Zombies have spawned on the map yet, then using the Nuke won't instantly end the round. While you don't score any points for killing Zombies with a Nuke, you do earn a flat 400 points. If you can help it, try to use the Nuke toward the end of the round to ensure you don't deprive yourself of significant points.

CARPENTER

This power-up repairs all of the barricades on the level. This doesn't happen instantly—it takes a few seconds to go around and fix all the barricades. While this can be useful when you're on the run from a large Zombie horde, it does rob you of potential repair points. On the other hand, picking up the power-up gives you 200 points.

INSTAKILL

This skull-shaped power-up makes any damage you inflict on a Zombie a one-hit kill. This is a great benefit any round, and it turns your wimpy pistol into an implement of the Zombie apocalypse. Never turn down an Instakill, but try to time the pick-up when many Zombies are around.

DOUBLE POINTS

This power-up doubles the points you earn while it's active. A hit that normally scores 10 points earns 20 when 2X is active. If you manage to get one of these early on, it can accelerate the steps of your strategy.

MAX AMMO

This is the most valuable power-up you can find, and it's the most common one. This power-up is the only way to refill the ammo on weapons you earn from the Mystery Box. This power-up fills your ammo for *both* of your weapons.

DEATH MACHINE

This drop is available only on the "Five" map, but it will also be available on some of the DLC maps. Death Machine gives you a giant minigun to use against the Zombies for a limited amount of time.

Power-ups can be stacked. Instakill + 2X in later rounds is an awesome combination will ensures plenty of money for upgrades.

Traps

The *Call of Duty: Black Ops* maps feature new traps. Traps activate temporarily once you pay their cost. They kill any Zombies that contact them, but you don't receive any points for those kills. Traps are important in later rounds, but avoid wasting points on them until you reach the double-digit rounds.

SURVIVAL TIPS

Never Try to Run Past a Zombie… If you get anywhere near a Zombie, it can slow you down enough to hit you multiple times. Always shoot a Zombie when it comes at you down a narrow corridor.

…Unless You Have Jugger-Nog. The Jugger-Nog Perk dramatically increases the number of hits you can take before you go down. This makes it possible to rush past small groups of Zombies, even in narrow spaces. Just be very careful there's enough room for you to sprint by before you make the charge. If you get stuck, even Jugger-Nog won't save you.

Keep the Barricades Up as Long as You Can. Having barricades in place significantly slows large Zombie groups and keeps the horde waves manageable. If you leave one Zombie at the end of a round, run around and repair all the barricades, even if you aren't getting points for the repairs.

Zombies Don't Drop Power-Ups Unless They Get Past the Barricade. Keep this in mind in the early rounds. It makes sense to let some Zombies into the area so you have a chance to get early power-ups.

The Last Zombie Goes Berserk. Each round, the last surviving Zombie tends to go berserk—even normally slow-moving Zombies come running at you with full force. You can prevent this "Bubble Bobble" effect by keeping two enemies alive at the round's end for putting up barricades.

Headless Zombies Can Still Kill You. When you kill a Zombie with a headshot, it invariably blows his head clean off. However, this doesn't mean the Zombie can't hurt you. After losing its head, a Zombie tends to move several steps. If it runs into you during those final steps, it can kill you.

Don't Get Cornered—Ever. If you get cornered, it's almost always game over. You need an escape path at all times, and you should never back yourself into a corner. The first six rounds are the only times you can get away without moving continually. During those rounds, you can fend off the hordes with your back to a wall. Once you get past round six, movement is vital to your survival.

Barricade Points Have Limits. Each round, you can earn only so many points by barricading. Every round has a maximum. If you notice you aren't getting points by putting up a barricade, wait until next round to complete the barricade repairs.

Beware Double Zombies. Never, ever—even on Level 1—attack two Zombies standing on the same space. While your melee strike will likely hit one, the second Zombie will get you.

Stick and Move. Literally. Stick a Zombie with your knife, but immediately move backward after you hit. After round three, Zombies can endure several melee hits. Even if a Zombie looks pretty much dead (well, it *is* dead!), it might take a melee hit and keep on ticking.

Find a Wall Gun That You Like. Each level features several guns you can buy on the wall. These are the only guns that are always available to you regardless of your luck with Max Ammo drops. You need one gun that always has plenty of ammo. We provide map-specific gun recommendations, but everyone has a different fighting style. Experiment to determine which of the typical wall guns you favor.

Instakill is Awesome...but it doesn't make you invincible. Many a Zombie hunter has been killed by the greedy point rush that is Zombie Instakill. Resist the urge and stick to your strategy, even when you luck onto an Instakill.

Reload Before You Pick Up a Max Ammo. Max Ammo doesn't refill your current clip. Always reload both your weapons before you pick up the Max Ammo power-up.

You Can Repair Barricades while Facing Any Direction. To do so, move toward the barricade, hold the Interact button, and then use the Look analog to turn around and ensure Zombies aren't approaching you.

Turn Up Your Sound! Nothing delights a Zombie more than sneaking up on a helpless victim. It delights them so much, in fact, that they just can't shut up about it. Of course, you'll never know this if you can't hear them coming. Make sure your sound is adjusted loud enough to hear the Zombies coming—a surround system doesn't hurt, either.

Zombies Have a Tough Time Reaching You through Barricades. As long as there's a barricade between you and a Zombie, you can feel free attack it with melee or whatever attack floats your boat. However, such Zombies aren't *completely* helpless. They can still get you with a lucky grab if you stand too close.

Reset the Game. If you're playing in Solo mode and having trouble, try quitting and starting a new game. The game doesn't reload the random seed for the spawns, the random drops, the various Zombie waves, and other random elements. It's quite possible that you are just stuck on a tough set of waves.

Plan Your Escape Strategy at the Beginning of the Round. Always know where you're going to escape to if Zombies overwhelm you. Memorize the doorways, and make sure you never accidently follow a dead end (no pun intended). If you're playing Solo, pause the game and plan your strategy with the maps in this guide before the round begins.

MILKING POINTS

You can employ a few techniques to "milk" valuable extra points in the early rounds. If you're playing Co-Op, be sure to communicate your chosen methods with your teammates so you don't end up killing each other's Zombies.

GO FOR MELEE KILLS

In round one, melee kills are vital for extra points. The Zombies go down with one melee hit, and you get a ton of bonus points. In later rounds, soften them up with a couple of bullets before you go in for the melee kill. Once you reach round four, melee kills become extremely dangerous, and you should attempt them only in desperate situations, or when a solid barricade is between you and the Zombie.

USE YOUR WORTHLESS PISTOL FOR BONUS POINTS

Yes, you start the game with a seemingly worthless pistol. Well, it's worthless when it comes to killing Zombies; it's not worthless when it comes to racking up points. Zombies can take a full clip of pistol shots in later rounds. Each time you hit a Zombie with a non-lethal shot, you get 10 points. In Round one, Zombies can take six shots from your pistol and then go down with a melee hit. This technique tallies 180 points per Zombie kill.

LET THE ZOMBIES TEAR DOWN THE BARRICADES

Particularly in the early rounds, if you kill a Zombie before it tears down a barricade, you throw away whatever the point cap is for barricades on the round you're playing.

LET ONE OR TWO ZOMBIES SURVIVE AT THE END OF EACH ROUND

This technique allows you to run around the level with relative impunity to repair barricades, purchase the upgrades you want, and further familiarize yourself with the level. This can be a tricky technique, as it's sometimes difficult to determine exactly when you're facing the last Zombie.

STICK TO MELEE KILLS WHEN INSTAKILL IS ACTIVE

You can snag significant bonus points if you stick to melee kills when Instakill is active. Don't try to melee multiple Zombies (unless you have the Bowie Knife and Jugger-Nog), but melee kills against solo Zombies offer a significant points edge.

USE YOUR GRENADES

Grenades slow down Zombies by blowing off their legs, and they give you a ton of bonus points for incidental damage.

YOU MELEE FASTER WITH THE PISTOL

This is particularly useful in the early rounds, and if you have the Bowie Knife. While your pistol is out, you melee considerably faster than you do with a larger weapon.

USE THE TACTICAL CONTROLS SETTING

You melee a lot more and crouch a lot less on the Zombies levels than you do in the normal single-player campaign. Conveniently, a "Tactical" option for your button setup in the Options Menu inverts these two controls. Try switching them out to see if it helps you during those intense Zombies sessions.

THE SECRETS

***Call of Duty: Black Ops* has many secrets. These vary from the details of the Zombies level to Easter Eggs you can get by activating a terminal.**

We don't want to spoil anything for you, so be warned: this chapter is full of spoilers! Enjoy!

GETTING OUT OF THE CHAIR

You may have noticed in the single-player menu that you are actually in first-person perspective as Mason on the torture chair. If you are on the first screen *after* the "Press Start to Begin" screen, you can actually escape the chair!

Toggle the Fire and Alternate Fire buttons until Mason stands up. The room that you can access is very small, but a computer terminal is in one corner. You can do several things at this terminal:

Enter a Cheat Code

Several cheat codes work in the computer terminal. Using these can affect your achievements, so if you are playing on Xbox 360 or PS3, we recommend you use the Reset command before you start playing the game.

3ARC UNLOCK	This cheat unlocks all the levels in the campaign, including the bonus Zombies level and Dead Ops.
3ARC INTEL	This cheat unlocks all of the Intel pieces so you can look at them in the Main Menu. Be warned—this cheat disables your ability to earn the achievement for gathering all the Intel.

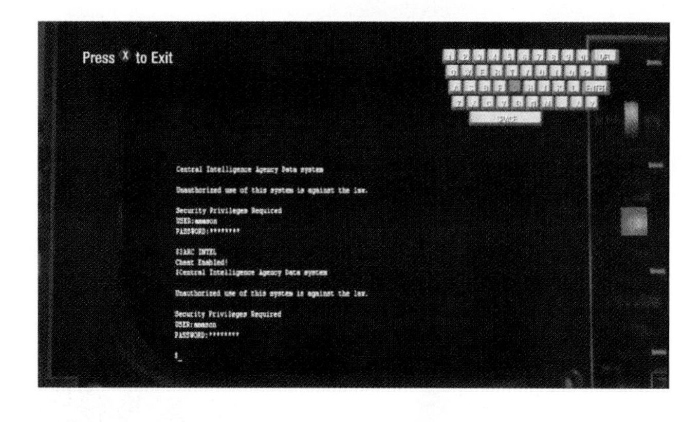

Hack the Terminal

The terminal provides access to a simulated Unix server, which allows you to read campaign characters' email, access production artwork, and read more background on the campaign's story.

- You can begin your hacking attempts by typing "HELP" into the terminal. This allows you to see all the commands available to you.
- Type "DIR" to see a list of assets in Mason's directory.
- Each file has a three-letter extension: TXT, SND, or PIC.
- To examine a file, type "CAT FILENAME.TXT"
- For instance, if you want to read Dad-Letter1.txt, type "CAT DAD-LETTER1.TXT"

You can also listen to sounds and look at pictures in the same way. The pictures in Mason's directory are primarily production artwork.

READ SOME EMAIL

Type "Mail" in the terminal to enter the mail system. Mail is operated by one-letter commands:

?	Help
I	Display Inbox
[n]	Read Message [n]
Q	Quit Mail

Type "I" to see the messages Mason has. Type the number of the message to display it in the terminal.

HACK INTO OTHER USER'S ACCOUNTS

When you're done with Mason's accounts, you may want to hack into some other users. To do so, you have to figure out their passwords. We don't want to give you all the details on that here, but we will give you a clue: you can find some of the other users' passwords by reading Mason's email and files closely.

- Type in "WHO" to see a list of all the users in the computer.
- Type in "LOGIN" to switch users.

PLAY ZORK

Even the C.I.A. occasionally needs some downtime with a video game. The entire *Zork* game is available on the terminal. You can access it by typing "ZORK".

Zork is an interactive fiction or "text adventure" game designed in the late '70s. It's notable for being the first in a long line of Infocom adventure games that brought interactive fiction to previously unseen heights.

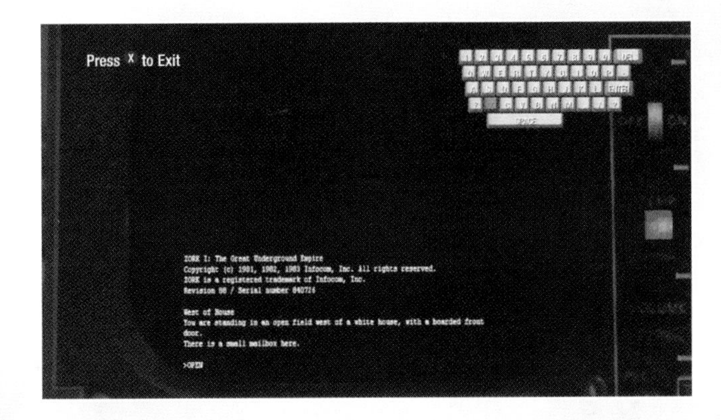

To play *Zork*, you type in simple statements, like "Attack Troll," to navigate through the world. Here are some basic commands to use in *Zork*:

N	Walk north
S	Walk south
E	Walk east
W	Walk west
U	Go up
D	Go down
TALK	Talk to an object
GIVE x y	Give someone (x) an object(y)
ATTACK	Attack something
TAKE	Take an object
USE	Use an object
OPEN	Open an object (usually an object like a door or chest)
SAVE	Save your current position
RESTORE	Load your save
I	Display your inventory
DIAGNOSE	Display your character's medical condition
G	Repeat last command (use this to continually perform the same action)
RESTART	Starts the game over
QUIT	Stops the game and gives you your score
SCORE	Displays your current score

Time in *Zork* passes each time you enter a command. Occasionally, you run into a challenge that requires you to wait for something to happen. The WAIT command ticks one turn for you. You can type Z instead of WAIT.

Zork also keeps track of your score—you receive a final score when your game is over. The object of *Zork* is to return as many trophies as you can to the trophy case in the house—doing so increases your score.

If you really want to tackle *Zork* on your own, here are some tips:

- Get a Keyboard (USB if you are using PlayStation 3, or a controller keyboard if you are using Xbox 360).
- Make a map as you explore.
- Look around each room to try to get clues of what you should pick up or interact with in each area.
- Use the "SAVE" command frequently.
- If you get stuck on a puzzle, bring in your friends and family to help you.
- If the game doesn't understand something you are trying to do, try phrasing it a different way.
- *Zork* only cares about the first six letters of a word—if you want to save some time, you can just type the first six letters of a long word like CANDLESTICK.

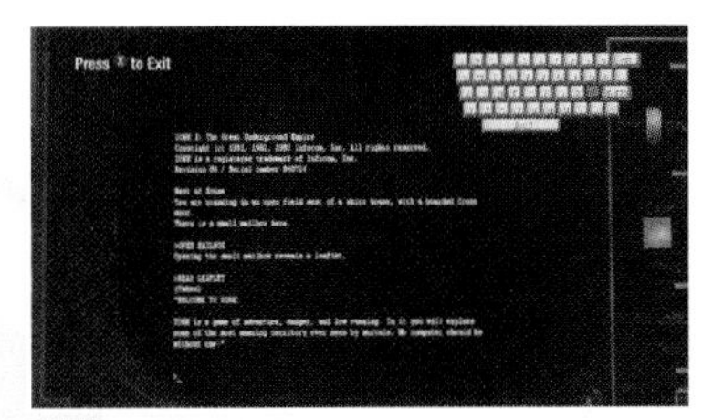

ZOMBIES LEVELS

We've put the level-specific Zombies strategies in this section because we reveal all the objects, areas, and weapons on each level. We feel part of the fun in Zombies is learning these levels on your own, so we didn't want to just throw the tips in the main part of the guide.

There are a lot more secrets to find, even beyond the following level guides. Keep your eyes open for hints as you explore the Zombies maps.

Kino der Toten

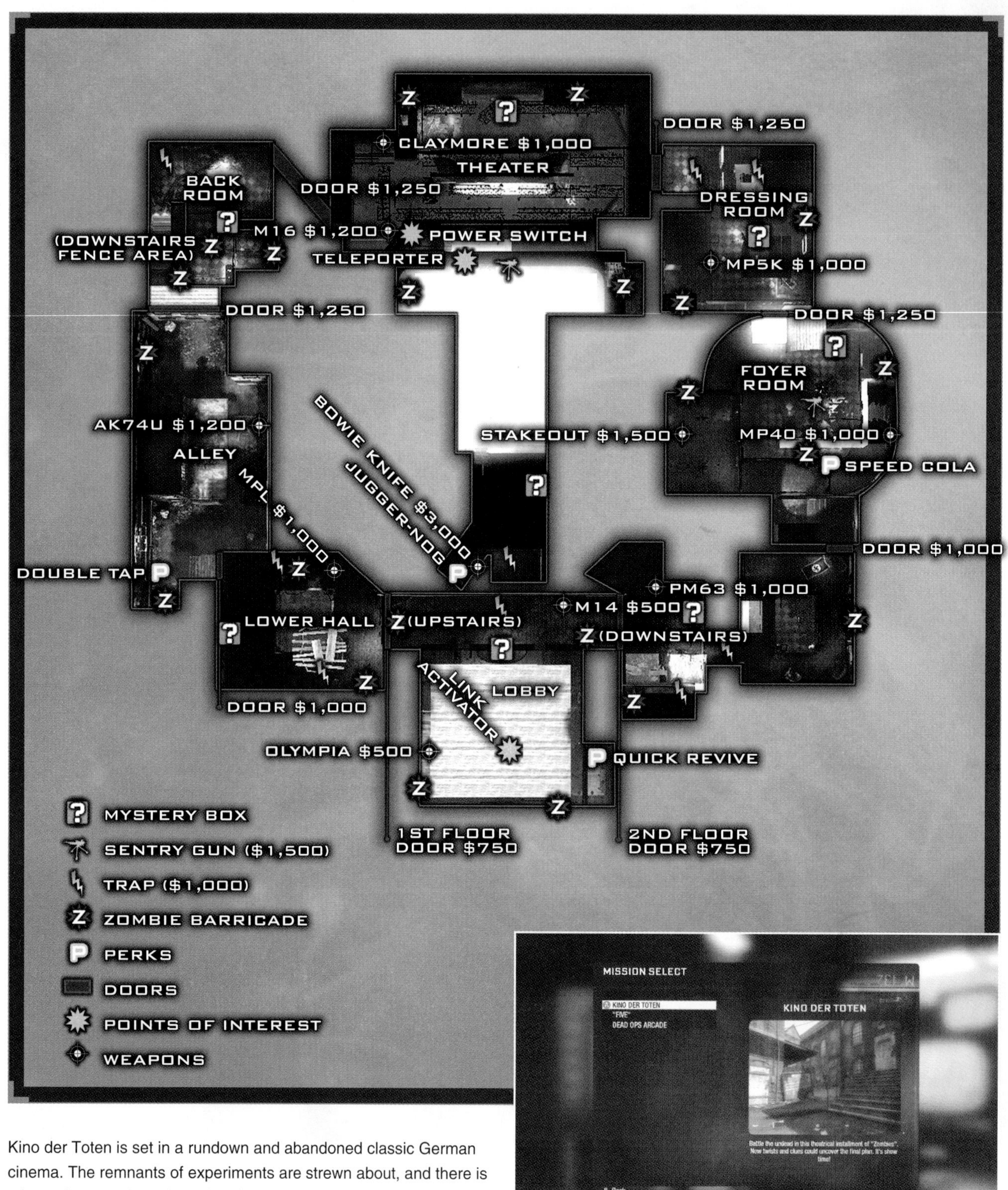

Kino der Toten is set in a rundown and abandoned classic German cinema. The remnants of experiments are strewn about, and there is a lot to discover through exploration.

Your primary goal on Kino der Toten is to make your way to the power switch. Restoring the power activates several level features: the teleporter to the projector room, the perk machines, a display for the location of the Mystery Box, and the many traps in the cinema.

TURNING ON THE POWER

To turn on the power, you have to make it halfway through the cinema to the backstage. There are two paths to the backstage area: the left alley path or the right dressing room path.

Deciding which path is "better" for your style only comes with practice on the map. If you want the MPL, but you want to follow the right-hand path, keep in mind that you can open the door up to the MPL and then proceed down the right-hand route. While this does cost more money, you can actually earn more money by waiting to activate the power until later rounds.

When you make it backstage, trigger the power switch located next to the M16. This raises the curtains on the stage, and it activates all of the previously mentioned level features. Furthermore, it opens the front doors to the theater area, creating a full loop for you to run.

One last note: turning on the power allows the Gas Zombies to spawn in, significantly increasing the difficulty of the waves.

USING THE TELEPORTER

The teleporter warps you to the projection room, which holds the Pack-a-Punch upgrade machine. To activate the teleporter, you must first initiate the link by holding the Interact button in the teleporter module located on the stage.

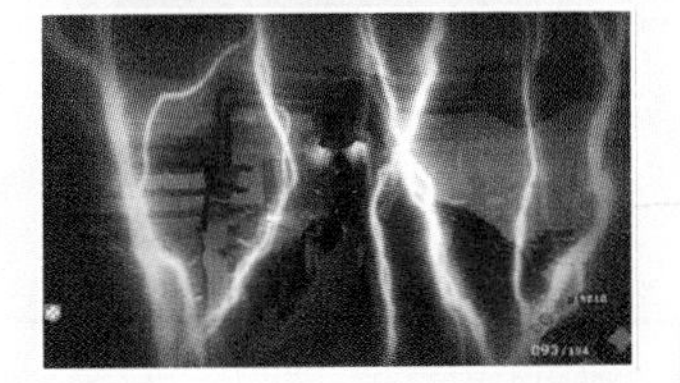

When you hear a click, the link is initiated. Now, head into the lobby area (where you started). When you were in this first room, you probably noticed that there was an odd pad on the ground. Stand on this pad and press the Interact button again—the teleporter is now good to go.

Fight your way back into the theater and stand on the pad to teleport to the projector room.

The projector room contains grenades on the wall and the Pack-a-Punch upgrade station. You can use this to improve any weapon significantly for 5,000 points.

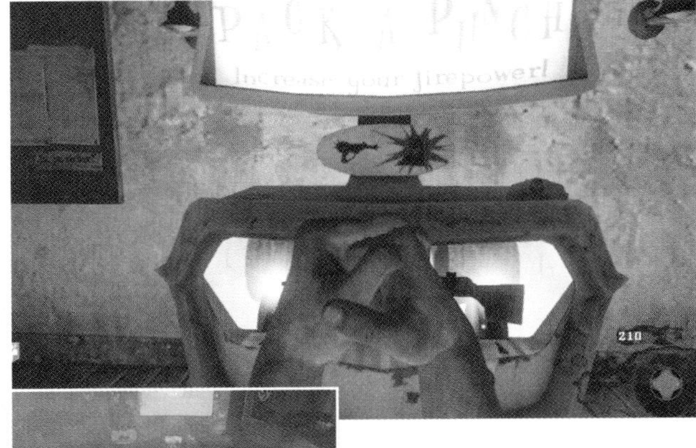

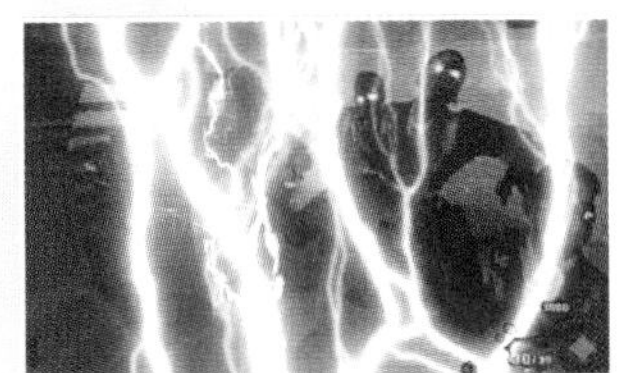

While you're in the projector room, you can look down on the Zombies below and freely fire on them. This is a great opportunity to toss down grenades or use a long-range weapon.

After 30 seconds, the projector room automatically teleports you back into the fray. You may wind up in a randomly selected room outside of the normal map. These rooms occasionally have power-ups.

An interesting note is that the teleporter can serve as a trap. Any Zombies in the teleportation chamber with you when you activate it are killed.

The teleporter requires a few minutes to cool down before you can activate it again.

HELLHOUND WAVES

Hellhounds can show up from round five onward. After their initial appearance, they return every four to six rounds.

Unlike with "normal" Zombie waves, you don't have to run to take on the Hellhounds. Just make sure you have plenty of ammo for your gun, and find a corner where you can see any advancing dogs from a good distance.

Stay in the corner and spray in controlled bursts at the dogs' heads as they charge you. If you get hit, sprint until your health goes back to normal. Dogs are much easier to handle if you have the Jugger-Nog perk.

TRAPS

You can activate traps by using points. They last for a few minutes, but they require a recharge before you can use them again. Zombies killed by traps do not provide points.

The cinema features three types of traps:

ELECTRIC TRAPS	These traps create an electrical wall, completely sealing off one passage in the cinema. Zombies are too stupid to know any better, and they continually run into the traps, getting zapped in the process.
FIRE PIT TRAP	This trap creates a fire in the middle of the room. Like the electric trap, Zombies just plow through the fire and perish before they reach you.
SENTRY GUN	These guns cost a bit more than the other traps, but they do a lot more. Sentry guns automatically target and destroy any Zombies in a 160-degree arc from where the gun is pointed. Sentry guns can help thin the Zombie herd, particularly at the beginning of the wave in the theater.

MYSTERY BOXES

There are many locations for the Mystery Box on this level. The Mystery Box is placed in one of several possible locations when you start the level.

When you turn on the power, a special sign at each potential box location displays a green light to show you the box's current location. As you use the Mystery Box, it eventually runs out of items and is teleported to a new spot.

STAYING ALIVE

When you turn on the power, the difficulty of the rounds increases significantly. You have to alter your strategy so that you constantly move in a forward direction. We recommend you move clockwise through the theater, continually advancing forward.

If you run into a large pack of Zombies going one way, turn and move in the opposite direction. The Zombies tend to clump together, so as long as you consistently take down one or two Zombies to clear your path, you should be able to keep moving and keep progressing through waves.

If you get stuck against a dead end, it could be game over. The Jugger-Nog and Bowie Knife upgrades make it easier to escape bad situations.

SOLO STRATEGY

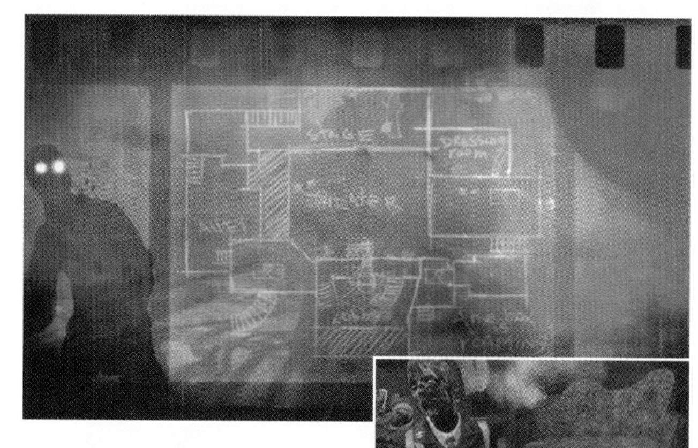

This general Solo strategy should get you to the double-digit rounds on Zombies. How far it takes you beyond that depends entirely on your skill.

The exact rounds in which you implement each step vary, because the amount of money you make fluctuates wildly, according to both the number of melee kills you perform and the random drops you find. Adjust your strategy accordingly if you have a lot of money, or not enough to proceed to the next step.

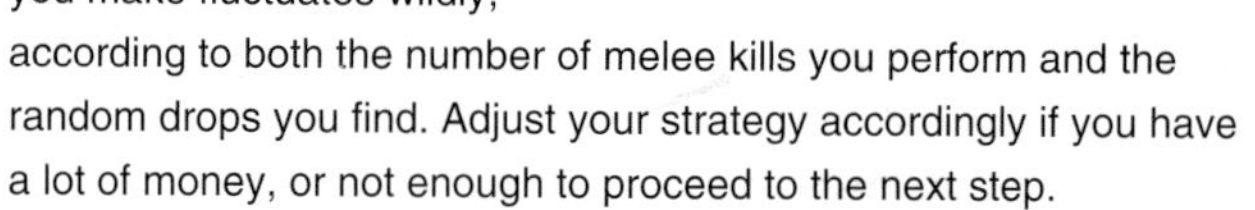

Feel free to modify this strategy for multi-play. Collectively, your team has slightly more resources, and can activate more traps and doors faster. Be warned—there are more Zombies in co-op, so some of these stages may be untenable.

ROUND 1

Let the Zombies tear down two barricades. If they attack a third, knife the Zombies trying to enter. Repair one of the barricades before the end of the round. Leave the second barricade to repair at the beginning of round two. Only use melee to kill Zombies this round.

Use your 500 starting points to buy a quick revive.

ROUND 2

At the start of the round, fully repair the barricade you left in round one. You can start repairing as soon as the second hash appears at the bottom of your HUD.

This round, you have to shoot the Zombies roughly 16 times (two clips) in the body with your pistol before you knife them. Do your best to melee-kill all of the Zombies on this round. Knife the Zombies through the barricade two or three times for a safe kill.

Don't buy anything this round.

ROUND 3

Make sure everything is boarded up at the start of this round. Hold out in this room for as long as you can with just your knife and your pistol. Pump 10 bullets into Zombies before you attempt to melee them if they are not behind a barricade. If you're out of ammo, don't worry about holding your ground.

When you can't hold them back any longer, unlock the door (cost: 750) and move to the lower hallway to purchase the MPL (cost: 1000). Finish off the rest of the wave with headshots via the MPL.

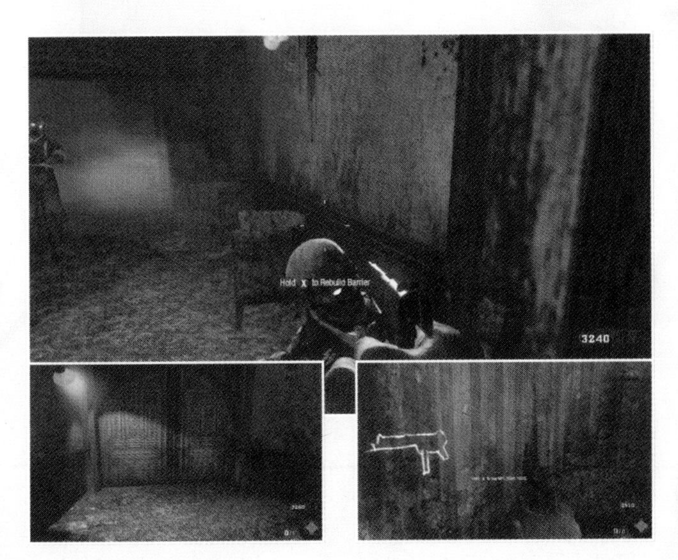

Try to hit your barricade points-cap by leaving the last Zombie alive and running around to repair each barricade.

WHEN YOU HAVE AT LEAST 7,000 POINTS

Your next move is to turn on the power. This costs 3,500 points just to unlock the doors. Hold out in the MPL room as long as you can. There are only two Zombie Barricades to keep up, and the Zombies funnel in directly at you.

You need more ammo before you're ready to move. You can either open the next door and buy the AK74u in the alley, or buy more MPL ammo directly.

If the enemy starts to overwhelm you, use your points to open doors. Whenever you enter a new area, you can be sure no enemies are there as long as most of the round's Zombies have already spawned in.

When you have at least 7,000 points, it's time to turn on the power. You don't have to do this all at once. In fact, we recommend you move slowly toward the power-generating room as the Zombies overwhelm you. This allows you to back your way toward the power room, and by the time you get there, you should have a lot of points. The more points you have *before* you turn on the power, the better.

Another reason not to rush is that the Gas Zombie crawlers don't show up until you turn on the power. In general, the Zombie waves should be much easier without the Gas Zombies around.

BUY JUGGER-NOG

By the time you get to the power room, it should be close to round seven or eight. The Zombies are very tough, and you need serious firepower to survive much longer. Wait until you're nearly cornered, and then open the last door to the theater. Once you're inside, continue backing down the staircase. This is an excellent spot to line up the Zombies and kill them one by one.

When you thin the Zombie wave considerably, move to activate the power on the stage.

Turning on the power opens up the loop, so you can now move freely in a full circle through the theater. Always having two ways out helps ensure your survival. Having looped back to the beginning, you can now buy another Quick-Revive in the lobby if you need it.

Sprint to the front of the theater and buy the Jugger-Nog. If you like to melee Zombies, consider the Bowie Knife—it's worth the 3K.

If you have about 4K left, buy the Claymores at the front of the theater as well. Claymores are useful, as they replenish two per round.

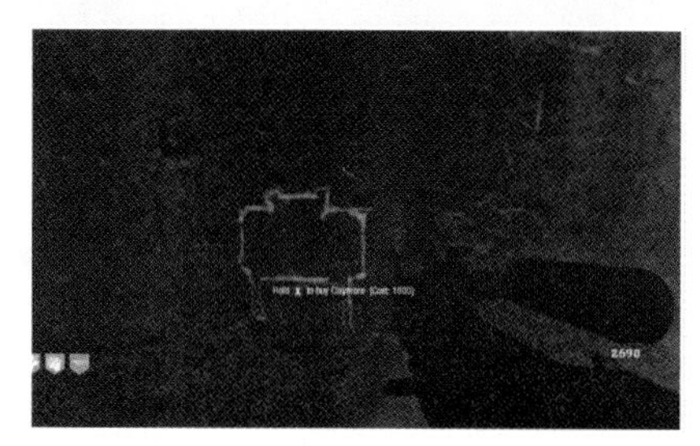

GET A GOOD RANDOM WEAPON

Now, you need to find a good random weapon. You should have about 3,000 left over for three random weapon tries. Locate the box using the map in the theater. Use the box until you get a weapon you like. You can get one of many good weapons, but normally you want something fully automatic that has a decent max ammo capacity.

We recommend the AUG, the HK21, or the Ray Gun. You can determine your favorite random weapon only via experimentation—everyone has different favorites.

UPGRADE YOUR RANDOM WEAPON

At this point, you should be encroaching on round 10. Consider opening up the rest of the theater to allow additional evasive options. Now that you have the Jugger-Nog, you should be able to sprint freely past small groups of Zombies without risk.

Remember to buy a new Quick-Revive if you get caught by the Zombies.

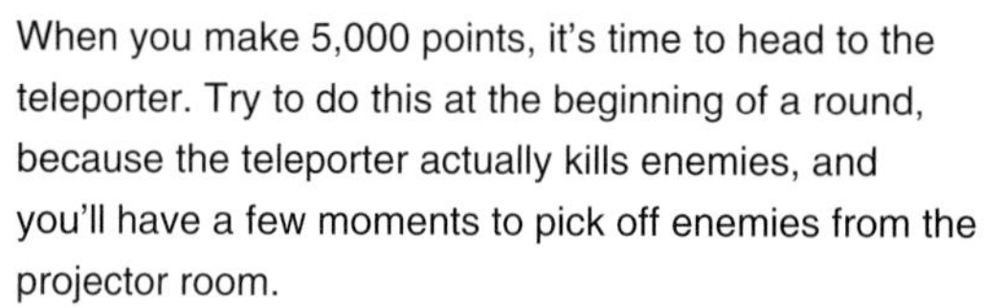

Your goal now is to survive long enough to have 5K points. Surviving past round 10 takes a lot of skill or a lot of luck. If you get cornered, consider deploying traps, as this gives you a couple minutes to take it easy, and it can help thin out a tough wave.

When you make 5,000 points, it's time to head to the teleporter. Try to do this at the beginning of a round, because the teleporter actually kills enemies, and you'll have a few moments to pick off enemies from the projector room.

LIVE LONG AND PROSPER

Once you have an upgraded gun, there is no best path. Just keep moving and saving up points. Consider getting the Speed Cola perk first, but avoid Double Tap, as it simply drains your ammo faster. Use the teleporter every other round to get a breather and eventually upgrade your second (wall) weapon.

Try to group the enemies behind you, keep them in sight, and move slowly through the house, picking them off slowly to get extra points. Only 24 that can appear in the cinema at any given time. The game doesn't spawn new enemies until those 24 are killed. Killing the Zombies slowly, helps ensure you don't get overwhelmed.

Always keep a wall weapon handy in case there's a shortage of Max Ammo power-up drops. How long can you last?

"Five"

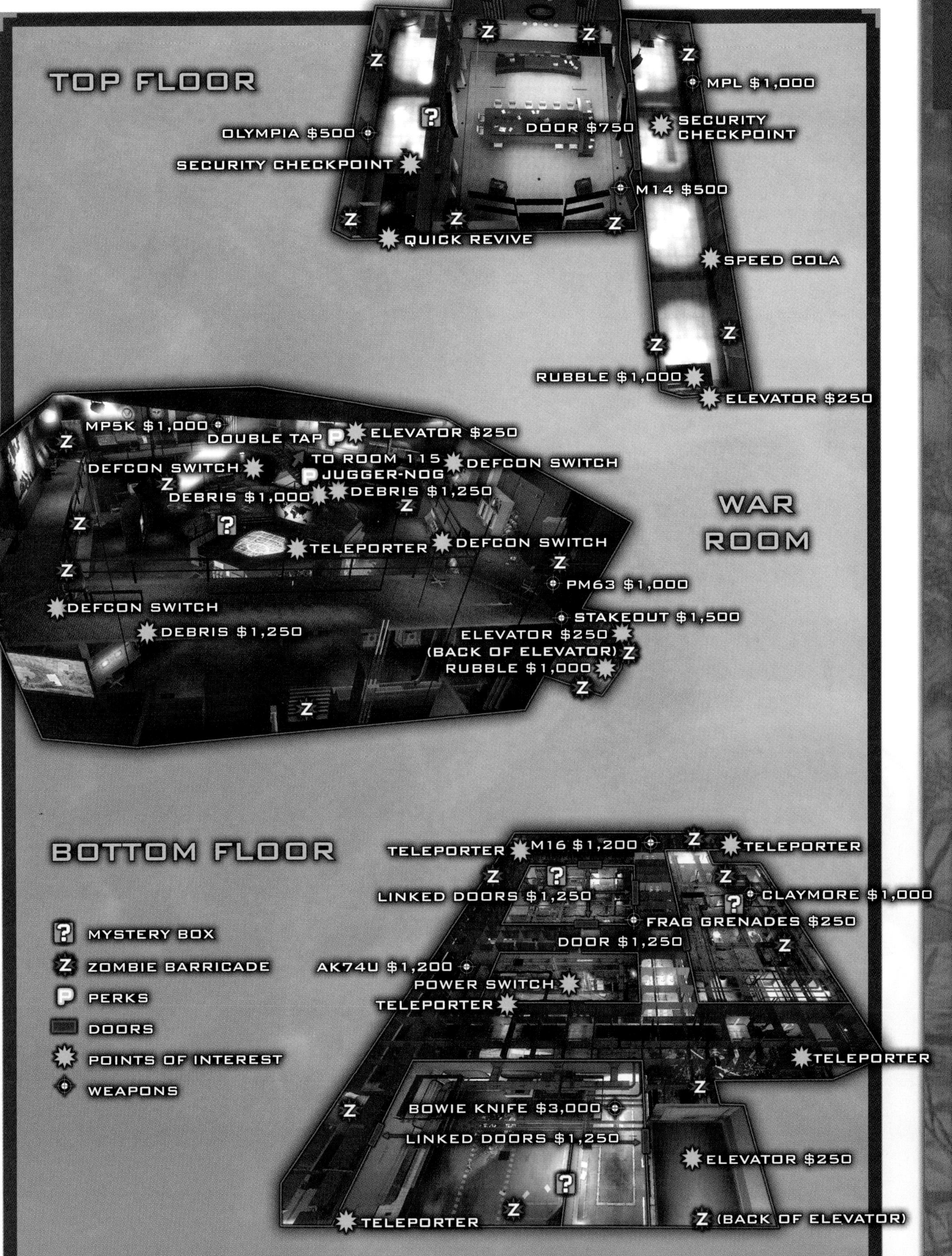
TOP FLOOR
MPL $1,000
OLYMPIA $500
DOOR $750
SECURITY CHECKPOINT
SECURITY CHECKPOINT
M14 $500
QUICK REVIVE
SPEED COLA
RUBBLE $1,000
ELEVATOR $250
MP5K $1,000
DOUBLE TAP
ELEVATOR $250
TO ROOM 115
DEFCON SWITCH
DEFCON SWITCH
JUGGER-NOG
DEBRIS $1,000
DEBRIS $1,250
WAR ROOM
TELEPORTER
DEFCON SWITCH
PM63 $1,000
DEFCON SWITCH
STAKEOUT $1,500
DEBRIS $1,250
ELEVATOR $250
(BACK OF ELEVATOR)
RUBBLE $1,000
BOTTOM FLOOR
TELEPORTER
M16 $1,200
TELEPORTER
LINKED DOORS $1,250
CLAYMORE $1,000
FRAG GRENADES $250
DOOR $1,250
AK74U $1,200
POWER SWITCH
TELEPORTER
TELEPORTER
BOWIE KNIFE $3,000
LINKED DOORS $1,250
ELEVATOR $250
TELEPORTER
(BACK OF ELEVATOR)
MYSTERY BOX
ZOMBIE BARRICADE
PERKS
DOORS
POINTS OF INTEREST
WEAPONS

You unlock "Five" by beating the single-player campaign on any difficulty.

"Five" takes place in the Pentagon and has you moving along three floors: the briefing room (top floor), the war room (second floor), and the basement (bottom floor).

In "Five," you play as one of four characters: Richard Nixon, John F. Kennedy, Robert McNamara, or Fidel Castro. This is probably the first game to pit historical characters against a horde of Zombies!

"Five" features many of the same things as Kino der Toten, including a power switch and the same set of wall weapons.

TURNING ON THE POWER

The power switch is located on the basement level, and it's actually slightly cheaper and easier to access than the power switch on the Kino der Toten map.

To get there, you have to clear your way to the elevator on the first floor(1750 to clear debris + 250 to ride elevator), and then clear your way to the elevator in the war room (2000 to clear debris + 250 to ride elevator).

Because it takes only about 4250 points to get to the bottom, you can do this as early as round three depending on your luck with points.

Once the power is on, all the perk machines are activated, the ability to set the Def Con level is unlocked in the war room, and the teleporters throughout the Pentagon are enabled.

THE TELEPORTERS

When you turn on the power, several teleporter pads become active. Use them to teleport randomly to other parts of the map.

If you use one of the four corner teleporters on the bottom level, it always teleports you to another pad on the bottom level. If you use the teleporter pad in the middle of the bottom floor, it randomly teleports you to either the war room (second floor) or the briefing room (top floor).

After you use a teleporter, a short cool-down period must pass before you can use it again. You can tell whether a teleporter is ready for use by the way it glows.

Inactive *Active*

BE WARNED

Zombies can freely follow you through the teleporters. If you teleport to a bad spot (the war room is very bad if many Zombies are around), you can quickly get overwhelmed and die. Make sure there's some distance between you and the Zombies following you before you teleport.

GOING DEF CON 5

To access the Pack-a-Punch room, you need to get the Def Con level to 5. To do this, you must activate all four switches in the war room—refer to the map in this guide.

When you activate all the switches, all teleporters lead to the special Pack-a-Punch briefing room. You can tell they are activated in this way by looking at the teleporter; inside, you can see the Pack-a-Punch machine.

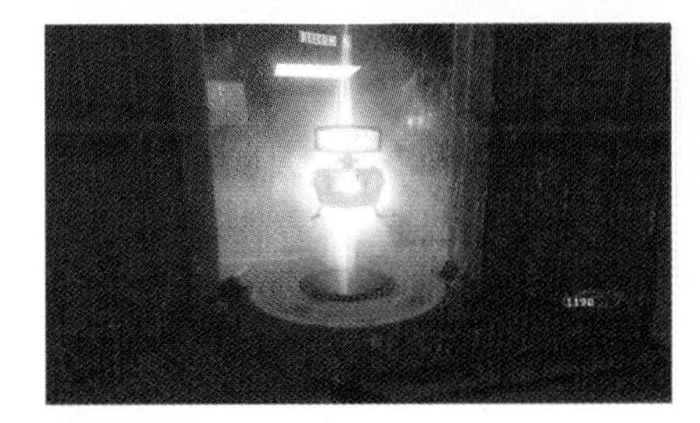

If you haven't entered the Pack-a-Punch room, you can hit Def Con 5 and let the portal stay up as a means of escape when things get hairy. Otherwise, you have about 60 seconds before the computer automatically counts back to Def Con 1. When it does, the area opens up and Zombies come flowing in—get ready to escape!

THE PENTAGON TECH

In order to trigger the Pentagon Tech you must turn on the power.

The Tech randomly appears within one or two rounds.

The Pentagon Tech is a very powerful scientist who steals all of the player's weapons. He hits the players one by one, no matter what area they occupy. While he may seem invincible at first, he can go down; it just requires some pre-planning and strategy.

The Pentagon Tech's hit points increase based on the round and the number of people in the game. Because of this, you want to get to the Tech as early as possible. With a little luck in drops and some extreme Zombie point-milking, you can trigger him as early as round four. However, if you want to have enough ammo to take him down, we recommend waiting to trigger him until round five or six.

To take on the Pentagon Tech, there are a few things you need to know:

Use Claymores: *Claymores are like free hits against the Pentagon Tech, and when they stack up, they inflict massive damage.*

Keep Two Weapons Fully Loaded: *You do not have enough time to reload your weapon when the Tech comes for you. Instead, switch weapons when your clip runs dry.*

Aim for the Head: *Aiming for the head inflicts a lot more damage.*

If He Gets Your Weapon, Don't Panic: *If the Tech gets anywhere near you, he grabs your weapon. Just switch to your backup weapon and chase after him, firing into his head.*

The More Damage He Takes, the Slower He Moves: *As the Tech takes damage, he moves slower so you have an opportunity to catch him before he gets away with your weapon.*

To kill the Tech, we recommend these steps:

- Activate the Tech as early as possible, but aim for round five or six.
- Buy the MPL as your first weapon. Have at least enough ammo for one clip.
- Buy the M16 as your second weapon. Have full ammo.
- Buy the Claymores.
- When you think a Tech round might be coming up, have everyone gather at the bottom-floor elevator. When the Tech spawns in, he comes out from the doorway where the power switch is just ahead.
- Lay down a lot of Claymores in the hallway, preferably four per person in the game. Have everyone aim with their M16s toward the doorway, ready for the Tech. When he emerges, shoot at either his head or at the front of the number trail.
- Keep firing and don't give up. Your goal is to kill him before he gets anyone's weapon. But even if he does grab your weapon, chasing him down and killing him later gets your weapon back, plus the Fire Sale.

After the Tech takes everyone's weapon, he runs around the lower area, where he moves randomly from teleporter to teleporter. You have about 60 seconds to pump him with enough ammo to kill him. Remember, getting headshots deals a lot more damage than melee attacks do at this point.

Killing the Tech rewards you with the awesome Fire Sale, a special event that allows you to buy weapons from the Mystery Box for only ten points. Also, a Mystery Box appears in all possible spots. If you sprint directly to a box, you should be able to get three uses before the sale ends. Killing the Tech before he gets anyone's weapon triggers a Bonfire Sale: the Pack-a-Punch cost is only 1000 instead of 5000. It also opens up the portal to PAP and bestows Fire Sale properties to Mystery Boxes.

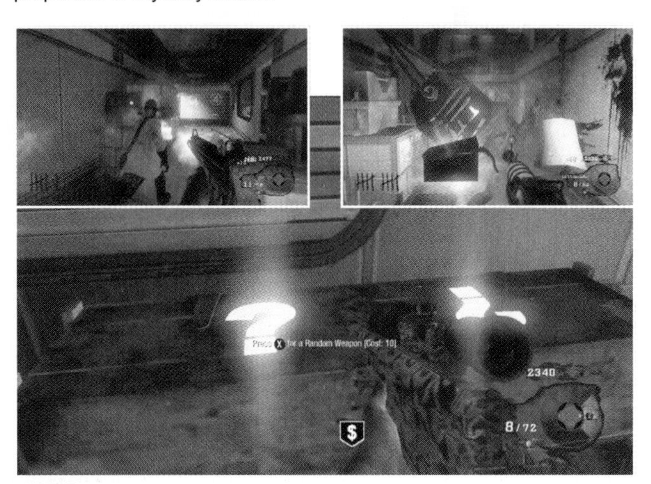

GLASS WINDOWS

"Five" features a unique type of Zombie barricade in the form of glass windows. Players can break glass windows with melee attacks and rebuild them for bonus points. However, points earned from barricades rebuilt in this manner do count toward your building cap.

MYSTERY BOXES

The top floor has two potential Mystery Box positions, while the middle floor has only one. The bottom floor has three Mystery Box positions, and the box always starts in one of these spots.

To figure out which room has the box, peak in through the rooms' windows. Here are the vantage points to determine if the box is inside:

Grenade Room

Claymore Room

Bowie Knife Room

Note: *"Five" features a special random weapon called Winter's Breath. This weapon has the ability to freeze Zombies.*

DEATH MACHINE

"Five" has a special power-up drop called Death Machine. This Power-up temporarily gives you access to the ultra-powerful Death Machine minigun. You can cut down Zombies at an incredible rate.

SOLO STRATEGY

Your Solo goal is to try to bring out the Pentagon Tech as early as possible to ensure he spawns with a minimum of hit points, making him easier to kill.

Again, you can do this as early as round four, but it's much easier on your resources to wait until round five or six so you have plenty of ammunition and Claymores.

ROUND 1

First round, repair enough to hit the 40-point cap.

Let the Zombies in to walk around. You need to luck into some Double Points or Max Ammo power-ups, and the Zombies drop them only if you let them in.

Don't buy the Quick Revive—you need every point, and you shouldn't have trouble with the Zombies until after the Tech round.

Do not buy the weapons in this area.

ROUND 2

Again, let the Zombies in to roam around. To kill a Zombie safely, shoot it six times with your pistol and then move in for a melee kill. This rewards you with 190 points per kill.

Zombies can take up to eight pistol shots in this round, but make sure you have enough ammo for all the Zombies. If you get a Max Ammo power-up, start using the extra bullets for extra points by hitting each Zombie eight times.

Don't forget to hit your repair cap.

Again, don't buy or unlock anything.

You may want to avoid using an Instakill power-up in this round, as it wastes some potential points you could get with your pistol.

ROUND 3

Round three is the first round in which the enemies are somewhat dangerous. Feel free to melee the first wave of Zombies through the barricades, but you'll get overwhelmed pretty quickly. When you do, move to open the first set of doors for 750 points.

Buy the MPL on the wall and use it to kill Zombies with headshots. If you aren't having luck with Double Points drops, you can milk some extra points by shooting Zombies three times in the body with the MPL and then finishing them off with the knife for 160 points.

Before you kill the last two Zombies, make sure you hit your points cap.

WHEN YOU HAVE ROUGHLY 7,000 POINTS

Don't head downstairs until you have 7,000 points. This is how much you need to clear the debris, use the two elevators, open the door to the Claymores, and either open the door to the Mystery Box room, or, if you're lucky, buy the M16.

This could happen at the end of round four, or as late as the end of round six. You shouldn't wait around longer than that, because the Tech will be very powerful on round eight and beyond (but still killable).

The best place to defend during rounds four through six is with your back to the elevator door—feel free to clear the debris. Keep the barricades up on the two windows to your left and right, and be ready to make an emergency escape via the elevator if you get overwhelmed.

The MPL should do you well, but you may need to purchase some extra ammo between rounds.

Whichever round you go downstairs, leave two or three Zombies wandering around before you go.

Take the elevator to the war room. Clear the debris that leads to the next elevator (two pieces of debris for 1,000 each). Now, spend 250 to go downstairs.

Go to the room with the Claymores first and purchase a set.

Now, if the Mystery Box is in this room, you're in luck. You should also have enough points to buy the Claymores and the M16. If the Mystery Box isn't in this room, head outside and figure out where it is.

Open the door to the Mystery Box room or buy the M16—or do both if you have enough points—you only need 30 points for the Tech round. Head to the middle room and turn on the power.

Now use the teleporters to return to the war room. If you don't go to the war room, head back through the teleporter and try again (it's random). In the war room, trigger all the Def Con switches to go to Def Con 5.

Leave the Pack-a-Punch room and return downstairs. Move to the elevator and kill the wandering Zombies when they find you. If you have Claymores, lay down two at the elevator entrance (facing out) before the end of the round.

Now might be a good time to get more ammunition for your MPL as well.

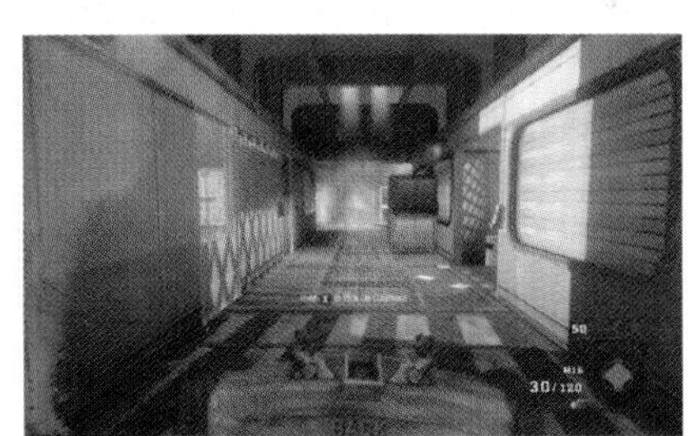

PENTAGON TECH ROUND

The facility's lighting should now go blue to indicate you've activated a Pentagon Tech round. If you have Claymores, you should have two more to plant in the elevator entrance. The Pentagon Tech has only one way to get at you: through the Claymores.

If you didn't have enough points to get the Claymores, use cooked grenades and your machinegun to take down the Tech before he disappears.

If he gets close to you, switch to your starting pistol so he steals that. If he gets your primary weapon, chase him through the teleporters. He has a fairly predictable pattern. Try to anticipate which teleporter he'll exit from on the bottom level.

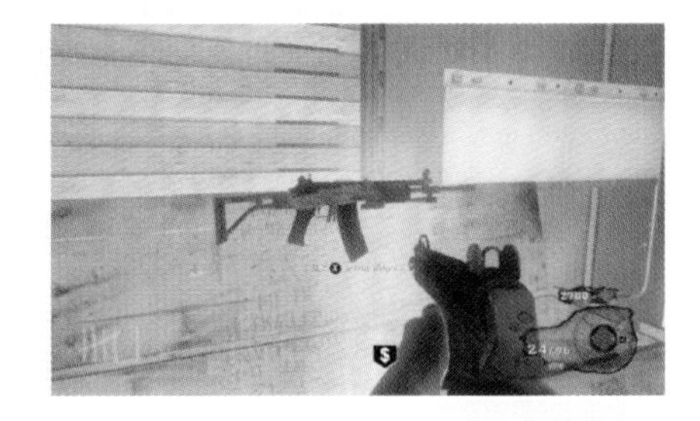

Killing the Pentagon Tech activates the Fire Sale. All uses of the Mystery Box cost only 10 points. Sprint to the box and start using it—you can get a maximum of three uses before the sale ends. Be careful, the next round doesn't wait to start. Zombies will be on you as soon as you're done with the box. If you kill the Tech before he steals any weapons, you trigger a Bonfire Sale (described on page 168).

BEYOND ROUND 5

At this point, it's up to you to stay alive. "Five" is an extremely difficult level compared to other Zombies levels, and getting a good weapon from the box requires some luck. Like other levels, keep moving, conserve your ammo, and find a good pattern to move through the teleporters.

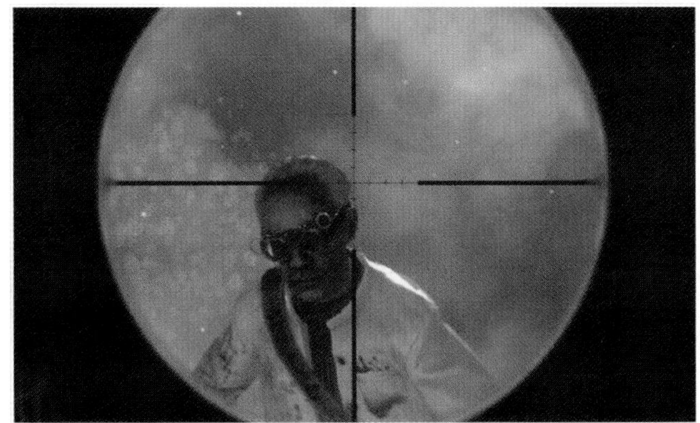

DEAD OPS ARCADE

Dead Ops arcade is a special game mode with gameplay based on classic dual-stick arcade shooters, like *Smash TV* and *Robotron 2010*.

Dead Ops is a Zombie mode. Once you complete the single-player campaign, you can unlock Dead Ops Arcade by typing "DOA" into the Main Menu terminal. After that, you can access the game mode from the Zombies menu.

Levels

While the maps you encounter in Dead Ops are random, they do have some predetermined patterns. Every four rounds, you gain access to a teleporter that takes you to a new area with a different theme. Additionally, occasional special rounds either give you bonus items or set up a particularly difficult round.

You can blast your way through 40 levels in Dead Ops. The later levels have distinct themes that make them more challenging.

Island	1-4	Basic Level, No Traps.
Town	5-8	Traps
Prison	9-12	Traps, Multi-Level Areas
Temple	13-16	Traps, Choose Your Fate Room
Factory	17-20	Traps, Stampeding Cows
Rooftop	21-24	Extra Traps, Multi-Level
Street	25-28	Traps, Exploding Barrels
Bunker	29-32	???
Snow	33-36	???
Jungle	37-40	???

Weapons

Weapons are your bread and butter in Dead Ops, and they are required to progress on the harder stages.

Death Machine	An extremely powerful minigun.
Grenade Launcher	Rapid-fire frag grenades.
Rocket Launcher	Fully automatic rockets—not your grandfather's rocket launcher.
The Shotgun	Fully automatic spread-shot.
The Flamethrower	Massive flames engulf your enemies.
The Ray Gun	Green lasers ricochet off objects.

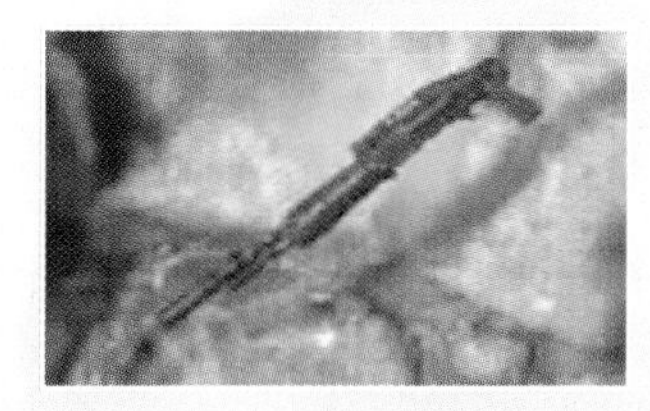

When you pick up a weapon, it lasts a temporary amount of time. A bar appears under your score, representing the amount of time you have left with the weapon. When the timer runs empty, you're back to your regular machinegun.

Firing a weapon significantly decreases the amount of time you have with it, so hold your fire until enemies are upon you.

Power-Ups

Barrel Barrier	Two barrels circle your hero, knocking over any Zombie foolish enough to get close to you.
Electric Coconuts	Similar to Barrel Barrier, except you get four electrified coconuts circling you. These coconuts shock and kill any Zombies that get close enough.
Bear Barrier	When you get this, you are surrounded with caring bear love. The barrier is not impenetrable, but it does fend off most attacking enemies.
Speed Boots	These boots effectively double your speed for a short duration, making it easy to dodge the enemy.
The Monkey	When you get this power-up, a clanking monkey drops on the ground. As long as you don't shoot the Zombies, they will move in toward the monkey. After a few seconds, it explodes, taking the Zombies with it.
The Chicken	This chicken orbits around you and fires the same weapon you do. It lasts for about two minutes before it self-destructs. You can have multiple chicken power-ups following you.
Sentry Gun	This power-up drops a sentry gun wherever you pick it up. The gun picks off any Zombies in the area. It's a great #2 in a Solo game.
Extra Life	You can find extra lives randomly in the form of power-ups.

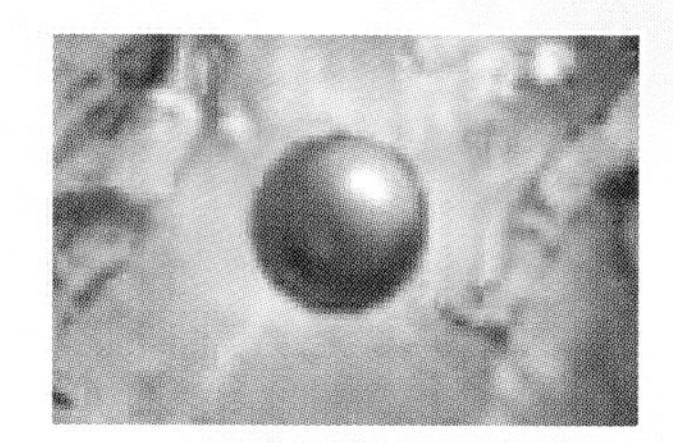

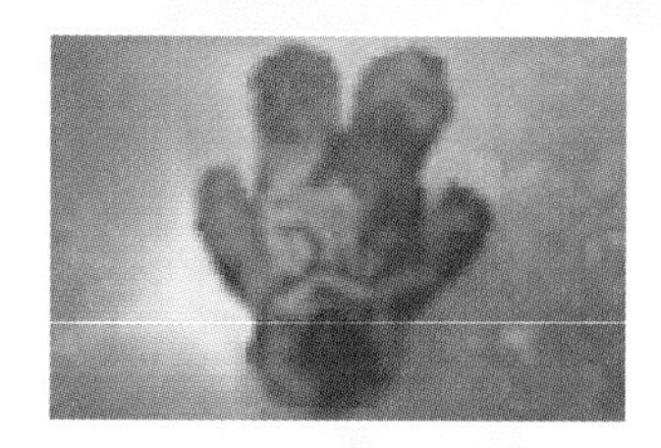

Vehicles

In addition to all those crazy power-ups and weapons, you can also occasionally find a vehicle power-up. There are two types of vehicle power-ups:

The Beast	The Beast is a tank with massive firepower, and it can freely run over Zombies. Use it to cut through enemy lines with grenade-lobbing goodness.
The Devil's Chariot	The Chariot is an attack chopper that you control for massive effect. Move around the area with great speed as you fire your ultra-powerful MGs.

Special Attacks

You also have access to two special attacks in Dead Ops.

The Tactical Nuke is activated with the Aim Down Sight button. It drops from the sky, killing all Zombies currently on the map. This emergency weapon can get you out of any jam.

The Speed Boost button zips you across the map, bowling over any Zombies too slow to get out of your way. This is a great power-up to use when you're cornered and there aren't many Zombies on the map.

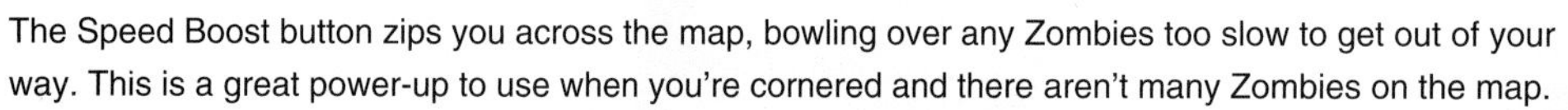

It can also be useful for grabbing a good power-up that's surrounded by enemies. Both the Tactical Nuke and Speed Boost abilities have drops of their own. You can see the counters for these two weapons next to your extra lives.

Fates

After you get to round 13, you eventually run into a random room in which you must "Choose Your Fate." Run to one of the doors to get one of the following permanent power-ups. These power-ups last forever and are much better than a normal power-up.

Furious Feet	You permanently move faster, making it much easier to avoid Zombies.
Fire Power	You have the Death Machine weapon permanently.
Fortune and Fortitude	Power-ups last longer and you gain your points multiplier quicker.
Friendship	This gives you a permanent Chicken power-up, effectively doubling all of your shots for the rest of the game.

Traps

Tesla traps appear on every level after the first four. As you reach higher levels, the traps become more dense. While these traps can kill you, they can also kill Zombies. Trick Zombies into running over them.

Points Multiplier

As you accumulate Zombie kills and loot, your points multiplier increases. The higher your multiplier, the more points you get for everything. This in turn results in more extra lives.

You earn an extra life every 200,000 points. A high multiplier is key to having enough lives to make it to the later rounds.

INTEL CHECKLIST

OPERATION 40		
Intel 1	Near the RPG in the shed, just before you enter the villa.	Page 20
Intel 2	In the bedroom in the villa, after Castro.	Page 22
Intel 3	At the top of the moving staircase in the first hangar.	Page 24

VORKUTA		
Intel 1	The second floor of the slingshot building.	Page 29
Intel 2	The first floor of the armory.	Page 34
Intel 3	Behind Reznov when he gets on the motorcycle.	Page 35

EXECUTIVE ORDER		
Intel 1	The third floor of the communications tower.	Page 43
Intel 2	Inside the room, opposite the wall you destroy with C4, on top of the workstation in the corner.	Page 46
Intel 3	In the headquarters room to the right of the final tunnel.	Page 49

S.O.G.		
Intel 1	Across from the LAW sandbags.	Page 55
Intel 2	In a bunker on napalm hill.	Page 56
Intel 3	Near the shell-shocked soldier in the collapsing tunnel.	Page 58

THE DEFECTOR		
Intel 1	In a side room just after you meet Reznov.	Page 64
Intel 2	In a building during the street battle.	Page 65
Intel 3	In a building across from the MG during the last battle.	Page 66

NUMBERS		
Intel 1	The doctor's lab at the very start of the level.	Page 70
Intel 2	Just after the roof slide.	Page 73
Intel 3	Behind where you drop down, just before you drop down to the final slide to the ground.	Page 76

PROJECT NOVA		
Intel 1	The second Floor of the first building you enter.	Page 80
Intel 2	In Hangar 2/3 through the base.	Page 81
Intel 3	Just before the last set of steps before you jump off boat.	Page 85

VICTOR CHARLIE		
Intel 1	Around the corner to the left, after killing the VCs sleeping in the hammocks, before the doorway to the VC eating from a bowl.	Page 88
Intel 2	In the house behind the first rat tunnel.	Page 90
Intel 3	Down the left rat tunnel after the split.	Page 93

CRASH SITE		
Intel 1	Right at the start, before you board the boat.	Page 95
Intel 2	In the middle of path after you disembark the boat.	Page 99
Intel 3	The flare-lit area after you jump off the wing.	Page 100

WMD		
Intel 1	Just in front of the entrance to the barracks.	Page 105
Intel 2	The second floor of the comm tower.	Page 110
Intel 3	In the final lab area on the table with the explosive barrels.	Page 112

PAYBACK		
Intel 1	In the waterfall room on the shelf.	Page 117
Intel 2	In front of the green tent before you board the Hind.	Page 118
Intel 3	In the dark left corner in the final cavern chamber.	Page 125

REBIRTH		
Intel 1	To the left after you kill the first enemy.	Page 127
Intel 2	In the Nova 6 gas chamber.	Page 130
Intel 3	In the suburban house during the gas attack.	Page 133

REVELATIONS		
Intel 1	After the first set of double doors on top of the cigarette machine.	Page 139
Intel 2	After the morgue area, down the hall to the right, in a bucket.	Page 139
Intel 3	In the inbox on top of the desk in the office area.	Page 139

REDEMPTION		
Intel 1	At the front of the first large cargo crate on the ship's deck.	Page 143
Intel 2	Under a desk in the control room before you rendezvous with Weaver.	Page 145
Intel 3	Under the desk before the final numbers-broadcasting area.	Page 149

ACHIEVEMENTS & TROPHIES

Earning all of the Achievements or Trophies (hereafter referred to as simply "achievements") in *Call of Duty: Black Ops* is no easy feat. There are 50 achievements to earn. You earn most by playing through the single-player campaign, but a few require you to go online.

The *Achievement/Trophy Guide* immediately below does not contain any spoilers, but the *Complete Achievement & Trophy List* that follows it does contain some spoilers, as we give the specifics on how to earn each individual achievement.

ACHIEVEMENT/TROPHY GUIDE: GUIDE TO 100%

Step One: Single-Player Campaign Veteran Playthrough

Your first step is to play through the game on the Veteran difficulty. This difficulty is extremely challenging, so just focus on surviving. Don't worry about any of the extra achievements or gathering the Intel.

Use the Intel list in the Secrets chapter to keep track of which Intel you find during your playthrough. This makes it much easier when you go back to get all the Intel later.

Step Two: Gather Remaining Intel Pieces

Refer to the Intel list in the Secrets chapter to get any of the Intel pieces you missed on your first playthrough. Each level in *Call of Duty: Black Ops* contains three pieces of Intel—you must find them all for the achievement.

Step Three: Mop Up Miscellaneous SP Achievements

With the exception of the Light Foot achievement, you can earn all of these miscellaneous achievements on any difficulty. Refer to the specific info in the following *Complete Achievement & Trophy List* for details on how to earn them.

Step Four: Zombies

The Zombies achievements are the hardest in the game. Refer to the Zombies chapter for extended survival strategy, and check the following achievements below for details on the specific achievements you need to earn.

Some of the Zombies achievements are much easier to achieve with a team of players. Two achievements—Sacrificial Lamb and See Me, Stab Me, Heal Me—require at least one other player.

Step Five: Online

There are just three achievements to earn in the multiplayer game. You can earn them somewhat easily—refer to the list below. One requires that you perform well in Ranked matches online.

Step Six: ???

A few achievements are way too secret to mention in this spoiler-free section. If you want to see what they are, go all the way to the end of the *Complete Achievement & Trophy List*, to the "Ultra-Secret" section.

COMPLETE ACHIEVEMENT & TROPHY LIST
REGULAR CAMPAIGN ACHIEVEMENTS & TROPHIES

You automatically earn each of these achievements for completing levels in the campaign.

SACRIFICE

Xbox 360	10 Gamerscore
PS3	Bronze Medal
Description	Ensure your squad escapes safely from Cuba

Complete the level Operation 40.

GIVE ME LIBERTY

Xbox 360	10 Gamerscore
PS3	Bronze Medal
Description	Escape Vorkuta

Complete the level Vorkuta.

VIP

Xbox 360	10 Gamerscore
PS3	Bronze Medal
Description	Receive orders from Lancer

Complete the level U.S.D.D.

A SAFER PLACE

Xbox 360	10 Gamerscore
PS3	Bronze Medal
Description	Sabotage the Soviet space program

Complete the level Executive Order.

LOOKS DON'T COUNT

Xbox 360	10 Gamerscore
PS3	Bronze Medal
Description	Break the siege in the battle of Khe Sanh

Complete the level S.O.G.

SOG RULES

Xbox 360	10 Gamerscore
PS3	Bronze Medal
Description	Retrieve the dossier and the defector from Hue City

Complete the level The Defector.

BROKEN ENGLISH

Xbox 360	10 Gamerscore
PS3	Bronze Medal
Description	Escape Kowloon

Complete the level Numbers.

NEVER GET OFF THE BOAT

Xbox 360	10 Gamerscore
PS3	Bronze Medal
Description	Find the Soviet connection in Laos

Complete the level Crash Site.

SOME WOUNDS NEVER HEAL

Xbox 360	10 Gamerscore
PS3	Bronze Medal
Description	Escape the past

Complete the level Project Nova.

CLARITY

Xbox 360	10 Gamerscore
PS3	Bronze Medal
Description	Crack the code

Complete the level Revelations.

STAND DOWN

Xbox 360	35 Gamerscore
PS3	Silver Medal
Description	Complete the campaign on any difficulty

This is rewarded after you complete the level Redemption.

VETERAN CAMPAIGN ACHIEVEMENTS & TROPHIES

You earn bonus achievements for completing campaign levels on the Veteran difficulty setting.

COLD WARRIOR

Xbox 360	25 Gamerscore
PS3	Silver Medal
Description	Complete "Operation 40," "Vorkuta" and "Executive Order" on Veteran difficulty

DOWN AND DIRTY

Xbox 360	25 Gamerscore
PS3	Silver Medal
Description	Complete "SOG and "The Defector" on Veteran difficulty

IT'S YOUR FUNERAL

Xbox 360	25 Gamerscore
PS3	Silver Medal
Description	Complete "Numbers," "Project Nova" and "Victor Charlie" on Veteran difficulty

NOT TODAY

Xbox 360	25 Gamerscore
PS3	Silver Medal
Description	Complete "Crash Site," "WMD," and "Payback" on Veteran difficulty

BURN NOTICE

Xbox 360	25 Gamerscore
PS3	Silver Medal
Description	Complete "Rebirth" and "Redemption" on Veteran difficulty

BLACK OP MASTER

Xbox 360	100 Gamerscore
PS3	Gold Medal
Description	Complete the campaign on Hardened or Veteran difficulty

SPECIAL CAMPAIGN ACHIEVEMENTS & TROPHIES

There are a lot special achievements to earn in the single-player campaign. We tell you the specifics of how to earn them here.

DEATH TO DICTATORS

Xbox 360	15 Gamerscore
PS3	Bronze Medal
Description	Take down Castro with a headshot
Level Earned	Operation 40

To earn this achievement, you have to kill Castro with a single headshot. This is an easy shot to make.

SLINGSHOT KID

Xbox 360	15 Gamerscore
PS3	Bronze Medal
Description	Destroy all slingshot targets in 3 attempts
Level Earned	Vorkuta

Earn this achievement by demonstrating perfect aim in the slingshot sequence early in the level. Aim a bit above your targets to demolish them successfully. Here's exactly where you should fire for the three targets:

VEHICULAR SLAUGHTER

Xbox 360	25 Gamerscore
PS3	Silver Medal
Description	Destroy all enemies on vehicles during the prison break
Level Earned	Vorkuta

To earn this achievement, kill all the enemies that appear on vehicles in the Vorkuta level's final escape sequence. We've identified some of the enemies you have to kill for the achievement here:

TOUGH ECONOMY

Xbox 360	15 Gamerscore
PS3	Bronze Medal
Description	Use no more than 6 TOW guided missiles to destroy the tanks in the defense of Khe Sanh
Level Earned	S.O.G.

Earn this achievement at the very end of the S.O.G. level.

There are six tanks to kill, so that means you can't miss with any of your TOW guided rockets. If you mess up a shot, wait for the tanks to kill you so that you can restart from the previous checkpoint.

THE DRAGON WITHIN

Xbox 360	15 Gamerscore
PS3	Bronze Medal
Description	Kill 10 NVA with Dragon's Breath rounds
Level Earned	The Defector

As long as you use the flame rounds with the shotgun you receive at the beginning of this level, you can't miss the achievement. You should earn this before you leave the starting office complex.

RAINING PAIN

Xbox 360	15 Gamerscore
PS3	Bronze Medal
Description	Rack up a body count of 20 NVA using air support in Huê City
Level Earned	The Defector

Use your helicopter radio liberally as you move through the streets of Hue City in the second part of Raining Pain. This should come without too much trouble.

DOUBLE TROUBLE

Xbox 360	10 Gamerscore
PS3	Bronze Medal
Description	Use only dual-wield weapons to escape Kowloon
Level Earned	Numbers

You start the level with dual weapons, and you must use only other dual weapons. You can tell if a weapon is a dual-wield type when you stand over it.

We recommend attempting this only on Recruit difficulty, because dual weapons have very limited range, and several sequences are difficult without a long-range weapon.

LIGHT FOOT

Xbox 360	30 Gamerscore
PS3	Silver
Description	Escape the ship with 2:15 left on the timer in Veteran
Level Earned	Project Nova

This is the most difficult achievement to earn in the single-player campaign, as it means you must escape the boat without getting killed in less than 45 seconds after Reznov sets the bombs.

We recommend you play through the level a few times on easier difficulty to chart your route through the enemies. When you feel you know the path perfectly, you essentially need to sprint the whole way. Don't stop to fight enemies; just keep moving and don't stop for anything. Did we mention you should avoid stopping?

You can fire at enemies before you get to the end, but don't slow down. Be sure to find a Sten before you activate the bomb in order to have two weapons during this sequence. Instead of reloading when your PPSH gets low, switch to the Sten.

UP-CLOSE AND PERSONAL

Xbox 360	15 Gamerscore
PS3	Bronze Medal
Description	Silently take out 3 V.C.
Level Earned	Victor Charlie

If you follow the walkthrough for this level, you should get this automatically. Simply use melee attacks to kill the three V.C. depicted in the following screenshots to earn the achievement.

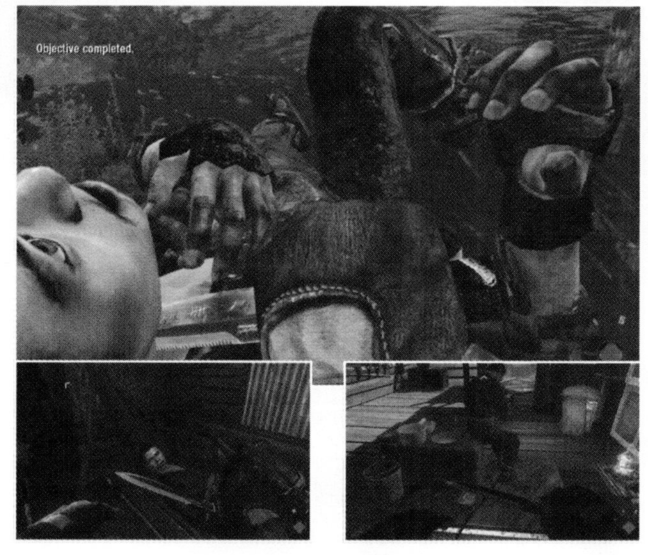

HEAVY HAND

Xbox 360	15 Gamerscore
PS3	Bronze Medal
Description	Use the Grim Reaper to destroy the MG emplacement
Level Earned	Victor Charlie

After you clear out roughly half of the village on this level, you can find a Grim Reaper near a downed soldier on the docks. This missile launcher is designed to take down the ZPU mounted on a boat floating on the river. Use it to take down the ZPU, but hang onto the missile launcher.

When you make it through the next house, a V.C. MG is positioned at the top of the next hill. Use the Grim Reaper to destroy the MG and earn this achievement.

LORD NELSON

Xbox 360	25 Gamerscore
PS3	Silver Medal
Description	Destroy all targets and structures while making your way up the river.
Level Earned	Crash Site

This is a straightforward achievement, but it requires you to be patient and thoroughly cover the shorelines with fire as you move up the river. This level never rushes you ahead, so just be sure to destroy all structures and enemies in the area before you move further up the river.

For the PT boat sequence, be sure to destroy the structures in the area before you destroy the PT boat itself. The PT boat is the last target, so you should earn the award shortly after you destroy it.

PATHFINDER

Xbox 360	50 Gamerscore
PS3	Silver Medal
Description	Guide the squad through the Soviet outpost without getting them killed
Level Earned	WMD

To earn this achievement, you have to get through the RSO portion of the WMD level without failing. Complete up to the barracks prior to the point where Hudson hides in the snowy bushes with the Crossbow.

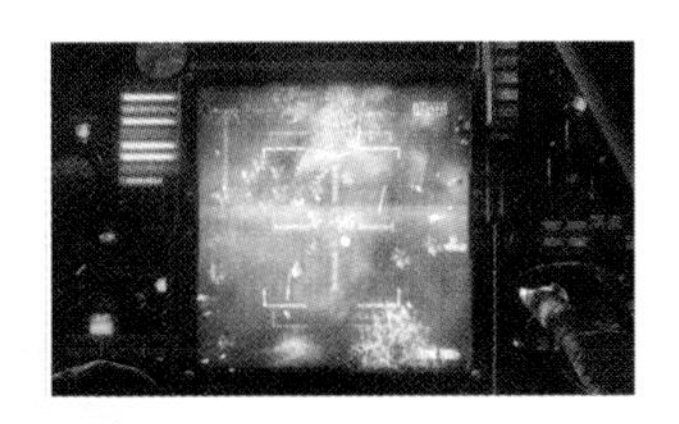

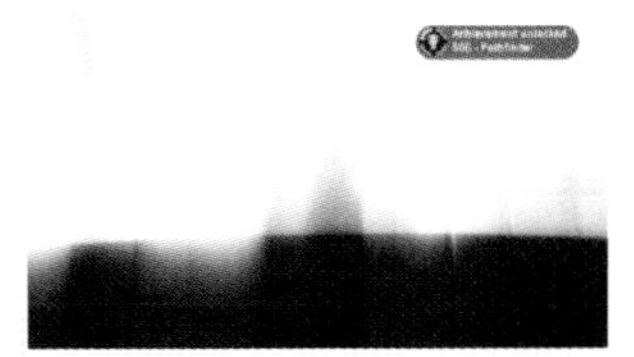

MR. BLACK OP

Xbox 360	50 Gamerscore
PS3	Silver Medal
Description	Enter the Soviet relay station undetected
Level Earned	WMD

This is a very difficult achievement to earn, but the walkthrough does a great job of outlining a stealth route through the enemy defenses leading up to the relay station. Follow the walkthrough step by step to earn this achievement.

WITH EXTREME PREJUDICE

Xbox 360	25 Gamerscore
PS3	Silver Medal
Description	Get to the POW compound in the Hind using only rockets
Level Earned	Payback

Halfway through this level, you and Woods fly a Hind. Keep your finger off the Fire button to avoid using the MG through the entire sequence to earn this achievement. We recommend you attempt this on the Recruit difficulty setting.

RUSSIAN BAR-B-Q

Xbox 360	15 Gamerscore
PS3	Bronze
Description	Incinerate 10 enemies with the Flamethrower attachment in the POW compound.
Level Earned	Payback

Just before you find the POWs on this level, an enemy drops an AK-47 with Flamethrower attachment. Grab this and proceed to kill 10 enemies before the end of the level. Like the With Extreme Prejudice achievement, we recommend you attempt this on Recruit difficulty, because it can be dangerous getting close enough to an enemy to light him on fire.

I HATE MONKEYS

Xbox 360	15 Gamerscore
PS3	Bronze
Description	Kill 7 monkeys in under 10 seconds in the Rebirth labs
Level Earned	Rebirth

This achievement is more challenging than you might think.

It's best to do this with Reznov in the first part of this level. Just before you get to the experiment room (the room with the large Nova 6 chamber in the middle), a group of monkeys is in cages at one corner of a hall. Drop a couple grenades in the corner, and then open up on the monkeys with your shotgun.

If you don't get it the first time, try again by committing suicide with a grenade—there's a checkpoint just before this area.

NO LEAKS

Xbox 360	50 Gamerscore
PS3	Silver
Description	Make it through the NOVA 6 gas without dying on Rebirth Island
Level Earned	Rebirth

We recommend you try for this achievement on Recruit difficulty. Halfway through the level, you have to wear a hazmat suit to get through a cloud of Nova 6. While you wear the suit, your health is represented by the damage your suit suffers. This means you don't automatically regenerate health.

You must get through this entire sequence without getting killed to earn this achievement. Keep to cover and avoid taking hits at all costs; you can't get this one by rushing ahead.

DOUBLE WHAMMY

Xbox 360	15 Gamerscore
PS3	Bronze
Description	Destroy both helicopters with one TOW guided missiles from the deck of the ship
Level Earned	Redemption

This difficult achievement requires excellent accuracy and timing. To take down both birds with one stone, you need to explode the Valkyrie early by pressing the Fire button exactly when the rocket is positioned between the two choppers. This takes some patience, as the helicopters must be flying next to each other for one Valkyrie to hit them both.

If you miss and accidently take down one helicopter, fire a rocket pointblank at the ground to commit suicide and retry from the checkpoint.

FRAG MASTER

Xbox 360	15 Gamerscore
PS3	Bronze
Description	Kill 5 enemies with a single frag grenade
Level Earned	Any Level

This requires a bit of luck, as the enemies must be very tightly clustered for you to kill all five with one blast. Using the Grenade Launcher attachment does not count toward this achievement.

SALLY LIKES BLOOD

Xbox 360	15 Gamerscore
PS3	Bronze
Description	Demonstrate killer economic sensibilities by taking down 3 enemies with a single bullet
Level Earned	Any Level

Zombies is also your best bet for earning this achievement quickly—try to get the Zombies in a line, and take down three with one shot from a high-penetration weapon like the FN Fal. The M16 can also do the job, but its rapid fire might make the task more difficult than a rifle.

This does not work with a shotgun, because the shotgun fires shells, not bullets.

UNCONVENTIONAL WARFARE

Xbox 360	15 Gamerscore
PS3	Bronze
Description	Use the explosive bolts to kill 30 enemies
Level Earned	Any Level

This achievement is cumulative over levels. However, if you die, you lose all crossbow kills since your last checkpoint.

Two campaign levels give you access to the explosive crossbow bolts: Executive Order and WMD.

CLOSER ANALYSIS

Xbox 360	15 Gamerscore
PS3	Bronze
Description	Find all the hidden Intel
Level Earned	All Levels

Each campaign level except for U.S.D.D. features three hidden pieces of Intel. For a complete list of Intel locations, check the Intel section of the Secrets chapter.

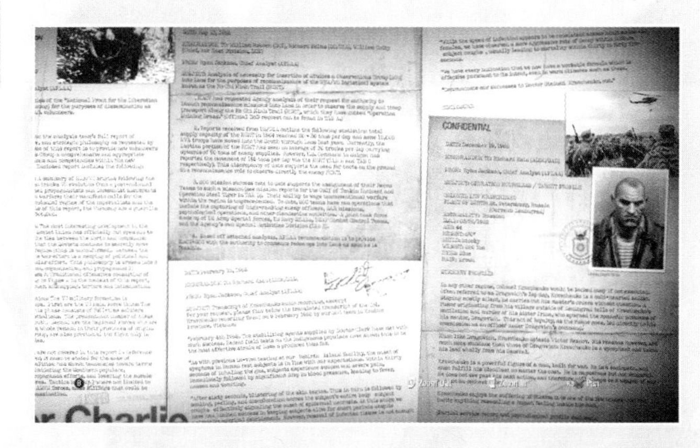

SPECIAL CAMPAIGN ACHIEVEMENTS & TROPHIES

There are only three Multiplayer achievements to earn.

DATE NIGHT

Xbox 360	15 Gamerscore
PS3	Bronze
Description	Watch a film or clip with a friend

Load up the Theater Mode in Multiplayer, invite a friend, and watch something with him or her to earn this achievement.

IN THE MONEY

Xbox 360	20 Gamerscore
PS3	Bronze
Description	Finish 5 Wager Matches "in the money"

Wager matches are a new game type in Multiplayer. You can gamble COD Points against other players in this mode. This mode requires you to play against random people online.

To finish a Wager Match "in the money," you must place third or higher in the final standings.

READY FOR DEPLOYMENT

Xbox 360	15 Gamerscore
PS3	Bronze
Description	Reach rank 10 in Combat Training

Combat Training is a new game mode for Call of Duty: Black Ops. You can play with your friends (or by yourself) against bots in Deathmatch and Team Deathmatch games. You can earn this by playing four or five games against the bots.

ZOMBIE ACHIEVEMENTS & TROPHIES

Zombies achievements are the most difficult to earn in the game. Patience, practice, and knowledge are key to surviving long enough to earn these.

THE COLLECTOR

Xbox 360	20 Gamerscore
PS3	Bronze
Description	In Zombie mode, buy every weapon off the walls in a single game

You need a lot of points to get every weapon. For complete weapon locations, check out the map-specific Zombie strategy in the Secrets chapter.

To get every weapon, focus on buying wall weapons only, and avoid spending money on areas that don't have access to wall weapons. Depending on your point-earning strategy, you have to make it roughly to round 12 in Solo to have enough points to buy all weapons and unlock the necessary areas.

Don't forget that Frag Grenades, Claymores, and the Bowie Knife all count as wall weapons.

If you follow the tactics outlined in the level-specific strategies, you should make it to the double digits in Solo with some practice.

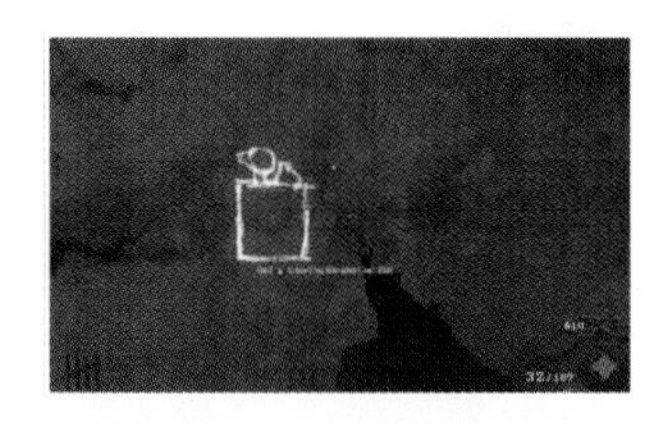

HANDS OFF THE MERCHANDISE

Xbox 360	15 Gamerscore
PS3	Bronze
Description	Kill the Pentagon thief before it can steal your loadout

The Pentagon thief is a special enemy you encounter in the "Five" Zombies level. Killing him isn't easy, but we have a strategy for you in the Secrets chapter.

You unlock the "Five" level after completing the game once on any difficulty.

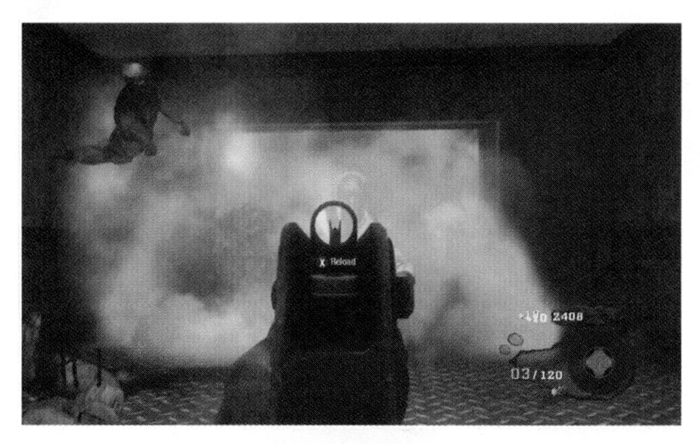

SACRIFICIAL LAMB

Xbox 360	15 Gamerscore
PS3	Bronze
Description	Kill 6 Zombies after getting shot by a Pack-a-Punched Crossbow bolt

You can receive the Crossbow from the Random Weapon Crate. To earn this achievement, you can have a friend upgrade the Crossbow with the Pack-a-Punch perk, and then have him or her shoot you with it. Once the explosive bolt is attached to you, run into a large group of enemies.

SEE ME, STAB ME, HEAL ME—SECRET ACHIEVEMENT

Xbox 360	15 Gamerscore
PS3	Bronze
Description	Throw a Pack-a-Punched Ballistic Knife at a downed ally to revive him from a distance

The Ballistic Knife is another weapon you procure from the Random Weapon Crate. If you upgrade one with the Pack-a-Punch upgrade machine, you can revive your teammates with it. This is a seriously challenging achievement and requires you to assemble a well-oiled anti-Zombie team.

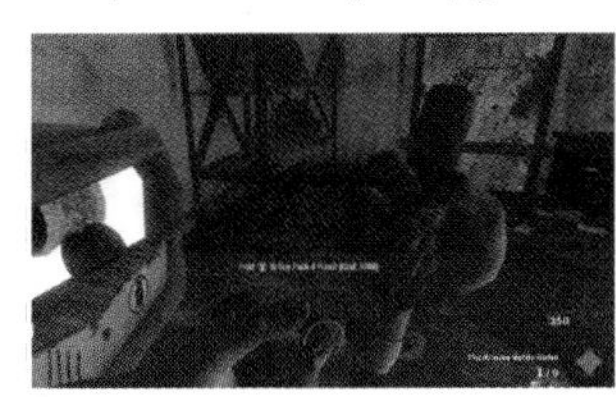

ULTRA-SECRET ACHIEVEMENTS & TROPHIES

"INSERT COIN"

Xbox 360	5 Gamerscore
PS3	Bronze
Description	Access the terminal and battle the forces of the Cosmic Silverback in Dead Ops Arcade

Enter "DOA" into the Main Menu's terminal. After you unlock it in the terminal, it then appears unlocked in the Zombies menu.

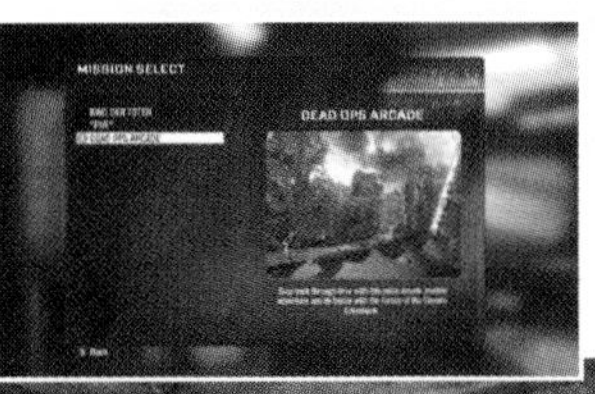

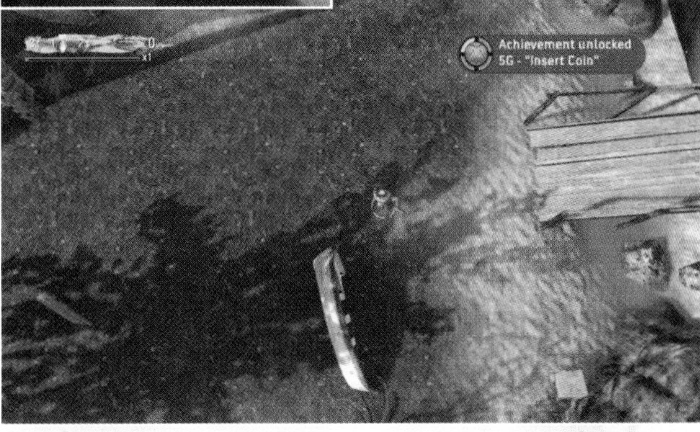

EASY RHINO

Xbox 360	10 Gamerscore
PS3	Bronze
Description	In Dead Ops Arcade, use a Speed Boost to blast through 20 or more enemies at one time

In Dead Ops Arcade mode, you can activate a special attack called the Speed Boost. Do this by pressing the Fire button.

You can earn this achievement on the first or second level of Dead Ops Arcade. Avoid killing Zombies and keep them at a distance. The Zombies will naturally group up as you move around. Keep avoiding the Zombies until they are in one tight group following you around the map. When a lot of Zombies are in this group, point directly into the group with a Speed Boost.

If you don't get the achievement, it just means there weren't enough Zombies in the pack—try the same strategy on the next level.

JUST ASK ME NICELY

Xbox 360	15 Gamerscore
PS3	Bronze
Description	Break free from the torture chair

To break free from the torture chair, you have to be on the Main Menu screen. Here, you actually play as Mason. To break free and explore the torture chamber, press the Aim Down Sight and Fire buttons rapidly. You should see Mason get up, and then you can explore this small area.

EATEN BY A GRUE

Xbox 360	15 Gamerscore
PS3	Bronze
Description	Play Zork on the terminal

Once you get up and earn the Just Ask Me Nicely achievement, you can use a computer terminal in the room. This terminal has the classic Activision text adventure Zork installed. Type "ZORK" into the terminal to start the game and earn this achievement.

MULTIPLAYER BRIEFING

Welcome to *Call of Duty: Black Ops* multiplayer. If you're a longtime *Call of Duty* fan, you'll find a lot to like here. If you're a fresh recruit, we've done our best to give you the tools you need to survive and thrive online.

Look through this chapter for a broad overview of the various multiplayer gameplay features in *Call of Duty: Black Ops*. Visit the Armory chapter for a more in-depth discussion, and then check out the Maps and Modes chapters for a look at all the battlefields and gameplay types. The Special Ops chapter holds the real bare-metal advice for playing online. Finally, the Reference section at the end is a good place to look if you seek information about equipment or other data.

OVERVIEW

You can enter *Call of Duty: Black Ops* multiplayer alone or with your party through any number of matchmaking playlists.

You can also play private, custom games with your friends, or even play offline in Combat Training against AI bots.

If you're just starting, we recommend running through the campaign, then hopping online with some friends. Multiplayer veterans may want to jump right online, while new players can ease the transition into multiplayer by checking out Combat Training against bots.

Multiplayer Modes

Matchmaking in *Call of Duty: Black Ops* is largely divided among the game's various play modes. Some modes are restricted to no parties (generally Free for All), but most allow you to bring your friends. A few playlists are explicitly for larger parties—large team battles, essentially—though most games are 6v6 affairs.

CALL OF DUTY: BLACK OPS MULTIPLAYER MODES

MODE	DESCRIPTION
Free for All (FFA)	Every man for himself. First player to the score limit wins.
Wager Match	Six-player FFA. Top three players earn CODPoints (currency). Bottom three lose it.
Team Deathmatch (TDM)	Team vs. team deathmatch. First team to the score limit wins.
Search & Destroy (S&D)	Two teams, offense and defense. One bomb, two bomb sites. Either team wins by eliminating the other. Offense wins by planting and defending the bomb until it detonates; defense can win by defusing it.
Demolition	Two teams, offense and defense. One bomb, two bomb sites. Offense wins by detonating the bomb; defense wins by holding out for the full time limit.
Sabotage	Two teams, one bomb, one bomb site for each team. Either team wins by planting and detonating the bomb.
Domination	Two teams, three capture points. Holding a point raises your team score; reach the score limit to win.
Capture the Flag (CTF)	Two teams, two flags. Capture the enemy flag to win.
Headquarters	Two teams, multiple Headquarters. Headquarter moves around the map randomly; secure and hold the Headquarter location to earn points. First team to reach the score limit (or outscore the other team by the time limit) wins.

Multiplayer Combat

The multiplayer combat experience is very different from the single-player campaign. Depending on your personal experience with the *Call of Duty* series, multiplayer combat may be new to you as well.

Multiplayer combat is very fast and very lethal. Most guns kill in no more than a few shots, and many types of attacks can kill instantly. Standing out in the open means a quick trip to the grave.

Survival in *Call of Duty: Black Ops* depends on your situational awareness, your movement skills, your stealth, and your aim. In most situations, the player who outthinks and outsmarts his opponent, and gets the jump and the first attack, wins the fight. Learning to be the player with the upper hand at all times is extremely important.

If you're new, learning online can be painful, but *Call of Duty: Black Ops* now includes Combat Training with bots. If you're totally green, we recommend experimenting a bit there—but don't be surprised to find that players online don't always play the way bots do.

Combat Training can help improve the fundamentals of your play—class outfitting, movement, aiming and firing weapons—but it can't help you with the mental aspect of defeating other human players. That's the difference between winning and losing online. Once you're comfortable with the basics, get online and start playing!

ADS: AIM DOWN SIGHTS

Any time you see ADS in this guide, we're talking about aiming down the sights of your weapon.

WELCOME BACK

For returning veterans of the *Call of Duty* series, we've prepared this section to give you a quick overview of the changes to the game.

Customization

Character and gear customization has been given a big upgrade.

In addition to weapon Attachments, you can now customize your reticules and even the scope tint, as well as create an entirely personal and custom emblem that you can then stamp on all of your weapons!

And yes, if someone picks it up your weapon (or watches your Killcam), he or she sees your emblems and any scope customization.

There's more: Your Clan Tag is actually embossed right onto your weapons. It is also possible to colorize your Clan Tag!

Camouflage has been extended, as well. In addition to being able to camo your weapon, you can now apply facepaint to your character.

Perks

Stopping Power is gone. This has several significant effects, notably on the performance of Sniper Rifles and weapons equipped with Silencers. It also limits the number of normal guns that can perform a two-shot kill.

Partially to compensate for this change, Assault Rifles have all moved to a 40-30 damage profile.

The other Perks have been reorganized and adjusted, with some additions and removals, as well as shuffling which Perks are available in each Perk slot. See the Perk overview section later in this chapter for a quick look, or check the detailed Perks overview for a more thorough investigation.

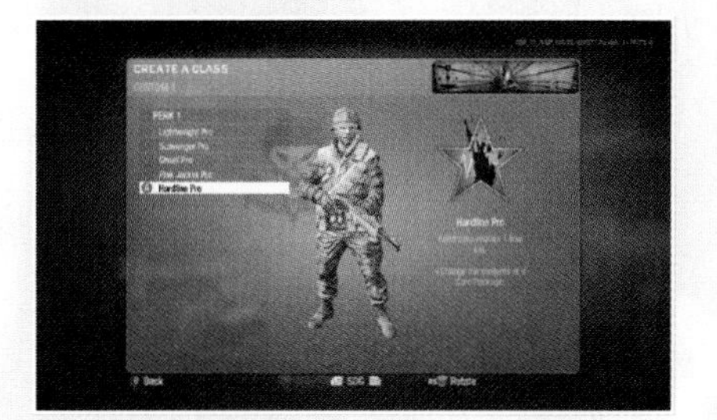

Loadout Changes

There's a greater emphasis on Assault Rifles and Submachine Guns (SMGs) this time around, with a large number of each available.

Shotguns can no longer be used as secondary weapons.

More options have been added to primary and secondary grenade types, and all deployable items have been moved to a new Equipment category; this includes C4 and Claymores.

Killstreaks

Killstreaks have completely changed across the board—see the Killstreaks sections for more specific details.

Of greater importance, Killstreaks *no longer contribute to Killstreak Chains*. That is, if you use an RC-XD and kill two players with it when you're already at three kills, your streak remains at three kills. If you want to get your 5 Killstreak, you have to get those next two kills the old fashioned way.

As a result, the highest accessible Killstreaks top out at 11 Kills—achievable, though still challenging.

Deathstreaks are removed. This means no more swearing when you fail to kill someone due to Painkiller, but it's also a bit harder to break out of a determined spawn camping if the enemy team is organized. Be prepared!

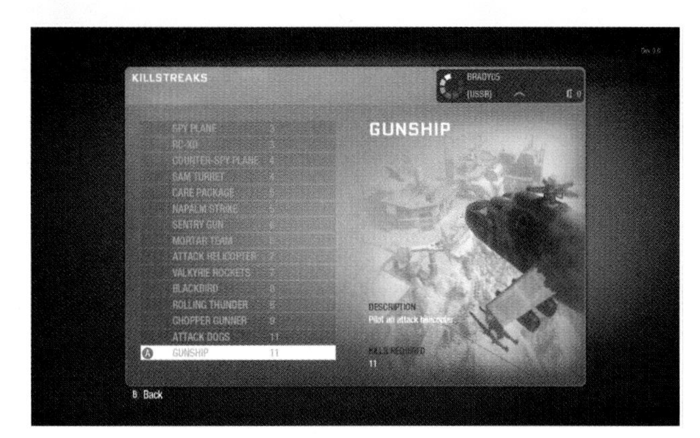

Unlock System

Weapons are still "unlocked" by gaining levels, but *all* items (including weapons) are now purchased with CODPoints.

CODPoints are earned as a fraction of the Match XP that you gain during a match. Ten percent of the Match XP that you earn is given as CODPoints.

You can also acquire CODPoints by playing Wager Matches, by completing Contracts, or by gaining levels. Again, 10% of all the XP you earn over time is funneled into your CODPoints.

You can unlock any items in any order with CODPoints: new Perks, Killstreaks, Attachments, Camo, Emblems, anything you want. The only restricted items are weapons, which you must first access by leveling; and Pro Perks, which must have their Challenges completed to unlock for purchase.

Leveling and Prestige

Level 50 is now the maximum, but there are 15 Prestige levels to aim for.

Prestige levels still unlock additional Custom Class slots, as well as some rare camo, and a few other goodies.

Contracts

New to *Call of Duty: Black Ops*, Contracts are special challenges that you can "buy in" with CODPoints. Once you accept a Contract, you're given a certain amount of live, online game time to complete the contract.

Succeed, and you earn more CODPoints. Fail, and you lose your investment and have to wait for the available Contracts to refresh.

Just like Challenges, a variety of Contracts are available. Unlike Challenges, the available Contracts vary from day to day.

Theater Mode

A major new addition is the ability to record and play back game video. You can even edit this video, stitch it together into a new video, and then save it to your personal online filespace, where it can be shared with your friends.

Expect a whole new generation of action videos to show up online...

Theater mode also includes the ability to take screenshots of any moment in time during a recording, and you can upload them to your personal filespace.

Statistics

Treyarch has packed in a massive suite of statistics-tracking tools, allowing you to drill down to an amazing level of detail about your entire online performance profile.

Want to know where you hit enemies most often? How accurate you are with a specific weapon? Which Killstreaks yield the most kills for you? No problem! It's all stored.

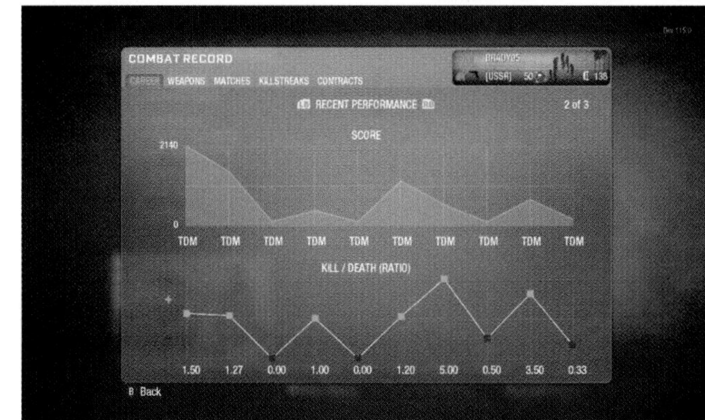

GAMEPLAY TWEAKS

Explosives Attenuated

In general, Explosives are somewhat less potent across the board. Most deal less damage or have a smaller radius. Using most secondary Launchers slows your movement speed considerably.

Explosives also do *not* restock with Scavenger (even Pro), and you receive only one Claymore by default.

Also, a few powerful Perks are resistant to explosives and secondary grenades.

That said, you can still build some very nasty bombardment classes with the right kit. See the detailed section on Custom Classes for more on this topic.

No More Quickscopes

Sleight of Hand no longer gives its ADS bonus to precision scopes. As a result, it's no longer possible to Quickscope with Sniper Rifles. Keeping your distance or swapping to a secondary weapon is advisable. On the upshot, Scout Pro now doubles weapon switch speed, so switching to a pistol is near instantaneous, and any other weapon is quite fast as well.

CUSTOM CLASSES

While you begin your *Call of Duty: Black Ops* multiplayer career without the ability to customize your classes, after completing just a few matches, you unlock your first five Custom Class slots.

PRESTIGE CLASSES

Gaining Prestige ranks unlocks additional Custom Class slots.

You can rename and configure each of these Custom Classes to your liking. You should decide how you configure your classes by what goals you are pursuing.

If you're trying to level up quickly, we recommend diversifying your classes as much as possible and cycling between them each round, or even each death! Doing so gives you the most possible Challenge completions over time, increasing your experience and CODPoint accumulation.

If you're more concerned about winning objective mode games, configure one or more classes (typically at least an offensive and a defensive class) specifically for that mode. This could be as minor as equipping a Tactical Insertion in CTF or Demolition, or as major as completely revamping a few classes with custom Perks and combat gear to suit the mode and map.

Finally, if you care most about simply performing well, configure your classes with your personal favorite weapons, equipment, Perks, and Killstreaks, mixing those you perform best with and those that are the most broadly effective across many maps and modes.

Primary and Secondary Weapons

When you create a class, you choose one primary and one secondary weapon.

PRIMARY WEAPONS

	Submachinegun
	Assault Rifle
	Light Machine Gun
	Sniper Rifle
	Shotgun

Broadly speaking, Shotguns and Sniper Rifles are useful for ultra-close or ultra-long-range combat, while Assault Rifles are middle of the road. SMGs are for close-medium, and Light Machine Guns (LMGs) for medium-long.

SECONDARY WEAPONS

	Pistol
	Launcher
	Special

Secondary weapons fill more specialized roles. While your primary weapon is generally strongest within a certain range band, secondaries have a different function.

Pistols are a great backup weapon if you have to reload mid-fight, or if you get surprised at close range with an LMG or Sniper Rifle.

Launchers are useful for flushing campers out of their hiding spots, and for clearing an objective point or chokepoint of multiple enemies.

Specials are just that—the Crossbow and Ballistic Knives fill unique roles. Generally speaking, the Crossbow has some properties of a Launcher, and Ballistic Knives are useful mostly for stealthy builds.

Combat Gear

In addition to your Primary and Secondary weapons, you also have to choose from an array of specialized combat gear. These equipment choices allow you to adjust the overall effectiveness of your build in a variety of combat situations.

LETHAL

	Frag Grenades
	Semtex
	Tomahawk

Lethal gear is exactly what it sounds like: tools that are used to kill. In the case of Frags and Semtex, they're used much like Launchers, for flushing out campers, targets behind cover, or multiple enemies clumped up at an objective or chokepoint.

The Tomahawk is a special weapon, great for adding some zest to stealth-based classes.

TACTICAL

	Willy Pete
	Decoy
	Nova Gas
	Flashbang
	Concussion

Tactical options are used mostly to give you more options on the battlefield. Using Tactical grenades intelligently can result in easy kills, or give you protection against enemies.

Willy Pete creates a smokescreen for temporary cover, while Decoy grenades can distract or attract enemy attention.

Nova Gas, Flashbangs, and Concussion grenades are all disruptive tools that can disorient or stun your opponents.

Nova Gas is additionally useful for flushing enemies out of cover, or creating an unsafe area at an objective or chokepoint for enemy forces.

EQUIPMENT

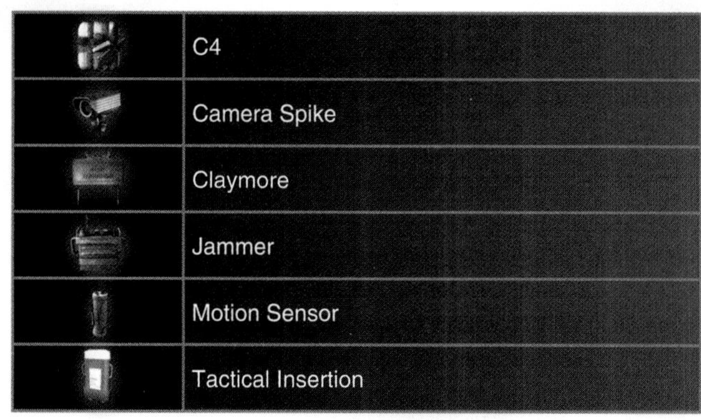

	C4
	Camera Spike
	Claymore
	Jammer
	Motion Sensor
	Tactical Insertion

Equipment gives you a range of useful tools. Claymores and C4 are additional lethal implements ideal for protecting an entrance or an objective.

Motion Sensors and Camera Spikes can be used to set up a perimeter if you're camping in an area, or to provide your team early warning of enemy presence in a critical objective location.

The Jammer is useful for aiding the defense of a fixed area on the map, or it can be placed near common chokepoints to disrupt enemy pushes.

Finally, the Tactical Insertion is most useful in certain objective modes, where controlling your spawn location can be vitally important for maintaining offensive pressure.

Perks

Perks are special abilities that enhance your character in various ways. Each of your Custom Classes can equip up to three Perks.

The three Perk slots each offer a distinct set of Perks; that is, Perk slot 1 provides several unique Perk choices, as do Perk slots 2 and 3.

Each Perk begins as a "basic" version. By completing certain specific Challenges unique to that Perk, you can unlock the ability to upgrade the Perk to a "Pro" version.

Pro Perks function similarly to their base versions, but with an additional bonus on top, making them stronger Perks all around.

PERK RUSHING

For your first trip to rank 50, we recommend simply acquiring Pro perks as you play naturally, going after the Perk Challenges in whatever order is most enjoyable for you.

Once you Prestige however, we recommend quickly identifying and pursuing the Pro Perks that are your favorites, as well as the ones that have the most power in your favorite game modes.

BASIC PERK OVERVIEW

PERK SLOT 1

PERK	EFFECT	PRO EFFECT
Flak Jacket	Reduces Explosive Damage.	Immune to fire damage, can throw back frag grenades safely.
Ghost	Undetectable by Spy Plane and Blackbird.	Undetectable by aircraft, dogs, IR, and sentries. No red name or crosshair when targeted.
Hardline	Killstreaks require one fewer kill.	Can change the contents of a Care Package.
Lightweight	Move Faster	No Fall Damage.
Scavenger	Pick up ammo from fallen enemies and replenish Lethal grenades.	Start with extra mags, replenish Tactical grenades.

PERK SLOT 2

PERK	EFFECT	PRO EFFECT
Hardened	Increased bullet penetration.	Increased damage to aircraft and turrets, reduced flinch and recoil when shot.
Scout	Hold breath longer.	Faster weapon switching.
Slight Of Hand	Faster reloading.	Faster ADS with non-scoped weapons.
Steady Aim	Increased hip-fire accuracy.	Quicker aiming after sprinting, quicker recovery from knife lunges.
Warlord	Equip two Attachments on primary weapon.	Start with one extra Lethal and Tactical grenade (except smoke).

PERK SLOT 3

PERK	EFFECT	PRO EFFECT
Hacker	Detect enemy equipment and explosives.	Ability to sabotage enemy equipment, turrets, and crates. Invisible to Motion Sensors.
Marathon	Longer Sprint.	Unlimited Sprint.
Ninja	Silent movement.	Completely silent, and enemies are louder.
Second Chance	Pull out your pistol before dying.	Survive longer, and teammates can revive you.
Tactical Mask	Reduces the effect of flash and concussion grenades.	Protects against gas grenades, reveals locations of flashed or stunned enemies.

Killstreaks

Killstreak rewards are given for maintaining a Killstreak (consecutive kills without dying). When you score three or more kills in a row without dying, you unlock the ability to employ a Killstreak.

Killstreaks have a wide range of effects. Some are straightforward offensive weapons, useful for attacking an objective area, open area, or chokepoint.

NO MORE KILLSTREAK CHAINING

It's no longer possible to gain a higher Killstreak by scoring kills with a lower Killstreak.

If you want an 11 Killstreak, you have to earn 11 kills in a single life, with your own gear—kills earned with lower Killstreaks do *not* increase your streak.

Others provide a team wide radar benefits, and a few act explicitly to protect you and your team from opposing Killstreak rewards.

Killstreaks earned are saved and *do* persist from life to life. As long as you don't use them and the match doesn't end, you can freely stock up on Killstreaks as much as you want, and use them when you feel they most benefit you or your team.

CALL OF DUTY: BLACK OPS KILLSTREAKS

KILLS	KILLSTREAK		EFFECT
3	Spy Plane		Displays enemy locations on minimap
3	RC-XD		Remote controlled explosive RC car
4	Counter-Spy Plane		Completely disables enemy minimap
4	SAM Turret		Airdrops a placeable SAM turret that destroys enemy air support
5	Care Package		Airdrops a random Killstreak reward or ammo crate
5	Napalm Strike		Targeted Napalm airstrike
6	Sentry Gun		Airdrops a placeable Sentry Gun
6	Mortar Team		Target three locations to bombard with artillery support
7	Attack Helicopter		Calls in helicopter air support
7	Valkyrie Rockets		Airdrops a Valkyrie launcher with two remote controlled missiles
8	Blackbird		Displays enemy locations and movement on the minimap, cannot be shot down
8	Rolling Thunder		Targeted massive bombing airstrike
9	Chopper Gunner		Take control of a high powered Gatling gun on an orbiting helicopter
11	Attack Dogs		Call in attack dogs that hunt down and eliminate enemy forces
11	Gunship		Take full control of an attack helicopter armed with minigun and rockets

WEAPON CUSTOMIZATION

Once you select your primary and secondary weapons, you can then further customize them by choosing from a variety of Attachments and camouflage.

Attachments

Attachments can be fitted onto all primary weapons and most secondary weapons.

Attachments act either to improve a weapon's basic function, or to add new or altered functionality. An example of the former would be adding a precision scope or an extended magazine. Examples of the latter include an under-slung grenade launcher or dual wielding.

All Attachments must be purchased with CODPoints. All Attachments for a given weapon are immediately available for purchase once you acquire access to the weapon. Thus, you're limited only by what you can afford to unlock immediately.

Camouflage

Camo, along with Emblems and your Clan Tag, can be applied to a weapon to customize its appearance.

While camo is often a matter personal style, you can change your camo to match the map on which you're playing if you want to squeeze every little bit of effectiveness out of your loadouts.

RANKS

As you complete matches online, you earn Experience (XP) that increases your level.

There are 50 Rank levels through which to progress, and each new rank unlocks a new weapon or other feature for your use, and awards you some CODPoints as a bonus.

Once you hit maximum Rank, you have the option of *Prestiging*. This resets you to the first level and re-locks all weapons, Attachments, Perks, and Killstreaks.

The only things you retain access to are your Custom Emblem, Clan Tag, and access to playlists.

However, Prestiging does come with some Perks—you unlock additional Custom Class slots, and you can work your way toward Gold Camouflage for your guns.

RANK #	RANK TITLE		MIN XP	XP TO NEXT	CP EARNED
1	Private 1		0	300	1000
2	Private 2		300	900	1000
3	Private 3		1200	1500	1000
4	Private First Class 1		2700	2100	2500
5	Private First Class 2		4800	2700	1000
6	Private First Class 3		7500	3400	1000
7	Specialist 1		10900	4100	2500
8	Specialist 2		15000	4800	1000
9	Specialist 3		19800	5500	1000
10	Corporal 1		25300	6200	2500
11	Corporal 2		31500	7100	1000
12	Corporal 3		38600	8000	1000
13	Sergeant 1		46600	8900	2500
14	Sergeant 2		55500	9800	1000
15	Sergeant 3		65300	10700	1000
16	Staff Sergeant 1		76000	11800	2500
17	Staff Sergeant 2		87800	12900	1000
18	Staff Sergeant 3		100700	14000	1000
19	Sergeant First Class 1		114700	15100	2500
20	Sergeant First Class 2		129800	16200	1000
21	Sergeant First Class 3		146000	17400	1000
22	Sergeant Major 1		163400	18600	2500
23	Sergeant Major 2		182000	19800	1000
24	Sergeant Major 3		201800	21000	1000

(continued on next page)

(Ranks continued)

RANK #	RANK TITLE	MIN XP	XP TO NEXT	CP EARNED
25	Lieutenant 1	222800	22200	2500
26	Lieutenant 2	245000	23500	1000
27	Lieutenant 3	268500	24800	1000
28	Captain 1	293300	26100	2500
29	Captain 2	319400	27400	1000
30	Captain 3	346800	28700	1000
31	Major 1	375500	30100	2500
32	Major 2	405600	31500	1000
33	Major 3	437100	32900	1000
34	Lieutenant Colonel 1	470000	34300	2500
35	Lieutenant Colonel 2	504300	35700	1000
36	Lieutenant Colonel 3	540000	37200	1000
37	Colonel 1	577200	38700	2500
38	Colonel 2	615900	40200	1000
39	Colonel 3	656100	41700	1000
40	Brigadier General 1	697800	43200	2500
41	Brigadier General 2	741000	44800	1000
42	Brigadier General 3	785800	46400	1000
	Major General 1	832200	48000	2500
44	Major General 2	880200	49600	1000
45	Major General 3	929800	51200	1000
46	Lieutenant General 1	981000	52900	2500
47	Lieutenant General 2	1033900	54600	1000
48	Lieutenant General 3	1088500	56300	1000
49	General	1144800	58000	2500
50	Commander	1202800	59700	2500

CONTROLLER TIPS

Most controller settings are fairly straightforward, but a few noteworthy options can directly affect your gameplay: specifically your controller layout and the sensitivity. Controller layout issues don't apply on the PC, though sensitivity still does.

Tactical Config

One controller option allows you to swap the position of Crouch and Melee. By doing this, you can more easily crouch or go prone while still moving. This can be important in combat, as going prone when you take a long-distance shot and then quickly ducking down behind cover can save your life.

With the new "dive to prone" this controller option also allows you to sprint, dive, and turn while still being able to aim.

The downside to switching this option is losing instant melee strikes, which can get you killed in close-quarters, face-to-face knife fights.

Spend some time playing around with each option; depending on how you normally play, you may find one or the other suits your preferences.

Sensitivity

Sensitivity can have a significant impact on your performance. On a console controller, higher sensitivities allow you to turn more quickly to respond to threats, and are generally more effective with weapons that require less precise aim—good for CQB weapons like SMGs and Shotguns.

Lower sensitivities give you more precision at a distance—better for Sniper Rifles and LMGS. The tradeoff, of course, is that you can't turn as quickly, which makes you more sluggish in CQB battles.

Spend some time playing around with different sensitivities; don't just leave it at the default. With some experimentation, you may find that you prefer a higher or lower setting than the default.

PRIVATE MATCHES AND COMBAT TRAINING

While most multiplayer takes place online in matchmaking, it is entirely possible to set up private matches with just you and your friends.

Not only is this just plain fun, you also have a tremendous amount of control over the settings in a private game. Want to tinker with available classes, Killstreaks, player health, the HUD, or other settings? No problem!

You can set up whole new game types by playing around with game settings, and the only place you can do this is in private matches, not in public matchmaking games.

Combat Training

Combat Training is a new feature in the *Call of Duty* series, pitting you against AI bots on any of the available multiplayer maps.

Combat Training uses a profile that's entirely separate from your online one—that is, you "level up" and rank up in Combat Training totally separately from your online profile.

Combat Training is great if you're new to *Call of Duty* and want some basic experience fighting and exploring the maps without getting trounced by veterans online.

Just be aware that, while Combat Training is great for learning the levels and experimenting with loadouts and weapons, the bots make good target practice. They don't work cohesively together like a skilled team, nor do they behave or respond quite like a human player. As long as you keep that in mind, you can get some useful practice in Combat Training.

Combat Training *can* be played with friends, but you *cannot* play objective game modes—only Team Deathmatch or Free for All.

THEATER MODE

New to the series, *Call of Duty: Black Ops* adds the ability to record your games as films, save them to your local hard drive, or upload them to your shared filespace online.

You can splice together clips from your films, tweaking variables like camera perspective to your heart's content, and turn them into movies. And you can upload the results for all your friends to see.

You can also take still screenshots of any moment in a match. Nailed the ultimate kill? Snag a shot and send it to your friends.

Recordings aren't just a fun tool for bragging rights; they can also be a very useful instructional tool. Got spanked badly by another player or a team online? View the footage and look at exactly what your opponents did that was so effective.

PLAYERCARD

Your Playercard is your personal database, where you can access a host of useful functionality.

- Configure your visible in-game Playercard
- Change your Clan Tag
- View Challenges
- View your Combat Record
- Check the Leaderboards
- Visit your File Share
- Check your recent Games
- View Community content

Most of the options are straightforward, but the Combat Record bears special mention, as it contains a wealth of information and statistics about your online performance. Take a look to see how you're doing and what you can work on to improve.

After Action Report (AAR)

Once a match is completed, you get a breakdown of everyone's performance in the game, and the match is stored in your personal history.

You can look through the AAR to see how you did, who was your worst Nemesis, and who the star players were in the match.

We've prepared this chapter as a detailed briefing on weaponry, equipment, Perks, and Killstreaks, and more.

CUSTOM CLASSES

Custom classes allow you to configure your weaponry and Perks to best suit your role in combat. You can create a highly stealthy class for flanking and sneaking behind enemy lines, or an aggressive, explosive class with a lot of firepower and almost unlimited ammunition.

You should always have a range of classes kitted out to suit the various modes you enjoy playing. What works well on one map or mode may not be quite as effective on another. Plus, it's just plain fun to mess around with different configurations, effective or not.

A custom class consists of your primary and secondary weapons, one each of a Lethal, Tactical, and Equipment selection, and three Perks, one from each of the three Perk categories.

Additionally, you can choose three Killstreaks from any you have unlocked, though these are the same for all of your custom classes.

Your custom class slots should be used to create a selection of classes that suit your personal preferences, the game mode you're playing, the map, and if you're playing with an organized team or running solo.

There is no *wrong* way to build a custom class, but certain combinations of weapons, combat gear, and Perks work very well together.

Weapon selection is intensely personal. The way the weapons are balanced within a given category, there is rarely one vastly superior choice for an SMG or an Assault Rifle. Instead, it comes down to what you find most comfortable. Choosing the right *type* of weapon for the map and mode is generally more important than choosing one specific weapon within a particular weapon class.

Reading through this chapter should provide you with the necessary information to make educated decisions about your custom classes—all the better to lay the smack down online.

PRIMARY WEAPONS

Submachine Guns (SMGs)

SUBMACHINEGUN ADVANTAGES

- Fast Movement Speed
- Fast ADS Time
- Fast Movement While ADS
- High Rate of Fire
- Good Hip-Fire Accuracy
- Rapid Fire Attachment

SUBMACHINEGUN DISADVANTAGES

- Rate of Fire Drains Ammo Quickly
- Inaccurate at Long Range
- Low Damage at Medium to Long Range
- Poor Penetration

Combat Role	CQB, Rapid Assault
Best On	Small to Medium maps
Optimal Range Band	Close to Close-Medium

AK47U

SKORPION

SPECTRE

SMGs provide *mobility*. This is an advantage that must be exploited by playing aggressively and actively. If you want to fight at long range or camp out and guard an area, there are better tools for the job.

On the other hand, for aggressive, forward play, SMGs are ideal. In objective-based modes where reaching a target quickly is important, or combat situations where flanking the enemy position rapidly can result in a rout, SMGs are the perfect weapon for this task.

Because SMGs have good accuracy when fired from the hip, you can "spray and pray" at close ranges without needing to Aim Down Sights (ADS) and still reliably score kills, something that most other weapon types can't accomplish as easily.

SMGs ADS quickly, and you retain a larger portion of your movement speed while ADS-ing. So, when you do need to take a more careful, aimed burst at a distant target, you can do so while remaining reasonably mobile.

SMGs typically have slightly faster rates of fire than Assault Rifles, granting them faster time to kill at close range, usually in exchange for accuracy at medium to long range. You *can* kill at a great distance with an SMG, but it's harder to do than with an Assault or Sniper Rifle.

SMGs also usually have the worst penetration values, meaning they aren't your best choice for overwatch on terrain that has a lot of cover.

SMGs share very similar statistics in their family, with only a few notable outliers. A few SMGs have 20-round magazines: the Skorpion, MAC11, PM63, and Kiparis.

The Spectre, MP5k, and AK74 have 30-round mags, while the Uzi and MPL have 32-round magazines.

Excepting the smaller mag SMGs (which benefit greatly from Extended Mags), deciding what SMG to use is mostly personal preference, based on the weapon's recoil profile and Attachment availability.

All of the SMGs have slightly different spread patterns and different amounts of recoil. Some can be used effectively out to medium range (or longer with a scope and careful trigger control), while others are better used up close from the hip, without worrying about targets at a distance.

SMGs have a greater mix of allowed or disallowed Attachments than other weapon types. Take a look at the charts to see which weapons best match your personal favorites.

Consequently, while you may prefer a few SMGs for longer-range work, you still probably want to switch between a few based on the size of the map you're playing, to best suit the map and your preferred Attachments.

Assault Rifles

ASSAULT RIFLE ADVANTAGES

- Good Accuracy
- Burst Fire and Semi-Auto Options
- Greatest Attachment Variety
- Three Types of Firing Modes

ASSAULT RIFLE DISADVANTAGES

- Weaker than Specialist Weapons in Their Preferred Range
- Automatic ARs Require Controlled Bursts to Maintain Accuracy

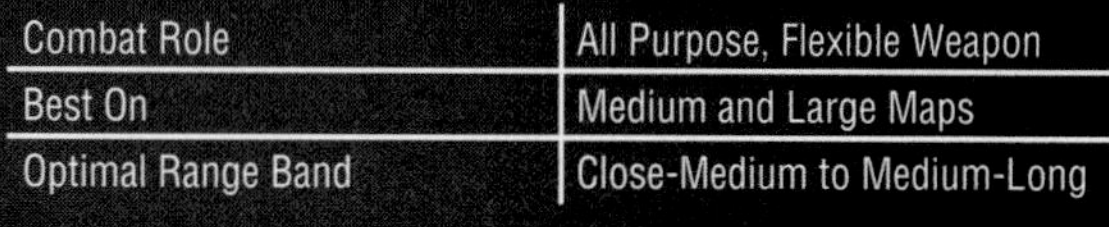

Combat Role	All Purpose, Flexible Weapon
Best On	Medium and Large Maps
Optimal Range Band	Close-Medium to Medium-Long

AK47

M16

FN FAL

When you aren't quite sure what to use, an Assault Rifle gets the job done—this makes them great "default" weapons.

As a general rule, Assault Rifles are at their best at medium range. Some ARs with specific Attachments can be modified to perform better at shorter or longer distances, through scopes or secondary weapon Attachments.

Assault Rifles have *average* mobility, in terms of movement speed, ADS times, and movement speed while ADS.

Assault Rifles have average to good penetration and can be quite effective at killing targets through thin cover.

There are three varieties of Assault Rifle: fully automatic, three-round burst, and semiautomatic. Most are fully automatic, two each are burst or semiautomatic.

Fully automatic Assault Rifles are effective at any range from close to medium, but to use of them at longer ranges, you must exercise trigger discipline. You should be familiar with the term, "short, controlled bursts." Firing at full auto at a distant target, especially using a precision scope, makes scoring a kill very difficult.

The M16 and G11 are burst-fire Assault Rifles that are very strong from medium to long range. They can reliably put rounds on target out to great distances. With a precision scope, they can almost act as Sniper Rifles in terms of battlefield utility.

The M14 and the FAL are semiautomatic Assault Rifles that depend on your trigger finger for their rate of fire. They have the twin advantages of precision and high damage. If you have good aim, you can score kills with rapid and precise shots. But if your personal accuracy, target tracking, and trigger finger aren't up to par, avoid these guns.

'SHOTGUN' BURSTS

The M16 and G11 both fire three-round bursts that can instantly kill a target at ultra-close range.

Consequently, you can occasionally get lucky in a close-range firefight and simply drop your opponent before he has a chance to respond with any sort of automatic weapon, even a CQB specialist like an SMG.

Naturally, against a real Shotgun, it tends to come down more to who gets the drop on the other player.

Scoring very long-range kills with these two guns is difficult, as they lack the automatic follow-up shots of burst weapons. And at shorter ranges, they can fall prey to fully automatic weapons. But at any distance between those two extremes, they can be very effective.

Assault Rifles can use many types of Attachments, including an under-slung Grenade Launcher, Shotgun, or Flamethrower, giving them additional flexibility. They can also fit scopes for accurate medium- to long-range shooting, silencers for stealthy conflict, or custom magazines for heavy firefighting power.

A properly chosen and customized Assault Rifle can work well on almost any map or game mode. Generally, you should spend time with each of the three Assault Rifle classes and figure out which firing mode you prefer. Narrow down your selection to one of those three classes, depending on the map and game mode, and finally add an appropriate Attachment.

The automatic and burst-fire Assault Rifles have 30-round magazines, the Galil uses a larger 35-round mag, and the M14 and FAL have 20 rounds.

Shotguns

SHOTGUN ADVANTAGES

- One-Shot Kills at Close Range
- Effective When Hip-Fired
- Good Mobility

SHOTGUN DISADVANTAGES

- Very Short Range
- Slow Reload Time
- Small Ammo Capacity

Combat Role	CQB, Urban Combat
Best On	Small Maps, Medium Maps with High Structure Density
Optimal Range Band	Extremely Close to Close

OLYMPIA

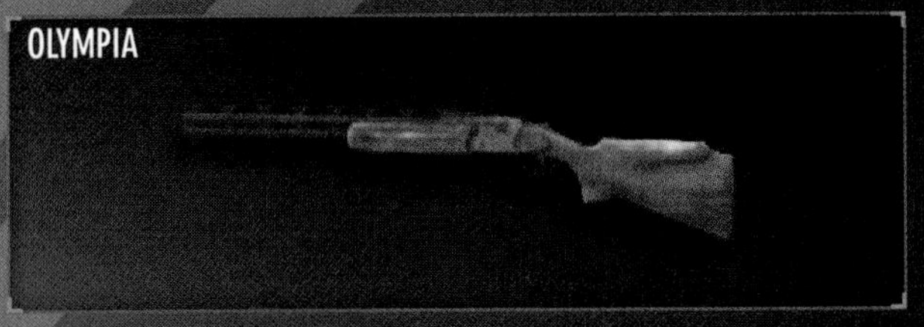

STAKEOUT

HS10

SPAS-12

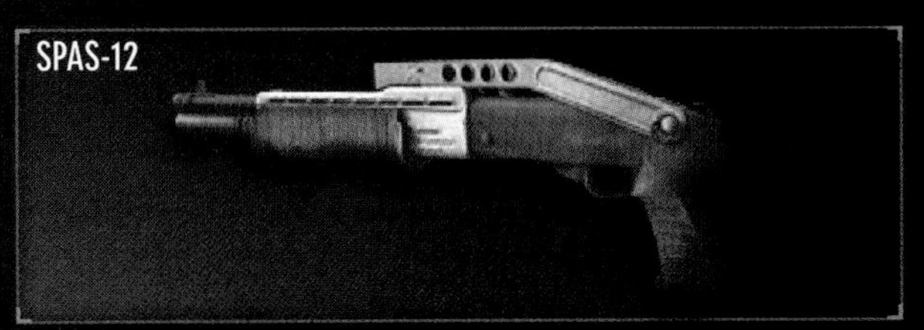

Shotguns are a close-range specialist tool. They should only be used on small maps, or on medium or larger maps if you're certain that you can *force* a close-range engagement.

Shotguns at close range are exceedingly lethal. Of the other weapon classes, only burst Assault Rifles and Sniper Rifles have a decent chance to kill you in one shot, and neither is as quite as reliable in close quarters.

Because of the Shotgun's one-shot kill capability, you can win fights in tight confines against any Pistol, SMG, Assault Rifle, or Light Machinegun, even if you're spotted and take a hit before you score your killing blow.

Shotguns are also deadly because they do not need to be used ADS at close range. You can simply aim and fire from the hip. This also means you're moving at higher speeds relative to most of your close-range targets, particularly if you're using the Lightweight and Hardened Perks.

However, outside of very close range, Shotguns become less effective. The various shotguns trade off damaging power with ammo capacity and fire rate, being either single-shot (the Olympia and Stakeout) or semiautomatic (the SPAS and HS10).

Of the two types, the Olympia and Stakeout are better at guaranteeing a close-range, one-shot kill, while the SPAS and HS10 are slightly more effective at taking down a target a short distance away.

Because Shotguns are so limited at a distance, forcing a close-range engagement is critical to your success. Pull these out when the map is small, or if the game mode you're playing focuses combat into concentrated areas.

When using a Shotgun, it's very important to take a secondary weapon that gives you additional options. A good Launcher or the Crossbow can give you some ability to fight at a distance. Once you score a kill and steal someone else's Assault Rifle, LMG, or Sniper Rifle, you'll have a complementary set of weapons that's deadly wherever you choose to fight.

Perks are also very important when you use a Shotgun. For Perk Slot 1, Ghost and Lightweight can help to close the distance safely. In Perk Slot 2, Hardened can help keep you moving and keep your aim on target up close if you get tagged in the open. Alternatively, Sleight of Hand helps compensate for a Shotgun's reloading deficiency. In Perk Slot 3, both Marathon and Ninja are helpful for getting in close.

If you choose a Shotgun with the intention of stealing someone else's weapon to round out your kit, consider taking a Perk that complements a different primary weapon. This is a risky choice, as some Perks are very important for getting that first kill, and there's no way to know exactly what your spoils of war will be.

Light Machine Guns

LIGHT MG ADVANTAGES

- Large Magazines
- High Penetration
- High Damage

LIGHT MG DISADVANTAGES

- Controlled Bursts Must be used at a Distance to Maintain Accuracy
- Poor Hip-Fire Accuracy
- Slow Movement Speed
- Slow ADS Speed
- Loud and Highly Visible

Combat Role	Area Suppression
Best On	Medium and Large Maps
Optimal Range Band	Medium to Long

HK21

RPK

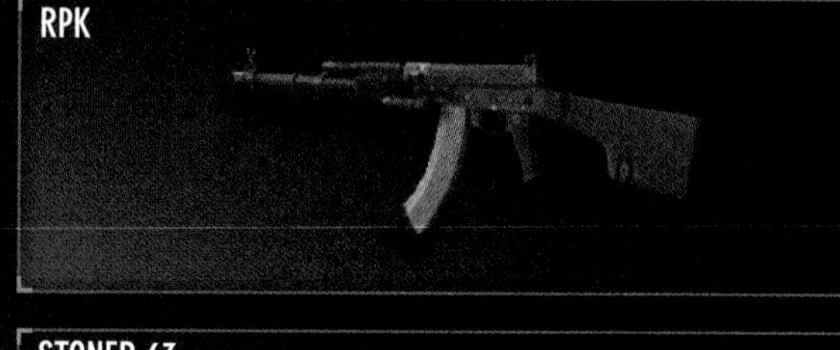

M60

STONER 63

Light Machine Guns are powerful long-range killing machines. With their large magazine sizes, they can also suppress an area with covering fire for extended durations, giving your teammates time to move in while you cover an area.

Like Sniper Rifles, LMGs *do not lose damage at a distance.* Most other weapon types inflict a range of damage values, dealing more damage at shorter distance and less damage, down to a minimum amount, at long distance. However, LMGs deal one flat damage value at any range.

Consequently, an LMG reliably kills a target in the open within a certain number of shots. LMGs also have the bullet penetration and ammo capacity needed to punch holes through walls and the enemies behind them.

Of the LMGs, the HK21 deals the lowest damage, at roughly four shots to kill. In exchange, it has the least recoil of any LMG, with a surprisingly tight bullet grouping, even when fired in moderate bursts.

The RPK and Stoner 63 are tied at roughly three shots to kill. They're very similar weapons, with only slight magazine size differences and different recoil profiles. The RPK can also use Dual Magazines, which the Stoner cannot.

Finally, the powerful M60 delivers a two-shot kill at any distance. The M60 also has the largest base magazine size (100 rounds) and an absurd 200-round magazine when fitted with Extended Magazines.

Spend time with each LMG, using them primarily at medium to long ranges, and determine which you prefer in terms of its accuracy profile and possibly its iron sights. They have different rates of fire and recoil patterns. You may prefer the accuracy of the HK21 over all the others, or the RPK or Stoner, or the sheer power of the M60 if you have the trigger discipline needed at long range.

Light Machineguns are powerful, but they pay for this power in several ways. First, and most critically, they significantly slow your movement speed and reduce the time you can sprint. This makes them very undesirable weapons for objective-based game modes that require a great deal of movement. They're at their best when you can set up shop at a distance, pick a trafficked area, and let loose.

Second, LMGs have slow ADS times, awful hip-fire spread, a very slow weapon switch time, and the longest reload times in the game. All of these attributes make them poor choices for close-range combat. Bringing along a Pistol in your secondary slot for close-range engagements is advisable.

Finally, LMGs are loud, have a distinct firing noise and bright muzzle flash, especially if you fire on full auto for any length of time. As a result, you can attract unwanted attention easily, especially if you mow down an entire enemy team over an objective. Your worst enemy is a Sniper, another LMG user, a precise Assault Rifle user with a long-range scope fitted, or a burst AR and good aim. Any of those weapons can take you out of your camping spot fairly easily, so be alert for those threats.

LMGs are most useful at longer ranges, so you must either become accustomed to their iron sights, accept the tradeoff of not using Extended or Dual Mags (generally not a good idea), or be willing to take the Warlord Perk to give you a precision scope and upgraded mags.

Be sure to exploit their ammo loads and penetration power. As you play the various maps in different modes, you get a feel for where enemy players move and hide out. If you suspect someone is hiding out of sight in a common camping spot, go ahead and take a few shots—you can spare the ammo, and at the very least confirm their presence.

With an LMG in particular, if you track a target that ducks into cover, *don't stop firing.* You'll be surprised at the materials an LMG can punch through to finish off a target.

If you think of yourself as a dangerous long-range turret when equipped with an LMG, you aren't far off the mark. LMGs are Sniper Rifles for players who are willing to get loud and a little messy. If a sniper is thinking "one shot, one kill," the machinegunner should be thinking "20 shots, three kills."

Using an LMG, think about the map as you would using a Sniper Rifle. The comparison isn't exact—Sniper Rifles can be lethal from different locations than LMGs. Nevertheless, you want to find an area where you can set up shop that has good line of sight on a key objective or multiple routes and chokepoints.

However, LMGs are very distinct from Sniper Rifles in that they can still be extremely effective and dangerous at medium range. The main reason to keep your distance is to exploit the LMG's damaging and penetrating power, coupled with its magazine size. This eliminates the threat from Shotguns, and greatly reduces the danger from SMGs and many ARs, leaving only a handful of weapons that can effectively attack you.

That said, if the situation calls for it, don't hesitate to set up behind cover at medium range covering a key area—you can mow down multiple targets with frightening speed, and the enemy team runs out of bodies before you run out of bullets.

Sniper Rifles

SNIPER RIFLE ADVANTAGES

- Potential for One-Shot Kills at a Very Long Range
- Effective Area Suppression at Very Long Distances

SNIPER RIFLE DISADVANTAGES

- Very Weak at Close Range
- Requires High Accuracy to be Effective
- Distinctive Firing Sounds

Combat Role	Long Distance Assassination
Best On	Medium and Large Maps
Optimal Range Band	Medium-Long to Long

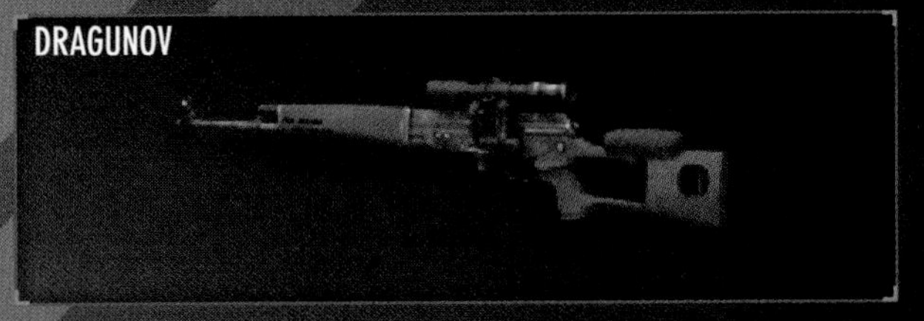

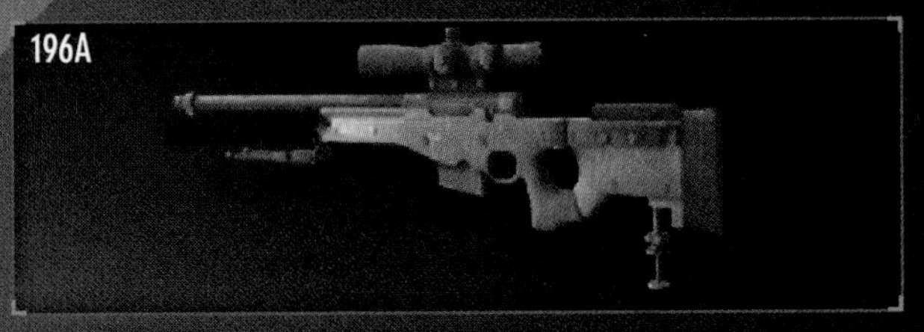

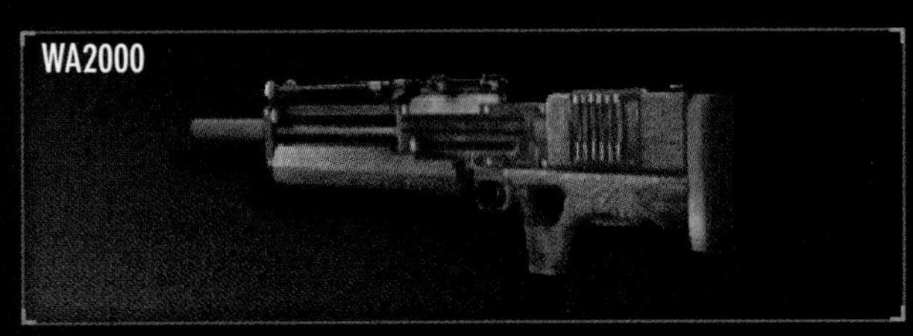

The antipode to Shotguns, Sniper Rifles in *Call of Duty: Black Ops* are ultra-long-range specialists.

With the capability to kill in a single shot at any range, and the precision scopes to accurately target at long distances, Sniper Rifles are ideal for removing campers at a safe distance, particularly those covering an approach that would be difficult or impossible for other weapons to handle.

A Sniper Rifle is also the best counter to *another* Sniper Rifle. In some cases, having a sniper on your team specifically to counter-snipe can be helpful. Otherwise, a good enemy sniper can suppress your team at very long range.

Sniper Rifles deal consistent damage regardless of range. All Sniper Rifles kill in two shots, or one shot to the upper chest or head. The L96A1 bolt-action has slightly stronger stopping power, killing with a hit to the stomach or above.

Otherwise, your choice of Sniper Rifle mostly comes down to a balance between recoil and magazine size. The Dragunov, WA2000, and PSG1 are all semi-auto rifles with decreasing magazine sizes, but also decreasing recoil.

In exchange for the ability to score one-shot kills at very long ranges, Sniper Rifles demand a unique set of skills from their users. To use a sniper scope, you must first line up and hold your breath to steady your shot. In addition, you can hold your breath for only a short time before you lose your concentration and your view begins to veer wildly while you recover your breath.

If you hold your breath and then release it, you also suffer a slight wobble in the scope. So, in most cases, you should hold your breath only a fraction of a second before you take your shot.

Sniping well takes practice, plain and simple. There's no substitute for the steady aim and concentration you need.

It's also very important to locate good sniper perches from which to take your shots. Ideal locations are positioned a great distance from your target area and have good lines of sight to key objectives, chokepoints, and common travel routes. A perfect location also has routes to your position that you can monitor, but finding such locations is rare on every map and every game mode.

Sniper Rifles have good mobility; exploit this to stay on the move. You can use your movement speed to get to a position and to move to another area once you're spotted (very important).

Many players *hate* snipers, so you can expect plenty of unfriendly attention once you take out more than a few enemies. Always be ready for retaliation. Staying put in one spot is a good way to eat a long-range retaliatory shot or a grenade lobbed through the window. Change your position regularly when you know the other team is focusing on you.

You can exploit this quirk of player behavior. Using C4, Claymores, the Camera Spike, or the Motion Tracker can be very helpful for protecting yourself from retaliation.

The Scout Perk is also custom tailored for snipers, as it lets you hold your breath longer when using a sniper scope. With the Pro upgrade, it lets you switch weapons in half the time. It's perfect for swapping to a secondary Pistol or, even better, a stolen weapon when an enemy nears your position.

Sniper Rifles are not great weapons at close range. It's almost always a better idea to swap to a Pistol or other secondary weapon instead of hoping for a lucky hip-fire shot.

'SHOTGUN' SNIPERS

Much like a three-round burst Assault Rifle, a Sniper Rifle *can* potentially kill a target at very close range with a single shot.

However, this is extremely unreliable, as the Sniper Rifle's hip-fire spread is the worst of all weapons. The bolt action or semi-auto fire rate is worse than any automatic weapon, as is your ADS time in comparison to other weapons.

If you get lucky, you may down an assailant at close range, but quickly switching to a secondary weapon is usually a better idea for more consistent results.

SECONDARY WEAPONS

Secondary weapons supplement your primary weapon with another option, either for emergency backup (all Pistols) or for additional tactical options (the Launchers and Specials).

Pistols

Combat Role	Backup Weapon

PYTHON

M1911

Pistols are very useful secondary weapons. Their primary advantage is switching speed. You can switch to Pistols faster than any other weapon type in the game. They're also very accurate, with only the full-auto CZ75 and Python having any significant recoil.

Consequently, they're ideal if you use a primary weapon that's poor at close range (Sniper Rifles, Light Machine Guns), or if you run out of ammo mid-fight and need to finish off an enemy. In almost all situations, it's faster to swap to a Pistol and continue firing than it is to reload.

Unsurprisingly, Pistols don't make a great "main combat" weapon. They have shallow magazines, significant damage falloff at a distance, and, with one exception, they can't be equipped with precision scopes for improved mid- to long-range combat.

With one exception, pistols are semiautomatic, so you need a quick trigger finger and a steady hand to get the most out of them in CQB.

The ASP, M1911, and CZ75 have nearly identical damage profiles, so determine which one to use by magazine size and the Attachments you prefer. The Python deals more damage at close range and a distance than the other pistols.

The CZ75 can be equipped with an Attachment that gives it full-auto capability. This greatly increases its recoil, making it a much less accurate weapon, but it also increases its lethality considerably in close quarters.

The Python can deal two-shot kills at close range without needing a headshot, making it a great choice for quickly dispatching single enemies. Its small magazine makes it less suited to engaging more than one foe at a time.

LAUNCHERS

Combat Role	Crowd Control, Camper Removal, Anti-Materiel

Launchers are explosive tools useful for defending objectives, clearing out crowds, blasting campers out of their hidey-holes, and destroying enemy air power or ground-based equipment, including SAM and Sentry turrets.

Launchers also work well with the Hacker Perk, as it lets you find equipment to blast, and it typically alerts you to a nearby camper, who you can then take out with an explosion.

The Scavenger Perk does *not* resupply the explosive ammunition that all Launchers use. However, Scavenger Pro grants you additional starting explosive ammunition.

When equipped, Launchers slow your movement speed—be careful about using them while you're visible in the open.

M72 LAW and RPG

M72 LAW

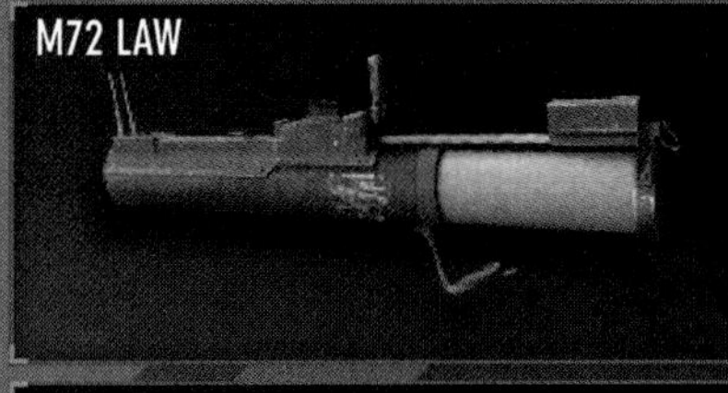

RPG

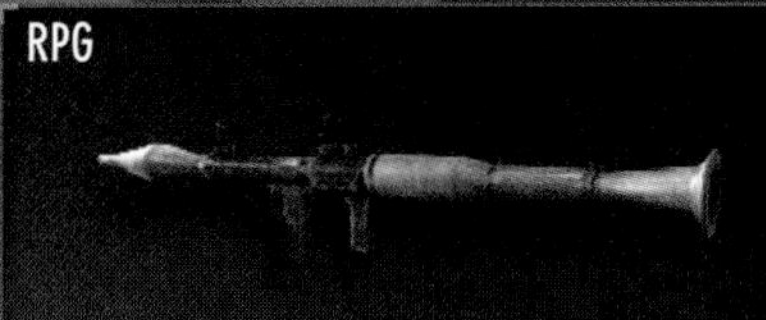

The LAW and the RPG fulfill somewhat similar battlefield roles—both fire a single explosive in a straight line.

The difference is that the LAW is single shot and tracks aircraft, while the RPG has two shots and has no homing capability. In fact, the RPG is rather inaccurate at a distance, with a tendency to drift off target.

Both weapons are suitable for bombing objective locations and are especially good at clearing out a Headquarters point or a camper in a room with an open window or door.

Both weapons are also generally quite bad to use on targets out in the open, especially those that can both move to evade the relatively slow-moving projectile and shoot you with much faster-moving bullets.

Strela-3

The Strela-3 is a specialist anti-air launcher, designed to take down Spy and Counter-Spy Planes, Attack Helicopters, Chopper Gunners, and Gunships.

You can also shoot down the carrier craft that drop supply crates, causing them to drop their package early. SAMs, Supply Drops, Sentry Guns, and Valkyrie Rockets are all vulnerable to this.

If you have the room, we recommend equipping at least one of your custom classes with this launcher. You never, *ever* want to let an enemy Chopper Gunner or Gunship, much less an Attack Helicopter, rampage unopposed.

If heavy enemy air support comes on the field and you happen to die, quickly switch to your class with the Strela-3 and take it down. In extreme circumstances, you may even want to suicide to get it out more quickly, eliminating the enemy air power before it deals any damage to your team.

China Lake

The China Lake is a grenade launcher that fires contact fuse explosives in an arcing path.

Grenades fired from this launcher require a minimum distance to arm, so you can't perform pointblank "rocket" explosions on the nearby ground or walls. A direct impact hit on another player is fatal, but we don't recommend going for those sorts of shots!

With practice, you can fire grenades from this launcher with extreme accuracy at a distance. There is no wobble in the flight path, so it's entirely possible to take out hiding campers by lobbing a grenade through the window. The contact explosion nearly guarantees a kill if your aim is good.

The China Lake is very effective against clusters of enemies, generally near objectives or at key chokepoints where most of the enemy team is moving at the same time. In matches with larger numbers of players on each team, the Grenade Launcher becomes proportionally more powerful.

MORTARING

A particularly dastardly China Lake or Grenade Launcher tactic is to bomb Domination, Demolition, S&D, or Sabotage objective points from long distance—as in, very, very long distance, entirely out of line of sight.

Because grenades launched from the underslung Grenade Launcher Attachment or the China Lake launcher don't wobble in flight, their trajectory is always the same for each shot.

Find a spot on the level that has clear landmarks to line up your crosshairs, take the shot, and have a spotter help you adjust your aim. With a little practice, you can plant grenades on target from out of sight 100% of the time.

This won't win you any friends on the other team, but it racks up kills fairly easily, particularly in Domination.

SPECIALS

Finally, the two pieces of specialist gear are unique weapons.

Ballistic Knife

BALLISTIC KNIFE

The Ballistic Knife is actually Ballistic *Knives*, a matched pair that can be used with deadly effect for lunging stabs, just like your normal combat knife.

In addition, the Ballistic Knife can be fired at enemies. You're given two shots, and the knife can be retrieved from the ground or your opponent's body…

Ballistic Knives are well suited to CQB classes that rely on stealth, as they give you the ability to take down an enemy at a distance quietly. If you're careful, you can then recover your knives and continue stalking the enemy.

Ballistic Knives are difficult to use, and require practice to aim the projectile accurately. If you plan to take these knives for anything other than occasionally humiliating your foes, we recommend taking them on nearly all of your classes for practice, and using them in all sorts of situations. Another option is to play a lot of Sticks and Stones Wager Matches to get good with them!

You need to practice, because otherwise, in most situations, you can get more mileage out of your other secondary options.

Crossbow

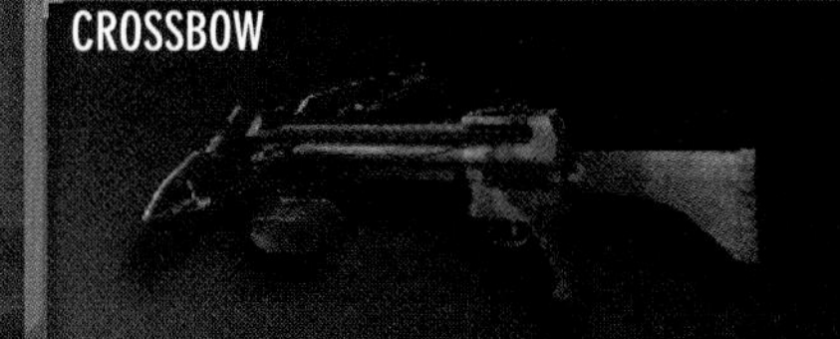

CROSSBOW

The Crossbow comes with two explosive tipped arrows that can be fired a good distance. These bolts stick to any opponent you manage to hit dead on, resulting in a fatal explosion.

You can hit the ground near an enemy, particularly an immobile camper, and still score a kill.

A stick is always lethal, but the delay preceding the explosion can give the doomed enemy just enough time to kill you. More embarrassingly, your target can sprint into range to take you both out with the explosion.

The Crossbow provides a good combination of explosive power, range, and accuracy in one package, though it has a slow reload speed, and the tracer is a dead giveaway to your location.

Spend some time with the Crossbow or play Sticks and Stones Wager Matches, just like the Ballistic Knives! Learn how to aim the arcing projectile, and you can get good use out of this tool.

Plus, sticking fools is just plain awesome.

ATTACHMENTS

Attachments can customize and personalize your weapons.

Attachments can improve a weapon or widen its utility, increasing its effectiveness in a greater variety of combat situations.

The Attachments available to each different primary weapon, as well as and Pistols, vary widely, so this section provides an overview.

Precision Sights

Precision Sights can give you an edge in accuracy when aiming at targets at medium to long range.

Both Red Dot and Reflex sights can be fully customized with unique targeting reticles and lens colors—not always for effectiveness, sometimes taking out your target with a pink heart is just the right thing to do…

RED DOT SIGHT

The Red Dot is the simplest and most straightforward of the various optical sights. It's also very slightly misleading. By default, it's in fact a simple red dot, but it's also fully customizable.

You can configure the RDS to have any combination of reticle appearance, color, and lens tint to match your personal crosshair preference.

The RDS is not a zooming scope; it's purely for assisting you in aiming at medium-range targets.

The RDS is slightly more effective on an Assault Rifle than an SMG, simply by virtue of the fact that Assault Rifles have less damage falloff and higher minimum damage than SMGs. This makes Assault Rifles more appropriate for engaging at medium range (or farther).

REFLEX SIGHT

The Reflex Sight is an alternative to the RDS, giving you a holographic image suspended in a deeper housing.

The Reflex Sight does have the disadvantage of being somewhat more affected by light glare than the RDS, which can interfere with your aim in a few places on certain maps, but this isn't a major issue in most situations.

The Reflex Sight is otherwise essentially identical to the RDS, including the ability to customize the color and shape of the reticle and the color of the lens.

Play around with both the RDS and the Reflex on various weapons to see which you prefer using.

WARLORD

The Warlord Perk allows you to equip two Attachments on your Primary weapon.

For example, you could use a custom magazine and a sight, or a suppressor and a custom mag, at the same time.

Remember that this allows you to customize your initial weapon only. It does not affect any weapon you pick up in the field, so if your highly tweaked weapon is important, consider pairing Warlord with Scavenger, so you can always reload your favorite toy.

The Masterkey shotgun, Flamethrower, and Grenade Launcher Attachments *cannot* be combined with any other Attachment using Warlord. If you want to use one of those Attachments, take a different Perk!

You can only use one sight and one custom magazine on a weapon at the same time. This includes ACOG, Red Dot, Reflex, Infrared, Variable Zoom, or Low Power Scope for the scopes, and Extended Mag or Dual Mag for custom magazines.

On SMGs, Dual Wield and Rapid Fire exclude the use of Extended Mags or Dual Mags.

A WORD ABOUT IRON

When you're not using a scope, you're using a weapon's iron sights, which are the gun's normal, standard-issue sights.

New players are often uncomfortable using iron sights, preferring to use a precision sight instead. This is totally fine—if anything, an Assault Rifle with a Red Dot Sight can be considered the bog standard *Call of Duty: Black Ops* weapon to which you can compare every other weapon and Attachment.

However, you may eventually find that you want to use other Attachments on your weapon. Without using the Warlord Perk, that means getting comfortable with the iron sights.

There's no substitute for experience here—spend time using every weapon with its standard iron sights. Some weapons have very nice, very clean irons that are just as easy to use at long range as a precision sight, and they have the added advantage of keeping more of your screen clear.

Others have slightly less comfortable irons, either because they're simply harder to use at a distance, or because they're very obscuring of your target.

As with recoil patterns, iron sights are a matter of personal preference. Learn what weapons use iron sights that you like—those are the guns on which you can more easily use non-precision sight Attachments.

ACOG SIGHT

The Advanced Combat Optical Gunsight, or ACOG, is a precision scope that provides enhanced zoom at the cost of slightly slower ADS time and lowered effectiveness at shorter ranges. Take the ACOG when you want to use your weapon at roughly one range band farther than you normally would, but be aware of the ADS and zoom handicap at closer ranges.

The ACOG can be used on Sniper Rifles, where it works in reverse, essentially reducing the range of your rifle by one range band. The advantage here is that the ACOG does not require holding your breath, allowing you to take quicker sighted shots with your Sniper Rifle. If you're planning to fight on the move with a Sniper Rifle, try the ACOG.

Curiously, the Python pistol can be equipped with an ACOG. This isn't a totally absurd option, as the Python has the best long-range damage of the pistols. But don't expect to take on a true long-range weapon successfully with it very often. It's mostly an extra long-range option for a Shotgun primary.

We don't recommend fitting the ACOG on SMGs in most situations. SMGs have fast damage falloff, and they deal low minimum damage at a distance. So, while an ACOG enables you to *see* targets clearly at longer ranges, actually killing them is more difficult. That said, some of the SMGs with good accuracy profiles can be reasonably effective at a distance with an ACOG equipped.

Consider using either Steady Aim or Sleight of Hand with the ACOG. Steady Aim gives you increased hip-fire ability, which is useful if you don't want to ADS your ACOG, while Sleight of Hand can help with the ADS time. Unlike the RDS or Reflex Sights, ACOGs have a fixed set of scope crosshairs. The specific crosshair depends entirely on the weapon to which you mount it. There are several different types, generally varying by the nationality of the manufacturer.

LOW POWER SCOPE

The Low Power Scope is unique to the G11 Assault Rifle. It functions very similarly to the ACOG, though it has the significant disadvantage of considerable sway.

If you don't mind compensating for the sway, the LPS gives the G11 longer range without forcing you to use a Variable Zoom scope, which requires you to hold your breath for accurate shots.

The G11 has no other scope options, so if you don't like the iron sights or the Variable Zoom, this is your only option—consider it a tradeoff for the G11's superior accuracy profile.

VARIABLE ZOOM SCOPE

The Variable Zoom Scope is a Sniper-style scope that provides multiple levels of high magnification, long-distance zoom. As with all Sniper-style scopes, it requires holding your breath to steady your aim.

The Variable Zoom scope is a nice piece of gear for a Sniper Rifle, as it allows you to adjust your magnification level to best fit the target area you're monitoring, which the default scope does not allow.

Play around with the Variable Zoom scope on your preferred Sniper Rifle—you may find you prefer it to the default scope.

The G11 Assault Rifle can also fit this scope, giving it the longest-range precision scope option of all Assault Rifles, and it has the accuracy to take advantage of the range, but it does weaken your ability to fight effectively at medium ranges.

INFRARED SCOPE

The Infrared Scope is a specialist tool that gives you a bright white outline on hostile targets in your scope in any lighting conditions. This makes the Infrared Scope ideal for targeting enemies in dark areas, and picking out enemy silhouettes in windows or hiding in camping spots is extremely easy.

The downside is that the Infrared requires steadying your aim to shoot accurately, which can make scoring a kill difficult with Assault Rifles. LMGs and Sniper Rifles both fare better, but choose this scope carefully depending on the map and mode you're playing—it isn't a good choice for general running-and-gunning.

SMOKESCREEN

Infrared Scopes can pierce smoke grenades. Pair your scope with Willy Pete and Scavenger for a very nasty combination. Continually blind your enemies with smoke, cover objectives, block chokepoints, and then shoot them through the smoke!

Magazines

Magazines help minimize the problem common to all ballistic weaponry: reloading!

EXTENDED MAG

Extended Mags do what you'd expect: increase your available ammunition per magazine. Generally, the increase is around 50%, though there are some exceptions.

Notably, LMGs benefit tremendously from Extended Mags, and we recommend taking them in almost all situations.

DUAL MAG

Dual Mags are taped magazines—by taping two magazines together, this allows you to reload extremely quickly. We're talking Sleight of Hand speeds without Sleight of Hand equipped!

Dual Mags are nice, but the reload bonus applies only to the first reload of each new magazine pair. That is, you get one quick reload, and then your next reload is normal speed as you introduce a new taped magazine pair.

You can "skip" the slow reload by firing a single bullet and reloading, but we strongly recommend avoiding this habit, as it lights you up on the minimap and exposes your location via sound. And you put yourself at risk if someone walks around the corner while you're performing your setup reload. But, if you must, the option is there—at least bring a Suppressor!

Weapon Attachments

The following Attachments are limited almost exclusively to Assault Rifles. The only exception is the Grenade Launcher, which has a special version that can be equipped on the AK74U SMG.

GRENADE LAUNCHER

The Grenade Launcher Attachment functions almost identically to the China Lake grenade launcher. Activate the underslung Grenade Launcher, and you can fire a ontact fuse grenade in an arcing path.

he AK74U is unique among all SMGs, as it's the only one that can quip a specialist weapon Attachment.

lowever, the AK74U pays for this privilege, as its grenades lack the ontact fuse. This makes the weapon significantly less deadly, but it's still iseful for clearing small rooms of enemies or an objective target area.

MASTERKEY

The Masterkey is an underslung shotgun. This can be quite useful on an automatic or semiautomatic Assault Rifle, as it gives you a solid close-range option with the otential to one-shot kill, especially if you aim for the head. We lon't recommend using the Masterkey on the burst ARs, as they're lready the next best thing to a shotgun at close ranges.

)therwise, the only real downside to the Masterkey is that you must earn to recognize the situations that are likely to involve CQB. Switch o it before entering buildings, when traveling in areas with lots of cover, or if you suspect you're being flanked by a lone enemy. Surprising an SMG gunner with a shotgun blast to the face is always gratifying.

The Masterkey lacks the power, ammo capacity, or semi-auto firing of the full-fledged Shotguns, but it does provide a very useful secondary function for most Assault Rifles.

FLAMETHROWER

The Flamethrower is a very specialized weapon Attachment. It gives you the ability to fire a short-ranged (and short-lived) jet of fire, perfect for cooking enemies at close ranges or torching a room from just outside a door or window.

However, the Flamethrower does have some significant disadvantages. First, it's totally nullified by Flak Jacket Pro, so if you see a target showing that heavy armor silhouette, skip the burner.

Second, it takes time for the Flamethrower to do its work, time that an enemy at close range can use to kill you in retaliation.

And finally, the Flamethrower has sharply limited ammunition. It burns through its fuel quickly, and reloading a Flamethrower canister removes all remaining ammo in the tank you discard. Normally, you're given two extra tanks, so be sure to use them as completely as possible before reloading.

Unique Attachments

Specialist Attachments have unique effects, and may not be "attachments" at all, in the cases of Dual Wield and Rapid Fire.

SUPPRESSOR

The Suppressor is a very powerful Attachment. Equipped on any weapon, it eliminates the red dot blip on the minimap from firing your gun, and it reduces, but does not ompletely eliminate, the sound your weapon makes while firing.

he Suppressor is powerful because many players tend to depend eavily on their minimap for locating threats. Good players also use ound to locate enemies. The Suppressor eliminates the first and educes the second.

he tradeoff is that the Suppressor increases damage falloff. It does ot *reduce* damage, but rather, it closes the range at which your veapon hits its minimum damage.

s an example, let's say the Skorpion SMG has a maximum-to-ninimum damage range of 50-20. At close range, it kills in two hots. At long range, it requires five shots to kill. A Suppressor auses the Skorpion to hit for 20 damage at a much closer range han it would without the device attached.

Suppressors have a dramatic impact on the SPAS Shotgun, a significant impact on SMGs, and a reduced but still noticeable impact on Assault Rifles.

Generally, you can expect to need the maximum number of hits for any target at long range, and quite often at medium range. This means four shots instead of three for Assault Rifles, and four to five shots for most SMGs or Pistols at a distance.

Because of the minimum damage of the FAL and M14, both are good candidates for a Suppressor. They still kill in three shots at a distance, or two shots if you can land a headshot. Similarly, the M16 works very well with a Suppressor, as its burst-fire nature means that you still aren't likely to need more than two or three trigger pulls at a distance.

There is one exception to this damage rule, and that is Sniper Rifles. A Suppressor placed on a Sniper Rifle *does* reduce its damage output, meaning that you need two shots to kill a target, regardless of the distance or the body location you hit.

The ability to kill silently at a distance is powerful, but it comes at a cost, demanding more accuracy from you. If you really want to snipe suppressed, we recommend an accurate semi-auto Sniper Rifle, and possibly Warlord to take both a Suppressor and Extended Mags.

Suppressors are powerful tools. They can allow you to operate behind enemy lines for an extended period. Or, if you mix up your position at mid range, you can pick off targets without drawing the enemy team's attention.

Because Suppressors don't provide a "visible" benefit like a Grenade Launcher Attachment or Dual Wielding, and because they it a bit *more* difficult to score kills at a distance, it can be easy to discount their power.

Don't make that mistake—suppressed weapons are very powerful, and learning to use them well is important in many game modes.

DUAL WIELD

Dual Wielding gives you extra firepower at a significant cost in accuracy and ammo consumption, as well as the total loss of your ADS.

Taking Dual Wield on Pistols, SMGs, or the HS10 Shotgun lets you take down targets at close ranges very easily. But it almost entirely removes your ability to fight targets at a distance.

If you plan to use Dual Wield, we recommend either taking Steady Aim (to give you *some* ability to fight at a distance), or using it only on your Pistols, so you still have another option for fighting at a distance.

Scavenger and Sleight of Hand are both useful for Dual Wielding, as you chew through ammunition at a ferocious rate when you use two weapons, and reloading quickly is also important for survival.

RAPID FIRE

Rapid Fire is a specialist Attachment for SMGs. It increases the equipped weapon's rate of fire at the cost of greatly increased recoil.

Rapid Fire reduces your time to kill—that is, how fast your enemy goes down from the time you squeeze the trigger to the time the last lethal bullet hits them. But it does not change the damage of your weapon in any way.

Rapid Fire increases close-range lethality somewhat less than Dual Wielding, but it also does not completely strip your ability to fight at medium range. You can still ADS, and with careful trigger control, you can take down targets at a distance.

Rapid Fire does have a noticeable impact on your weapon's accuracy profile, so you may want to take advantage of Steady Aim.

As with Dual Wield, Rapid Fire benefits from Scavenger, as ammunition can be a serious concern when you burn through it so quickly. Sleight of Hand is also useful, as you tend to reload more frequently.

GRIP

The Grip is a specialized Attachment that can be equipped on only a few weapons.

Equipping a Grip reduces the weapon's recoil, slightly increasing its overall accuracy profile. The Grip is a solid choice for improving your kill rate at longer ranges. This benefit isn't quite applicable to the Stakeout, the only Shotgun that can use the Grip, but it's also the only Attachment that weapon can take!

Pistol Attachments

A few Attachments are specific to Pistols.

UPGRADED IRON SIGHTS

Upgraded Iron Sights are simply tritium-highlighted sight posts, giving your pistol's irons slightly better visibility. In general, we don't recommend taking this over the other Pistol Attachment options.

FULL AUTO UPGRADE

Unique to the CZ75, this Attachment gives the CZ75 the ability to fire in fully automatic mode.

This makes the CZ75 a very nice secondary weapon for a Sniper Rifle or LMG, as you have a pocket machine pistol for dispatching close-range threats.

This Attachment does give the CZ75 massive recoil though, so don't expect to pick off targets at a distance without very careful trigger control.

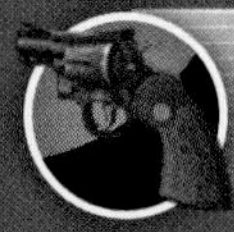

SNUB NOSE

The Snub Nose Attachment for the Python changes the weapon's damage and accuracy profile, trading ten points of maximum damage for greatly improved recoil control.

This changes the weapon roughly from a 50-30 to a 40-30, eliminating the ability to two-shot kill enemies at close range. This is a big sacrifice, but the accuracy improvement is substantial, and you keep the Python's elevated minimum damage compared to other pistols, so it's more effective at taking down enemies at a distance if you have good aim.

SPEED RELOADER

The Speed Reloader is the third unique Attachment for the Python, and it's a very useful one. With a Speed Reloader equipped, you can reload the Python fully with a six-shot clip. Without it, the Python must be reloaded one bullet at a time.

Note that, oddly, a Python without the Speed Reloader can be reloaded more quickly, but only if you've fired just a single shot—not exactly a typical use scenario.

Attachments Allowed

Submachine Gun Attachments

ATTACHMENT		AVAILABLE ON THESE WEAPONS
Extended Mag		MP5K, Skorpion, MAC11, AK74, Uzi, PM63, Spectre, Kiparis
Dual Mag		AK74, MPL
ACOG Sight		MP5K, AK74, Uzi, MPL, Spectre, Kiparis
Red Dot Sight		MP5K, MAC11, AK74, Uzi, MPL, Spectre, Kiparis
Reflex Sight		MP5K, MAC11, AK74, Uzi, MPL, Spectre, Kiparis
Grip		Skorpion, MAC11, AK74, Uzi, PM63, MPL, Spectre, Kiparis
Rapid Fire		MP5K, Skorpion, MAC11, AK74, Uzi, PM63, MPL, Spectre, Kiparis
Suppressor		MP5K, Skorpion, MAC11, AK74, Uzi, MPL, Spectre, Kiparis
Dual Wield		Skorpion, MAC11, PM63, Kiparis
Grenade Launcher		AK74 only. No contact fuse.

Assault Rifle Attachments

One benefit of Assault Rifles is that, with two exceptions, they can use all ten of their available Attachments.

ATTACHMENT		AVAILABLE ON THESE WEAPONS
Extended Mag		All Assault Rifles
Dual Mag		All Assault Rifles
ACOG Sight		All Assault Rifles
Red Dot Sight		All Assault Rifles
Reflex		All Assault Rifles
Masterkey		All Assault Rifles

Assault Rifle Attachments (cont.)

ATTACHMENT		AVAILABLE ON THESE WEAPONS
Flamethrower		All Assault Rifles
Infrared Scope		All Assault Rifles
Grenade Launcher		All Assault Rifles
Suppressor		All Assault Rifles
Grip		M14 only.
Low Power Scope		G11 only.
Unique to the G11, the Low Power Scope is somewhere between an ACOG and a Sniper Rifle scope. Unfortunately, while it has Sniper Rifle levels of view sway, it does not allow you to hold your breath and steady your aim.		
Variable Zoom		G11 only.
A Sniper Rifle style scope, this Attachment gives you the ability to use the G11 at long distances with considerable accuracy. The tradeoff is that you lose ADS time and the ability to use the G11 comfortably at close-medium to medium ranges.		

Shotgun Attachments

ATTACHMENT		AVAILABLE ON THESE WEAPONS
Grip		Stakeout only.
Suppressor		SPAS only.
Dual Wield		HS10 only.

Light Machine Gun Attachments

All Light Machine Guns have access to Extended Mags, ACOG, Red Dot and Reflex Sights, and the Infrared Scope.

The RPK can use Dual Mags, and the M60 can use a Grip.

ATTACHMENT		AVAILABLE WEAPONS
Extended Mag		HK21, RPK, M60, Stoner63
Dual Mag		RPK only.
ACOG Sight		HK21, RPK, M60, Stoner63
Red Dog Sight		HK21, RPK, M60, Stoner63
Reflex Sight		HK21, RPK, M60, Stoner63
Grip		M60 only.
Infrared Scope		HK21, RPK, M60, Stoner63

Sniper Rifle Attachments

All Sniper Rifles have access to Extended Mags, Suppressors, and multiple scopes: ACOG, Infrared, and Variable Zoom.

ATTACHMENT	AVAILABLE ON THESE WEAPONS
Extended Mag	All Sniper Rifles
ACOG Sight	All Sniper Rifles
Infrared Scope	All Sniper Rifles

ATTACHMENT	AVAILABLE ON THESE WEAPONS
Variable Zoom	All Sniper Rifles
Suppressor	All Sniper Rifles

Pistol Attachments

Pistol Attachments vary depending on the specific pistol you're using, with the Python and CZ75 having some of the more unusual Attachments.

ATTACHMENT	AVAILABLE ON THESE WEAPONS
Dual Wield	ASP, M1911, Makarov, Python, CZ75
Upgraded Iron Sights	M1911, Makarov, CZ75
Extended Mag	M1911, Makarov, CZ75
Suppressor	M1911, Makarov, CZ75

ATTACHMENT	AVAILABLE ON THESE WEAPONS
Full Auto Upgrade	CZ75
ACOG Sight	Python
Snub Nose	Python
Speed Reloader	Python

LETHAL / TACTICAL / EQUIPMENT

Grenade Usage

Learning how to use your primary and secondary grenades well is an important part of your training as a skilled *Call of Duty: Black Ops* player.

If you're new, we recommend learning how to move and shoot first, but adding grenades (and later, Equipment) to your skillset is very important. Use Lethal Grenades to flush campers out of their cover or hiding spots, to clear an objective, to toss into crowds of enemies, or to cover a retreat.

You can use Tactical Grenades to help win a firefight, distract an enemy, assist your teammates, or cover a retreat or an advance.

One quick tip: Never throw grenades mid-firefight with an active enemy who has his eyes on you. The time it takes to prime and throw the grenade is enough for you to get killed.

Also, be aware of the noise that using a grenade makes. Alert and skilled opponents react to the sound, and even a blind opponent hit by your Flashbang can easily fire at the only door into his room when you dash through!

Sometimes, faking out an enemy with a Tactical Grenade is more valuable than trying to stage a frontal assault supported by a grenade toss.

Lethal

Lethal Grenades, or throwing axes, in the case of the Tomahawk, are supplementary tools for taking down your foe.

Grenades have the distinct advantage of indirect fire. That is, they can kill a target behind cover, in a room, or around a corner.

For both Frag and Semtex Grenades, part of their power isn't simply killing, but also flushing a target out of cover. Even if the explosion doesn't kill your targets, it may scare them out of hiding. If the blast damages them, all the better to make the kill easier for you or a nearby teammate.

Grenade spam, that most hated tactic, is still possible if you take Scavenger, and moreso if you pack Warlord Pro for the extra grenades. While it's generally effective (and annoying) in most modes, it's especially lethal and useful in Headquarters or Domination, where you can be assured of your target's location.

The Flak Jacket Perk acts to counter this tactic, and is nearly vital when you play Headquarters or Domination in an objective-grabber role. You gain both heavy resistance to explosive damage and the ability to shrug off fire, plus the occasional bonus of safely tossing back a Frag Grenade.

FRAG

Frag Grenades have a three-and-a-half-second fuse, and can be "cooked" by holding them for up to three seconds. Each second, your reticle visually pulses, so it's very easy to time exact Frag Grenade throws.

With practice, you learn exactly where a Frag will explode depending on how long you cook it. Once you know these distances instinctively, you can actually airburst Frag Grenades to kill enemies.

This is a very effective use of Frag Grenades. Done properly, it gives the enemy no time whatsoever to evade the Frag or throw it back. Frag Grenades bounce and roll around terrain, so they're ideal for getting behind cover, into a room, or around a corner.

A quick-thinking enemy can pick up and throw back Frag Grenades, but as long as you cook them before throwing, at best your target can throw the grenade out of lethal range—better than the humiliating return throw that takes out you or your teammates!

TOMAHAWK

The Tomahawk is a special lethal weapon that you can throw to score an instant kill if it connects. You can even bounce the Tomahawk off the ground to score a bank-shot kill.

The Tomahawk can be retrieved, whether you hit or miss your target; just don't get killed trying to pick the 'hawk back up!

The Tomahawk has a few advantages over normal grenades. It's stealthy and instantly lethal if it connects, and it can be used at almost any time to "interrupt" an action, such as sprinting, reloading, or even climbing over an obstacle.

However, you do lose the ability to flush targets out of cover, and using the Tomahawk is an acquired skill that demands practice. Play Sticks and Stones Wager Matches to brush up on your 'hawking skills!

SEMTEX

Semtex is a sticky grenade that adheres to the first surface or enemy (!) that it touches, and then explodes.

Semtex has reduced power compared to its last outing in the *Call of Duty* series, and it has a very short throw range.

Because Semtex is sticky and does not roll (nor can it be thrown back), it's ideal for close-range explosive work when you need to get a target behind a piece of cover or up in a room. You can simply stick the Semtex on a nearby wall or ceiling and let the blast do its work.

Tactical

Tactical Grenades are exactly that—grenades that increase your tactical options. Each can be useful in a variety of situations, and several are extremely useful or critical in objective modes.

Tactical Grenades have varying throwing speeds. Decoy and Concussion Grenades actually throw more quickly than smoke, flash, or gas grenades.

Note that the Tactical Mask Perk has both offensive and defensive bonuses to Tactical Grenades. On offense, it lets you know exactly the direction of a target that has been hit by a Tactical Grenade. This is a powerful tool for locating and eliminating blinded or stunned enemies.

On defense, it all but eliminates the effect of Tactical Grenades used against you, which is a powerful benefit when protecting a Headquarters, Domination point, or other key objective or chokepoint area.

WILLY PETE

These white phosphorous grenades create a cloud of smoke. They do actually inflict a tiny amount of damage on impact, and they momentarily stun a target hit by the initial light blast.

However, the main purpose of these grenades is not damage or disorientation, but instant cover creation. Dropping a Willy Pete Grenade creates a thick cloud of obscuring smoke, fully blocking line of sight for a short time.

The uses for this are numerous: creating cover in the open to sprint across a dangerous area; covering an objective area while you secure it; blinding a camper; or making good use of the Infrared Scope.

In most objective modes, at least one team member should always carry smoke. In cases where you cannot rely on your teammates to do so, be sure to bring smoke on at least one of your custom classes. Having the cover of smoke when planting or disarming a bomb, securing a control point, or sprinting across open ground with a flag is very important.

NOVA GAS

Nova Gas is a powerful new addition to the roster of Tactical Grenades in *Call of Duty: Black Ops*. When deployed, Nova Gas Grenades create a thick cloud of caustic, toxic gas. This gas does deal damage, and does kill enemies if they remain in it for too long. In addition, the gas disorients, causing slowed movement and badly blurred vision.

In many ways, Nova Gas is the best possible combination of a Lethal and a Tactical Grenade, as it damages, slows, and disorients all in one package.

Nova Gas Grenades lobbed on objectives can lock down the point by keeping enemies off these teammates. Snipers or campers can be flushed out of their hidey-holes, because they cannot remain in the gas safely. In general combat situations, Nova Gas can give you an easy victory by slowing and blurring the vision of your mark.

There are only two downsides to Nova Gas: one is that it's on the slower, Flashbang side of the grenade-tossing speed contest; and the other is that it can be nullified by the Tactical Mask Perk.

Even so, Nova Gas is a very strong grenade, and we strongly recommend using of it—and learning to avoid it—as much as possible.

FLASHBANG

Flashbangs release a blinding flash and concussion that whites-out the screen of anyone unfortunate enough to be facing it, including you!

If the explosion occurs close enough, even looking away doesn't completely stop the blast's effects, though doing so does reduce them slightly. Flashbangs are ideal for clearing occupied rooms of enemies, temporarily blinding them as you sprint to cover, or for closing distance.

Flashbangs do take longer to throw than Concussion Grenades, so it's important to time the throw and the attack carefully. Thrown at the right height and angle, it's possible to airburst a Flashbang, blinding anyone below or around the blast.

They work very well when used with a teammate, as you can toss the grenade and have it explode at almost the same time your teammate assaults the position. This provides maximum time to take out any blinded enemies in the area.

While they're powerful, Flashbangs do have a few major weaknesses. First, you have no way of knowing how blinded your targets are. They might be completely whited out and unable to retaliate in any way, or they might be only mildly dazed and facing the door. Full-auto fire from a blind enemy is still dangerous if he's aiming in the right direction.

Because enemies often suspect an attack from a certain direction, stealth and surprise are the Flashbang's advantages. If you can blind a target that doesn't know where you're attacking from, they're as good as dead.

CONCUSSION

Concussion Grenades are powerful tools for mobile combat. When hit by a Concussion Grenade, enemy targets are nearly stopped in their tracks, as their movement is staggered and they almost completely lose the ability to turn.

Consequently, if you're running any sort of mobile loadout, you can stun a target and move to hit them from the side or rear for a near-guaranteed kill. If you happen to stun someone who is already facing away from you, he or she has no chance of turning in time to retaliate.

Concussion Grenades have the benefit of throwing more quickly than other types of grenades, which also makes them more useful for high-speed combat. Even in the thick of a firefight, you can often find time to get behind cover, lob a Concussion Grenade, and either eliminate your targets or sprint away to safety.

Concussion Grenades have a minor blinding effect, but be aware that they do not otherwise impair aiming or firing. So, if you're in the frontal arc of a stunned target, you can still be taken down. Don't expect a Concussion Grenade to work perfectly for storming a defended room or other tough defensive position.

Concussion Grenades work best as a mobile combat aid against enemies in the open, and they excel at that task.

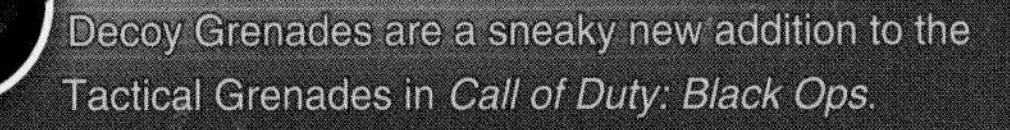

DECOY

Decoy Grenades are a sneaky new addition to the Tactical Grenades in *Call of Duty: Black Ops*.

When deployed, a Decoy Grenade creates a fake burst of gunfire sounds, causing an aural distraction and a blip to appear on the minimap. Because players are so tuned in to hunting targets on their minimap without carefully examining the situation, it's very, very easy to bait players with Decoy Grenades.

Decoys work best when the area in which you use them is relatively quiet. One additional red dot in the middle of a large-scale firefight is likely to go unnoticed. However, a single blip on an otherwise empty minimap, especially deep in enemy territory, is very likely to demand investigation.

You can use Decoys to draw attention away from you, or to bait enemies into coming toward you. Both tactics are helpful, either for slipping past a defended area or for drawing enemies out of a favorable position, into one that you can exploit, generally with them lined up in your sights.

Multiple teammates using Decoy Grenades simultaneously can create a more realistic "assault," especially if you back it up with a few tossed grenades and some real gunfire. In some objective modes, this can cause more enemies to shift their positions to investigate.

Experiment with Decoys; they're a powerful psychological weapon. Just be aware that overuse in a given match can reduce their effectiveness. Canny opponents won't fall for the same trick repeatedly, but sometimes even once is enough.

Equipment

A new category in *Call of Duty: Black Ops*, Equipment is gear that can be deployed into the world. It can also be retrieved, including C4 and Claymores!

This is excellent for setting up defensive strongholds and then gathering up your gear and moving out.

Equipment used well in isolation is useful, but when it's used well as a team, it is extremely powerful.

It can be very difficult to break a defensive lock on an objective position by a team that uses Camera Spikes and Motion Sensors to spot flankers, along with Jammers, Claymores, and C4 to disrupt and kill attackers.

The Hacker Perk is designed explicitly to counter Equipment, causing these items to show up as bright red, visible *through* objects in the world. You can then hack the objects to turn them against their former owners, or just outright destroy them.

Explosives work well for taking down Equipment, though you can also destroy it by simply shooting or meleeing it.

CAMERA SPIKE

The Camera Spike is a powerful reconnaissance tool. Placed anywhere on the map, it sends a black and white video signal highlighting enemy forces in bright white as they pass in front of the camera.

The camera is placed in the direction and angle you're facing when you deploy it, so line up the facing and then drop the camera.

Once placed, the camera automatically replaces your minimap with the camera view. To cycle it, simply press the Equipment button again to swap between your minimap and the camera.

Note that the camera's field of view is not quite as wide or high as your own, so you have to experiment with placement to find the best line of sight.

A great rule of thumb when placing the Camera Spike is to treat it as a visual "tripwire." Look for locations where you can set up the camera to cut a long line across a common movement path. Place it correctly, and no enemy without the Ghost Perk can cross the line toward your defended position without alerting you to their approach.

Pop open your map and think about drawing a straight line from the camera across the area you want to protect. If you can find a location that bisects any possible approach vectors to your position, you have a good camera spot. When you go to place the camera, try to put it in out-of-the-way or darkened areas to avoid its detection for as long as possible. Even if it's destroyed, you still get the early warning in most situations, and saving your life even once means the Equipment does its job.

The camera is very useful for long-range camping. With a Sniper Rifle, LMG, or even an Assault Rifle, you can set up shop in a likely location and use the camera to protect you from enemy flanking or assault attempts.

On its own, the camera is helpful, but when used with a team employing efficient communication, it can be downright deadly. Just two players with carefully placed cameras can make excellent "tripwires" across almost any possible approaches to a defensive position. In an objective mode, and with good communication, no enemy forces can get in range without your entire team knowing the position from which they're attacking.

C4

C4 is a powerful remote-detonated explosive. Placed carefully, it can cover an objective or an approach to your position with ease.

C4 doesn't make a great "grenade," but it can be used in that capacity in some situations, especially if you happen to be close to a large enemy group oblivious to your presence.

C4's downside is that it requires your constant attention to be truly effective. There are a few exceptions, but they generally require either good teamwork and communication or certain specific objective modes.

To wit: In Domination, the voiceover announcer and HUD elements inform you when a point is being taken. Pre-placed C4 means you don't even need to watch in order to score kills. Listen for the announcement or spot the glow of a point under attack, click the detonator, laugh devilishly.

You can use C4 in Headquarters and bomb-planting modes (S&D, Demolition, and Sabotage). However, HQ is dangerous because explosives often fly into a Headquarters location, and they can cause a potentially lethal chain reaction. At the very least, they can simply waste your C4. In bomb modes, carefully placed C4 can possibly take out a bomb planter or defuser, but this usually requires either your own eyes on the target or a very alert teammate.

You can shoot C4 to cause it to explode, which is useful either for destroying enemy C4 or for detonating friendly C4 prematurely if you see an opportunity to inflict damage.

It's possible to use C4 to guard an approach to your position if you're on defense. However, a Camera Spike, Motion Sensor, or Claymore is usually a better choice, as all three do the job without requiring your direct attention.

There are three points of possible failure with a C4 detonation: your attention, your reaction time, and the explosion itself, which may not always prove fatal. As a result, relying on C4 to protect you or your teammates from flankers isn't a great idea unless you're in a position where the planted C4 is clearly visible in your normal firing arc.

Remember that you do not need to press the Equipment button to detonate your C4—you can double-tap reload to quick-detonate it. This allows you to throw a C4 pack and airburst it, or quickly detonate planted C4 on reaction as needed.

You can place C4 one at a time, or both packages can be dropped at the same time. In the latter case, both detonate with one activation of the detonator. C4 sticks to surfaces in the same manner as Semtex (though not to players). Thus, you can hide C4 by sticking it to a ceiling or wall rather than just throwing it on the ground out in the open.

TACTICAL INSERTION

The Tactical Insertion is a very special piece of Equipment with a unique ability: it allows you to set your own respawn location. This has several significant gameplay implications. Most notably, it's a vital tool in Demolition, and it's very useful in Capture the Flag.

It's generally less powerful in other gameplay modes. However, for anyone who loves camping in certain areas or respawning behind enemy lines, it can still be put to good use. Once placed, a Tac Insert has a distinctive glow at a distance: green if it's friendly, red if enemy. If you aren't careful where you place a Tactical Insertion, an enemy can easily spot it. Tactical Insertions can be destroyed by moving over them and holding reload, by shooting them, or with an explosive from a distance.

While Tactical Insertions are very strong offensively in Demolition and CTF, they're a double-edged sword in all modes. If enemies kill you near your Insert and they're aware of it, you may give up a double kill for free. The same applies if one enemy kills you and another enemy teammate is near your Insert. An especially canny opponent may kill you, let you respawn and place another Insert, kill you again, and then kill you a third time when you respawn. Place those Inserts carefully!

Remember that you can cancel an Insertion during a Killcam. If the enemy that killed you is near your Insert and you suspect they're aware of it, cancel the Insertion and go for a normal respawn. Losing your forward position is painful, but giving up a multi-kill is more painful.

Tactical Insertions also have a very obnoxious use for boosters. By colluding with an enemy player, one can use them to quietly rack up high-end Killstreaks by hiding out in a corner of the map and feeding kills. Pay careful attention to the scoreboard, and use Hacker (or plain common sense and your teammate map) to seek out and eliminate these abusers.

The Tactical Insertion's power on offense is multiplied if all or most of your team uses them. On some maps, finishing the second bomb location in Demolition can be very difficult. With your entire team respawning even halfway closer to the bomb point, you can massively reduce time lost to travel across the map. Similarly, having your offensive force in CTF using Inserts can make running the flag much easier.

In a variety of objective modes, stealthy classes can use Tactical Insertions behind enemy positions very effectively. While you risk giving up a double kill, you can likely deal much more damage to the enemy team by spawning behind them. Spawns can be fairly predictable in some game modes, and Tactical Insertions let you exploit player expectations, punishing opponents with a silenced bullet from behind.

JAMMER

The Jammer is a powerful defensive tool. When placed, it creates a large area of radar jamming that also shuts down any enemy Equipment within its radius.

The Jammer has two circles of effectiveness. As a player moves closer to the center ring, his or her radar gets more and more fuzzy until it's completely snowed out, totally eliminating the minimap.

It's best to use Jammers on defense, either placed around a key objective or chokepoint or placed centrally on the map, giving the greatest possible coverage.

Because Jammers have a fixed radius that does not change with map size, they're more powerful on smaller maps.

Jammers are doubly nasty when multiple teammates deploy them. Two or three Jammers can cover a very large stretch of terrain, large enough to guarantee that no enemies approaching a defended position can use their minimaps.

On offense, Jammers can still be useful, thanks to their ability to disable enemy Equipment. Bring one along and deploy it when you get close to a known enemy position.

To find and eliminate a Jammer without Hacker, you can triangulate its position based on the fuzziness of your minimap. Approach the fuzz from two directions, and then home in on the Jammer's likely position. Just don't get so distracted by the Jammer that you let an enemy take you down!

CLAYMORE

The Claymore is a very simple and very effective piece of explosive Equipment.

You can place the Claymore anywhere you wish. It has a front-facing motion sensor that detonates the device a split second after it senses an enemy in its frontal arc.

Place the Claymore facing away from doorways, stairwells, and other entrances, not toward them. You want the Claymore to trip and explode as the target moves past it. If you plant a Claymore facing a doorway, it detonates harmlessly behind an enemy as he or she sprints over it.

Instead, if you place it off to the door's left or right, facing inward at an angle, it's almost impossible to avoid.

Claymores are not foolproof. They can be evaded, destroyed, or negated by Ghost, Hacker, Flak Jacket, Lightweight, as well as simple caution and a few well-placed bullets or an explosive.

But even in situations where your Claymore fails to get the kill, it can still alert you to an enemy in your vicinity. If that enemy happens to be damaged as a result of the blast, so much the better.

Because you get only one Claymore, you should choose its placement carefully. Try to use it to cover the weakest, hardest-to-cover approach to your position, or place it in a very high traffic area to guarantee a kill and start your Killstreak on its way.

MOTION SENSOR

The Motion Sensor is another powerful defensive tool. Although it lacks the Jammer's broad utility, it compensates by being much more dangerous to enemies who unknowingly stumble into its range.

The Motion Sensor projects a small radius of detection that tracks any enemy movement, giving you perfect intelligence on their position.

As a result, if you're camping out at long range or guarding an objective, the Motion Sensor can easily protect you from flankers or stealthy enemies who lack Hacker Pro.

Be aware that the Motion Sensor has a limited range, and it does not help teammates at all—they cannot see your Motion Sensor pings. It's therefore much less helpful to your team than the Jammer. However, if you're good about communication, you can still alert teammates to an enemy presence.

Due to its short range, the Motion Sensor does not work extremely well with mobile builds. But you can use it to cover a small area while you operate behind enemy lines. This is particularly useful if you know roughly where enemies are spawning, and you want to avoid being surprised by a stray traveler.

PERKS

Perks provide powerful, game-changing abilities and bonuses to your custom classes. Choosing the right set of Perks to match your equipment and personal playstyle is an art, and is best refined over time with plenty of practice and experimentation.

This section provides an overview of each Perk's effects and their implications on the battlefield.

There really aren't "stronger" or "weaker" Perks, but rather situational Perks. Their effectiveness depends on the mode and map you're playing, as well as your loadout, and your own personal preferences.

Perk 1

LIGHTWEIGHT

Lightweight increases your movement speed. Exactly how much of a benefit you get from this Perk depends on your equipped weapon. SMGs and Shotguns move the fastest, followed by Sniper Rifles, Assault Rifles, and Light Machineguns.

Lightweight is a simple Perk, but its effects can be dramatic. In objective modes, it can let you blitz an objective and guarantee that only another player with Lightweight can intercept you.

Lightweight is extremely useful for offensive flag-running in CTF and blitzing bomb points in S&D, Demolition, and Sabotage. It's also great for getting to Headquarters in HQ and reaching the back lines in Domination.

In normal combat, it lets you quickly reach key conflict points on a map, travel through a flanking route more quickly, escape from a losing battle, or move faster to land a lethal knife kill.

Lightweight is effective with Marathon and either an SMG or a Shotgun. This lets you close the distance to fully exploit your close-ranged weaponry. It can also be useful with a Sniper Rifle or Assault Rifle. We don't recommend taking Lightweight with an LMG in most situations.

Lightweight is very strong at the start of a match. In some modes, you may wish to have an SMG/Lightweight/Marathon build specifically at the start of a round. You can use it to get into position and either secure a key objective or potentially flank the entire enemy team. Once the initial wave of team spawns has dispersed, you can then switch to a different class.

Other than the obvious uses in objective modes, Lightweight's effects are generally more subtle in normal TDM or combat around objectives. We recommend you avoid making heavy use of Lightweight for normal combat until you have a good feel for travel through the levels.

Learning when Lightweight can give you a decisive positional advantage takes time. Its effects aren't immediately obvious in a straight fight. You need to have a good feel for map flow before you can really see how helpful Lightweight can be.

LIGHTWEIGHT PRO

The Pro upgrade gives you near immunity to falling damage. You can still die from a lethal fall, but any nonlethal fall doesn't hurt you at all.

In most situations, this is simply a nice bonus, but on some maps, you can get a lot of mileage out of this by sticking to high ground, safe in the knowledge that you can leap from tall buildings without fear of dying on impact.

On some maps, this facilitates an easy getaway from combat, even if you take a hit or two while jumping.

SCAVENGER

Scavenger causes slain enemies to drop ammo packs. These packages replenish your primary and secondary weapons' ammunition, as well as Lethal Grenades. Scavenger packs do not replenish explosive weapons of any other kind.

Scavenger's power increases the longer your average lifespan is. If you play a very run-and-gun build prone to dying quickly, you won't get much use out of Scavenger.

On the other hand, if you're a more cautious player, Scavenger can allow you to defend a fixed position almost indefinitely. Or you can operate "behind enemy lines," picking up replenished grenades and ammo from your victims to continue your Killstreak.

This benefit is usually more pronounced on medium to large maps, where you have time to pick up the supplies and get out of sight. Smaller maps, with their high rate of conflict and frequent close spawns, give you less of a chance to catch a breather. And typically, one tends to waste less ammo and grenades in tight confines.

Scavenger is perfect for an Assault Rifle build operating on defense or offense. Be sure to bring along Frags or Semtex to benefit from the grenade restocking.

SCAVENGER PRO

Scavenger Pro has two significant benefits. The first is that it fully loads your ammo for all weapons, including explosives. The second is that Scavenger packs now reload Tactical Grenades as well as Lethal Grenades.

Between the two benefits, Scavenger Pro turns you into a sort of walking one-man army, capable of holding an area for an extended period or laying siege to a defended position with a barrage of grenades and explosives.

GHOST

Ghost gives you immunity to Spy Planes and Blackbird detection.

Because players tend to rely very heavily on their minimap to spot enemies, Ghost and a Suppressor renders you all but invisible to the enemy team. If they don't see or hear you, you don't exist.

Even without a Suppressor, you can still take advantage of Ghost by waiting until a Spy Plane is in the air and then making an aggressive move toward known enemy positions.

Keep aware of your position relative to your teammates and the enemy. By moving away from your teammates, you can ensure that the enemy team heads toward the red dots visible from their Spy Plane or Blackbird, completely missing you as you slide up on their flank.

Ghost is very useful for any build that needs to get close to be effective, so it's great with Shotguns, SMGs, or ARs if you prefer to fight up close or behind enemy lines.

We strongly recommend pairing Ghost with a Suppressor if you plan to engage CQB behind enemy lines. Firing an unsilenced round with no friendly blips near you on the radar can be a death sentence.

GHOST PRO

Ghost Pro upgrades Ghost from very good to downright amazing. With Ghost Pro, air support won't target you, attack dogs ignore you, Infrared scopes don't highlight you in white, and Sentry Guns ignore you. Not only that, but your red name does not show up, and you don't highlight red under enemy crosshairs.

Ghost Pro makes you very, very difficult to spot, and it allows you to ignore all forms of air support completely.

Ghost Pro doesn't change the basic utility of Ghost; it just makes it more effective at its job. The lack of a red name or crosshair highlight is the biggest benefit to covert ops in enemy lines, but the other benefits are also very helpful.

INVISIBILITY

If you're running with a full party, get everyone to run Ghost Pro for a few games.

There's nothing quite as amusing as hearing, "Enemy Spy Plane," and ignoring it completely.

This can actually be extremely effective as a team build, especially if all of you run Silencers and use Ninja. They'll never see your team on the minimap or hear you coming.

FLAK JACKET

Flak Jacket is the answer to your explosive-hating prayers. Flak Jacket slices any explosive damage you receive by a massive 65%, meaning that anything but a direct explosive hit won't kill you. You can stand near C4, walk past Claymores, breeze by Semtex or Frag Grenades, and sprint through RPG and Grenade Launcher fire.

Flak Jacket is most useful when you know you're going to take explosive damage, rather than simply because you don't like explosives. If you aren't certain you'll take explosive fire, there are better choices to improve your effectiveness.

When can you be certain of that? In objective modes. Particularly in Headquarters, but also in Domination, and to a lesser extent in the other modes.

Flak Jacket can be useful on offense or defense, but it's generally most useful on offense, when you have to seize a location or plant a bomb under fire. When the enemy knows where you must be in order to win a game mode, you can be certain to encounter explosives there.

Flak Jacket does not save you from a concentrated barrage of explosives by multiple players, but it does let you last longer, and it absolutely saves you from stray explosions. In game modes where games are won or lost by seconds of time alive, Flak Jacket can mean the difference between victory and defeat.

Consider keeping an offensive objective build that equips Flak Jacket. If you run into heavy explosive fire, you can use that class to help weather the storm.

FLAK JACKET PRO

Flak Jacket Pro gives a few minor but nice upgrades to the basic explosive resistance. First, it gives you immunity to fire damage. This protects you from any Flamethrowers or Napalm Strikes you may encounter—minor, but handy.

To abuse this a bit, use Napalm Strike to saturate an objective area, and then move in and secure it while the Napalm is en route. Mix this with a smoke grenade, and you become pretty difficult to root out!

Finally, Flak Jacket Pro lets you safely throw back Frag Grenades almost without fail. Any time you pick up a Frag to toss back with this Perk active, it resets the grenade's timer to 2.5 seconds. That's plenty of time to carefully aim and throw the pineapple with a return-to-sender message stamped on it.

HARDLINE

Hardline drops the number of kills required for any Killstreak by one.

This seems like a minor change, but it actually has a profound impact on the frequency of Killstreaks you generate. It's less noticeable for very high-end Killstreaks, but taking any of the six or below streaks can greatly increase their frequency.

Hardline is especially powerful when paired with Spy Plane, Counter-Spy Plane, and SAM Turret, giving you almost total denial of enemy radar and air support. At the same time, it gives your team constant two-kill Spy Planes.

You can also use the lower Killstreaks by stocking up a ton of RC-XDs and then unleashing them all in sequence when their explosive power is most needed.

Hardline won't dramatically increase the frequency of higher streaks for you, but it does help.

Because you can most fully exploit Hardline by running low streaks and stockpiling them, you may want to set an upper limit of five or six kills for your streaks, and then make sure to die and reset your streaks when you hit your highest Killstreak.

If you do this with your team supporting a Spy/Counter-Spy/SAM setup, you can seriously hamper the effectiveness of the enemy team's Killstreaks and general combat effectiveness. This simultaneously grants your own team the aid of near-constant radar sweeps. You can also use Care Packages to great effect, accumulating quite a few in a given match.

HARDLINE PRO

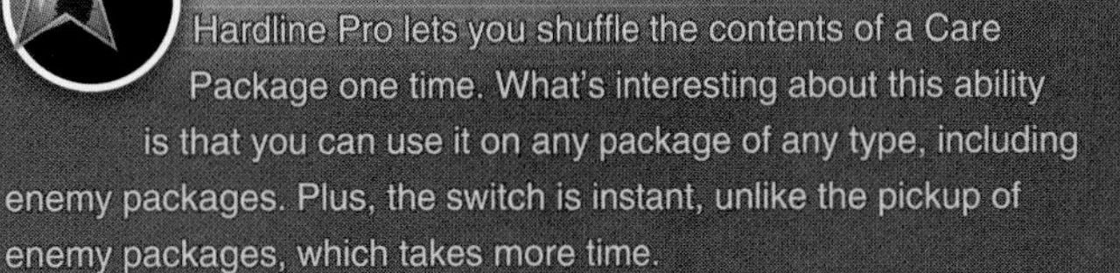

Hardline Pro lets you shuffle the contents of a Care Package one time. What's interesting about this ability is that you can use it on any package of any type, including enemy packages. Plus, the switch is instant, unlike the pickup of enemy packages, which takes more time.

Because of this fact, when combined with Hardline's basic ability, you can run SAM Turret, Care Package, and Sentry Gun to get three chances of different Killstreaks, all for the low entry cost of a five-kill streak.

You can also use the ability to reshuffle a dud friendly drop, or to sabotage a high-powered enemy drop when you don't have the time to secure the crate.

Incidentally, this is one of the better ways to aim for a Death Machine or Grim Reaper if you really, really want to play with one. One last note: if you encounter a package that you cannot switch with Hardline Pro, it has been booby-trapped with Hacker Pro. Beware!

HARDENED

Hardened increases bullet penetration.

This is a very straightforward Perk, but its power and utility vary significantly depending on the map you're playing. On any map with a lot of cover or buildings, its power increases. In more open maps, it's a lot less useful, though it can still be helpful with the Pro version (see below).

It's generally more effective to take Hardened with weapons that have poor penetration than it is to take it with guns that already have good penetration; the extra penetrating power can be overkill.

The other issue with Hardened is that it very much depends on your own firing behavior to be effective. If you rarely take shots at enemies behind cover, you won't fully utilize this Perk.

We strongly recommend taking Hardened and then unloading gratuitous amounts of ammo into every enemy you see, think you see, thought heard, spotted on the minimap, heard about from a teammate, or read a rumor about in the news.

The idea here is that you gradually get a feel for how well your weapon penetrates with Hardened, and how and where enemies move through a map.

Also remember that you can use the hit markers you get through a wall to track a target. With practice, you can even track a running target through a wall and take it down.

HARDENED PRO

Hardened Pro increases the utility of Hardened by increasing damage to aircraft and turrets. It also substantially reduces flinching and recoil when you're hit by enemy fire. Hardened Pro's bonus against aircraft and turrets is most useful with high-damage weapons that have good magazine size, Assault Rifles and LMGs in particular.

Remember that you can shoot down Spy and Counter-Spy Planes easily with accurate fire from an AR or LMG. This is true even without Hardened Pro, but this Perk makes doing so much easier and faster. If you're diligent, you can deny an enemy recon power just by using your equipped weapon, without needing an anti-air launcher or SAM turret. Taking down Attack Choppers is a bit more dangerous. An LMG can manage it, but expect to draw hostile attention by firing at any airborne chopper.

The flinch and recoil protection are useful with almost any weapon. The reduced flinch means you're barely slowed at all when you take fire. This makes it a very useful Perk for running-and-gunning builds of all sorts.

Reduced recoil helps keep your shots on target when engaging in a heads-up firefight. If your view stays on target but your opponent's jerks wildly when you tag him, you're more likely to come out standing.

These bonuses are especially noticeable when engaging in CQB and hip-firing your weapon. You can continue to move at full speed, without suffering either the ADS or flinch penalties from getting shot.

BULLET PENETRATION

Bullet penetration in *Call of Duty: Black Ops* is handled by giving each weapon a penetration power and then comparing that to the thickness (and permeability) of the object you shoot.

Some objects, despite their appearance, are totally impenetrable to bullets; only practice teaches you these subtleties.

In most cases, penetration works how you would expect. Thin walls or light cover is easily penetrated, even by lighter weapons, while thick brick, concrete walls, or hard cover require LMG or Sniper Rifle fire to punch through.

The angle of the shot also matters. The more cleanly you penetrate an object (a perfect 90-degree perpendicular shot to the surface you're targeting), the more damage that passes through to your target on the other side.

Hardened indirectly increases damage by allowing a greater percentage of your bullet's power to survive passing through a wall. It also allows weapons to punch through surfaces they otherwise could not.

Hardened does not increase base bullet damage; it only increases the share of damage that passes through a surface.

SCOUT

Scout allows you to hold your breath longer.

This straightforward Perk is almost exclusively useful for Sniper Rifles, though a few other weapons can equip scopes that require steadying by holding your breath.

Scout is helpful for a sniper, particularly a sniper in training. But you may find that as your skill increases, you need to hold your breath for less time to land a shot. Oddly, this makes Scout less useful as you improve.

Scout does allow you to hold your breath and stay honed in a target that you're waiting to emerge from cover. You can cover a key route or chokepoint for a longer period with a primed shot. However, you can similar results by watching the area and then steadying your shot a split second before you fire, as long as your aim is good.

If you're just beginning to snipe, we strongly recommend using Scout to help improve your accuracy. As you improve and get faster, you can either keep Scout for the Pro benefit, or swap it out for a Perk 2 option that better suits your play style.

STEADY AIM

Steady Aim improves hip-fire accuracy, reducing the normal spread factor by a multiplier of 0.65.

This is a substantial improvement, generally bumping a gun one step up the accuracy scale, from Sniper to LMG to AR to SMG, more or less. For weapons that are already accurate or effective at short-range hip-fire (SMGs and Shotguns), Steady Aim is less vital, but it can still be useful to ensure your rounds stay on target at a greater distance.

Steady Aim is very useful for the run-and-gun player, because ADS-ing takes time, and movement speed while ADS is reduced. Firing from the hip has neither of those disadvantages. Coupled with the fact that bullet impacts slow player movement and cause view recoil, the first player to score a hit in a CQB is often the victor. Steady Aim helps you get that first hit and get hip-fire kills at a moderate distance with SMGs.

Steady Aim is also helpful when Dual Wielding or using Rapid Fire, options that substantially penalize accuracy. Steady Aim can help make up for the lost accuracy and improve your odds of a quick kill while wasting less ammunition.

SCOUT PRO

Scout Pro provides the very handy benefit of cutting weapon switch times in half.

This allows you to switch to a secondary Pistol almost instantly. Even weapons that are slow to bring up, like Shotguns, LMGs, and Sniper Rifles, are readied more quickly.

You can exploit Scout Pro by taking down a foe and then stealing his weapon. Scout Pro lets you switch weapons fast enough to make good use of a Sniper Rifle (or LMG!) and a primary weapon stolen from a fallen soldier.

STEADY AIM PRO

Steady Aim Pro adds two bonuses built for the run-and-gunner. First, it reduces the delay after sprinting before you can take aim with your weapon. Second, it cuts in half the recovery time after a knife lunge.

Both bonuses are very useful to an aggressive player using an SMG or Shotgun, though they can be helpful to an offensive AR user as well.

Quicker aiming after sprinting can reduce the number of deaths you suffer from sprinting into a combat engagement, which is very near first place on the list of Things You Should Not Do Online. Meanwhile, faster knifing recovery is useful in any CQB situation.

SLEIGHT OF HAND

Sleight of Hand cuts your weapon's reload time in half.

This very useful Perk is helpful to almost any weapon, but it's especially useful to weapons with shallow magazines (20-round SMGs), slow reloading (Shotguns), or weapons that burn a lot of ammunition quickly (Dual Wield or Rapid Fire equipped weapons).

Sleight of Hand is very helpful, but it can also encourage some bad habits. In general, reloading is a risky maneuver, as it leaves you completely vulnerable to any nearby enemy. Because you often reload just after a firefight, an enemy honing in on the red dot, the death marker, and the noise is likely to show up at this inconvenient time.

Sleight of Hand helps minimize this danger, but it can get you in the habit of constantly reloading your weapon, even if you use only a few rounds to down your target. Meanwhile, a second or third enemy might be en route to your position. This is especially bad if you switch to a build without Sleight of Hand but continue your reloading habits.

Be mindful of why and when you reload, and Sleight of Hand can provide a useful benefit for you, especially with the weapon types mentioned above. Just don't get in the habit of mashing reload when you're five rounds down in a 30-round magazine.

SLIGHT OF HAND PRO

Sleight of Hand Pro provides the excellent bonus of halving ADS time for any weapon except those equipped with a precision sniping scope.

This reduced ADS time makes Pistol and SMG sighting lightning fast. Assault Rifle times become very quick, and LMG times become fast enough to use more safely in medium-range engagements.

Cutting down ADS time can increase your chance of scoring a kill in a firefight where you spot an enemy in the open who can see you. You're all but guaranteed to line up the first shot more quickly than your opponent does.

This is a very useful benefit for almost any weapon type, though you lose its bonuses if you're Dual Wielding.

WARLORD

Warlord allows you to equip two Attachments on your Primary weapon. There are some restrictions on what Attachments can be combined: only one precision scope, only one weapon Attachment on an AR, only one magazine Attachment, Rapid Fire and Dual Wield cannot use enhanced magazines. In general, Warlord lets you trick out your weapon to be a bit more effective in more situations.

Warlord is most useful when you want a very specific combination of Attachments that fit a particular build. It's very important that those Attachments be more useful to your build than the other benefits a Perk 2 slot would provide.

Consider pairing Warlord with Scavenger once your average life expectancy improves. A double Attachment weapon is less attractive if you run out of ammunition and have to swap out your upgraded weapon for someone else's normal weapon.

WARLORD PRO

Warlord Pro grants you an extra Lethal and Tactical Grenade (excepting smoke) when you spawn.

This gives you a little added firepower. Again, when paired with Scavenger, this lets you stockpile a truly ruinous collection of bombardment materiel.

This Perk is useful in all modes, but it's especially useful when using Lethal Grenades and Nova Gas or smoke to protect or assault an objective.

Perk 3

MARATHON

Marathon doubles the length of time you can sprint.

How useful this is depends on what weapon you're lugging around. SMGs and Shotguns let you run a good distance, ARs and Sniper Rifles slightly less, and LMGs the least of all.

Marathon is very important in any mode that requires rapid mobility, which is almost all of them on offense. It's also useful for quickly cutting off chokepoints before the other team arrives or for reaching key camping spots and contested overlooks.

However, Marathon can be a dangerous Perk. Sprinting blindly around corners is one of the absolute most common ways to die online. Don't get into this bad habit, and especially don't let Marathon encourage it.

MARATHON PRO

Marathon Pro is a straight upgrade. Once it's unlocked, you can sprint an infinite distance.

This is a vital Perk for run-and-gun classes, and still important for many others. Even slow-moving LMGs benefit tremendously from this Perk, as they can use the infinite sprint distance to get into position and better exploit their power.

Definitely work on unlocking this Perk quickly to make full use of Marathon.

In many objective modes, having a Lightweight/Marathon Pro class with an SMG is extremely useful as an objective-blitzer.

Our warnings about sprinting around corners apply doubly with Marathon Pro. It's very, very easy to fall into the habit of sprinting everywhere around the map. This is a good way to get yourself killed by campers, cautious players, or surprise encounters. Mind those corners!

NINJA

Ninja silences your footsteps. This is a very powerful Perk in FFA and S&D, and it's still extremely useful in almost all modes, especially on offense.

Ninja is odd in that it can be functionally useless against a newer, unaware player or someone with a poor audio setup. However, it's more useful against good players.

Most skilled players rely heavily on sound to warn them of enemy presence, whatever their radar might say. Ninja removes the warning that footsteps give.

Remember that you can crouch to move silently without Ninja, but the ability to move normally and sprint quietly is extremely powerful.

If you enjoy running stealthy builds, operating behind enemy lines, or going on offense, Ninja should be a staple Perk for you.

NINJA PRO

Ninja Pro is an extremely powerful upgrade to the basic Ninja Perk.

First, it silences you completely. All forms of movement, falling, mantling, equipment rustling, and so forth are totally silent. Because Ninja only silences footsteps, there are plenty of other ways to give away your location beyond firing your gun, and alert players take advantage of them.

Second, Ninja Pro makes all enemy sounds louder. This is a ridiculously strong bonus. Used well, it can almost feel like cheating. You can clearly hear enemy movements a good distance away, sometimes even through walls.

We strongly recommend upgrading Ninja to Pro status quickly; it's a very strong, very useful upgrade.

SECOND CHANCE

Second Chance causes you to drop to the ground with your pistol out for 10 seconds after you take damage that would normally be fatal. If you don't have a pistol in your build, you get a "free" M1911 to use instead.

In a normal firefight, this usually gives you just a split second to fire a few shots before whoever took you out finishes the job—make those shots count. If you die from a headshot or a knife kill, you don't go into Second Chance.

Second Chance can be somewhat useful if you're running a CQB build. It gives you a chance to ruin the Killstreak of whoever takes you down. At greater distances, pulling off the retaliation kill is less likely. You can crawl very slowly in Second Chance, and if you hold reload, you instantly expire.

One note for both Second Chance and Second Chance Pro: If you're still moving when you drop to the ground, you start crawling immediately. This has the unfortunate side effect of dropping your pistol temporarily. Do this in combat, and you aren't likely to pull off any Second Chance shots.

If you plan to use Second Chance regularly, discipline yourself to stop moving the instant you take lethal damage so you can aim and start shooting as soon as you fall. With practice, this can help you score those retaliatory kills more often.

SECOND CHANCE PRO

Second Chance Pro is a very nice upgrade. It increases the length of time you stay alive for 30 seconds. More importantly, teammates can revive you if they get to you in time! Oddly, contrary to Second Chance, Second Chance Pro's revival ability is more useful on a build that fights near home, closer to teammates. If a few stray shots from long range take you down, you have a much better chance of crawling behind nearby cover and having a teammate revive you.

A particularly nasty option is to have most of your team run medium-range or longer builds and Second Chance Pro. In some objective modes, this can force the other team to work extra hard to make their kills stay dead.

HACKER

Hacker causes enemy Equipment and any explosives to show up as bright red and visible through walls at a short distance. Hacker is very useful on offense. It's also useful for covering objectives, as you can quickly spot unpleasant surprises that the enemy team may have set up nearby.

Using some of your own explosives, you can get rid of enemy Equipment from a distance. Traveling the map on offense, you can often use the location of a Claymore or Motion Tracker to find a nearby camper.

With a bit of deduction, you can nail said camper with an explosive through a nearby window. In some cases, you can just shoot him straight through a wall if you have the right gun for the job.

HACKER PRO

Hacker Pro offers two very useful upgrades to Hacker. Firstly, you can sabotage enemy Equipment, Sentry Turrets, and crates of all types.

Sabotaging enemy Equipment or turrets causes them to "join your team," while sabotaging a crate of any sort causes it to become booby-trapped. Any enemy opening the crate triggers a lethal explosion.

Secondly, Hacker Pro makes you invisible to Motion Sensors. Against enemies sitting on defense or camping near a Motion Sensor, this is as good as invisibility. They tend to trust their Motion Sensors to cover their backs. You can punish them for this, as long as you're quiet on your approach!

Hacker Pro simply enhances Hacker's basic combat role, giving you more options on offense or operating in enemy terrain.

TACTICAL MASK

Tactical Mask is a useful defensive Perk that renders you nearly immune to Flash or Concussion Grenades.

Tactical Mask is great when you go for objectives where you expect grenades of all types to hammer you. But, because it depends on the enemy team using those grenades, you may or may not get a lot of mileage out of this Perk.

Tactical Mask on its own is reasonably useful, but we strongly suggest getting the Pro version as quickly as possible, as it's an important upgrade.

TACTICAL MASK PRO

Tactical Mask Pro adds Nova Gas to the list of protections. This is extremely important, because without the Pro upgrade, the gas still forces you off objectives, even if you're protected from Flash or Concussion Grenades.

Also, Tactical Mask Pro causes your crosshair to "point" in the direction of an enemy hit by your own Flashbangs or Concussion Grenades. This is a very useful bonus when you use either type of grenade on offense. With practice, you can increase your grenade kills.

Communication also makes Tactical Mask Pro more useful. You can lob grenades into areas to test for enemy presence. You can then notify your teammates of where the hit marker indicator detects enemies.

We recommend pairing Tactical Mask Pro with Flak Jacket for offense in objective modes where you expect to eat normal explosives. Or pair it with Scavenger and Concussion Grenades, Flashbangs, or Nova Gas to get the most out of the hit detection upgrade.

Carrying Nova Gas can let you abuse your own immunity to it. Toss gas to blind enemies, sprint in, and finish them off without worrying about gassing yourself.

KILLSTREAKS

Killstreaks are powerful rewards earned for racking up consecutive kills in one life.

Killstreak rewards have many battlefield applications. Some are offensive, some are defensive, and some can be used in tandem with teammates' Killstreak rewards for greater effectiveness.

If you're new to *Call of Duty: Black Ops* online, you might find that the higher Killstreaks feel out of reach. With practice, your average lifespan should increase and your average Killstreak will climb higher.

It's true that playing cautiously and more defensively is usually a safer route to high-end Killstreaks, compared to playing aggressively or going for objectives on offense. As a result, it's extremely important to pick a set of Killstreaks that supports your chosen role. Taking Rolling Thunder, Chopper Gunner, and Attack Dogs as your default setup is rarely a good idea.

HARDLINE

The importance of Hardline Pro when choosing Killstreaks can't be overstated. Not only does it make racking up low-end Killstreaks extremely easy, its ability to manipulate the contents of dropped packages is also extremely useful.

In any build running most of its Killstreaks for six or less kills, we recommend using Hardline to amp up your Killstreak output per match.

In any build running two or more "package" drops, consider taking Hardline Pro to exploit its drop reshuffling.

If you run a low streak setup, consider dying as soon as you hit your top reward. Avoid this if you're a key defender or in the middle of securing an objective. Otherwise, resetting your streak to get more rewards on the field can be very helpful to your team.

Resetting streaks in this manner is the key to accumulating a truly absurd number of RC-XDs or Spy and Counter-Spy Planes per match.

- You can choose up to three Killstreaks, and they are set for all of your custom classes.
- You cannot select more than one Killstreak reward for the same number of kills. For example, you can pick only one between Spy Plane and RC-XD.
- Killstreaks that can kill enemies do not contribute kills toward subsequent Killstreaks.
- Killstreaks can be stockpiled, and they persist after death. Nothing prevents you from storing 10 RC-XDs to use at the end of a match if you can pull it off.
- The Hardline Perk reduces by one the kills required to earn any Killstreak reward.
- The SAM Turret, Care Package, Sentry Gun, and Valkyrie Rockets Killstreaks all deliver packages to the battlefield. These can be shot down in midflight and can be changed by Hardline Pro or booby-trapped by Hacker Pro.
- Care Packages and packages changed by Hardline Pro have a greater chance of low-end Killstreaks and no chance at all of Gunship or Attack Dogs.
- Extremely rarely, Care Packages or packages reset by Hardline Pro may award the Death Machine or Grim Reaper streaks.
- To reset your Killstreaks once you earn your top reward, your character must die, either intentionally or not!

Suggested Killstreak Combinations

TEAM SUPPORT

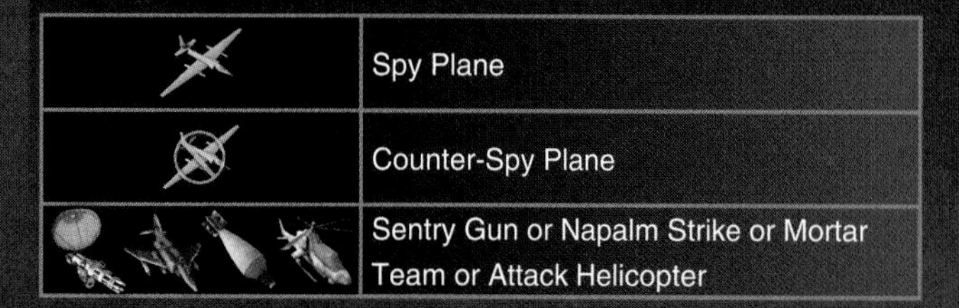

	Spy Plane
	Counter-Spy Plane
	Sentry Gun or Napalm Strike or Mortar Team or Attack Helicopter

This setup gives you constant aerial cover, shuts off the enemy team's minimap, and nullifies their Spy Planes or Blackbirds, as well as a lot of Equipment. It also gives you a finishing Killstreak that can be useful in a variety of situations.

If you're running offense, we suggest taking Attack Helicopter, as you can fire and forget, letting it do its work while you do yours.

On some maps, the Attack Helicopter can inflict serious damage to the enemy team. But in certain objective modes, or if the enemy team is aggressive about destroying air support, the Mortar Team or Napalm Strike might be more useful to cover an objective or bombard an enemy position.

Remember that Napalm Strike is extra useful if you or someone on your team runs Flak Jacket Pro.

Finally, the Sentry Gun is the most defensive option of the four. If you know you're playing defense, or the objective mode you're playing is friendly to Sentry Guns, take it. Even if you're busy on offense, you can still drop the gun behind friendly lines and let a teammate place the Sentry while you head out.

OBJECTIVE BOMBARDMENT

ANY THREE OF THE FOLLOWING

	RC-XD
	Napalm Strike
	Mortar Team
	Valkyrie Rockets
	Rolling Thunder

This build brings the pain to enemies covering objectives. You can use explosive RC cars and well-timed Napalm, Mortars, Valkyrie Rockets, or a carpet-bombing Rolling Thunder to deliver devastating bombardments to objectives.

Coordinate your actions with your teammates. If you call in the strikes, teammates can prepare to blitz an objective at almost the exact same time the area is hit with your explosive payload.

If you or a teammate has Flak Jacket Pro, you can call in Napalm Strikes on the target area and ignore the flames to secure an objective.

Flak Jacket also protects from your own Mortar Strikes to some extent, but trying to secure an objective amidst a shell barrage isn't the safest job.

Be sure that you or your teammates are in position to blitz the objective area just as the strikes start to land. Coordinating this build is the key to success.

EFFECTIVE BOMBARDMENT

For Napalm Strikes, Mortar Teams, and Rolling Thunder, it's very important to have a Spy Plane in the air just before you call in the strike.

Knowing exactly where the greatest concentration of enemy players is, and where they're likely moving, enables you to inflict the maximum damage.

Even the RC-XD and Valkyrie Rockets benefit from this knowledge, so try to ensure that you have Spy Plane coverage before you use your bombardment Killstreaks.

If you can't guarantee that a teammate will call up a Spy Plane, swap out your lowest Killstreak for your own Spy Plane—it's that important.

PACKAGE FRENZY

	SAM Turret
	Care Package
	Sentry Gun

Run this build with Hardline Pro, and you get three chances per life to accumulate packages—and you can reset them with Hardline Pro's reshuffle ability.

This gives you a chance to see the rare Death Machine and Grim Reaper rewards. More importantly, it gives you three chances to rack up anything from a Mortar Team to a Blackbird.

PACKAGE BAITING

You can use any build running package drops to bait the enemy team.

Toss packages out in the open and then set up shop nearby to cover them. Many enemies instantly go for a package if they don't see anyone in plain sight. This can let you rack up easy kills.

Just be sure you can trust your teammates. Otherwise, they may grab your bait!

GOING THE DISTANCE

	Spy Plane
	Blackbird
	Chopper Gunner or Gunship or Attack Dogs

The very high-end Killstreaks generally require some preparation and dedication on the battlefield to acquire.

To secure them, we recommend running your favorite custom class and then taking Spy Plane and Blackbird.

It's also helpful to make a "prep run" in which you get a Spy Plane or two first, die, and then activate the first Spy Plane once you hit a three-kill streak. From there, work to stay alive using your Spy Plane coverage to reach your Blackbird.

If you can hit your Blackbird safely, you'll almost always secure the top streak because it's such a powerful informational advantage.

As a general rule, medium- to long-range builds have an easier time reaching high-end streaks than CQB builds, simply because CQB is riskier all around.

This build also has the side benefit of aiding your team while you pursue your top-end Killstreak—Spy Planes and Blackbirds are never a bad thing.

PACKAGE TIPS

The SAM Turret, Care Package, Sentry Gun, and Valkyrie Rockets all call in a chopper to drop a crate containing your Killstreak reward.

Because of this delay, we don't recommend running any of these streaks on offensive builds, as you rarely have time to find a safe place and wait for the drop.

In general, these Killstreak rewards are more useful on defense, or when covering a static objective location.

In some cases, you may want to stockpile a few of these rewards and then drop them all quickly at the start of a round or during a lull in the action.

On most maps, it's safest to drop the packages either near your team's starting spawn or off in an area that receives little traffic.

Remember that calling in a package always attracts a bit of enemy attention. Be ready for this, and take up station in nearby cover.

Packages of all sorts can be picked up by you (quickly), a teammate (more slowly), or an enemy (also slowly).

Hardline Pro can shuffle a package's contents, and Hacker Pro can booby-trap them to create a bomb.

In some situations, it's a good idea to drop packages near defenders and let them take the rewards. As long as the packages are used intelligently to help your team, everyone wins!

SPY PLANE: 3 KILLS

The Spy Plane calls in an aerial reconnaissance mission that provides regular scanner sweeps of the battlefield.

Each sweep updates your entire team's minimaps with enemy positions, current at the time of the sweep.

Note that enemies using the Ghost Perk do not show up on these sweeps. So, don't assume you're completely safe if you don't see any nearby blips on your minimap.

Remember that you can hit the Pause Menu to see a full map of the battlefield. Bringing up this map just as a Spy Plane comes online can give you a very good sense of the enemy team's overall position.

If multiple friendly Spy Planes come online simultaneously, the frequency of the scanning sweeps increases. Generally, this isn't a good use of Spy Planes—if one is already online when you earn yours, wait until the active one falls off before you activate it.

Consider keeping a Spy Plane in reserve to activate when you enter enemy territory.

RC-XD: 3 KILLS

The RC-XD grants you control of a remote control car strapped with explosives.

When you activate it, you crouch down and man the controls. Be sure your meatspace body is safely tucked away while you drive your RC car around the battlefield!

You can powerslide with the RC car and use one burst of nitro speed to quickly reach a target or evade enemy fire.

Several maps feature special RC-car-only routes, all the better to reach objectives or flank an enemy position.

When it's triggered, the blast from the RC-XD is projected mostly forward in front of the car, so try to aim your detonation appropriately.

Enemies can shoot RC-XD. And, because it makes a very distinctive noise as it drives around the map, try to get it into position and detonate it quickly, or you might lose your toy to an alert enemy.

The RC-XD is ideal for clearing an objective area or for removing a particularly annoying camper from a distance.

Stock up your RC-XDs and use them to remove key threats rather than using them immediately. Remember that your character's body is out of commission for the duration of the car ride, so it's important that your mobile bomb helps your team as much as you would!

COUNTER-SPY PLANE: 4 KILLS

The Counter-Spy Plane calls up an aerial electronic warfare flight that completely jams the enemy minimap. It shuts down Spy Planes and Blackbirds, and renders Motion Sensors useless.

The Counter-Spy Plane is an extremely powerful Killstreak because players tend to rely heavily on their minimaps. This makes the Killstreak an ideal weapon to assist your team, weaken the enemy team, and give you cover as you move behind behind enemy lines.

When you acquire a Counter-Spy Plane, save it until you need to make an offensive push. The radar blocking gives you some cover and functions in some ways as a team-wide Suppressor upgrade; gunfire no longer gives the enemy a perfect fix on your location.

RECON DENIAL

Both the Spy Plane and the Counter-Spy Plane can be shot down.

You can shoot down either one with regular gunfire, though this is easier with Hardened Pro, a LAW, or the Strela-3. The SAM Turret also takes them down.

After a recon plane has been in the air for a short time, it flies away. If you don't kill it in that time, you lose the ability to remove it from the skies.

If you're running an AR or LMG with Hardened Pro, make a point of shooting down enemy Spy Planes or Counter-Spy Planes immediately. If you're persistent, you can severely weaken your enemy's recon efforts, giving your team a marked advantage.

SAM TURRET: 4 KILLS

The SAM Turret Killstreak calls in a package drop that grants you a placeable SAM Turret.

This turret fires at any enemy air support and provides Killstreak nullification of the Spy Plane, Counter-Spy Plane, Attack Helicopter, Chopper Gunner, Gunship, and potentially all four package drop streaks: Sam Turret, Care Package, Sentry Gun, and Valkyrie Rockets.

Not bad for a four-kill Killstreak!

There are a few caveats. First, the SAM Turret does have a line of sight. You have to place it in a position where it can fire up at the sky cleanly, and covering the entire map is usually impossible with a single turret.

Second, an enemy can easily destroy the turret, either up close with a single knife swing or Hacker Pro, or at a distance by simply shooting it.

You can pick up and move your SAM Turret. Feel free to do so if you spot enemy air support that needs repositioning to target.

CARE PACKAGE: 5 KILLS

The Care Package calls in a drop that provides a random Killstreak. This is the only way to get the Grim Reaper or Death Machine if you aren't running Hardline Pro.

A Care Package can contain any Killstreak except the very high-end streaks. Also, they have a greater percentage chance of awarding low-end Killstreaks. You never know what you'll get!

We don't actually recommend running Care Package in most Killstreak loadouts. It's usually a better idea to run a focused Killstreak setup that accomplishes a specific goal.

Care Packages are fun and can occasionally reward you with a higher Killstreak, but the odds are weighted against that. Plus, a random reward doesn't always fit into any particular Killstreak strategy.

The one exception to this rule is if you're running Hardline Pro. In this case, the Care Package arrives at four kills and gives you another shot at reshuffling your reward.

THE GRIM REAPER AND THE DEATH MACHINE

Two very special rewards show up only in Care Packages or in packages reset by Hardline Pro. These are the quad-barreled Grim Reaper rocket launcher and the Chopper Gunner's Death Machine minigun.

These babies last until you run out of ammunition or die. Be sure you're covered by teammates and outside enemy territory before you activate these rare rewards!

Both weapons are extremely powerful, but you're still vulnerable, and you immediately become a high-priority target. Save these weapons until you have the best chance of dealing mayhem and destruction, and be sure to communicate with your team!

If you're actively hunting these Killstreaks, running the Package Frenzy setup with Hardline Pro gives you the best chance of seeing one in a match.

If you really want the best chance, bring some friends all running the same build and litter the battlefield with crates until your reward shows up!

NAPALM STRIKE: 5 KILLS

Napalm Strike calls in an airstrike on a targeted area, aimed in the direction you choose.

The strike delivers a burning payload of Napalm, incinerating anyone within the target zone and killing anyone foolish enough to walk into the flames after the strike lands.

Napalm is ideal for covering objective areas, but it's otherwise less useful for racking up kills. Even with a Spy Plane active, it's difficult to catch most of the enemy team in the open for any length of time.

Napalm is best used for covering objectives or for blocking off a specific chokepoint or route on the map.

Remember that Flak Jacket Pro provides immunity to fire damage, so it's possible either to exploit this or be denied a kill depending on the situation.

SENTRY GUN: 6 KILLS

Sentry Gun delivers a package by helicopter containing your shiny new turret.

This turret can be placed anywhere on the map and automatically attacks any enemy that moves within its frontal arc of fire.

The Sentry Gun is very lethal and kills anyone exposed in the open. But it does not track perfectly and multiple targets can overwhelm it. It can also fail to kill a target that gets behind hard cover quickly enough.

The Sentry is also vulnerable to attacks from the rear, enemies with Ghost Pro or Hacker Pro, explosives, and attacks from Hardened Pro bullets. Furthermore, a single melee strike takes it down. The Sentry Gun also eventually deactivates on its own.

Nevertheless, the Sentry can still be extremely powerful if it's placed carefully. It's very useful for covering objectives, and it can block off a route through a map. Used carefully, you can herd the enemy team down an alternate route.

Multiple Sentry Guns set up simultaneously are even more effective, especially if they're arranged to naturally cover each other. Look for high ground that has a good line of sight, long narrow corridors or alleyways, or open areas with a clear view to an objective. Avoid placing it in an area that has multiple routes in and out or in the open with its rear arc exposed.

You can use C4 or Claymores to help protect your turret. Place these defenses nearby to punish anyone who goes after your turret from its vulnerable rear arc.

MORTAR TEAM: 6 KILLS

The Mortar Team allows you to call in three precision artillery barrages on any three points on the map…or all three in one location. Each barrage drops two powerful explosive shells that kill anyone near the blast area.

The Mortar Team is very useful for removing or suppressing defenders long enough to get into position to secure an objective.

Using Mortar Strikes to take down mobile enemy forces is more difficult, even with a Spy Plane active. Because of the artillery barrage's delay, hitting most of the enemy team is difficult.

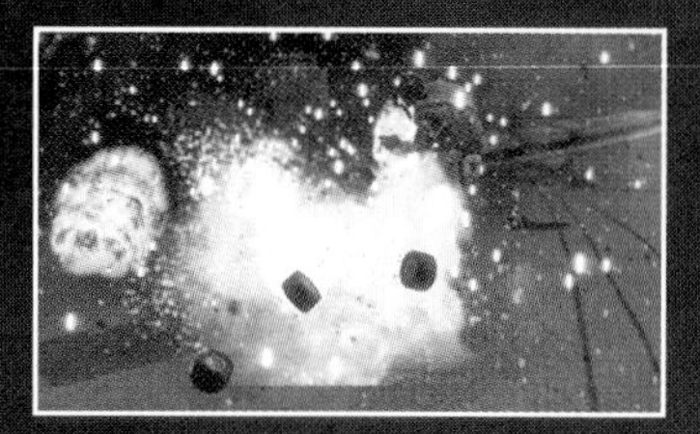

Much like the Napalm Strike, you can pound the enemy team if you save a Mortar Team for the start of a new round and drop the strikes on the most likely path out of their spawn area.

ATTACK HELICOPTER: 7 KILLS

The Attack Helicopter Killstreak calls in a friendly helicopter that automatically patrols the battlefield, shooting down enemy infantry.

You can choose the Attack Helicopter's initial placement on the battlefield. Position it to cover a key objective, or use a Spy Plane to have it cover the enemy team's location.

Left unchecked, the Attack Helicopter is very dangerous. If an enemy Attack Helicopter arrives on the battlefield, remove it as quickly as possible.

This chopper is a very useful streak, as it provides effective air support, allowing you to continue fighting on the ground without worrying about the chopper doing its job.

AIRSPACE FULL

Only one Attack Helicopter, Chopper Gunner, or Gunship can be active at a time. If an enemy chopper is taking up your airspace, shoot it down and replace it with yours!

VALKYRIE ROCKETS: 7 KILLS

Valkyrie Rockets arrive via package drop, so be sure to find a safe place to deliver these—you don't want them falling into enemy hands. Once acquired, using this streak puts the actual Valkyrie launcher in your hands, a specialized missile launcher that can fire two fully guided warheads.

You can control the missiles in flight, and the explosion they make on impact is very large. Fire the missile from a safe area and guide it to your chosen impact zone, or use a Spy Plane to find the largest concentration of enemy forces and go for a massive multi-kill.

To ensure you don't smack the missile into nearby terrain, try to find a launch site that lets you fire the missile vertically, and then guide it back down onto the battlefield.

It's possible to guide the missiles into narrow doorways or windows and detonate them inside buildings, which can be especially devastating if you catch multiple enemies indoors.

If you're playing an objective mode and you get your hands on this launcher, don't fire both missiles immediately—wait to use them until they're needed most.

You can manually detonate Valkyrie Rockets early; they don't need to impact to explode. Try air-bursting a Valkyrie over an enemy position or in the center of a room.

BLACKBIRD: 8 KILLS

The Blackbird activates a super-powered spy plane sweep that provides constant, realtime location and direction indicators of all enemy forces on the battlefield. Only enemies using Ghost Pro fail to show up on your entire team's minimap.

The Blackbird is an extremely powerful Killstreak that can tip the entire battle in your team's favor while it's active.

The Blackbird, unlike the Spy Plane, cannot be shot down once active. The only way to disable it is with a Counter-Spy Plane or indirectly with a Jammer. If the enemy unleashes a Counter-Spy Plane, make shooting it out of the sky your immediate priority, whatever weapon you're using.

Having an active Blackbird can enable your team to rack up high-end Killstreaks quickly in addition to the overwhelming informational advantage it provides.

Apart from unchecked Attack Dogs, a Chopper Gunner, or the Gunship, few other Killstreaks can deal as much damage to an enemy team as the Blackbird.

ROLLING THUNDER: 8 KILLS

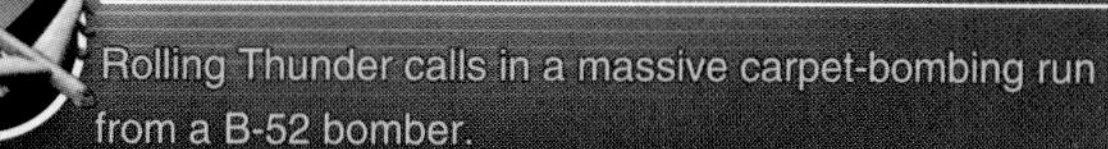

Rolling Thunder calls in a massive carpet-bombing run from a B-52 bomber.

This total-saturation bombing run covers a map from one end to another. Placed carefully, you can lay down a crushing no man's land across an objective and everything nearby.

Wait to use Rolling Thunder until just after a Spy Plane comes online. Check your Pause Menu map to verify enemy positions, and then call in the bombing run.

In objective modes, coordinate Rolling Thunder with your teammates. Allow them to get into position, and let them know just before you call in the strike, so they can capitalize on the damage it delivers.

CHOPPER GUNNER: 9 KILLS

Chopper Gunner places you on a helicopter's minigun as the chopper flies a circular path around the entire map.

From the air, you can fire infinite explosive minigun rounds on the helpless targets below you. If the enemy doesn't take out your ride quickly, you can inflict devastating casualties on their entire team.

Because the Chopper Gunner's route is automatic, there may be moments when you can't fire on the enemy due to the helicopter's position. How often this happens depends on the map and the enemies' locations.

You can expect enemy forces to scurry for hard cover as soon as you unleash the Chopper Gunner. Alert your teammates when you trigger the Gunner, and call out the locations of enemy forces that you can't target—the aerial recon can be almost as lethal as the minigun you wield.

Enemy troops are highlighted by red targeting boxes, though anyone with Ghost Pro is not highlighted. You only need to hit enemies' approximate locations to kill them, so feel free to fire through windows or doorways to nail targets that are just out of sight. Exploit the Chopper Gunner's movement to get new firing angles, taking down enemies who think they're safe in cover.

DEALING WITH AIR POWER

The Attack Helicopter, Chopper Gunner, and Gunship are all dangerous. You should never allow the enemy to keep them on the battlefield for any length of time, particularly the latter two.

The SAM Turret, LAW, RPG, Strela-3, or an LMG with Hardened Pro can take down air support. Note that any hostile attack on the choppers is likely to put you in their sights very quickly.

Of these options, the SAM Turret and Strela-3 are the safest choices. If you don't have a SAM Turret handy, keep a build with the Strela-3 handy once you unlock it.

It's far better to suicide once, change classes, and use your Strela-3 to take down a Gunship than it is to let the enemy rack up a massive killcount against your team.

Plus, trading one death for the crestfallen enemy's day you just ruined by shooting down his 11 Killstreak is always rewarding...

ATTACK DOGS: 11 KILLS

Attack Dogs calls in a pack of vicious canines that continuously pours the edges of the map and attacks any enemy forces.

Enemy fire can kill the dogs, but because so many arrive on the field, defending yourself from a dog strike is difficult at best.

Only targets with Ghost Pro remain untouched by the dogs. So, if you find yourself the victim of an enemy dog attack and you have access to Ghost Pro, quickly switch to a class that uses it and go hunting. Enemies who think they're safe with the dogs in the field make good targets.

Attack Dogs usually make your enemies try to hole up in areas with elevation or limited approach routes so they can shoot the dogs. Be ready for some urban hunting when you call in your own dogs.

When friendly Attack Dogs are active, you can almost always freely secure objectives. If you acquire the dogs at the end of a round in an objective mode, save them for the next round to get an easy win.

GUNSHIP: 11 KILLS

The mighty Gunship Killstreak puts you on the controls of your very own Attack Helicopter.

You have full control over the chopper—you can fly it around the level and fire its miniguns and rockets with abandon.

Enemy targets on the ground are highlighted the same way as they are in the Chopper Gunner. And again, only foes with Ghost Pro remain invisible.

As with Chopper Gunner, use your altitude and enemy marking to call out entrenched targets so your teammates can flush them out for you.

The Gunship has the potential to rack up massive kill totals if your enemies don't take action. If you wind up parked over an open enemy spawn position, they are in for a world of hurt.

If you hear an enemy Gunship hitting the field, immediately suicide and switch to a class with a Strela-3, or use other anti-air options. Never, ever let an enemy Gunship reign unopposed, or your team will pay for it.

An untouched Gunship usually ends the match in an FFA or TDM setting, and it usually results in the loss of all objectives in any mode that features them.

MULTIPLAYER MAPS

These map briefings give you an overview of the major features and terrain on each of the 14 multiplayer maps in *Call of Duty: Black Ops*.

It's very important to remember that the game mode you select for a map dictates the level's flow. High-traffic hotspots in Team Deathmatch may see little or no significant conflict in a Capture the Flag or Domination match.

We've included route maps to highlight a few primary travel pathways in Capture the Flag, Demolition, Domination, Sabotage, and Search & Destroy. Generally, you can expect to see enemy (and friendly) movement along these routes, as well as a good amount of fighting. Of course, each match will have its own personality, so consider the high-traffic paths marked on the following maps to be flexible.

If you need to avoid combat for one reason or another, staying off the hot routes is a good idea. Finding a good location to cover an objective is usually a matter of finding a spot with sight lines to both the objective and at least one hot route that sees a lot of traffic.

Conversely, if you want to hit an objective on offense, you can often find a safer route by avoiding the most obvious pathways to the objective. Coupled with a proper custom class, this approach can often inflict more damage than making a faster but more exposed assault.

When you want to drop a package on the level, areas away from routes and preferably near or behind your friendly spawn area are the safest places to use. This also applies if you seek a hidey-hole to use a guided Killstreak of any sort.

In Free for All, Team Deathmatch, and, to some extent, Wager Matches, it's easy to see the hotspots in-game by viewing the heatmaps of matches you've played. In most cases, they're exactly what you'd expect. Centrally located areas with many routes for ingress and egress are usually the hottest zones.

Surviving in the preceding modes is a matter of skirting hot zones to find targets. Avoid traveling through them as much as possible to limit your exposure to unfriendly eyes.

Headquarters is distinct among all objective modes in terms of flow; combat hotspots and routes change dynamically as the Headquarters moves around the map. See the Modes chapter to learn more about the implications of this.

Take the time to look over the HQ locations marked on the maps. After you spend some time playing, you should get a better feel for good routes to approach the HQ safely, cover the HQ, or cut off the enemy team.

On any map, good, solid *Call of Duty* play is always important. Stay behind cover, move quickly from cover to cover, don't sprint around blind corners, and be alert around doorways and windows.

Communicate with your teammates and learn the maps. By using the alpha-numeric coordinates on the map (these match up identically with the in-game minimap), you can quickly call out enemy positions and movement. A well-coordinated team that communicates is very tough to beat.

ARRAY

Terrain	Arctic
Key Features	Huge, centrally located communications array; open, snowy exterior.
Map Size	Large
Map Profile	Scattered exterior building cover. Some CQB in array interior.

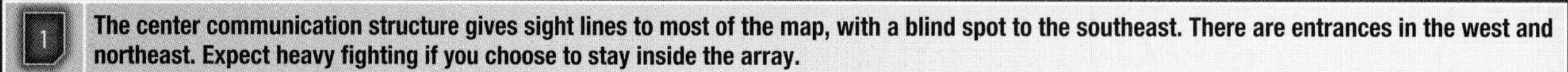

1	The center communication structure gives sight lines to most of the map, with a blind spot to the southeast. There are entrances in the west and northeast. Expect heavy fighting if you choose to stay inside the array.
2	This sniper tower provides excellent, elevated sight lines, but it's also highly exposed to incoming fire. Use with caution.
3	The map's eastern portion has a significant amount of cover. In most modes, it's not a hotspot for conflict. As a result, this area is good for moving around from the north to the south without coming into conflict with the level's more active central region. You can also use this area as a drop zone for packages.
4	The northwest hill acts as a meeting point for several pathways between the north and the south to the west of the array. As a result, expect plenty of combat in this area. Remember that the larger finished building acts as solid cover and blocks sight lines. Meanwhile, the smaller unfinished building is not a safe place to take cover.
5	The map's southwest isn't a great place to camp, but it does provide access to one of the two array entrances. You can get around the array safely by moving through its blind spot to the east.

Array is a large, snowy level set around a huge communication array station in the center.

The bulk of this level's conflict occurs in and around the communication array. The inner structure has sight lines to most areas outside, allowing any gunner inside to take out enemies in the open.

When you traverse the outer "ring," it's important to use the available cover to protect you from multiple sight lines. If you're careful and you move fast from cover to cover, you should have little to worry about from enemies inside the array. Keep your focus on external threats. Just be aware if someone in the array targets you—don't make yourself an easy target.

The level's northwest attracts action because it's an open area that the center structure's windows can cover. Several pathways and spawn points intersect in the area.

Be cautious about hiding out in the northwest. There aren't a lot of great places to hide. Because this area acts as a highway for conflict just outside the array, it's usually not a safe place in which to fight for any length of time.

Medium to long-range combat reigns supreme here, so bring your Assault Rifle or Sniper Rifle. You can make good use of an LMG, but the movement penalty is rough. Take Marathon to let you get around the map if you're insistent on using an LMG.

If you want to force shorter-range engagement, bring an SMG and go for the array itself. Don't bring a Shotgun because there's too much ranged combat and few areas where you can continually fight in close quarters.

SEARCH & DESTROY

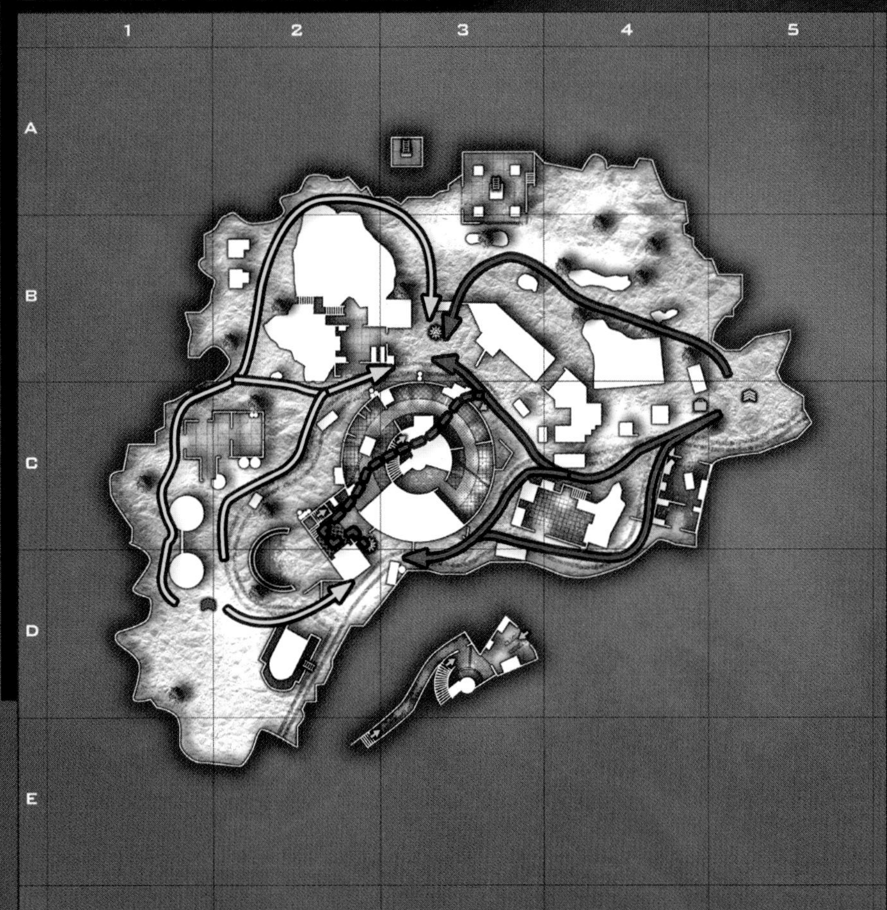

DOMINATION

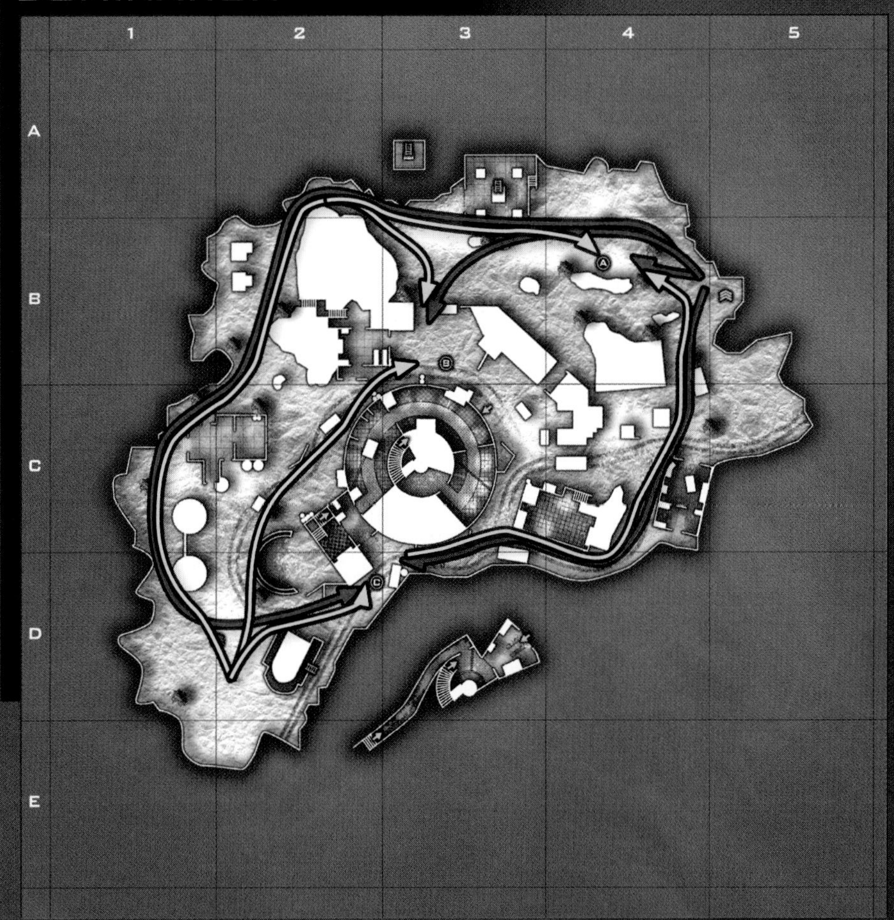

EQUIPMENT TIPS

	C4	Can be used at the entrances to the array itself, difficult to use as a booby trap elsewhere.
	CAMERA SPIKE	If you plan on sticking around in one part of the outer ring, you can use a Camera Spike to cover your blind spot.
	CLAYMORE	Not a lot of great chokepoints to cover, but it can block an entrance to the array.
	JAMMER	Fairly useful if placed in the array itself, less so in the outer ring. To clear the array, set one up before you assault it. Alternatively, place one inside once you've claimed it.
	MOTION SENSOR	Useful in the array, but due to the structure's size, covering all possible entryways isn't possible.
	TACTICAL INSERTION	Be careful where you place your Insertion—the glow can reveal it from a good distance.

SUGGESTED CUSTOM CLASSES

SILENT SERPENT

PRIMARY/ SECONDARY	PSG1/Crossbow	
ATTACHMENTS	Variable Zoom	
LETHAL/TACTICAL/ EQUIPMENT	Tomahawk/Decoy/Motion Sensor	
PERK 1	Ghost	
PERK 2	Scout	
PERK 3	Ninja	
KILLSTREAKS	RC-XD/Counter Spy Plane/ Mortar Team	

This class has you fully outfitted with everything you need to be the best sniper you can be.

WINTER WONDERLAND

PRIMARY/ SECONDARY	Enfield/Crossbow	
ATTACHMENTS	ACOG	
LETHAL/TACTICAL/ EQUIPMENT	Frag/Nova Gas/ Tactical Insertion	
PERK 1	Hardline	
PERK 2	Sleight of Hand	
PERK 3	Ninja	
KILLSTREAKS	RC-XD/Mortar Team/Valkyrie Rockets	

Put on your snowy best and cover long-range and close-quarters engagements with this class.

HEADQUARTERS

DEMOLITION

ARRAY

CAPTURE THE FLAG

SABOTAGE

CRACKED

WAGER MATCH VARIANT

Terrain	Urban
Key Features	Bombed-out central "hill" area; many damaged rooms and buildings.
Map Size	Medium
Map Profile	Intense building-to-building CQB. Many windows and doorways; dangerously exposed open streets.

1	The bombed-out and ruined center of the map is a constant hotspot. Avoid moving through here whenever possible.
2	The far southeast building has a window that provides sight lines all the way up toward B4, which is useful if you're using a strong long-range weapon.
3	This cracked building provides coverage of the western corridor up toward C2. However, be wary of your exposure to the east toward D3.
4	The two buildings at C3 and C4 are conveniently connected. Moving around in them provides plenty of cover and sight lines through the center and east of the map.
5	This building is the only structure on the map's northwest that has a window looking south. Use it with caution, because anyone in the center of the level can easily spot you and shoot through the thin wall.

KEY

	SOG Spawn
	NVA Spawn
	Bomb-Search & Destroy / Sabotage Modes
	Search & Destroy / Demolition Plant Site
Ⓐ Ⓑ Ⓒ	Domination Flags
	SOG CTF Flag
	NVA CTF Flag
	Headquarters Point
	Ladder
	SOG Sabotage Plant Destination
	NVA Sabotage Plant Destination
	Arrows are color-coded to match the levels that they lead to

Cracked is a small urban warfare map, the bombed-out remains of a riverfront Vietnamese city.

Cracked demands good situational awareness. Use caution when you set up for camping, or employ rapid movement and aggression to cover ground and take down your targets.

We recommend either running a CQB build with a Shotgun or SMG, or a build designed for medium-range combat with an AR or LMG. You can use sniping on this map, but few locations are completely safe from being flanked. Getting a good sight line over the entire level is impossible.

If you're going for CQB, use defensive and stealthy gear choices. You need to cross open streets and alleyways likely to be covered by campers in various buildings with longer-range weaponry.

If you can get behind the enemy position, you can deal a lot of damage with a CQB setup. This is especially true if you're running a silencer and opponents don't pick up on your presence until it's much too late.

For medium-range combat, consider camping to cover the alleys and streets. Many buildings with windows overlook various parts of the map. Because you can't cover all possible approaches, either work solo and bring equipment to cover your own tail, or communicate with your teammates to block routes from the enemy spawn to your position.

You become very vulnerable to long-range retaliation or an explosive lobbed through the window if you hang out for too long. Try one spot, grab a few kills, and then move to another position. At the very least, try another angle on the same area.

SEARCH & DESTROY

DOMINATION

EQUIPMENT TIPS

	C4	When you're advancing, C4 is useful as an extra explosive to toss into a room. When camping, you can plant it in an alleyway approach that you're already covering. You can occasionally use it to cover your six as well.
	CAMERA SPIKE	Very useful. Plant it at the end of one of the streets and slice a visual tripwire directly across the entire map. If the other team doesn't notice it, you always know when they're coming. Just watch out for people using Ghost Pro or smoke to evade your all-seeing eye.
	CLAYMORE	Very useful as well. If you're camping, drop it to guard one of the main entrances to your hideout. Even when you play aggressive, you're almost guaranteed to get a kill out of your Claymore if you place it properly in a high-traffic area.
	JAMMER	Strong in the center of the map. Cracked isn't a large map, and the Jammer can cover a lot of it, shutting down enemy equipment and blinding them as they approach midfield.
	MOTION SENSOR	Very helpful when camping. Be highly sensitive to enemy Motion Sensor usage on offense. Either run Hacker Pro or use a Jammer to shut down enemy Sensors.
	TACTICAL INSERTION	Very useful in a lot of modes. There are tons of nooks and crannies where you can hide a Tactical Insertion. If you're running a CQB build, bring an Insertion to move your spawn point once you get behind enemy lines. The only thing better than clearing out the enemy team once is doing it twice because you spawned behind them.

SUGGESTED CUSTOM CLASSES

WALL-EY

PRIMARY/ SECONDARY	HK21/Python	
ATTACHMENTS	Extended Mag/ACOG	
LETHAL/TACTICAL/ EQUIPMENT	Frag/Flashbang/Motion Sensor	
PERK 1	Scavenger	
PERK 2	Hardened	
PERK 3	Marathon	
KILLSTREAKS	Spy Plane/Sentry Gun/Attack Dogs	

This powerful combo keeps you stocked with ammo to spray through this map's many walls with deadly results.

PAIN TRAIN

PRIMARY/ SECONDARY	RPK/China Lake	
ATTACHMENTS	Extended Mag	
LETHAL/TACTICAL/ EQUIPMENT	Semtex/Nova Gas/Claymore	
PERK 1	Lightweight	
PERK 2	Steady Aim	
PERK 3	Marathon	
KILLSTREAKS	Counter Spy Plane/Care Package/ Sentry Gun	

Use this class to run-and-gun your way through the many buildings with plenty of rounds to spare.

HEADQUARTERS

DEMOLITION

CAPTURE THE FLAG

SABOTAGE

CRISIS

WAGER MATCH VARIANT

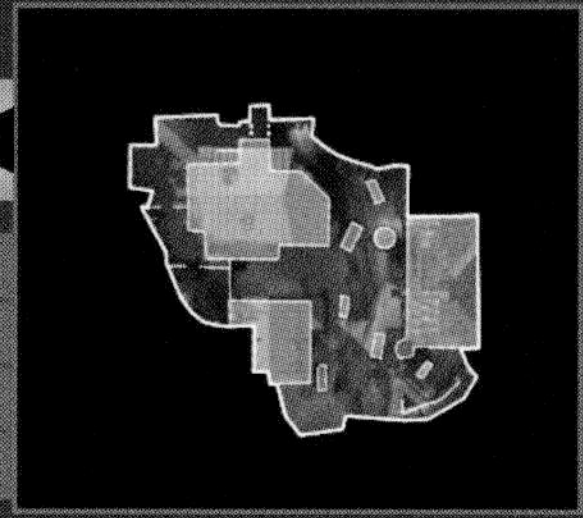

Terrain	Mixed beachfront and urban
Key Features	Centrally located missile base; beachfront landing zone (north); rundown buildings (south).
Map Size	Large
Map Profile	Mixed terrain. Combat ranges from mid-long-range to CQB depending on location.

1	This point encompasses two areas: a lower missile storage facility and an upper overwatch area that covers both the beach approach and the map's southern area, connected to D3. The lower missile base is connected to both halves of the map as well, but we don't recommend traveling through it.
2	There are many possible routes through the beach area, making it an extremely dangerous area to cover. You can use a ladder to climb a boulder on the western part of the beach, giving you a decent elevated position. Otherwise, we recommend moving swiftly through this area.
3	The southeast open area is at a meeting point between several routes to the map's south. As a result, it's often a hotspot for conflict. If you're traveling through this position, move quickly.
4	This building provides elevation, good sight lines, and multiple egress points if you're overwhelmed, including a route to the upper area. Try to lock down this point building to dominate the map's southern half.
5	This sniper tower has excellent sight lines over the map's southern part, but it's dangerously exposed. You can safely drop off the perch by mantling over the edge and dropping onto the vehicles to the west, southeast, or the stone post to the south. We recommend the southeast drop point, as it has the least exposure to the center area.

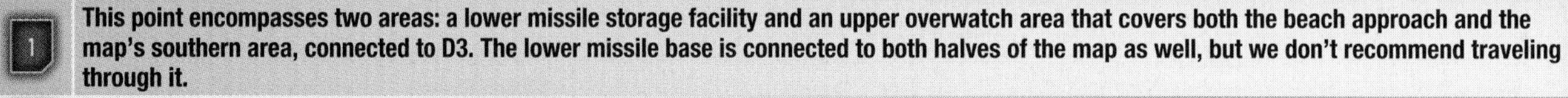

KEY

Icon	Meaning
	OP 40 Spawn
	Tropas Spawn
	Bomb-Search & Destroy / Sabotage Modes
	Search & Destroy / Demolition Plant Site
Ⓐ Ⓑ Ⓒ	Domination Flags
	OP 40 CTF Flag
	Tropas CTF Flag
	Headquarters Point
	Ladder
	OP 40 Sabotage Plant Destination
	Tropas Sabotage Plant Destination
	Arrows are color-coded to match the levels that they lead to

Crisis is a Cuban missile base featuring a range of terrain to over which to fight. In the north, a beachhead populated by several troop transports provides a wide-open firefighting arena with some coastal rocks as cover.

In the center of the map, an underground missile bunker provides a route between the north and south, or you can move over the top of it on the hill itself.

In the map's south, several old and partially ruined buildings offer a mix of CQB and midrange outdoor fighting.

Crisis is a flexible map for loadouts. The mode you're playing dictates what you choose. Almost any weapon setup can be effective depending on where you spend the bulk of your time fighting.

Because this is a multi-area, multi-terrain map, the multitasking Assault Rifle is always a safe choice, especially if you don't want to specialize into short or long-range combat.

In most modes, we don't recommend hanging around on the beach if you can avoid it. You're simply too exposed to long-range fire. Set up shop in the south of the map, preferably in the building connected to the hilltop. This gives you good access to much of the level, and plenty of cover on demand.

When moving around the map, try to avoid passing through the lower missile base area, unless you're packing a CQB build and you can take advantage of the dark, close combat.

SEARCH & DESTROY

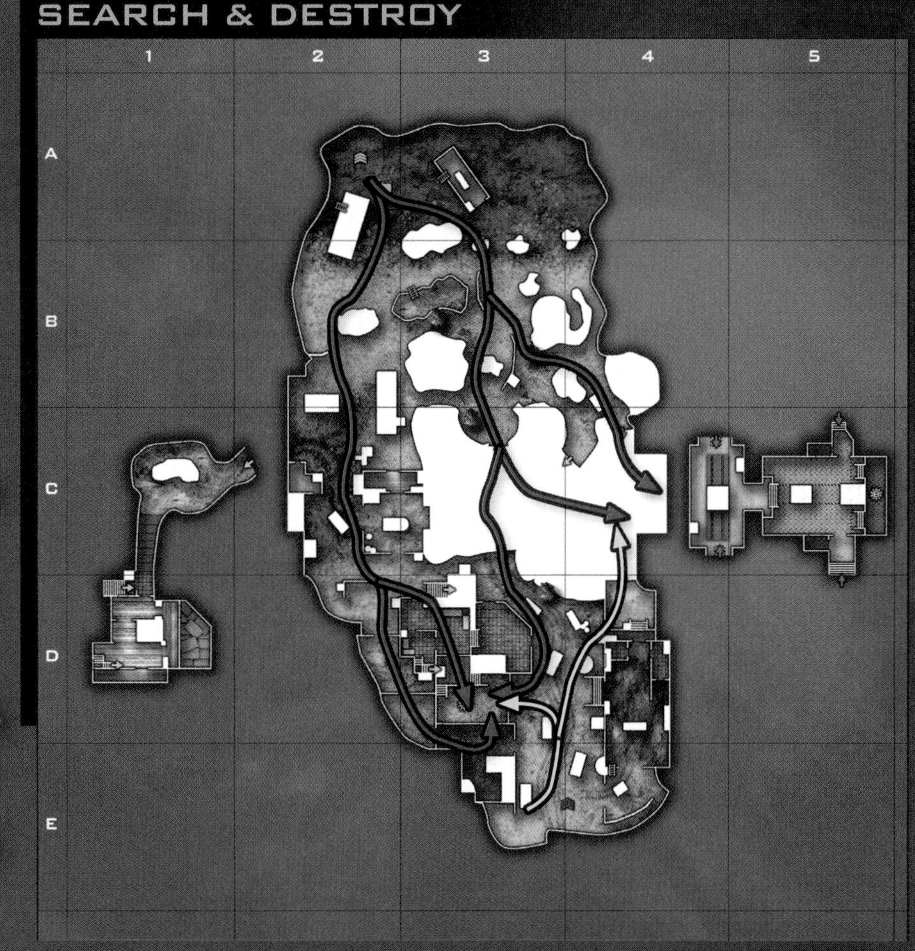

DOMINATION

EQUIPMENT TIPS

	C4	Limited utility here. There aren't a lot of key chokepoints to cover, and there are few defensive positions or camping spots to flush out. Save it for objective modes to cover specific objectives.
	CAMERA SPIKE	Moderate utility. If you're playing defense on an objective mode, it can provide useful visual coverage of one route between the level's north and south.
	CLAYMORE	Can be somewhat handy on defense, but again, there aren't many chokepoints on this map. However, setting one up on the hilltop or in the buildings to the south can often net you a kill.
	JAMMER	Handy in the center of the map, but there aren't many spots to hide it from enemy discovery. If you set one up, stay nearby to protect it —pick it up and move it if necessary.
	MOTION SENSOR	Very handy if you can drop one unnoticed near the middle of the map, as you can spot enemy forces traveling through the middle. Just be careful you don't mix up an enemy on the lower level with one on the upper!
	TACTICAL INSERTION	Useful in objective modes, as it's a good hike from one end of the map to the other. If you can shave off some of that time with an Insertion, it's worth bringing.

SUGGESTED CUSTOM CLASSES

THE SPORT

PRIMARY/ SECONDARY	Galil/Makarov	
ATTACHMENTS	IR scope & Suppressor/ Suppressor	
LETHAL/TACTICAL/ EQUIPMENT	Frag/Nova Gas/Tactical Insertion	
PERK 1	Ghost	
PERK 2	Warlord	
PERK 3	Ninja	
KILLSTREAKS	SAM Turret/Sentry Gun/Attack Dogs	

HEADQUARTERS

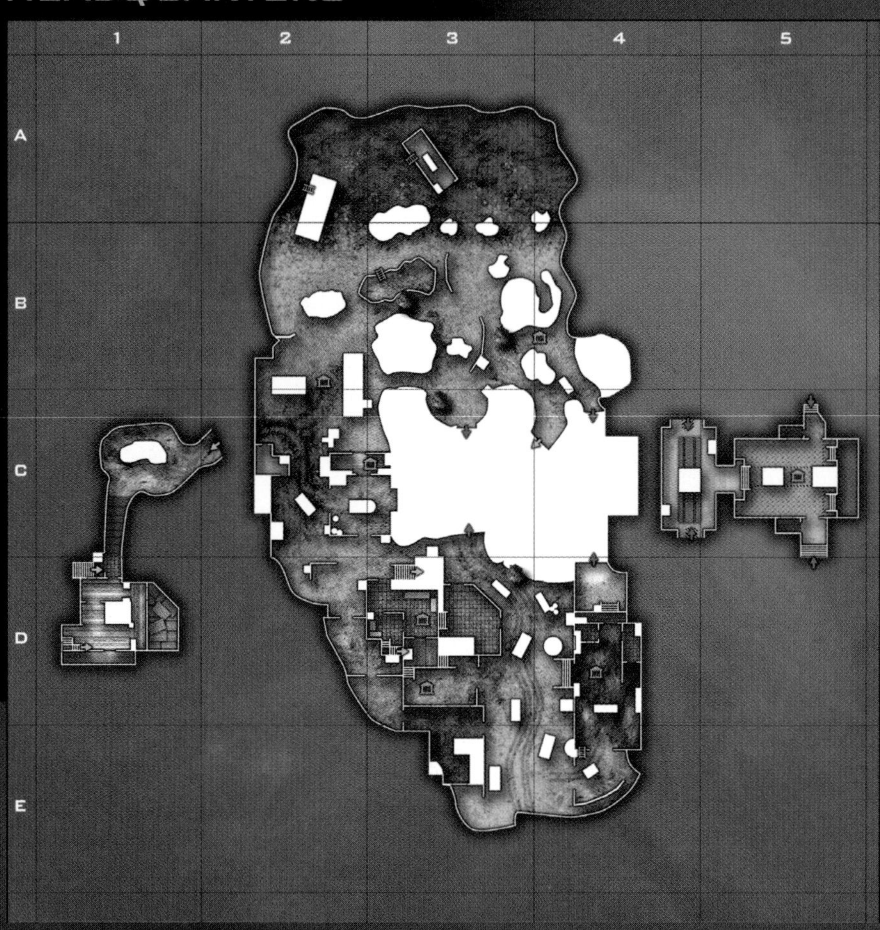

DEMOLITION

CRISIS

CAPTURE THE FLAG

1 2 3 4 5

A B C D E

SABOTAGE

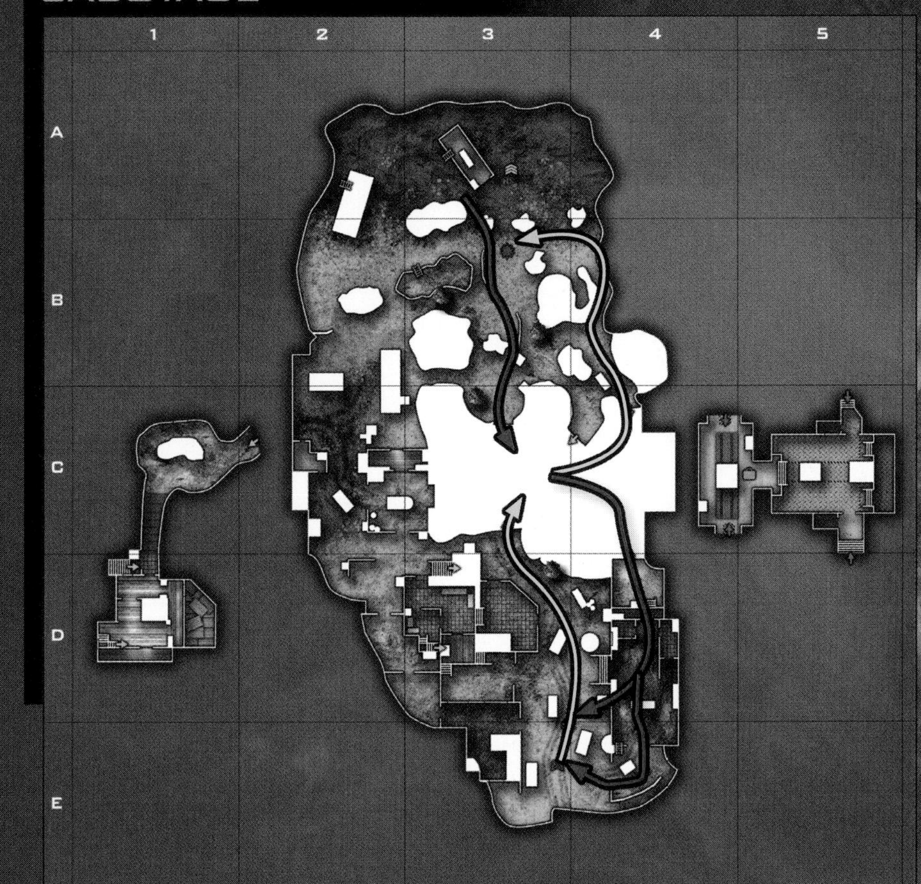

FIRING RANGE

Terrain	Urban military training grounds
Key Features	Multiple faux buildings and target dummy silhouettes.
Map Size	Small
Map Profile	CQB firing range; mix of urban structures and narrow pathways.

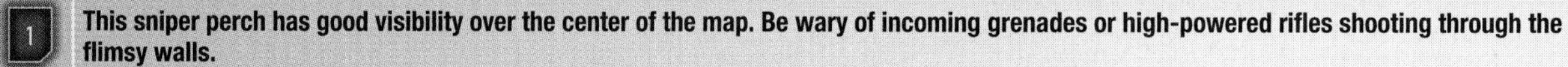

1	This sniper perch has good visibility over the center of the map. Be wary of incoming grenades or high-powered rifles shooting through the flimsy walls.
2	This area tends to see a lot of conflict; be cautious about traveling straight through in the open.
3	From the lower part of the range, you can travel to the upper-western half via three routes: north, center, or south. You can cover all three routes. Communicate with your teammates to find the safest path, or bring gear to force one.
4	You can climb up and into this building from three directions: south over a training target, in the building up a set of stairs, or from the north by climbing onto some sandbags or rocks.
5	The C3 building provides elevation and good coverage of multiple areas, but it lacks great defensive cover. Exploit the building's virtues, but be ready to bail out if you come under heavy fire.

KEY

	Black Ops Spawn
	Tropas Spawn
	Bomb-Search & Destroy / Sabotage Modes
	Search & Destroy / Demolition Plant Site
Ⓐ Ⓑ Ⓒ	Domination Flags
	Black Ops CTF Flag
	Tropas CTF Flag
	Headquarters Point
	Ladder
	Black Ops Sabotage Plant Destination
	Tropas Sabotage Plant Destination
	Arrows are color-coded to match the levels that they lead to

Firing Range is a small combat training ground.

Despite its small size, Firing Range has a lot of cover and plenty of interesting mini combat areas.

This map is ideal for SMGs, and Shotguns can do reasonably well. AR and LMG usage requires that you pick your fights carefully at a distance. This also applies to the Sniper Rifle, which can be better than you'd expect here, due to the long sightlines on the three east/west routes through the map.

There is a lot of cover, as well as multiple buildings with many entry and exit routes. This makes Firing Range a great map if you have good situational awareness and movement skills. It can be a nightmare if you aren't careful because you can get flanked easily.

When combat isn't channeled by an objective, most of the conflict concentrates around the central C2 grid area. Spend some time moving around these buildings and learning where you can climb, jump, or mantle to get around.

If you're traveling through the map east/west in an objective mode, note that there are only three possible channels through the level. Either pick your path carefully or bring gear to help force an entrance. Stealth won't work. Smoke, Flashbangs, explosives, and the Jammer can all help break through.

SEARCH & DESTROY

DOMINATION

EQUIPMENT TIPS

	C4	Potentially very useful for blocking the three east/west routes. Also quite useful in objective modes. The small spaces and buildings on this level make C4 detonations deadly.
	CAMERA SPIKE	Useful for covering any one of the three main routes, or for cutting a north/south tripwire on the map's western portion.
	CLAYMORE	Useful in the buildings, but harder to use on the main routes without it being spotted. Unlike C4, you can't go sticking a Claymore on a nearby wall or ceiling.
	JAMMER	Quite useful. The hard part is keeping it standing once the enemy triangulates its location.
	MOTION SENSOR	Very helpful on either the west or east side of the map, as you can use it to monitor incoming enemy positions easily.
	TACTICAL INSERTION	Save it. This map is too small to demand Tactical Insertion positioning.

SUGGESTED CUSTOM CLASSES

ERASER

PRIMARY/ SECONDARY	M60/Crossbow	
ATTACHMENTS	Extended Mag	
LETHAL/TACTICAL/ EQUIPMENT	Semtex/Willy Pete/Claymore	
PERK 1	Ghost	
PERK 2	Hardened	
PERK 3	Hacker	
KILLSTREAKS	SAM Turret/Napalm Strike/Rolling Thunder	

Gear up with this class and shred the plywood walls that populate this map. Use the supplied "stickable" explosives to dig enemies out of their tents.

MAVERICK

PRIMARY/ SECONDARY	G11/Ballistic Knife	
ATTACHMENTS	Variable Zoom	
LETHAL/TACTICAL/ EQUIPMENT	Frag/Flashbang/Camera Spike	
PERK 1	Scavenger	
PERK 2	Hardened	
PERK 3	Second Chance	
KILLSTREAKS	RC-XD/Care Package/Chopper Gunner	

Use the Camera Spike as your wingman with this class. Ice enemies from a distance with your variable-scoped assault rifle.

HEADQUARTERS

DEMOLITION

CAPTURE THE FLAG

SABOTAGE

GRID

WAGER MATCH VARIANT

Terrain	Arctic Urban Base
Key Features	Two large, centrally located structures; open, snowy field in the east.
Map Size	Small
Map Profile	Mix of interior CQB and mid-range, open fighting.

1 2 3 4 5

A B C D E

KEY

	Black Ops Spawn
	Spetznaz Spawn
	Bomb-Search & Destroy / Sabotage Modes
	Search & Destroy / Demolition Plant Site
Ⓐ Ⓑ Ⓒ	Domination Flags
	Black Ops CTF Flag
	Spetznaz CTF Flag
	Headquarters Point
	Ladder
	Black Ops Sabotage Plant Destination
	Spetznaz Sabotage Plant Destination
	Arrows are color-coded to match the levels that they lead to

1	The center of Grid is not a safe area. Avoid running through here if possible.
2	It's possible to mantle onto this thin wall from the north. Then you can jump into the window to the east to get into the D3 building quickly.
3	You can get into this window by mantling up from the ground level and jumping over, or by jumping across from the small building to the southwest.
4	This open field offers limited visual cover from trees and brush, but no hard cover. You may want to use it as an airdrop point.
5	This building is littered with RC-XD tunnels. If you're an RC enthusiast, go hunting in here. An extra tunnel leads into the creek from C3 to D4.

Grid is a small arctic level with a pair of multi-level office buildings facing each other. There are two other conflict zones: one to the west in front of a pair of concrete bunkers, and another to the east in an open field.

This is a relatively simple level. Much of the combat takes place in the center of the level and in the two buildings, as both teams struggle to dominate the elevated sight lines.

Simply by choosing where to fight, you can play this map effectively with either a CQB or a medium-range build. If you want to dominate the structures, take your CQB loadout. If you want to stay out in the open and pick off targets at a distance, go for one of your medium-range (or longer) setups.

Combat flow on this map depends heavily on the game mode you play. Because of the size, objectives change where the fighting focuses. Match your build with your preferred role and the objectives you need to tackle.

This is one of several maps that have special RC-XD tunnels. You can use them to drive your remote bomb while avoiding enemy attempts to shoot it. Tunnels run through the northern building, and one runs through the southern building's lower level.

If you're going for a CQB setup, either bring along a cooperative teammate to watch your back or bring equipment to do the job for you. Both structures have too many routes in and out to cover by yourself. You can enter the north building from the ground level, or you can jump into it from the truck in the center.

The southern structure has ground-level entrances, and two different jumps from the west and southwest can get you onto the second level quickly.

For longer-range combat, you're somewhat safer behind cover on the map's west half. There is very little hard cover on the field to the east, and it has very poor sight lines to the center of the map. Generally, you only want to be out there in a few specific objective modes, unless you're dropping a package or using it to traverse the map away from the central field.

SEARCH & DESTROY

DOMINATION

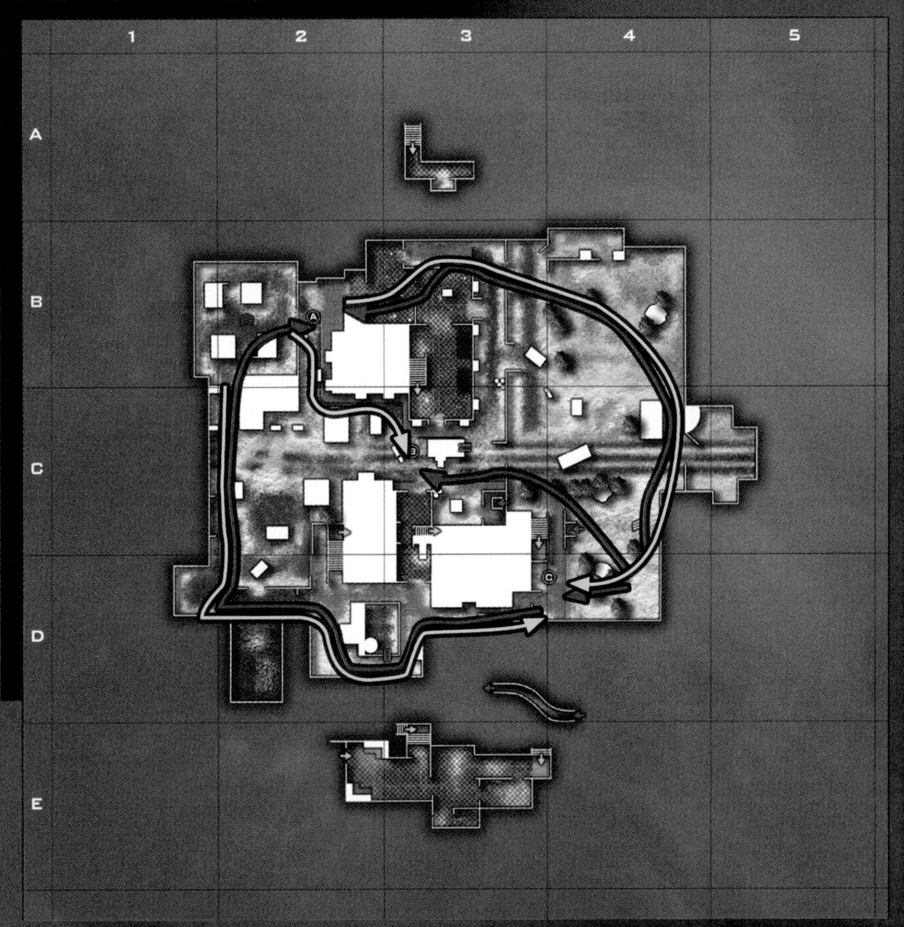

EQUIPMENT TIPS

	C4	Best saved for objectives. There aren't many key chokepoints you can cover easily.
	CAMERA SPIKE	Somewhat hard to use here. Because there are only two main buildings and they're open from three or four sides, covering multiple approach avenues is hard to do. You can use it in some objective modes to watch one path to the objective.
	CLAYMORE	Very helpful inside the buildings—almost a guaranteed kill if you place it properly.
	JAMMER	Quite effective in the center of the map. You can drop it in several corners inside the buildings, and it's guaranteed to cover a good chunk of the midfield.
	MOTION SENSOR	Very useful for camping out in either structure. This is your best choice for covering your back if you're camping alone.
	TACTICAL INSERTION	Only mildly useful on this map. There isn't a lot of ground to cover, and the most likely spots to drop your Insertions get a lot of traffic.

SUGGESTED CUSTOM CLASSES

IN COUNTRY

PRIMARY/ SECONDARY	Dragunov/CZ75	
ATTACHMENTS	Variable Zoom & Suppressor/Full Auto Upgrade	
LETHAL/TACTICAL/ EQUIPMENT	Frag/Decoy/Camera Spike	
PERK 1	Ghost	
PERK 2	Warlord	
PERK 3	Second Chance	
KILLSTREAKS	Counter Spy Plane/Attack Helicopter/Attack Dogs	

This quiet sniper class can keep you popping heads from a distance or shredding bodies up close.

LONG RANGER

PRIMARY/ SECONDARY	PSG1/Python	
ATTACHMENTS	Variable Zoom/Speed Reloader	
LETHAL/TACTICAL/ EQUIPMENT	Frag/Willy Pete/Motion Sensor	
PERK 1	Flak Jacket	
PERK 2	Scout	
PERK 3	Hacker	
KILLSTREAKS	SAM Turret/Rolling Thunder/ Gunship	

Dig in and snipe from a distance with the gear in this class. Use the Motion Sensor to get the drop on enemies closing in on you.

HEADQUARTERS

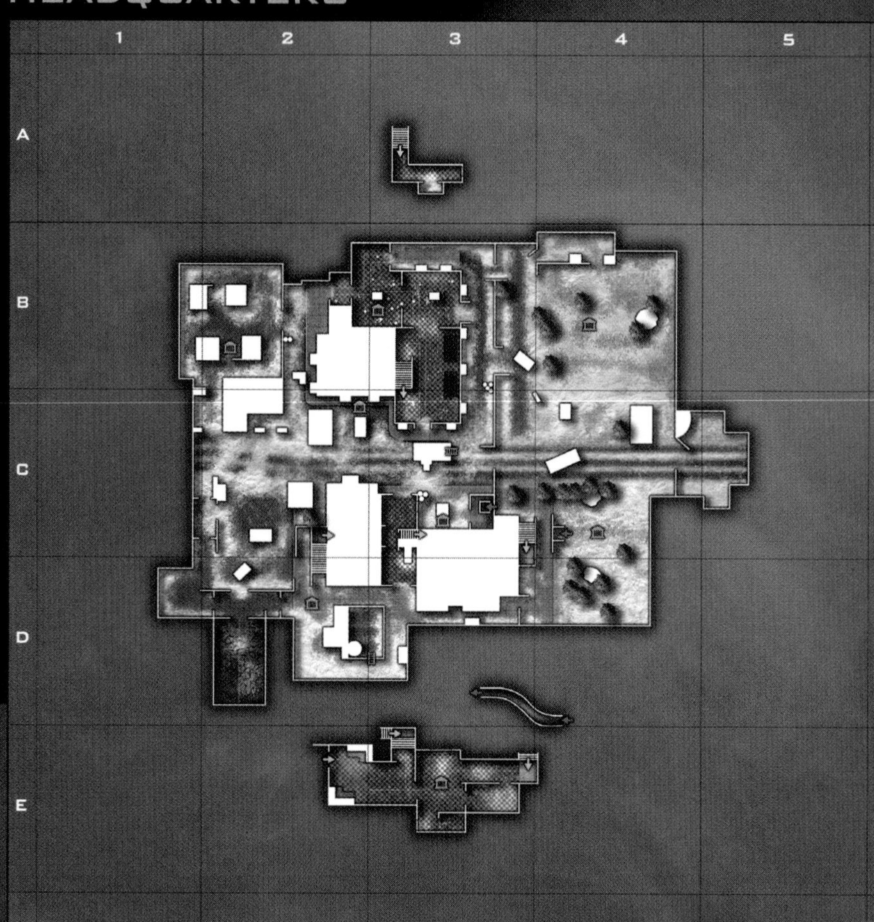

DEMOLITION

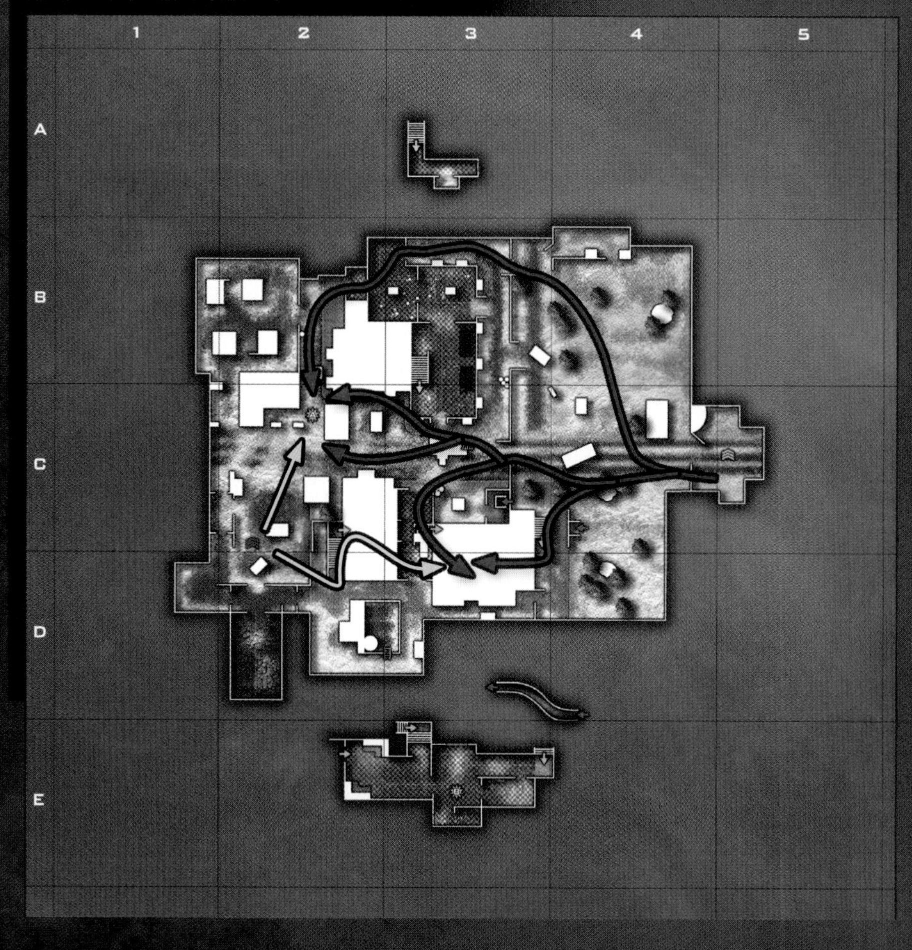

CAPTURE THE FLAG

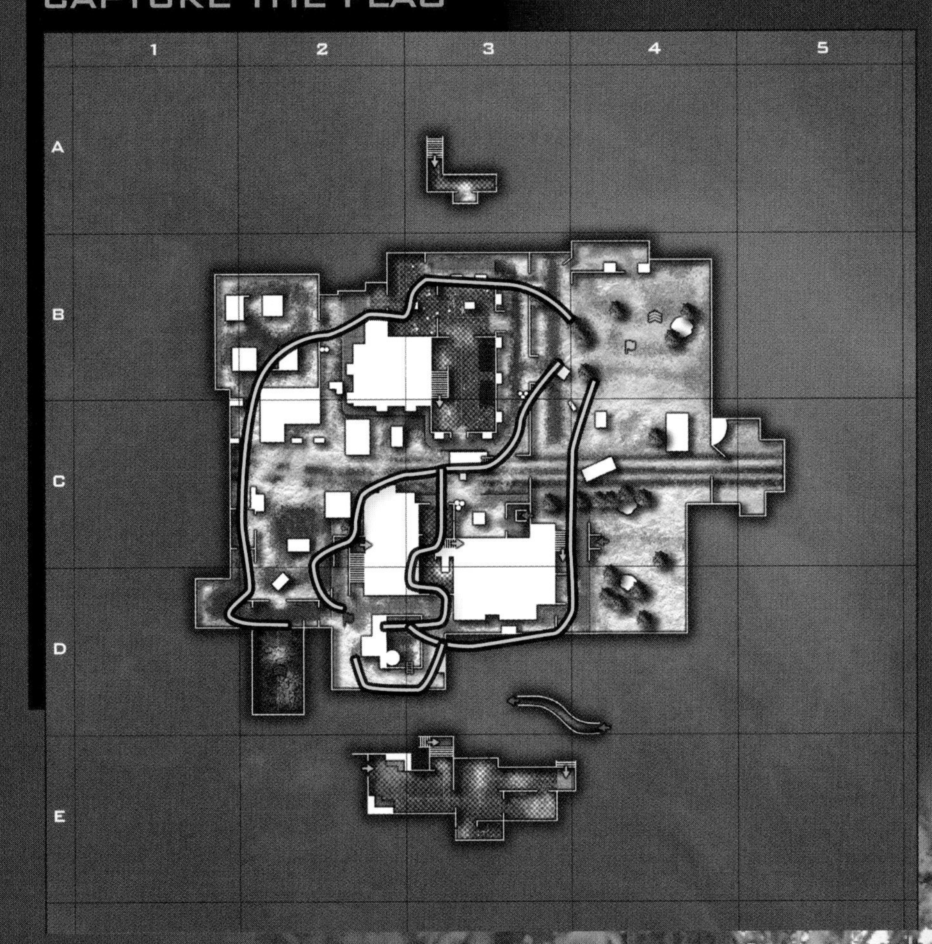

SABOTAGE

HANOI

WAGER MATCH VARIANT

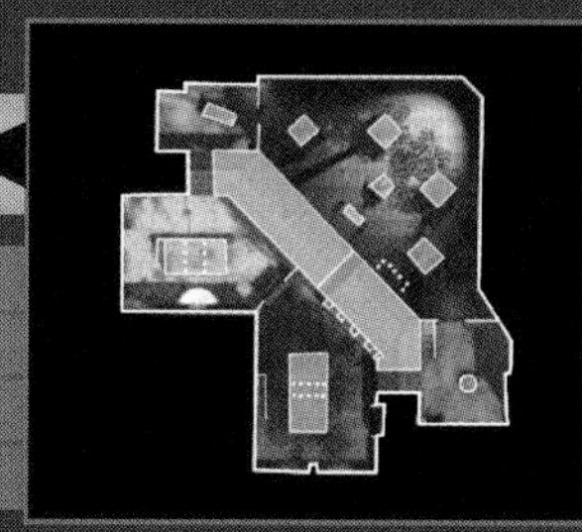

Terrain	Urban
Key Features	Open courtyards surrounded by long, narrow buildings.
Map Size	Large
Map Profile	Mixed mid- and long-range combat. Limited possibility of CQB in buildings.

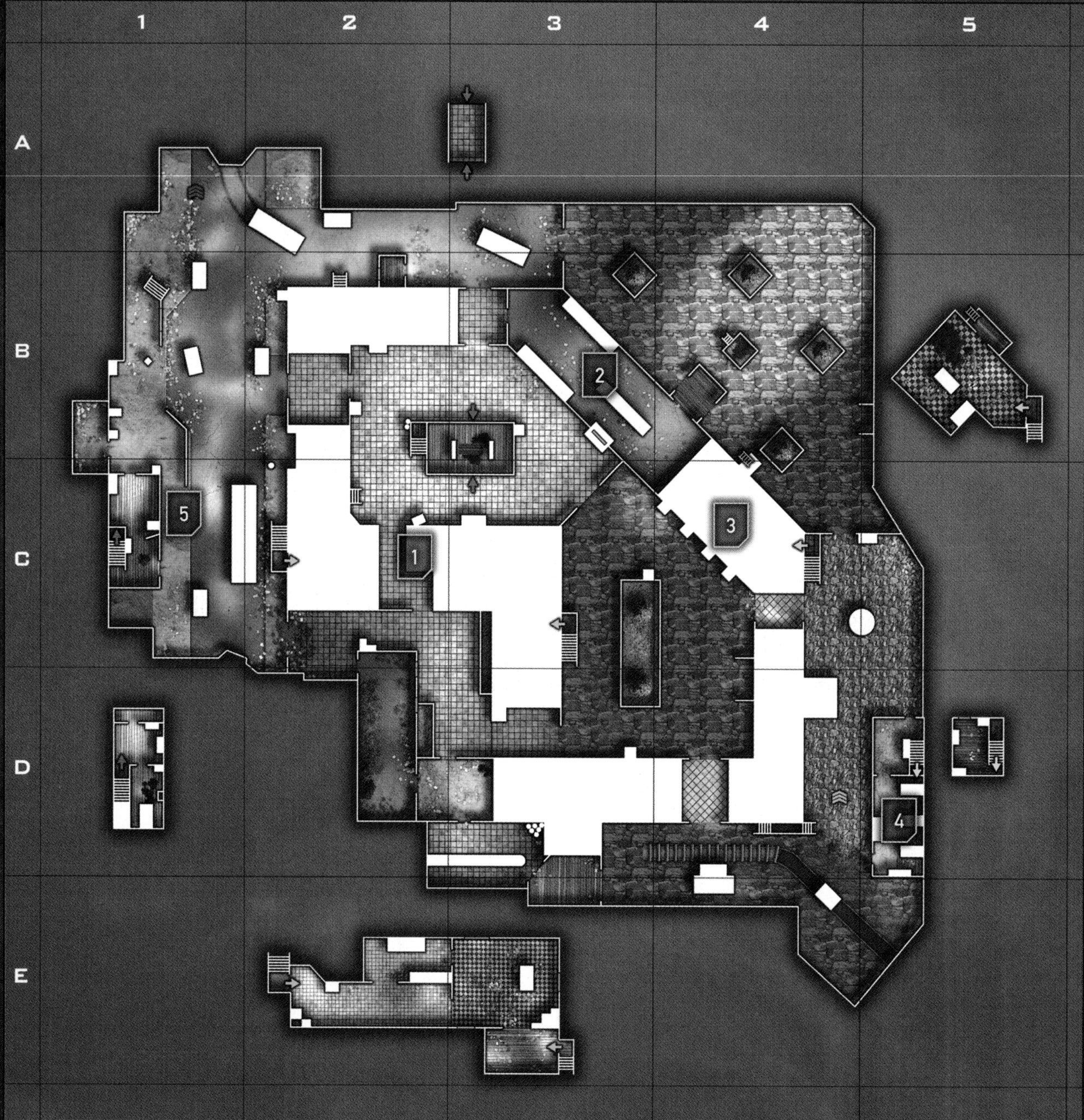

1	You can climb into the propaganda movie room from the execution grounds just north of this point. This is one of two second-floor rooms that offer good overwatch on multiple parts of the map.
2	This passage provides quick access between the inner and outer northeast areas, as well as a ladder leading up to the execution room at C4.
3	This execution room overlooks the planter in the center of the map, as well as another way in or out of the map's outer ring.
4	This building has two windows. You can exit one onto a rooftop, which provides good overwatch for the outer southeast ring area.
5	This building has two doors and windows on each of its two levels, giving you decent sight lines on the western outer ring area.

KEY	
	SOG Spawn
	NVA Spawn
	Bomb-Search & Destroy / Sabotage Modes
	Search & Destroy / Demolition Plant Site
Ⓐ Ⓑ Ⓒ	Domination Flags
	SOG CTF Flag
	NVA CTF Flag
	Headquarters Point
	Ladder
	SOG Sabotage Plant Destination
	NVA Sabotage Plant Destination
	Arrows are color-coded to match the levels that they lead to

Hanoi is a prison complex consisting of two inner courtyards surrounded by a perimeter of long, narrow buildings.

You can use a larger outer ring around the map for stealthy travel. This area typically doesn't see as much action as the buildings or center courtyards.

Hanoi has very unusual flow in all modes. Despite open buildings wrapping around the map's center, many buildings have limited access, and some have no access at all. Some have two floors, while others have only one.

As a result, combat tends to be broken up into discrete firefights that move around the level. Where they move depends on where people spot the action and where objectives force players to go.

A pair of two-story buildings is in the central prison ring: one to the east and one to the southwest. Try to control these structures. Two-story buildings are also to the west and southeast on the outer ring, but your problem here is player traffic. Generally, they're useful only on certain objective modes in which you're sure to see enemies cross your line of sight.

Whenever you can, avoid moving through the center courtyards. There are many ways in and out of them, they see a lot of traffic, and they offer almost no cover. If you move through them, watch enemy positions and keep friendly support nearby, or make sure you use a good stealth setup.

You can use the streets outside the prison to travel more safely from point to point. Try to hug the walls and any available cover, and avoid running into the middle of the streets.

SEARCH & DESTROY

DOMINATION

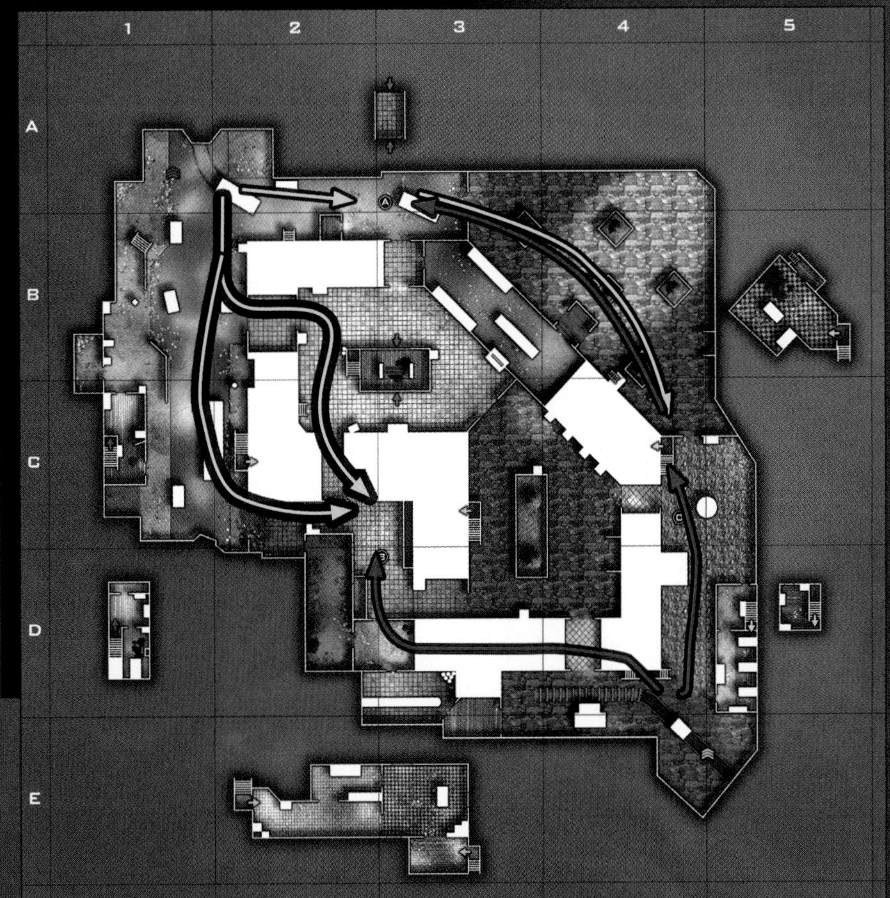

EQUIPMENT TIPS

	C4	Useful only in objective modes. Hanoi's irregular combat zones don't lend themselves well to chokepoints. Unless you're willing to sit and watch your C4 in one location, it's hard to get kills with it.
	CAMERA SPIKE	Potentially very useful in objective modes. There are clear sight lines on the outer streets and in some of the buildings. A well-placed Spike can cover one approach for you with ease.
	CLAYMORE	Fairly effective in the high-traffic, contested structures in C2 and C4.
	JAMMER	Varies. In objective modes, hiding one near your goal can be effective. Otherwise, hiding one near whichever building you're trying to hold can be helpful.
	MOTION SENSOR	Quite useful if you're trying to dominate either of the two-story buildings and want some protection from flankers.
	TACTICAL INSERTION	Very useful in objective modes. You must cross a fair amount of dangerous ground to reach your targets. A well-placed Insertion can save you a lot of time. Just be careful where you put it. This is a dark map, and the glow from your Insertion is easy to see.

SUGGESTED CUSTOM CLASSES

CANDLEPOWER

PRIMARY/ SECONDARY	AK47/Crossbow	
ATTACHMENTS	Flamethrower	
LETHAL/TACTICAL/ EQUIPMENT	Semtex/Nova Gas/Claymore	
PERK 1	Flak Jacket	
PERK 2	Sleight of Hand	
PERK 3	Tactical Mask	
KILLSTREAKS	Napalm Strike/Sentry Gun/ Chopper Gunner	

Light 'em up with this high-caliber, fiery kit complete with explosive-tipped crossbow!

SAVIOR

PRIMARY/ SECONDARY	Commando/Crossbow	
ATTACHMENTS	Flamethrower	
LETHAL/TACTICAL/ EQUIPMENT	Semtex/Decoy/Claymore	
PERK 1	Ghost	
PERK 2	Steady Aim	
PERK 3	Ninja	
KILLSTREAKS	Counter Spy Plane/Sentry Gun/ Blackbird	

Save your buddies and eliminate the enemy with extreme prejudice. This class can help you clean up the mess in Hanoi.

HEADQUARTERS

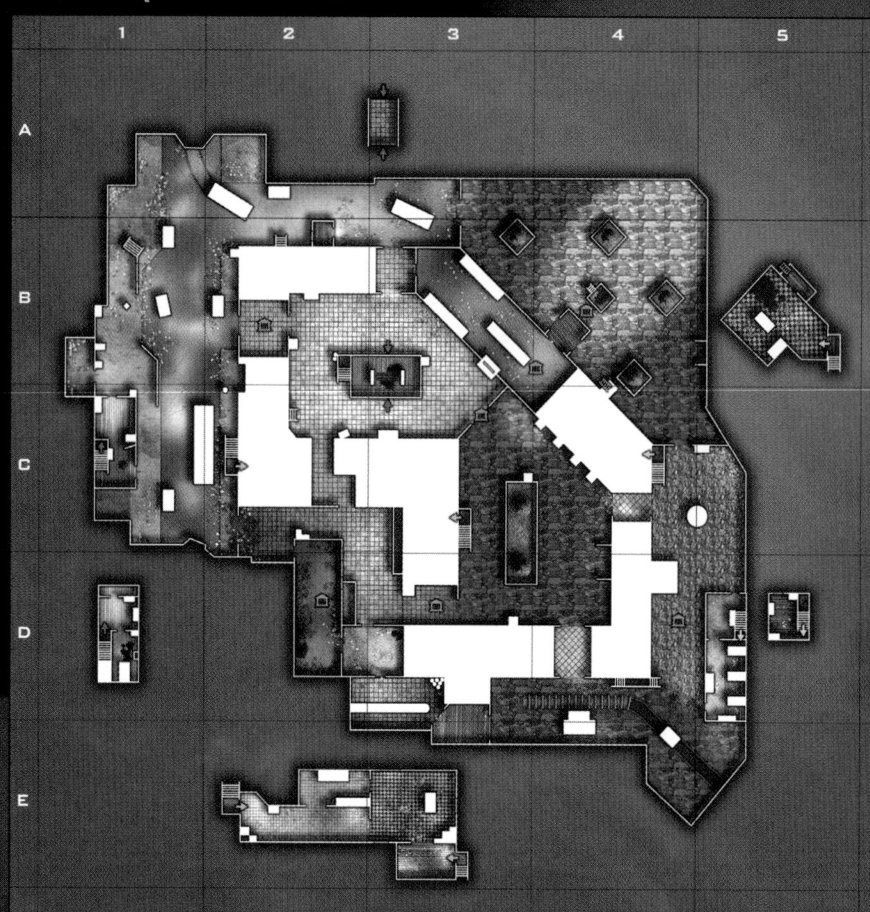

DEMOLITION

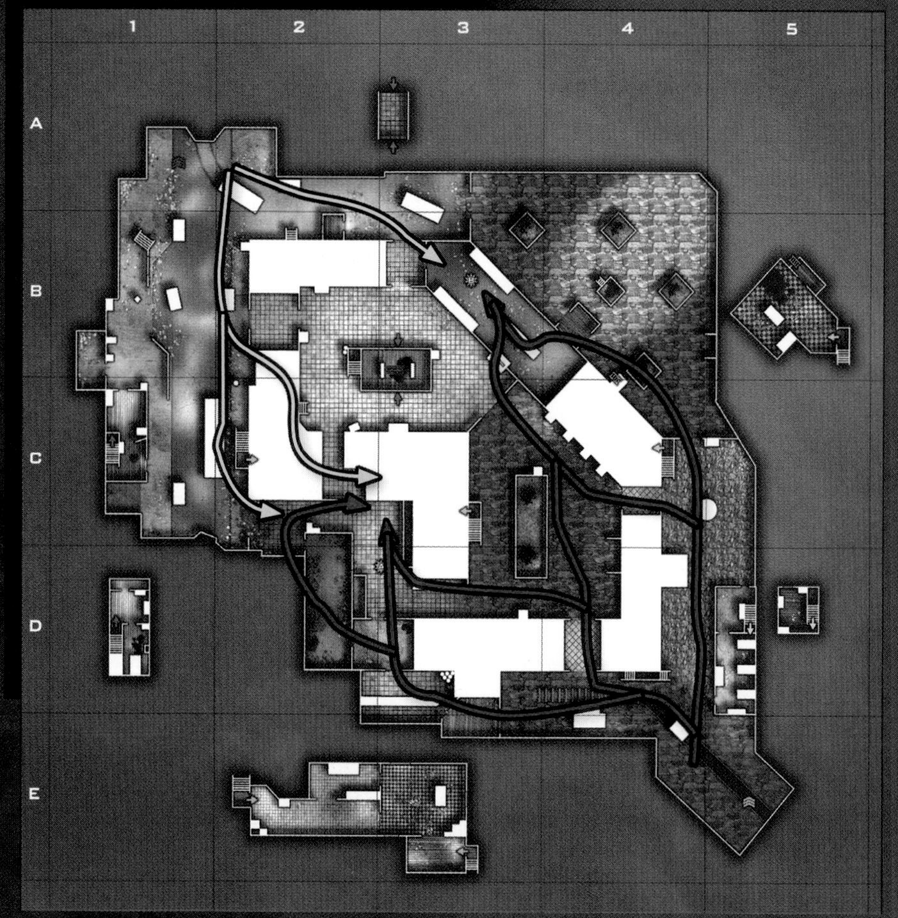

CAPTURE THE FLAG

SABOTAGE

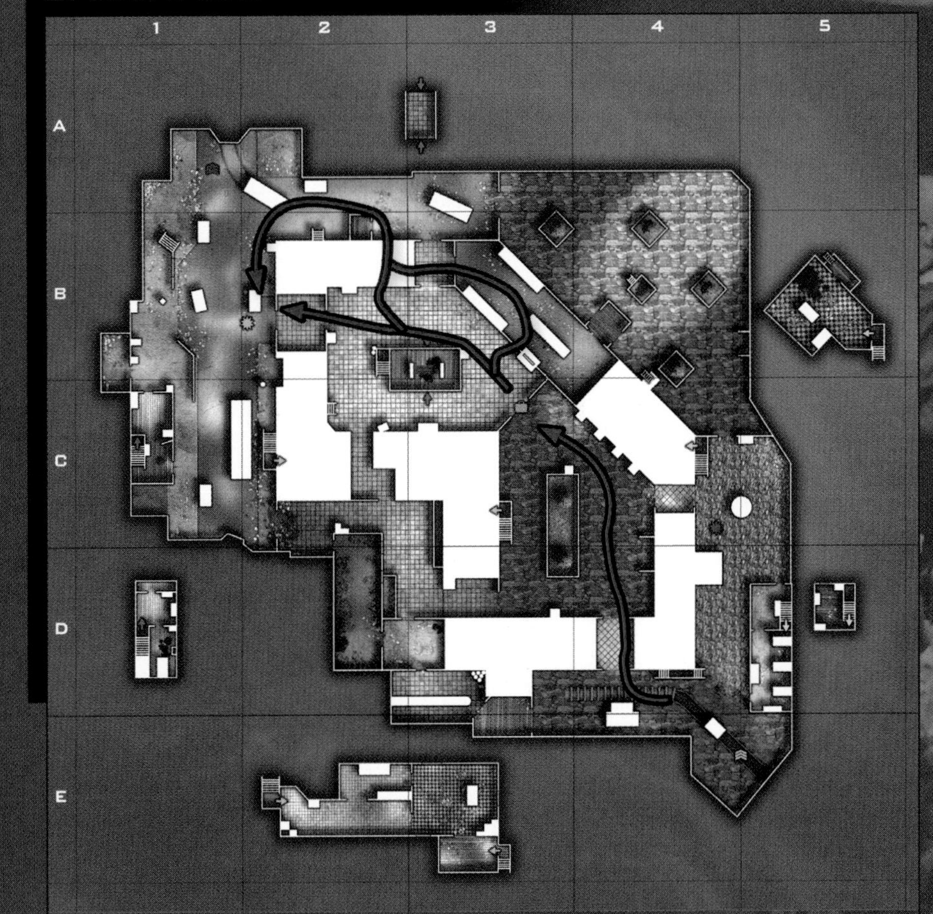

HAVANA

WAGER MATCH VARIANT

Terrain	Urban
Key Features	A broad city street marks the center path through the entire map.
Map Size	Medium
Map Profile	Intense CQB on both sides of the street; medium- and long-range firefights across the street.

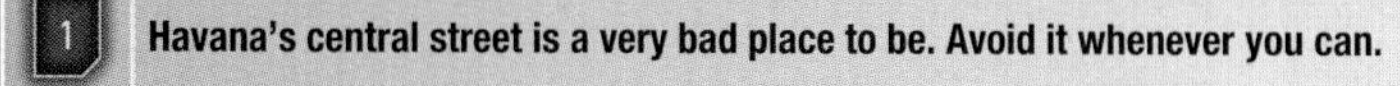

1	Havana's central street is a very bad place to be. Avoid it whenever you can.
2	Both this building and the opposing one at E3 are very similar. They have excellent sight lines up the central street, but they're vulnerable to snipers and flanking attacks.
3	Multiple routes lead in and out of this two-story hotel. Exploit its flexibility to mix up your path through the structure and to escape if you come under attack.
4	This hotel has two floors, but a less complex rear area. Therefore, evading pursuit is somewhat more difficult here than it is at the buildings across the street.
5	The rear alleys are a great way to travel north/south while avoiding the central street.

KEY

Symbol	Meaning
	OP 40 Spawn
	Tropas Spawn
	Bomb-Search & Destroy / Sabotage Modes
	Search & Destroy / Demolition Plant Site
Ⓐ Ⓑ Ⓒ	Domination Flags
	OP 40 CTF Flag
	Tropas CTF Flag
	Headquarters Point
	Ladder
	OP 40 Sabotage Plant Destination
	Tropas Sabotage Plant Destination
	Arrows are color-coded to match the levels that they lead to

Havana is an S-shaped street flanked by multiple small buildings. Plenty of cars and galleries offer limited cover on the main street. Back alleys and buildings provide safer travel north and south.

Much of Havana's combat takes place either at a distance on the main street or on the buildings to either side—a mix of hotels, restaurants, and residential structures.

Take your CQB builds up the east or west sides, or cover the street from the northeast or southwest using a long-range setup.

Depending on the mode, you're usually confined to one end of the street with your team. If you manage to push up to midfield, you may be able to use the balconies on the central street's east and west. Otherwise, avoid them because you're dangerously exposed from the front and rear.

The street itself is a no man's land. Avoid being out in the open on it unless you have a very good idea of exactly where the enemy team and your teammates are. Too many people can watch the street from too many locations to make navigating it a safe proposition.

The street's southwest and northeast ends are often objective targets, but you can also use them to catch a breather and drop off a package.

The two buildings at the north and south ends are ideal for LMGs, Sniper Rifles, or scoped ARs. They are also very obvious camping spots, so be ready for long-ranged retaliation if you set up shop inside one of them.

Of the two side paths, the east is more straightforward, with only a single two-level hotel providing passage. The west is a maze of buildings with a lot more crossover, making it ideal for sneaking through if you have the right loadout.

SEARCH & DESTROY

DOMINATION

EQUIPMENT TIPS

	C4	C4 can be useful early in a match, when the cars are still on the battlefield. Plant your C4 near a car in the street, and then set up shop covering the street from a distance. The resulting explosion is very large, not to mention very fatal to anyone nearby.
	CAMERA SPIKE	The Camera Spike is very useful for covering the street's far north and south bends. Set it up at one end, facing west or east. You get instant warning of anyone crossing into your back field. If you camp at the north or south buildings, this gives you easy warning of enemy forces.
	CLAYMORE	A Claymore can be very dangerous in the structures on the west side. You can often catch someone in the buildings to the east as well.
	JAMMER	Very useful on the west or east, where it blots out anyone's map coming into the CQB areas and shuts down nearby enemy gear.
	MOTION SENSOR	Useful if you patrol the east or west sides with a CQB setup. Just be careful because there aren't many safe places to camp in either area. Stay alert with your eyes and ears, as well as your sensor.
	TACTICAL INSERTION	You can hide an Insertion in a decent number of places around the map. However, it's risky due to the level's small size and the potential for it to be discovered, as there are so few viable routes north and south.

SUGGESTED CUSTOM CLASSES

STREET RAT

PRIMARY/ SECONDARY	AUG/China Lake	
ATTACHMENTS	ACOG Sight & Masterkey	
LETHAL/TACTICAL/ EQUIPMENT	Semtex/Concussion/Camera Spike	
PERK 1	Hardline	
PERK 2	Warlord	
PERK 3	Second Chance	
KILLSTREAKS	RC-XD/Sentry Gun/Gunship	

Blast second-story rooms and scope down the long streets with this class. Switch to the underslung shotgun for clearing this map's many rooms.

PORK CHOP

PRIMARY/ SECONDARY	HS10/RPG	
ATTACHMENTS	Dual Wield	
LETHAL/TACTICAL/ EQUIPMENT	Tomahawk/Nova Gas/Claymore	
PERK 1	Scavenger	
PERK 2	Hardened	
PERK 3	Second Chance	
KILLSTREAKS	RC-XD/Sentry Gun/Attack Dogs	

Clean up the streets with this devastating class. Clear rooms with the shotguns and streets with the RPG!

HEADQUARTERS

DEMOLITION

CAPTURE THE FLAG

SABOTAGE

JUNGLE

WAGER MATCH VARIANT

Terrain	Jungle
Key Features	Shallow creek winding through the center of the map; bombed-out village.
Map Size	Small
Map Profile	Mixed high/low elevation and mid-range combat.

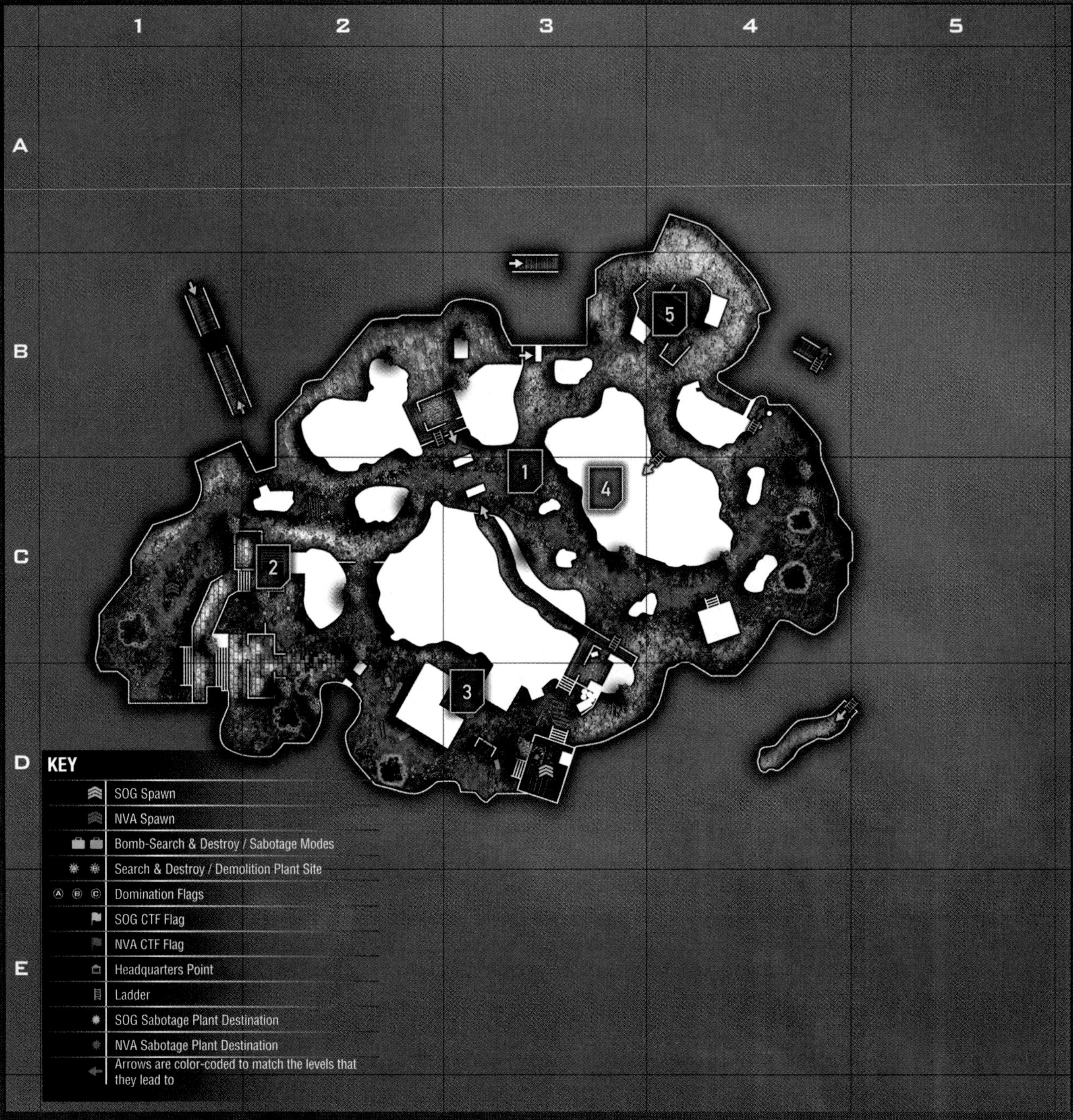

1	The lower central river is the danger zone on this map. Stay out of it and stay alive.
2	The ruins area has good cover and multiple paths through it. It acts as the meeting point between the river and the southern village.
3	The village exits north to the ruins and east out to the rice paddy fields. There isn't a lot of great cover here, so be careful about trying to set up camp.
4	This sniper perch has decent visibility, but it's also an extremely obvious camping spot. Hop up for a few kills, but don't stay too long, or you can expect unfriendly explosives at your feet.
5	This small bunker has good connectivity to other areas of the level, but it isn't a great place to hang out. Move through quickly, pick your destination, and keep moving.

Jungle is a small, intense, medium-range map with good connectivity and many blocked sight lines that prevent easy cross-map sniping.

Assault Rifles work very well here, though you can dip up or down a range band and use SMGs or LMGs effectively. Both extreme weapons, Snipers and Shotguns, are harder to use, though they can be effective if you pay careful attention to where you engage the enemy.

Jungle is divided into a few areas by ruins, boulders, and overgrown foliage. A blasted-out village sits beside an ancient set of ruins to the southwest. A makeshift sandbag bunker sits atop a hill in the northeast. Two small bridges pass over a shallow creekbed that winds through the center of the map. Finally, a dangerously open bombed-out area sits beside rice paddies to the southeast.

Oh, and don't walk in the fields, or a land mine could blow you to bits.

Because the map is chopped into many discrete sections, pay attention to the connections between the different areas. Always have a teammate (or some equipment) watching your back, as it's difficult to cover all the approaches alone.

The central area connects to all parts of the map, but it's also the most exposed. Try to minimize your time spent in the open near mid-field. Moving around the map's outer edges usually lets you concentrate on what's ahead of you rather than what's off to your sides and rear.

Spend some time getting familiar with each chunk of the map. Each one has distinct sight lines and approaches you need to learn.

Mobility is important on this level, because a whole team can push out to several different directions from the map's east or west sides. Be prepared to shift your position constantly to respond.

SEARCH & DESTROY

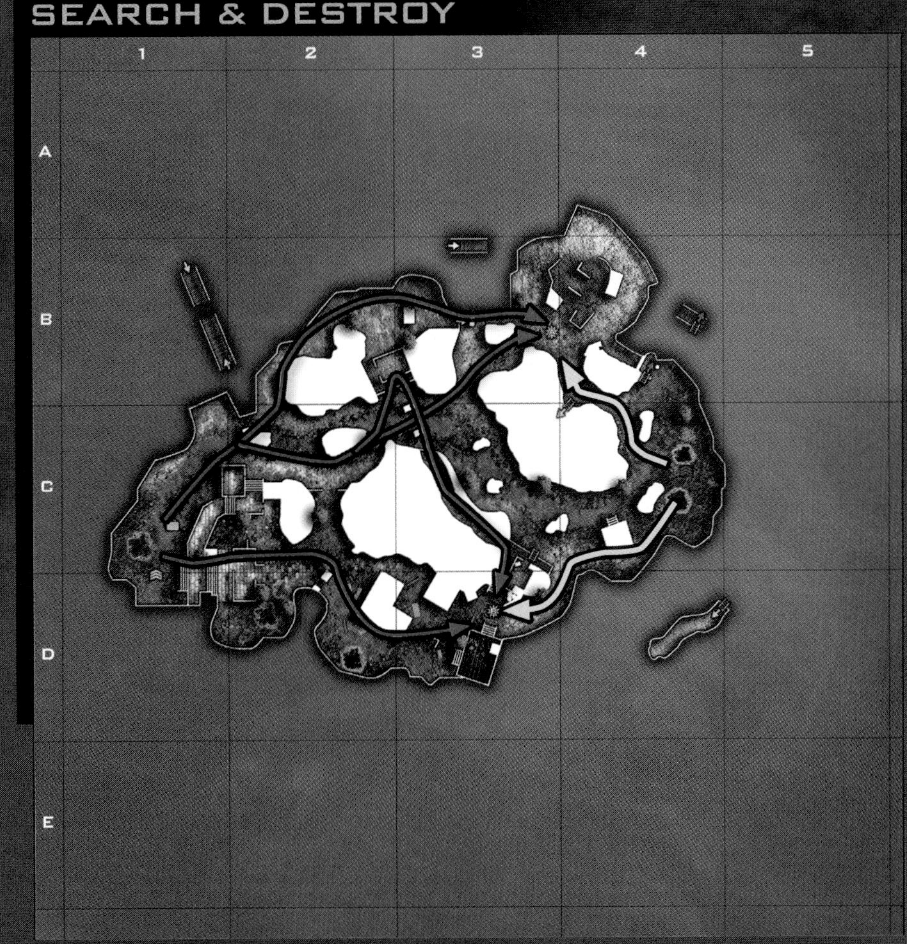

DOMINATION

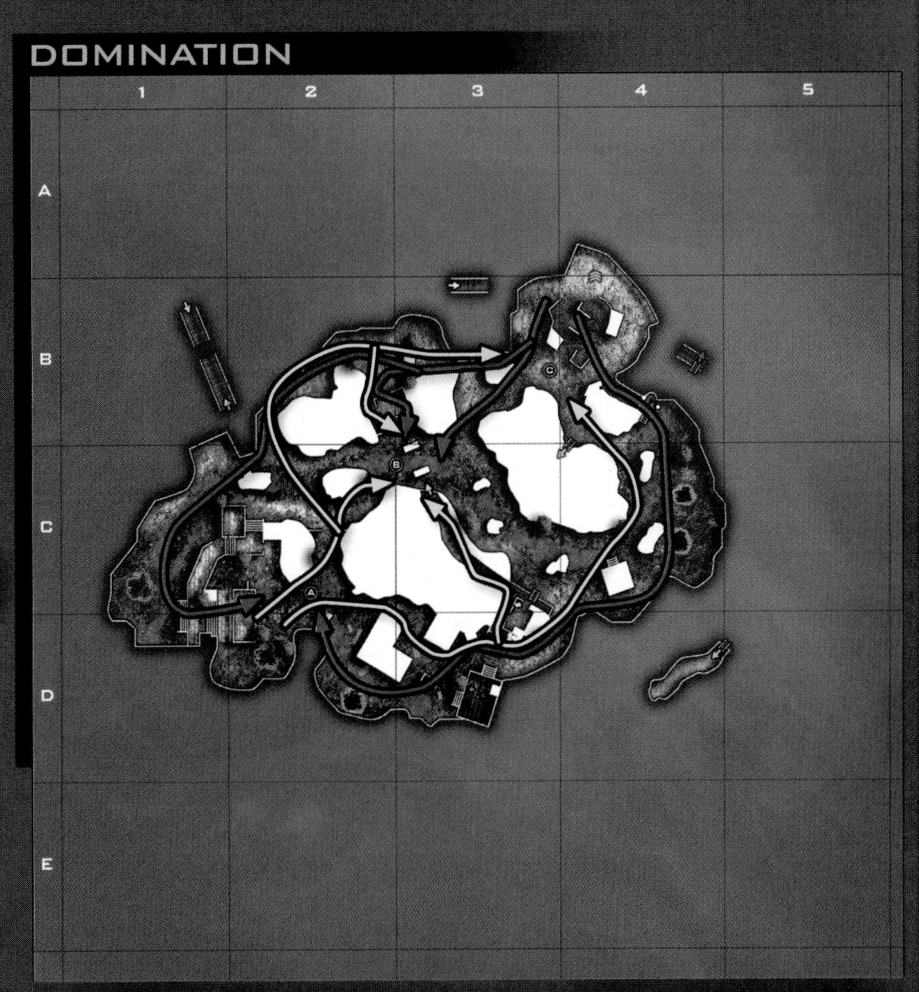

EQUIPMENT TIPS

	C4	A few key chokepoints, such as the bridges and the sniper perch, are ideal for planting C4.
	CAMERA SPIKE	Potentially useful in objective modes in the southwest and northeast, where you can use it to watch one approach. Safer to use if you have some teammates who can also keep you updated on enemy movements.
	CLAYMORE	Somewhat useful. You can use it in the ruins or village in the southwest, or near the bridge and ramp exits in the northeast.
	JAMMER	Effective but hard to hide. There simply aren't many places you can conceal a Jammer for long, though it's effective in mid-field as long as you can keep it active.
	MOTION SENSOR	Somewhat useful. With no significant urban structures, you usually don't have much time between the sensor warning and an enemy being on top of you. The Motion Sensor can be helpful in objective modes to cover a rear approach.
	TACTICAL INSERTION	Few hiding places and a small map size conspire to reduce the Insertion's utility here.

SUGGESTED CUSTOM CLASSES

P.O.W.

PRIMARY/ SECONDARY	M60/Crossbow	
ATTACHMENTS	Extended Mag & Grip	
LETHAL/TACTICAL/ EQUIPMENT	Tomahawk/Decoy/Claymore	
PERK 1	Lightweight	
PERK 2	Warlord	
PERK 3	Ninja	
KILLSTREAKS	Napalm Strike/Valkyrie Rockets/ Attack Dogs	

This class feeds your need to succeed in the jungle—plenty of ways to set up traps and send the enemy running from fire and dogs!

GET TO DA CHOPPA!

PRIMARY/ SECONDARY	L96A1/M1911	
ATTACHMENTS	Suppressor/Extended Mag	
LETHAL/TACTICAL/ EQUIPMENT	Frag/Willy Pete/Tactical Insertion	
PERK 1	Ghost	
PERK 2	Scout	
PERK 3	Hacker	
KILLSTREAKS	Napalm Strike/Attack Helicopter/ Chopper Gunner	

Take this class for the ultimate in jungle warfare. Find a nice high point, drop a Tactical Insertion, and fire away.

HEADQUARTERS

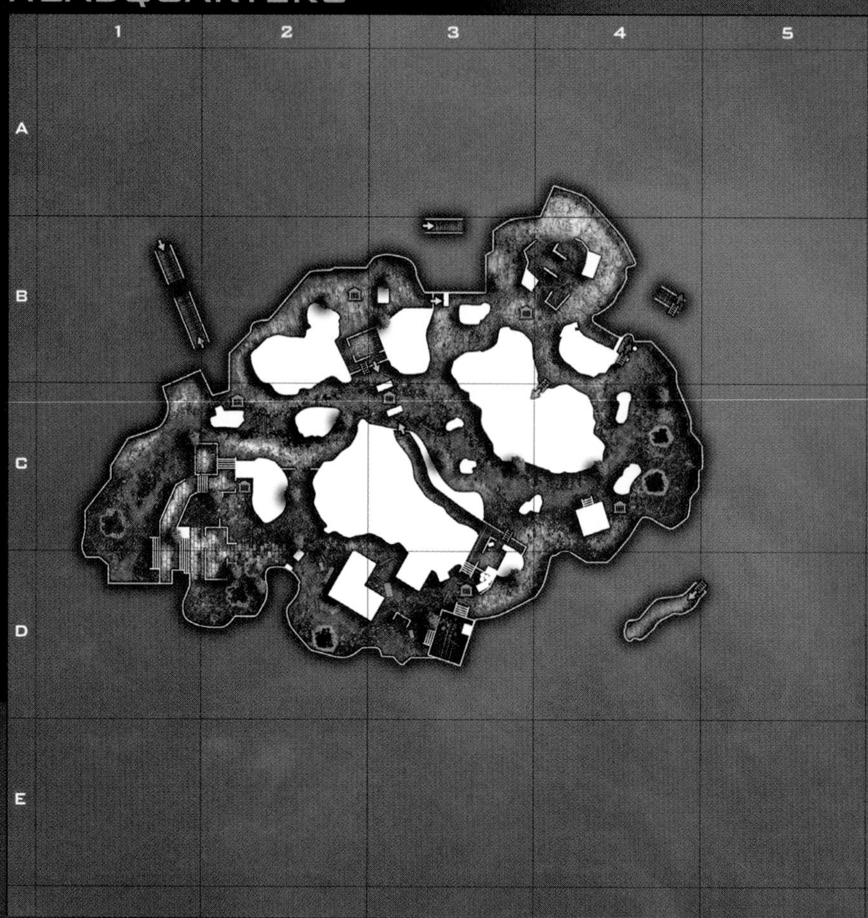

DEMOLITION

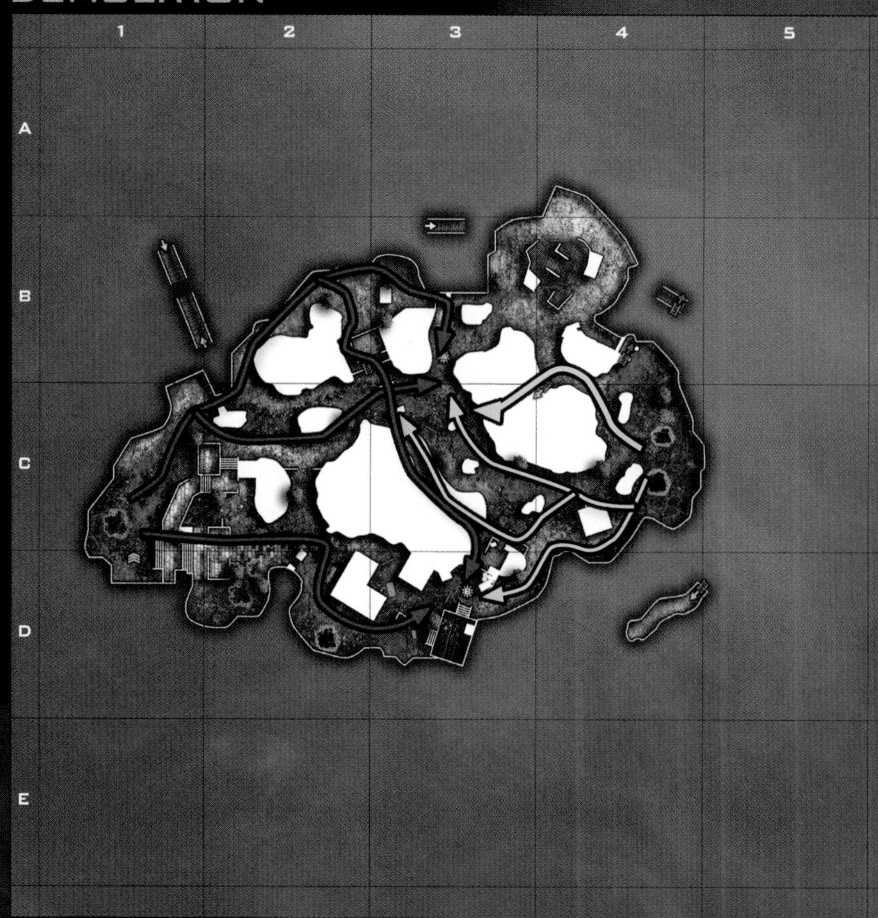

JUNGLE

CAPTURE THE FLAG

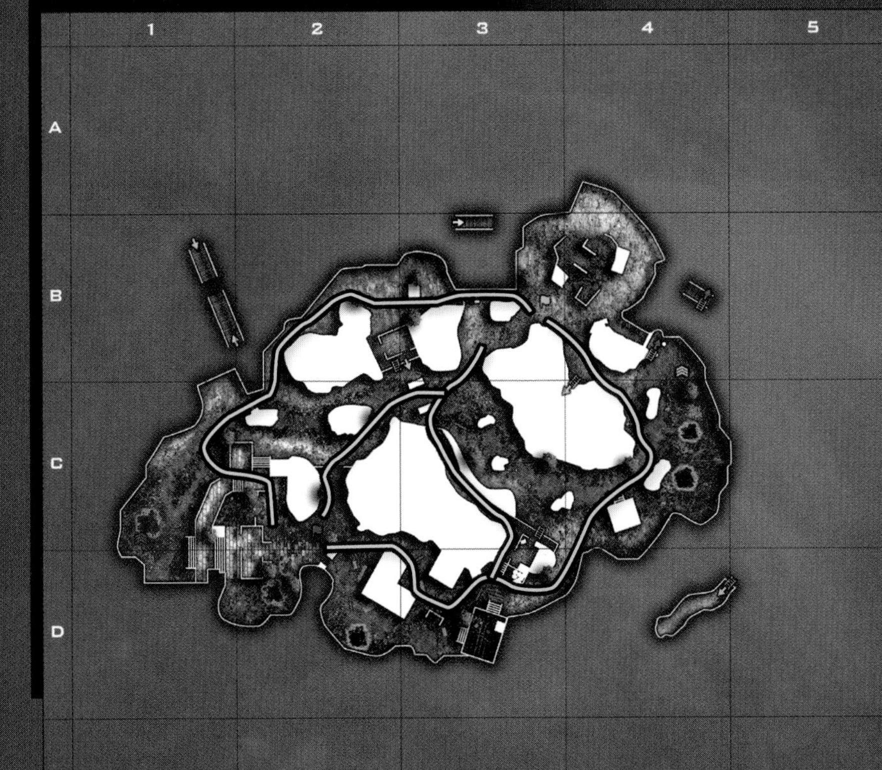

SABOTAGE

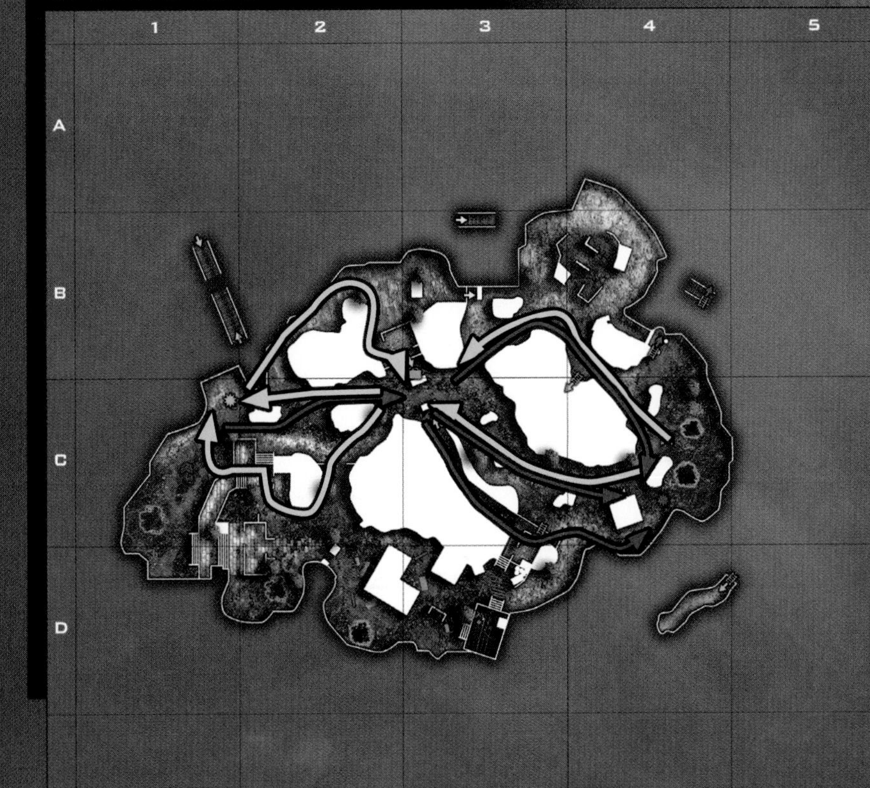

LAUNCH

WAGER MATCH VARIANT

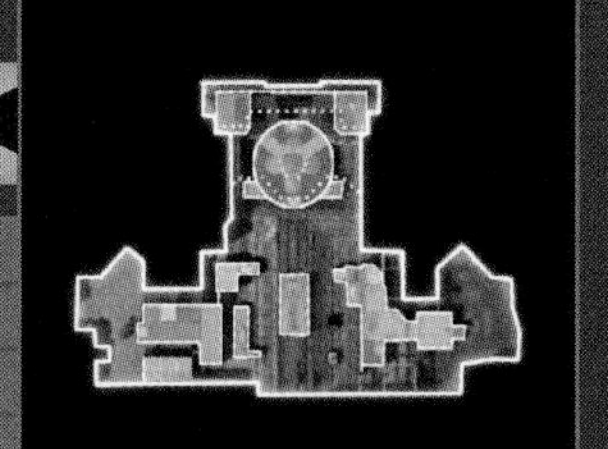

Terrain	Urban military compound
Key Features	Massive Soviet rocket in the center of the map.
Map Size	Large
Map Profile	Mixed mid- and long-range combat; many alternate routes to a large conflict zone in the center.

1	Launch's center area is a hotspot. Limit your exposure as much as possible when you move through here. Try to avoid fighting on the platform's raised center portion.
2	The western portion features multiple routes to the center. A single route leads to the lower missile launch area in the north.
3	The east is essentially a mirror of the level's western portion. It hosts the same multi-route access to the middle of the map and a single route leading to the missile launch pad in the north.
4	The missile launch area is important, as it can be accessed from the east, west, and from above.
5	These outer girders look unsafe, and they are, but you can jump out onto them, both to run between the eastern and western launch towers and to get a good sight line on the map's eastern or western edge. Just be aware that you have no cover, and you're vulnerable on the narrow beams.

Launch takes place on an impressive battlefield—a Soviet launch facility with a missile on the pad preparing to lift off. At the end of a match, the missile actually takes off! Make sure you aren't underneath it…

Launch consists of a large central section with a lower area beneath the rocket to the north, and two roughly similar areas to the east and west.

Multiple routes from the center lead to either the east or west. A few routes lead up and down to the area below the missile in the north. You can drop down into the launch room from above, follow stairs down from either launch tower, or descend the ramps from the map's east or west sides.

Most combat takes place at medium range, making Assault Rifles prime weapons. The distance between the sides is lengthy, but the raised central platform blocks the sight line, and the machinery further obscures the view.

If you're dead set on using an SMG, you can force close-quarters encounters if you lurk around the entrances to the center of the map. We don't recommend using a Shotgun in most cases here. Sniper Rifles can work very well in objective modes, covering the various approaches to either side of the map, and the center from north to south.

In general, the map's center isn't as safe as either side or even the north. Because it serves as the map's connective center, it gets a lot of traffic, and there are no areas to hide.

SEARCH & DESTROY

DOMINATION

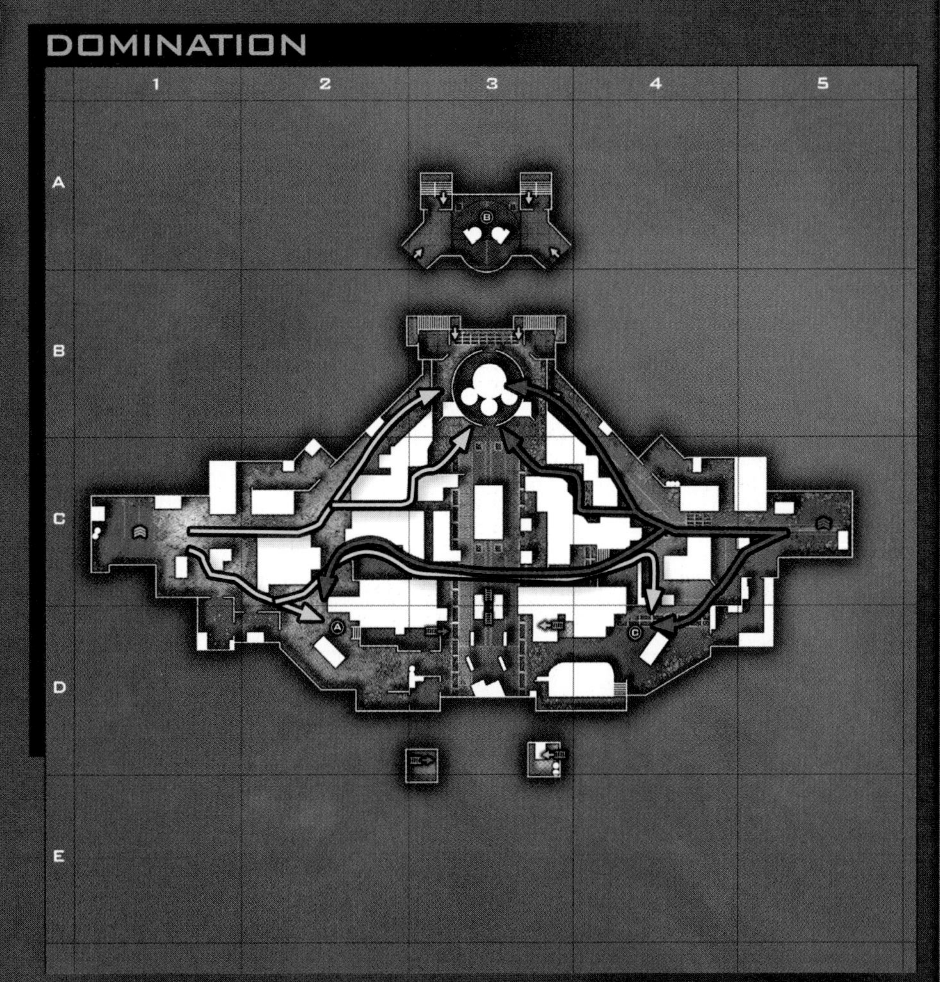

EQUIPMENT TIPS

	C4	You can use C4 to cover one of the routes to the east or west. Make sure you set up in a position that can monitor the booby-trapped route and at least one other route at the same time.
	CAMERA SPIKE	Very useful in the east or west. You can set up the camera facing north or south, creating a visual tripwire that alerts you to any enemy movement into your area.
	CLAYMORE	Use a Clamore in the narrow passages from the center to the edges of the map. You may not get a kill immediately due to the surplus of available routes.
	JAMMER	Fairly helpful on defense in objective modes. You can cover the east or west without much trouble. Safely planting a Jammer in the center is harder to do.
	MOTION SENSOR	Quite useful to place in the routes to the east or west. A single sensor can easily cover one or more routes.
	TACTICAL INSERTION	Quite helpful in objective modes. The tricky part is finding a safe place to plant the Insertion so that a traveling enemy doesn't discover it immediately.

SUGGESTED CUSTOM CLASSES

THE CHIEF

PRIMARY/ SECONDARY	UZI/Python	
ATTACHMENTS	Rapid Fire/ACOG	
LETHAL/TACTICAL/ EQUIPMENT	Frag/Willy Pete/Jammer	
PERK 1	Hardline	
PERK 2	Steady Aim	
PERK 3	Hacker	
KILLSTREAKS	RC-XD/Mortar Team/Rolling Thunder	

Use the rapid-fire UZI against enemies rounding this map's many corners. Unleash the Python/ ACOG combo for longer shots.

HOUSTON

PRIMARY/ SECONDARY	G11/CZ75	
ATTACHMENTS	Dual Wield	
LETHAL/TACTICAL/ EQUIPMENT	Semtex/Nova Gas/C4	
PERK 1	Lightweight	
PERK 2	Hardened	
PERK 3	Marathon	
KILLSTREAKS	Spy Plane/Care Package/Valkyrie Rockets	

Gas your enemies and stick 'em with C4 when you run this class. The Nova Gas grenade gives you a hit marker every time the gas hurts someone.

HEADQUARTERS

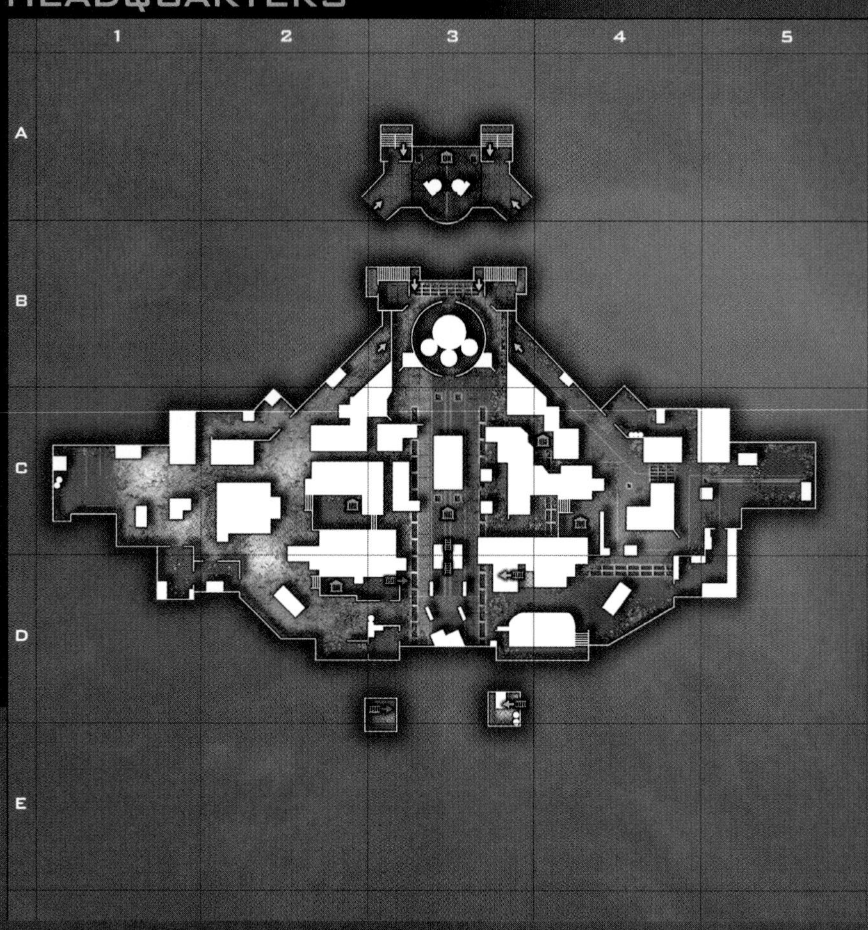

DEMOLITION

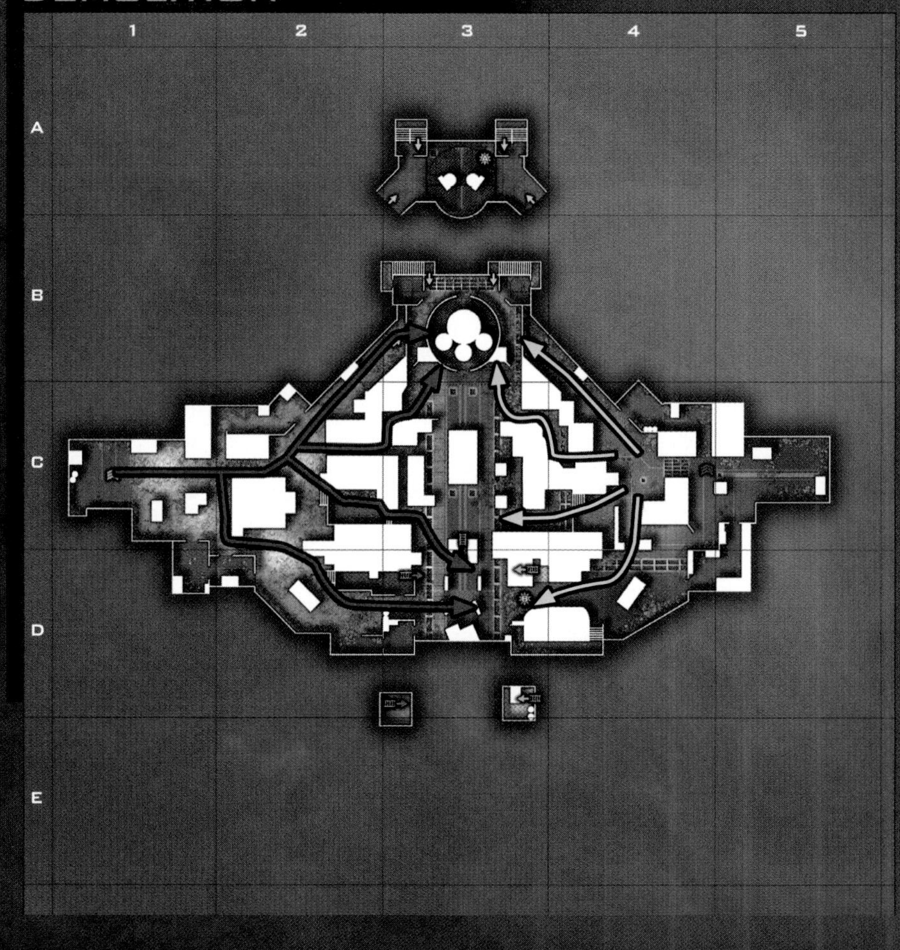

CAPTURE THE FLAG

SABOTAGE

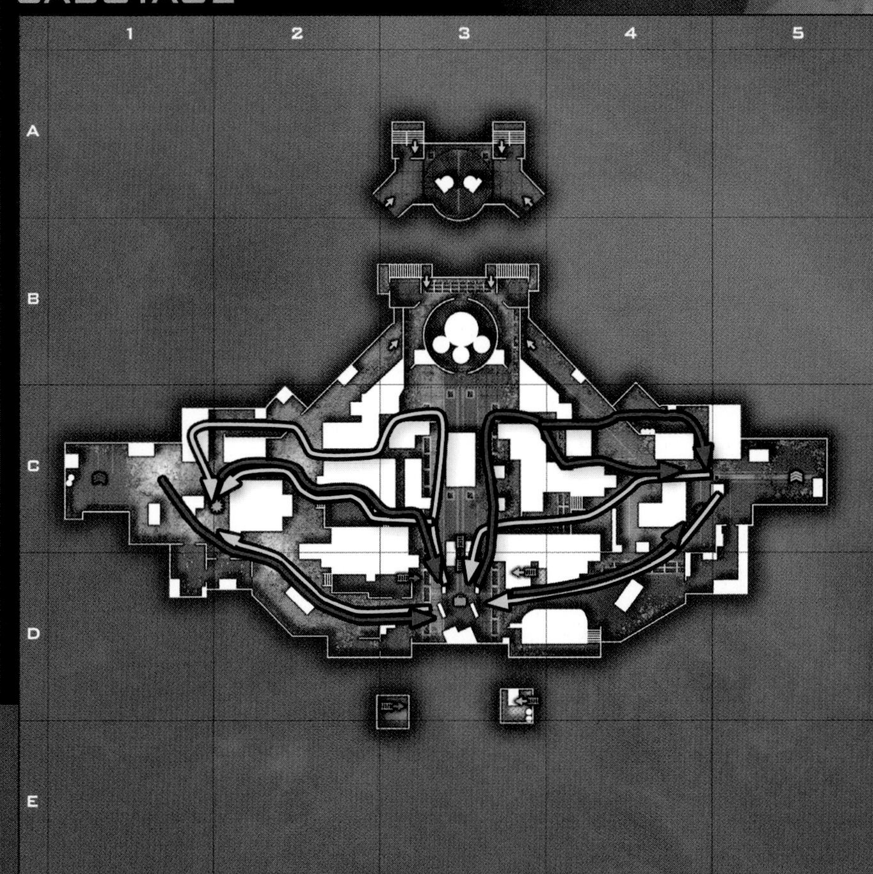

NUKETOWN

Terrain	Urban
Key Features	Fake houses.
Map Size	Very small
Map Profile	Intense CQB and short- to medium-range firefights.

1	As you might expect, the center of Nuketown is a killing field. There's a decent amount of cover, but its location makes it a high-risk area to traverse.
2	The buildings on the map's south and north ends are useful for the elevation and cover they can provide, but be ready to defend yourself from breaching enemy forces and explosives.
3	The backyards are open firefight areas, but be very careful about moving through them.

Nuketown is a tiny map with no safe places to camp. Bring your best CQB builds, stay alert, and keep moving.

This level is a fake American suburb out on a nuclear test field. At the end of the match, an atomic explosion in the distance levels everything!

Explosives are particularly nasty on this map. Because there is such a small area to traverse, they can inflict heavy casualties in either building or in the narrow pathways through the level's center.

Oddly, LMGs can be surprisingly nasty on this map, simply because you're so likely to encounter multiple enemies in close proximity to each other. The LMGs' large magazine sizes can help you take down many consecutive targets. LMGs can also pierce the limited cover. There aren't many places for your targets to hide once you have a bead on them.

Otherwise, we recommend running SMGs in particular, but Shotguns or Assault Rifles also work quite well. It's possible to snip, but we don't recommend it unless you're looking for a challenge.

Both of the buildings on this level are deathtraps. If you want to clean house, bring a Shotgun and some explosives, and sweep through the building. Then get out and keep moving until it's repopulated by more targets to hunt.

This map offers a nifty RC-XD route. You can pass through either fence in the backyards to find a secret that takes you from one end of the map to the other! Make sure you use your nitro boost to get over the rock jump halfway down the trail...

There isn't much to Nuketown. It's a very simple level, so expect short and vicious firefights no matter which mode you play. There's a decent amount of cover, so it forces you to fight a mobile, close-quarters combat style. You may find this highly enjoyable or extremely challenging depending on your mindset!

SEARCH & DESTROY

DOMINATION

EQUIPMENT TIPS

	C4	Fairly useful, simply as an extra explosive. Use it to good effect in either building, the back yards, or the faux center street.
	CAMERA SPIKE	Handy to alert you to targets running around behind either house. But what are you doing camping in that building? There's a grenade coming in the window!
	CLAYMORE	Consider the Claymore as close to a free kill as you can get. Drop it in either building, and if an explosive doesn't take it out, someone will trip it.
	JAMMER	Extremely effective in the north, center, or south of the map, but the hard part is keeping it standing for any length of time.
	MOTION SENSOR	Very effective in the center or in either building. As with the Jammer, the hard part is keeping it active.
	TACTICAL INSERTION	You really don't want to use the Tactical Insertion here, unless you like giving away double kills.

SUGGESTED CUSTOM CLASSES

KEY MASTER

PRIMARY/ SECONDARY	Enfield/Python	
ATTACHMENTS	Extended Mag & Masterkey/ACOG	
LETHAL/TACTICAL/ EQUIPMENT	Semtex/Nova Gas/Claymore	
PERK 1	Lightweight	
PERK 2	Warlord	
PERK 3	Second Chance	
KILLSTREAKS	RC-XD/Attack Helicopter/ Attack Dogs	

Open any door you wish with this class. Use the RC-XD to head outside the map and into enemy territory with a bang!

FILTHY HARRY

PRIMARY/ SECONDARY	Skorpion/Crossbow	
ATTACHMENTS	Dual Wield	
LETHAL/TACTICAL/ EQUIPMENT	Frag/Nova Gas/Jammer	
PERK 1	Hardline	
PERK 2	Hardened	
PERK 3	Tactical Mask	
KILLSTREAKS	RC-XD/Napalm Strike/Sentry Gun	

Come at them with a Skorpion in each hand. With this map's small size, you want the fast fire rate of these guns at your service.

HEADQUARTERS

DEMOLITION

CAPTURE THE FLAG

1 2 3 4 5

A B C D E

SABOTAGE

RADIATION

WAGER MATCH VARIANT

Terrain	Urban
Key Features	Centrally located access hatch; derelict Uranium processing facility to the north.
Map Size	Medium
Map Profile	Mix of medium- to long-range outdoor firefights and short- to medium-range indoor combat.

1	Use the buttons in the northern structure and the southern catwalk to open or close the central access hatch to the lower tunnel. Once the hatch opens or closes, a few seconds must pass before anyone can activate it again.
2	This structure provides access to the lower tunnel. It has decent cover and a few sight lines to the center of the map. Unlike the blockhouses at C3 and C4, this building is not mirrored on the east side of the map.
3	This small blockhouse has a sister structure in the southwest. Both provide limited cover but are in high-traffic areas, so neither is safe for long. Conveniently, both provide access ladders to the lower tunnel.
4	This large fuel storage room is one of three major routes through the level. You can pass through it on a catwalk to the north, at ground level through the center, up a ladder or stairs to the south, or even out through the south side.
5	You must access this rear walkway from the west via a conveyer belt that passes over a set of crushing grinders. Jump!

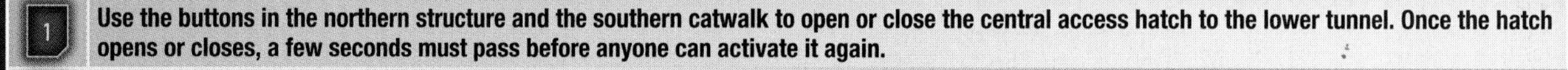

Radiation is a Russian refining facility for nuclear materials. The map itself is a mostly open stretch of ground from east to west. You can enter a large processing facility on the north side from almost anywhere on the level. A large tunnel in the map's center stretches under the level from east to west.

A set of doors is located in the center of the map. You canopen or close them via switches to the north and south. Players can drop down through the hatch to the central tunnel below.

This map is roughly symmetrical in terms of structures and cover around the map's center. Each side has a small blockhouse with a ladder accessing the tunnel to the hatch's northeast and southwest. Both sides have two-story buildings farther back to the northeast and southwest. These have sight lines toward each other across the center of the map.

The southern structure features a pair of narrow catwalks traversing the level—a low wall protects you from attackers in the center of the map.

The northern structure provides three different ways across the level and a boasts large, open area in the center for firefights.

You can enter the lower tunnel that stretches through the map at either end: from the blockhouses near the center, or through the access hatch if it's open. This tunnel offers little cover and provides clear sight lines for anyone waiting at the other end.

RC-XD tunnels pass through the map's east and west sides into the lower tunnel. They're perfect for sneaking an explosive car across the map or into the tunnel.

The least desirable way to cross the map is simply running across the center field on ground level. We don't recommend this.

You can mantle up and over the short walls to the north and south. You can actually mantle onto the north wall and then hop up to the building's second level to reach a control room that overlooks the storage tanks below.

SEARCH & DESTROY

DOMINATION

A rear catwalk inside the building passes around the map's extreme north edge. But watch out on the west side—the "ramp" down is actually a conveyor belt delivering rocks into crushing gears. Don't fall in!

As you can see, there are many routes through Radiation, but they boil down to north, center, or south, each offering a few options. When you move east/west, pay attention to enemy positions and choose your route appropriately. When you can, avoid fighting in the central field, which can have eyes on it from many different places.

EQUIPMENT TIPS

	C4	Given the number of routes, it's difficult to use C4 effectively anywhere but near objectives.
	CAMERA SPIKE	Helpful on defense in objective modes, you can use it to cover a few of the possible east/west routes.
	CLAYMORE	Not great. There aren't many narrow chokepoints. You can plant it in one of the mirrored blockhouses or sniper perches in the northeast or southwest.
	JAMMER	Fairly effective on either side of the level, or in the northern building. Very difficult to place centrally.
	MOTION SENSOR	Solid for covering one of the routes east or west. Just make sure you don't place it in an area where you can get mixed up on an enemy's vertical position.
	TACTICAL INSERTION	Though this map isn't large, getting across safely can be tricky in some modes. It's helpful to have a Tactical Insertion on the enemy's side of the map. The tricky part is finding a safe spot to hide it. Make sure no enemies are close enough to hear you plant it!

SUGGESTED CUSTOM CLASSES

SHOWSTOPPER

PRIMARY/ SECONDARY	G11/CZ75	
ATTACHMENTS	ACOG/Full Auto Upgrade	
LETHAL/TACTICAL/ EQUIPMENT	Frag/Willy Pete/Camera Spike	
PERK 1	Scavenger	
PERK 2	Sleight of Hand	
PERK 3	Ninja	
KILLSTREAKS	SAM Turret/Mortar Team/Gunship	

Use the three-round burst mode with the ACOG scope for long-distance accuracy. Whip out the fully automatic pistol for close encounters.

I'M FAMAS!

PRIMARY/ SECONDARY	FAMAS/M72 LAW	
ATTACHMENTS	Red Dot Sight & Dual Mag	
LETHAL/TACTICAL/ EQUIPMENT	Frag/Decoy/Motion Sensor	
PERK 1	Flak Jacket	
PERK 2	Warlord	
PERK 3	Ninja	
KILLSTREAKS	Counter Spy Plane/Mortar Team/ Blackbird	

Lay down the law and show 'em who's boss with this gear. You can eat grenades for breakfast and then toss them back to the chef.

HEADQUARTERS

DEMOLITION

CAPTURE THE FLAG

SABOTAGE

RADIATION

SUMMIT

WAGER MATCH VARIANT

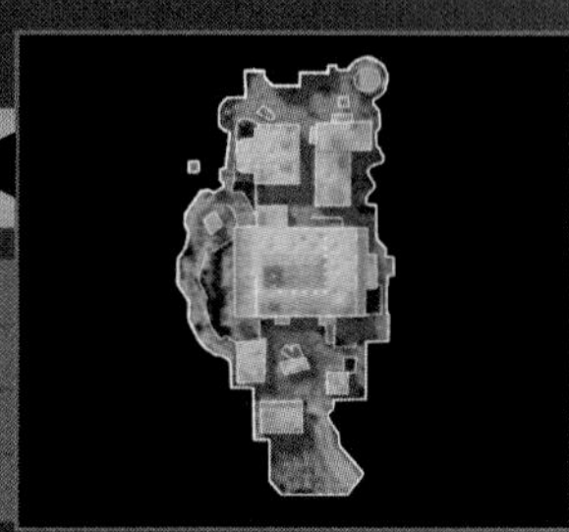

Terrain	Arctic Urban
Key Features	Large central installation serves as a focal point for battles.
Map Size	Medium
Map Profile	A mix of short-range and medium-range combat fought in and around a few key structures.

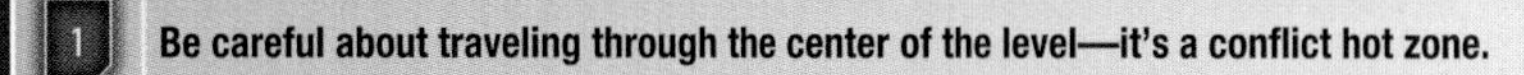

1	Be careful about traveling through the center of the level—it's a conflict hot zone.
2	You can hide out at the top of this cliffside pathway. Crouch behind the building and watch anyone coming up the cliff. This is safe only if your back is covered. Don't expect it to work more than once, but it can start an early streak for you.
3	The eastern path can take you into, above, or around the center structure. Use the variety of routes through this area to avoid and surprise enemies.
4	This outer catwalk has a clear sight line down through D4. With a good long-range gun, you can take down enemies crossing the bridge. Just don't hang out for too long, because you make an easy target once they know where you are.
5	Inside the center room, you can climb up onto the catwalk from one of the computers, break the glass, and jump outside to the tower just southwest of the C3 marker.

Summit, as you probably guessed, takes place in a small military facility atop a snowy mountain peak.

The map has a large central building that serves as a major focal point for many battles. Everyone has to pass through it or skirt wide around the dangerous outer mountainside ledges.

Essentially, there are three routes north/south through the map. The east and west routes take you out on the cliffs, while there are multiple options for going through the center structure.

Most combat takes place at medium range or shorter, though there are a few opportunities for long-range firefighting, mostly on the outer ledges.

In objective modes, the distinct geography of the level's northern and southern areas makes combat on either side quite different. Explore each side and get a feel for the sight lines.

SMGs and Assault Rifles both play well here, though you can also make do with other weapon classes if you choose your fights carefully.

The outer ledges to the east and west are dangerous to travel. There isn't much cover, and there aren't many tricks for concealing your approach. On the other hand, they provide a quick secondary route between the two halves of the level, so weigh the benefit against the danger.

Sniper Rifles or LMGs can do a very good job of locking down either outer route. If you're playing an objective mode, consider pairing with a teammate to block both outer routes across the map while your other teammates fight in the central room.

When you pass through the center, remember that you can get in and out of the room through several different routes: three on the bottom and four on the top. Depending on where the enemy is concentrated, mix up your entrances and exits to avoid or engage hostiles.

You can also climb up on top of the computers in the room's center. From there, jump and mantle onto the catwalk at the room's north edge. You canjump out the window on the west side to the narrow crow's nest that overlooks the western ledge.

SEARCH & DESTROY

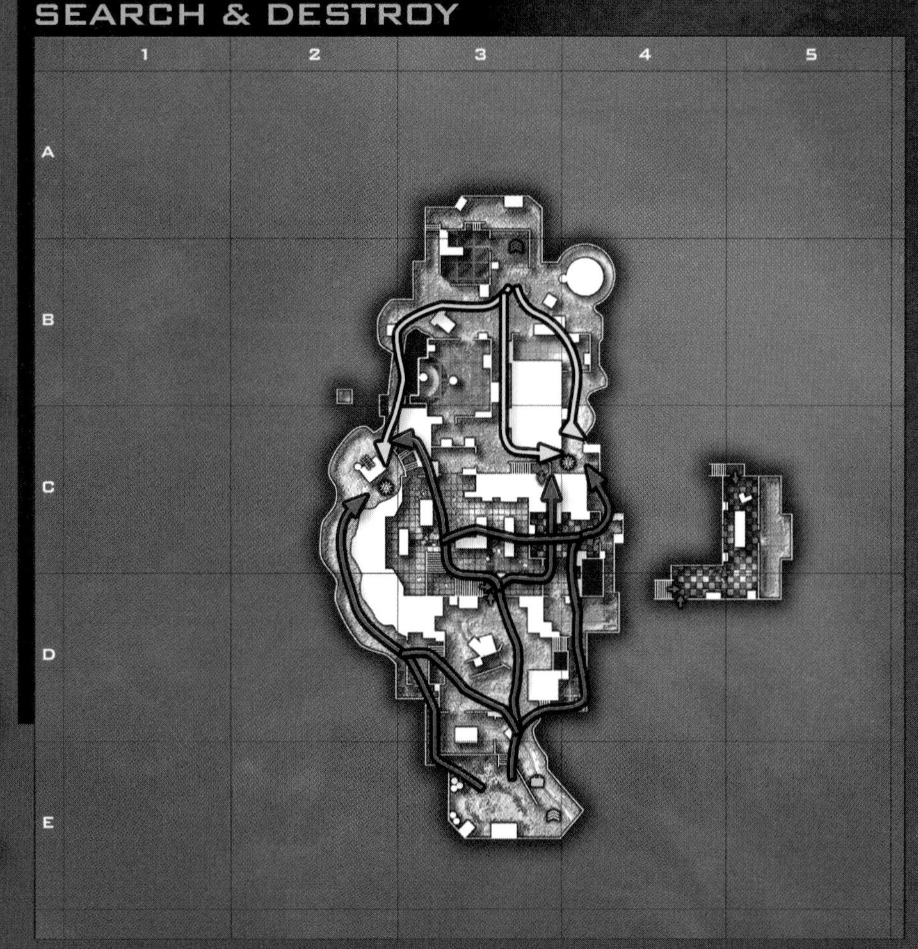

DOMINATION

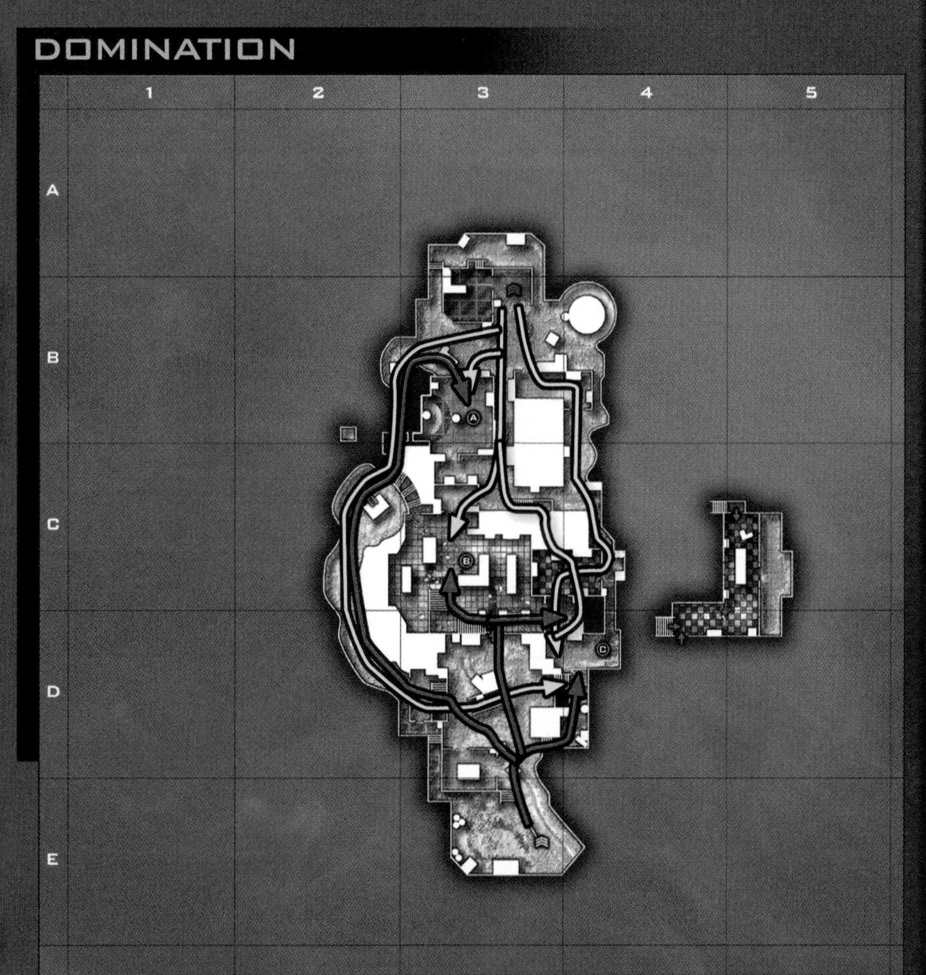

The catwalk and the crow's nest are both exposed, but they also have excellent fields of fire to enemies below. High risk, high reward!

You can sprint and jump to a tiny gondola that hangs off the map's western edge. This is a dangerous spot to camp, but you can occasionally surprise foes on the mountain ledge and take them out.

EQUIPMENT TIPS

	C4	Tough to use here—you can either mine one of the outer ledges or save it for objectives.
	CAMERA SPIKE	Very handy for covering one of the outer routes. Harder to place in a safe spot to cover the north or south exits from the central building.
	CLAYMORE	Useful on the outer ledges if placed carefully. Also effective at the main north and south entrances to the central structure.
	JAMMER	Very nice if you can keep it active in the central building. It can jam almost the whole center of the map.
	MOTION SENSOR	Very useful for guarding either of the outer ledges or a portion of the central building.
	TACTICAL INSERTION	Insertions can be quite helpful to bypass the dangerous ledges and central building once you break through to the other side. There are several out-of-the-way spots to hide your Insertion. Just don't let an enemy see you stepping out from behind the buildings to the far north or south!

SUGGESTED CUSTOM CLASSES

TOP GUN

PRIMARY/ SECONDARY	Stoner63/M72 LAW	
ATTACHMENTS	Red Dot Sight & Extended Mag	
LETHAL/TACTICAL/ EQUIPMENT	Frag/Flashbang/Claymore	
PERK 1	Ghost	
PERK 2	Warlord	
PERK 3	Second Chance	
KILLSTREAKS	Sentry Gun/Attack Helicopter/ Gunship	

Plenty of firepower and accuracy with this class. Don't forget to set your Claymore around a corner.

PLAYTIME EXTENDED

PRIMARY/ SECONDARY	Stoner63/Python	
ATTACHMENTS	Extended Mag/Speed Reloader	
LETHAL/TACTICAL/ EQUIPMENT	Semtex/Nova Gas/Claymore	
PERK 1	Scavenger	
PERK 2	Sleight of Hand	
PERK 3	Ninja	
KILLSTREAKS	RC-XD/Sentry Gun/Attack Helicopter	

This loadout has you wreaking havoc with nonstop heavy-weapon fire. Again, use your Claymores on this map's many corners.

HEADQUARTERS

DEMOLITION

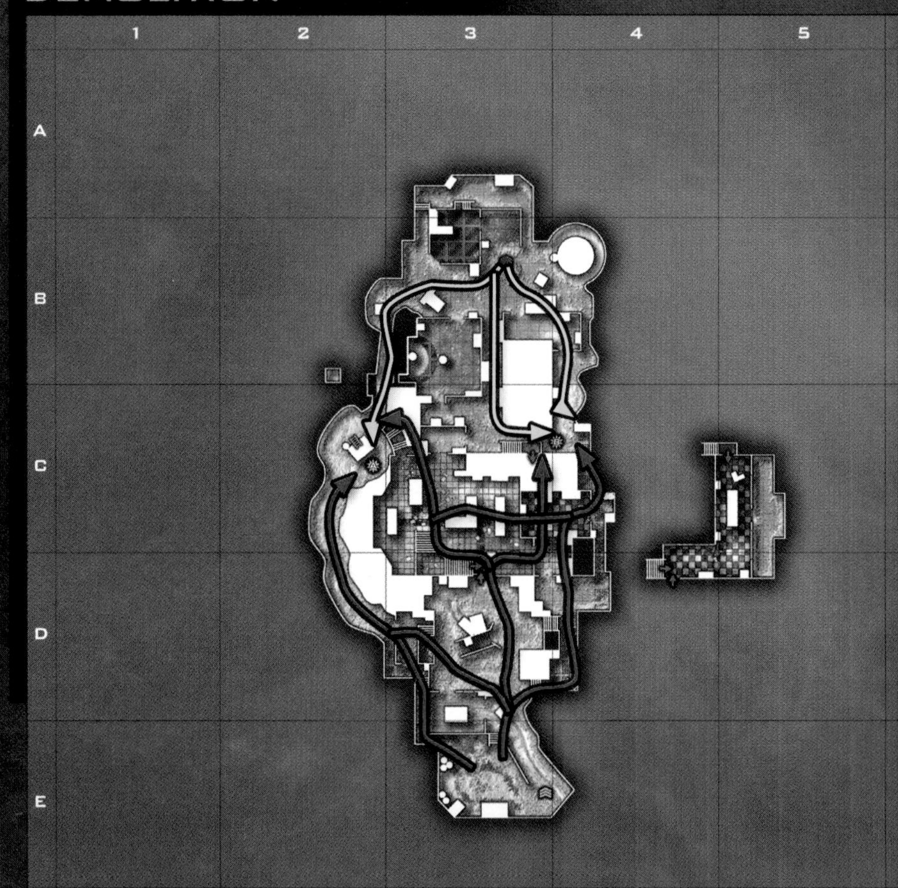

CAPTURE THE FLAG

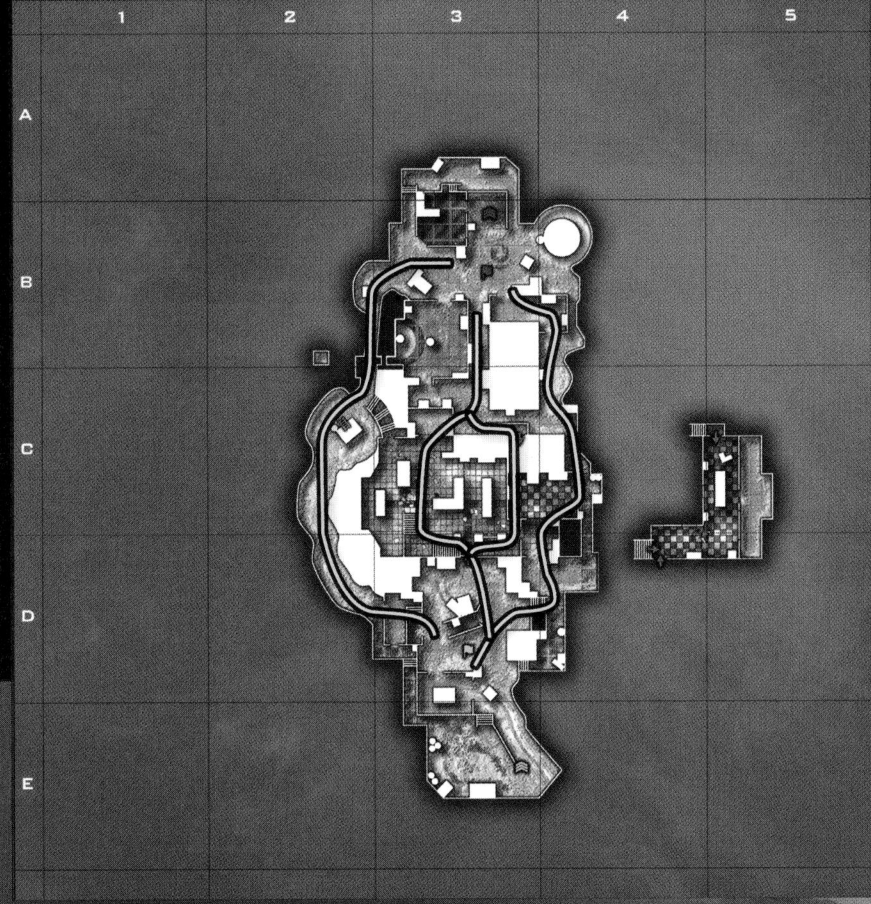

SABOTAGE

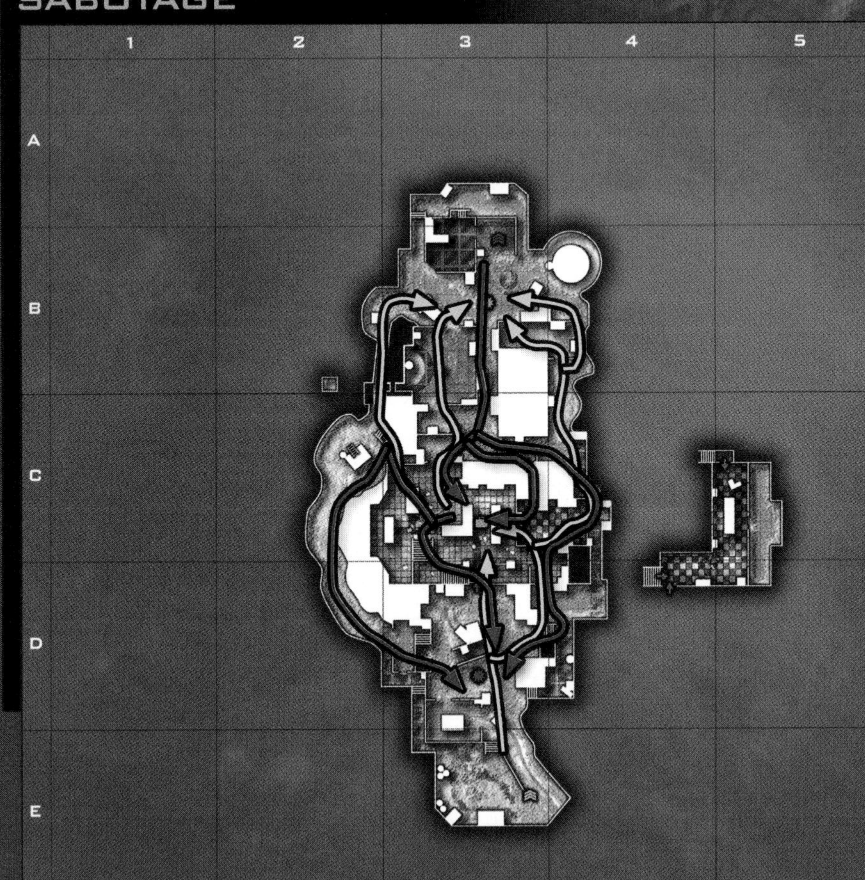

VILLA

Terrain	Urban
Key Features	Large fountain courtyard in the north; swimming pool area in southeast of villa.
Map Size	Medium
Map Profile	A mix of very open streets and yards, and a few simple buildings with some CQB within.

1	This grand building has a second level with two useful overwatch locations. One faces west toward the fountain at B3-B4, and the other faces south toward the pool at D4-D5.
2	This intersection of roads is a hotspot for travel. Be careful about moving through this area.
3	This outer area in front of the villa typically sees little traffic, making it a good location for calling airdrops.
4	This building has two useful windows: one faces east to the pool, and one faces west to the high-traffic streets at D3. Just be careful, as penetrating weapons or explosives easily target these small windows.
5	This building's upper floor has sight lines east over to the fountain, into the building at C5, and south along the street toward E3.

KEY

	OP40 Spawn
	Tropas Spawn
	Bomb-Search & Destroy / Sabotage Modes
	Search & Destroy / Demolition Plant Site
Ⓐ Ⓑ Ⓒ	Domination Flags
	OP 40 CTF Flag
	Tropas CTF Flag
	Headquarters Point
	Ladder
	OP 40 Sabotage Plant Destination
	Tropas Sabotage Plant Destination
	Arrows are color-coded to match the levels that they lead to

SEARCH & DESTROY

Villa is a mostly open level with a handful of structures. These provide key overwatch positions on the map's travel routes.

Most combat occurs at medium to long range in the open, though some CQB can break out in the eastern structures. Assault Rifles, LMGs, and Sniper Rifles can all prove effective here, thanks to the wide-open sight lines.

If you're using an SMG, be sure to confine yourself to fighting in and around the buildings. We don't recommend using a Shotgun here due to the long, open sight lines, which are not healthy for the dedicated up-close and personal type.

Because the villa's streets are so exposed, it's important to know where the enemy team is covering and take an alternate route. Failing that, be sure to bring smoke grenades; creating temporary cover can be important.

There are only a few major structures on this map, most concentrated on the eastern half. In the north around C4-C5, the large, two-level building provides passage north and south, and overwatch on the entire fountain courtyard to the west.

The two buildings to the south provide passage east/west into the pool courtyard area. They also provide overwatch on the streets to the west.

On the west side, one two-story building to the north can counter-snipe toward the major villa to the east. A less accessible building to the south lets you pass between C2 and D3.

The courtyard and streets offer relatively limited cover out in the open, so move carefully through the level, and try to avoid exposure in the open as much as possible.

The level's far west has no major objectives and little connectivity, so it generally sees very little traffic. Use it if you need to make a drop or control a guided Killstreak.

DOMINATION

EQUIPMENT TIPS

	C4	Other than chain-detonating a few parked vehicles, it's hard to use C4 to effectively block a route. Save it for the objectives.
	CAMERA SPIKE	Very handy. The long, linear paths are easy to cover with a camera, so you can watch two parts of the map at once.
	CLAYMORE	Useful in the eastern buildings. Harder to use effectively in the open streets to the west.
	JAMMER	Fairly effective in the east. Again, less useful around the west, as it's harder to conceal a Jammer there.
	MOTION SENSOR	Very useful for covering some of the intersections to see which way enemy forces are moving. You can also use it to cover the eastern buildings. However, keeping it active in the west is difficult, much like the Jammer.
	TACTICAL INSERTION	Not especially needed. It's hard to find a good place to conceal the Insertion's glow, and travel across the map is quick if you don't get intercepted by a bullet!

SUGGESTED CUSTOM CLASSES

IN-FIDEL

PRIMARY/ SECONDARY	FAMAS/China Lake	
ATTACHMENTS	Masterkey	
LETHAL/TACTICAL/ EQUIPMENT	Semtex/Nova Gas/Motion Sensor	
PERK 1	Scavenger	
PERK 2	Steady Aim	
PERK 3	Hacker	
KILLSTREAKS	Care Package/Sentry Gun/ Attack Dogs	

Take the gear in this class for the ultimate in room-clearing efficiency. Use the shotgun for room sweeps and the grenade launcher for campers.

UNLOCKED

PRIMARY/ SECONDARY	M16/Ballistic Knife	
ATTACHMENTS	Masterkey	
LETHAL/TACTICAL/ EQUIPMENT	Tomahawk/Flashbang/Camera Spike	
PERK 1	Ghost	
PERK 2	Sleight of Hand	
PERK 3	Marathon	
KILLSTREAKS	RC-XD/Counter Spy Plane/Attack Helicopter	

This class lets you run and reload much more quickly as you engage the enemy outside this estate.

HEADQUARTERS

DEMOLITION

CAPTURE THE FLAG

SABOTAGE

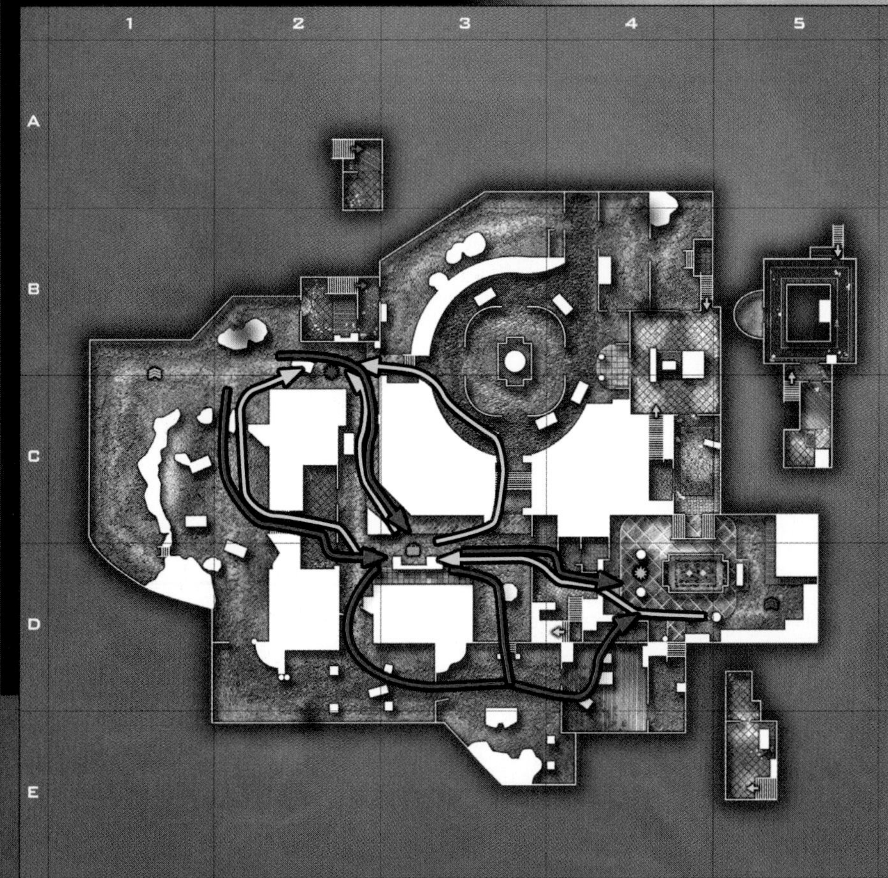

WMD

WAGER MATCH VARIANT

Terrain	Urban
Key Features	Large factory warehouses.
Map Size	Large
Map Profile	A mix of mid- and long-range, open-area fighting, with many different large buildings for CQB.

1	This path and, to a lesser extent, the route just west between C2-D2 are both hotspots due to the convergence of multiple paths. Be careful about walking in the streets.
2	You can climb up into a nice sniper tower here, but be careful because it's exposed and obvious.
3	A second sniper catwalk is up a ladder here. This one has the advantage of pipes and a rooftop you can jump to just to the west at the D3 building.
4	This building has multiple windows, multiple ingress and egress points, and a path over to the D3 building with a bit of parkour.
5	The D3 building offers good coverage of the central and southerly routes, as well as an exit that lets you travel over to the C3 building or along a catwalk east toward the C4 building.

KEY

Icon	Meaning
	Black Ops Spawn
	Spetznaz Spawn
	Bomb-Search & Destroy / Sabotage Modes
	Search & Destroy / Demolition Plant Site
Ⓐ Ⓑ Ⓒ	Domination Flags
	Black Ops CTF Flag
	Spetznaz CTF Flag
	Headquarters Point
	Ladder
	Black Ops Sabotage Plant Destination
	Spetznaz Sabotage Plant Destination
	Arrows are color-coded to match the levels that they lead to

SEARCH & DESTROY

DOMINATION

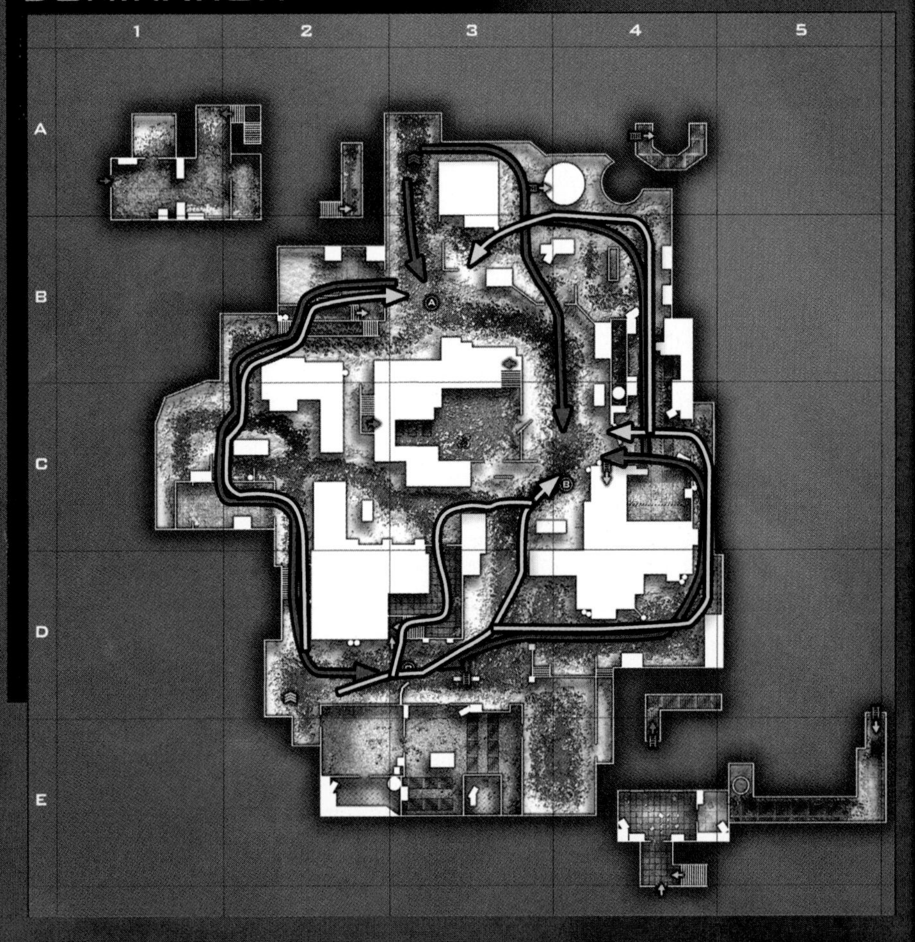

WMD is a large map and one of the more diverse levels in the game. There are many routes through the map and many different buildings to explore. You can climb up to elevated perches in quite a few places, or jump from rooftop to rooftop.

Almost any weapon type can be effective on WMD. It's simply a matter of picking your engagements carefully. If you plan to lurk in and around the buildings, bring your CQB loadouts. If you want to cover the outside streets and alleyways, bring your long-range kit.

Snipers can have a good time on this level. There are many clean sight lines and plenty of space to move around between positions. Revenge-seekers won't find it easy to pick you off. Just watch those windows; it's easy to get taken down if you don't spot enemies in the buildings.

Be sure to explore this map thoroughly. Examine all of the sight lines from each building so you know what you can shoot and areas to avoid as you traverse the map.

Learn all the various jumps you can make. You can climb and jump across several areas to get around the map in an elevated position.

Several routes between the north and south offer multiple branches along the way. Be very aware of your position and exposure to enemies traveling in the vicinity.

Many overwatch positions in the buildings can take out anyone in the open, so make a point of learning where these positions are. Either avoid them entirely, bypass them with the aid of smoke or stealth Perks, or fling explosives or Hardened bullets through the walls at the campers.

EQUIPMENT TIPS

	C4	C4 is tough to use here. The streets are broad and the buildings don't have many easily covered chokepoints. Save your C4 for objectives.
	CAMERA SPIKE	Very handy. You can use your camera to cover a road approach and watch a different direction with the naked eye.
	CLAYMORE	Useful in various buildings. You can usually rack up a kill or protect your back with careful placement.
	JAMMER	Helpful, but it's difficult to cover most of the level without multiple Jammers. Either get a teammate to bring a second one, or save the Jammer for an objective location.
	MOTION SENSOR	Very handy if you're lurking in a building. Cover the most dangerous entrance, and then focus your attention on overwatch duty.
	TACTICAL INSERTION	A good candidate. There are a lot of little hiding spots where you can tuck away an Insertion. In some objective modes, you can really exploit spawn point control.

SUGGESTED CUSTOM CLASSES

THE RUSH'N HOBO

PRIMARY/ SECONDARY	MP5k/M1911	
ATTACHMENTS	Rapid Fire/Dual Wield	
LETHAL/TACTICAL/ EQUIPMENT	Tomahawk/Willy Pete/Tactical Insertion	
PERK 1	Lightweight	
PERK 2	Sleight of Hand	
PERK 3	Marathon	
KILLSTREAKS	Attack Helicopter/Chopper Gunner/Gunship	

This class makes you mobile enough to catch the train in the distance on this map. With fast reloads and decent firepower, you can call in air support in no time.

SILVER BULLET

PRIMARY/ SECONDARY	AK47/Crossbow	
ATTACHMENTS	Extended Mag	
LETHAL/TACTICAL/ EQUIPMENT	Frag/Willy Pete/Jammer	
PERK 1	Hardline	
PERK 2	Hardened	
PERK 3	Marathon	
KILLSTREAKS	Care Package/Mortar Team/ Attack Dogs	

This gear allows quicker Killstreak acquisition and better bullet penetration.

HEADQUARTERS

DEMOLITION

CAPTURE THE FLAG

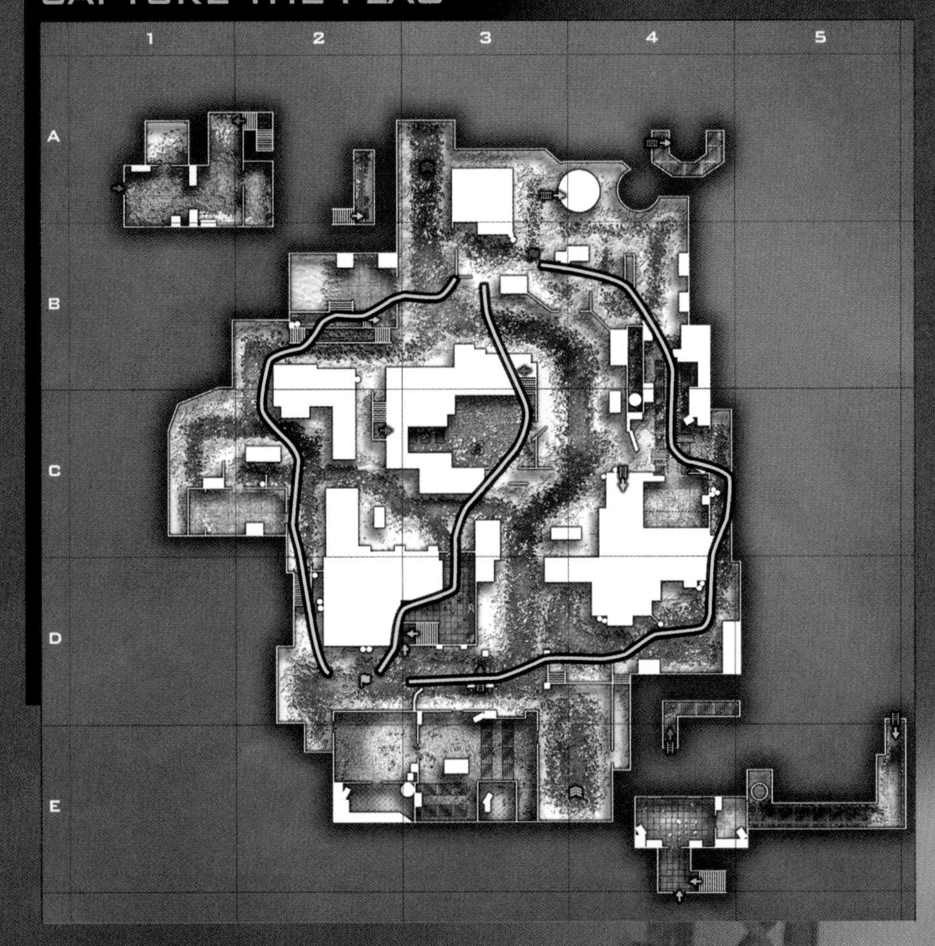

SABOTAGE

MODES

This section is designed to give you an overview of all game modes in Call of Duty: Black Ops multiplayer, as well as advice on how to thrive in each mode.

If you're new to the series, spend some time in all of the different online playlists to find what you like, then hone in on your favorites and see what you can learn to improve your game.

Successful teamplay in Search and Destroy or Domination is worlds apart from winning Wager Matches or TDM matches, and playing alone is different from playing with a few friends or a fully organized team.

Where appropriate, you'll find thoughts on team strategies for objective modes, as well as some tactics for the lone wolves out there who frequently run solo.

In almost all modes, organized teams are more effective than teams comprised of solo-minded players or small parties. But having fully organized team battles outside of clan matches is rare in general matchmaking. Expect to go on long winning streaks if you play with a team of organized friends against random players.

If you're looking for a bigger challenge, it's best to find online leagues and ladders, where you can schedule matches and find competitive teams to practice against.

FREE FOR ALL (FFA)

Every man for himself. First player to the score limit wins.

Free for All is the simplest multiplayer game mode in *Call of Duty: Black Ops*. Hop in and kill everyone in sight, win or lose.

Winning in Free for All

Unlike most other team modes, and very much unlike Team Deathmatch (TDM), Free for All is best won by getting kills at all costs, even at the cost of your own life.

Unlike TDM, you can easily have a negative kill/death ratio (k/d) and still win the match, because the first player to hit the score limit wins instead of the player with the fewest deaths.

As a result, you can go after FFA victory in two ways. One is to take an aggressive stance and patrol hotspots, looking to jump in on firefights and score kills. This is risky, because moving around a lot in FFA is dangerous. Still, this technique offers a better chance of yielding more kills quickly, which is what matters here.

The other option, if you simply can't stand giving up deaths freely, is to cordon off a section of the level as "yours," and kill anyone who enters your zone. Bring a Suppressed weapon and pick an area with only a few entrances and exits that you can cover easily.

Because of the spawning system, you're *very* likely to get shot in the back if you patrol around the map. If you set up shop with a stealthy build, in one part of the level, and some equipment to help cover you, you can rack up Killstreaks. This can help you hit the score limit faster.

Some key Perks in this mode include Ghost, Scavenger, Hacker, and Ninja. The tradeoff between Hacker and Ninja is a tough one, because without Hacker Pro, you're vulnerable to Motion Sensors as you move around the level.

Bring Spy Plane as one of your Killstreaks; the informational advantage is vital for staying alive and scoring kills.

Another option is to skip Ghost or Scavenger and take Hardline, specifically to get cheap Spy Planes and Counter-Spy Planes, and either Attack Helicopters or the SAM or Care Packages. Packages in general are dangerous in FFA. But, with Hardline you can reshuffle it, and you can easily use packages as bait. Toss one out, find a hidey-hole, and wait for some poor sap to try to jack your package.

If you're running Hardline with Counter-Spy Plane, you can potentially ditch your Suppressor, as you're "silenced" from radar while it's active.

If you're going for the zone defense tactic, bring a Motion Sensor or Camera Spike to cover one entrance to your area.

WAGER MATCH

New to *Call of Duty: Black Ops* is the Wager Match, a Free for All variant where you put your money where your mouth is. You pony up CODPoints for a chance to prove yourself in a six-player game. End up in the top three, and you get a payout—you are "in the money." End up on the bottom, and you get nothing.

Wager Matches can be one of four different game types, each demanding a different set of skills for success.

All Wager Matches are played in a special no-custom-classes arena. You use the weapons and tools provided, no classes, no Killstreaks, and, with one exception, no Perks.

All Wager Matches take place on special reduced-size variants of normal *Call of Duty: Black Ops* multiplayer maps. These are the same maps, but with outer areas blocked off to better suit the more "intimate" nature of the six-person FFA arena.

Wager Match Playlists

Three types of Wager Match playlists are available to you. The lowest level, Ante Up, allows parties. If you just want to blow off some steam with a few friends, Ante Up is the place to go.

Spend some time in the higher buy-in playlists if you really want to rack up CODPoints rapidly. A mix of Contract completions and Wager Matches can net you a lot of cash in a short time.

ANTE UP

A variety of Wager Match game modes with a low buy-in entry fee. Parties allowed.

WEEKEND GAMBLER

A variety of Wager Match game modes with a medium buy-in fee. No parties allowed.

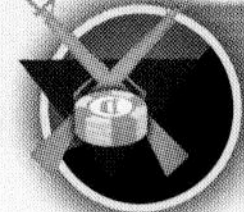

HIGH ROLLER

For the big spenders only. Entry fees start at 10,000. You can still vote, but you don't get to pick a specific Wager Match game mode. No parties allowed.

ONE IN THE CHAMBER

One pistol, one bullet, one bullet earned per kill. Miss, and you use your knife.

The current match leader shows up on your minimap as a gold dot. Once the number of players has been reduced, Spy Planes start flying over.

You have a limited number of lives in each round of One in the Chamber. Once those are exhausted, you had better hope your score is good enough to keep you in the money.

One in the Chamber demands precision aim, situational awareness, and very quick reactions. You have to make split-second decisions about when to shoot your one precious bullet, and if not, you must quickly sprint to close the distance and get the kill.

Avoid open areas and travel hubs. Patrol the outer reaches and pick off targets as they arrive. Skirt the interior of the map and kill any targets that foolishly get involved in multi-person battles.

Be careful around blind corners. Walking into melee range results in a roll of the dice—the less you play bad odds, the less chance you have of losing that roll. Let other players sprint around corners so you can knife them in the back.

Because Spy Planes begin flying over the battlefield once the number of players is reduced, you can't hope to camp out and win a match just by surviving. You must score points to finish in the money, so camping is a bad idea anyway. Just be aware that once the sweeps arrive, you need to be in a good position on the map to fight the remaining players.

STICKS AND STONES

A Crossbow, Ballistic Knives, and a Tomahawk. Axe someone with the Tomahawk, and you Bankrupt them.

As in One in the Champer, Spy Planes start arriving to speed up the match. Sticks and Stones is an awesome Wager Match mode that pits players against each other using nothing but projectile weapons.

This challenging mode is perfect for practice with the game's three special weapons: the Crossbow, Ballistic Knife, and Tomahawk.

Because Tomahawking another player Bankrupts them, you should always throw your 'hawk if you spot an opportunity. You can always retrieve it after the battle if you survive.

Of your two main weapon choices, the Ballistic Knife is a bit easier to use than the Crossbow. More importantly, it kills instantly. Use up your Knives first (and retrieve them if possible), then go for Crossbow kills.

You should also pull out your Crossbow if you spot a target at a distance or hiding in cover, where you can score a kill with an indirect explosion.

GUN GAME

Start with a pistol and work your way up through 20 levels of weapons.

Kill another player with the final weapon to win. Get knifed and drop down a level.

The Gun Game challenges your abilities with every weapon, from pistols to Assault Rifles to high explosives.

Speed counts here, as the first player to score a kill with every weapon wins, so you want to get into the thick of it as much as possible. Since scoring kills with your current weapon is the only thing that matters, don't worry about dying.

Getting knifed drops a player down one weapon level. Because it's very difficult to identify and stab the top player, this is more of a general penalty for losing a melee exchange than a practical tactic to thwart the current leader.

As a result, avoid getting into melee range unless you see a prime stabbing opportunity. The delay just might help you win, and if you get ahead in the arms race, you can really keep the pressure on other players.

Gun Game is a fun game mode. Unlike Sticks and Stones, which really refines your skills with those weapons, Gun Game is so hectic that it doesn't really train you with each weapon as much as simply using them in normal matches would.

SHARPSHOOTER

All players use the same weapon. Weapons change periodically.

Killstreaks give Perks and then score multipliers. Die, and you lose your Perks and multiplier.

Sharpshooter challenges all players to use a random gun with a random Attachment to score kills.

The weapon changes every so often, and all players receive a new random weapon to use.

Scoring Killstreaks in Sharpshooter matters, because your first three kills unlock temporary Perks for you, and then additional kills grant you a score multiplier.

If you can get a good streak going and keep it running once your multiplier is active, you have a good chance of running away with the win, even if another player gets a few more kills than you do!

As a result, this mode forces a mix of aggression and cautious play. You want to get kills to raise your score, but staying alive has big benefits.

TEAM DEATHMATCH (TDM)

Two teams battle for the top score. First team to reach the score limit wins.

Suggested Custom Classes

FULL-AUTOMATON

PRIMARY/SECONDARY	FAMAS/CZ75	
ATTACHMENTS	Red Dot Sight and Extended Mag/Full Auto Upgrade	
LETHAL/TACTICAL/EQUIPMENT	Frag/Decoy/Claymore	
PERK 1	Lightweight	
PERK 2	Warlord	
PERK 3	Ninja	
KILLSTREAKS	Spy Plane/Napalm Strike/Attack Helicopter	

This fully automated setup provides quick, quiet movement, the ability to of enemies, and plenty of ammo in your primary weapon.

TRAPPER

PRIMARY/SECONDARY	Commando/Crossbow	
ATTACHMENTS	Reflex Scope and Suppressor	
LETHAL/TACTICAL/EQUIPMENT	Tomahawk/Decoy/Motion Sensor	
PERK 1	Scavenger	
PERK 2	Warlord	
PERK 3	Ninja	
KILLSTREAKS	RC-XD/Attack Helicopter/Gunship	

Use this class to make your way around the perimeter of the map. Drop a Decoy grenade and a Motion Sensor to set traps along the way.

Winning in Team Deathmatch

Winning in TDM is all about staying alive and locking down the enemy team's spawn locations.

Unlike in FFA, where kills matter more, in TDM, your kill/death ratio is what wins or loses the game. It's better to go 5-0 in a TDM match than 15-20. Why? Because the second score is losing the game for your team *and* feeding enemy Killstreaks, which makes the situation worse.

In many objective modes, it's totally acceptable to give up kills to win a match, but in TDM, doing so hurts your team twice over. Don't do it!

Staying alive is the first pillar of TDM success. The second is spawn control.

In any TDM match, the initial spawn points for both teams are the same. After the first rush, the spawn points for each team can change. Learn where these spawns are and when they are likely to change.

As a general rule, if your team pushes too far into an enemy spawn, they immediately begin spawning elsewhere—sometimes behind your position.

As a result, the easiest way to win is to pinpoint the new enemy spawn and set up a defensive line to take down anyone who tries to escape. Your team can do this without pushing into the opposing spawn area.

This has the odd effect of slightly emphasizing longer-range weaponry. Short-range weapons demand pushing up to the spawn area to be effective. However, you can still guard an exit from the spawn area, rather than moving into it.

If your team gets pinned at a spawn, find a way to break out and get around the enemy team, both to flank them, and to start spawning elsewhere on the map.

With time, you eventually get a good feel for both the area of the current spawn, and where the next likely location is if it shifts.

Stick together in fights—not so close that you're ripe for a Grenade Launcher multi-kill, but in the same general area. This lets you call out targets and provide supporting fire for each other.

Another important point: The map's size has a huge impact on the importance of spawn control and mobility. On smaller maps, there's usually too much chaos to really lock down anything —the better CQB team wins. But on larger maps, being able to quickly identify the enemy position and relocate to is much more important.

Unlike other objective modes, there are no discrete offensive and defensive specialties. You're always playing a mix of offense when you push out from a spawn, or defense when you try to pin the other team. On smaller maps, those concepts dissolve entirely, and it's simply a fast-paced, free flowing battle.

One significant tactic is to run an entire team with stealth Perks and Suppressors. A fully Ghosted team with Ninja and a few Hackers is really tough to deal with as a group. Because Spy Planes and air support are useless, gunshots don't show up on the minimap, Equipment can be avoided, and even footsteps are hard to hear.

However, assuming you aren't fortunate enough to run with a fully organized group, you can still run some other useful configurations for TDM.

TEAM DEATHMATCH LOADOUT TIPS

Hardline and Scavenger are both useful Perk 1 choices, as Hardline can give your team Killstreak support more easily, and Scavenger can keep you fighting without having to swap weapons mid battle.

You've already learned the importance of Hacker and Ninja, but Second Chance Pro can also be very useful if you're fighting at a distance. Having a teammate revive you is as good as denying the other team a winning kill. Multiple players who fight at a distance with Second Chance Pro increase the odds that distant killshots instead result in no kill at all.

Most Perk 2 choices come down to matching them with your personal preference and your weapon. Hardened bears mentioning because it can help you get kills that would otherwise be difficult or impossible. This is important, because every kill counts more in TDM than in other modes. Consider using it if you're running an SMG or AR, where the extra penetration can really help you.

TDM is very flexible and accepting of many builds. Try various weapon and class loadouts, both to try different weapons and to experiment with class effectiveness.

In general, players have the most success in TDM with builds they're comfortable using. Your attention needs to be focused on the combat instead of working with unfamiliar gear.

Also, it's true that CQB is more dangerous than longer-range combat. If you're not confident in your close-quarters skills, run an Assault Rifle or longer-range build. Just keep in mind that TDM is a good place to get CQB practice if you're training.

Finally, running a stealthy build is always helpful in TDM, even if no one else on your team is doing so. If you plan to run on your own, stealth Perks are nearly mandatory. But if you spend most of the time near your team, they are less critical.

DOMINATION

The rules in Domination are simple. Three points to control A, B, and C. Control of Domination points increases your score. Hit the goal score first, and your team wins.

Suggested Custom Classes

SPEED DEMON

PRIMARY/SECONDARY	Skorpion/Ballistic Knife	
ATTACHMENTS	Extended Mag	
LETHAL/TACTICAL/EQUIPMENT	Tomahawk/Nova Gas/Motion Sensor	
PERK 1	Lightweight	
PERK 2	Steady Aim	
PERK 3	Marathon	
KILLSTREAKS	Mortar Team/Chopper Gunner/ Attack Dogs	

Get from point to point as quickly as possible with this loadout. Then drop a mortar on any points you don't already control.

BOOMER

PRIMARY/SECONDARY	HK21/China Lake	
ATTACHMENTS	Red Dot Sight	
LETHAL/TACTICAL/EQUIPMENT	Frag/Flashbang/C4	
PERK 1	Scavenger	
PERK 2	Sleight of Hand	
PERK 3	Marathon	
KILLSTREAKS	Spy Plane/Care Package/Mortar Team	

Lay down the explosives and keep 'em coming. This class setup restocks your gear so you can keep putting out the boom!

Winning in Domination

The easiest way to win a match in Domination is to hold two of the three points and lock the enemy team at the third point, preventing them from escaping their spawn area or securing another Domination point.

At the beginning of a match, each team spawns near A and C, with B usually being centrally located. Some maps string out the three points in a line, while others locate them in a triangle, or more unevenly.

Almost all maps feature two points that are easier to lock down, with the third (typically A or C) being the area where you should pin the other team.

In almost every map, B is the site of the heaviest fighting. It's by far the most dangerous and difficult of the three points to secure.

If you plan to capture points (and particularly B), bring a class specifically for doing so.

If you find you're on the "bad" side of the map, or if the fight at B is bogging down, it's often a very good idea to sneak around the map's edge and make a run at the opposite point (A or C).

Even one person can accomplish this, as so much attention is focused around the B point. Two or three players provide a much greater chance of success.

Understanding Domination's spawn behavior is very important. Teams usually spawn at or near the points they control. This is why locking down two areas and trapping the other team at one spawn location is desirable.

However, it's important to note that capturing all three points (Dominating) causes the enemy team's spawn to move. Because you can't predict where it ends up, this usually results in the immediate loss of one or more points. Don't let this happen if you're working with an organized group.

The only time we recommend going for a full Domination is when you're trailing in score and will lose the match without holding all three points for some duration!

Remember that points capture more quickly with multiple players on them. This is often key for securing B, where you may have only a few uninterrupted seconds to grab the point between enemy waves.

The downside to planting multiple players on a point is that your entire team is in the open and very vulnerable, especially to explosives.

HUD TIPS

Points being captured give you an audio alert and they flash on your HUD.

If you happen to be nearby when enemies are capturing a point, you can lob an explosive at it. Then quickly sprint to get a sight line to take down whoever is capturing it.

Team Tactics

OFFENSE

To secure a point on offense, eliminate any enemies on or near a point, and then capture it. Alternatively, you can distract nearby enemies long enough to capture it, and then quickly back off to cover the point, switching from offense to defense.

Be very careful about feeding kills in Domination on offense. Losing two points for short periods is not a losing situation, but feeding the enemy team into multiple Killstreaks can turn a tug of war into a lockdown.

If the enemy team does establishes a solid lock on two points, work with your team to push for their rear point. Or, make a dedicated push to flank the enemy position (*not* the center point) and clear them out. Dig out the campers before capturing the point.

You can attempt to push for a rear point or the defenders around the center in two ways. Either make a dedicated push with your entire team in one direction to overwhelm defenses, or split up and hit multiple routes at the same time.

Communicate enemy positions as you move. Even if you die going for a flank, you can still help break the lock if you quickly relay the enemy position to your team.

OFFENSIVE LOADOUT TIPS

For Tactical, bring Willy Pete or Nova Gas grenades, either to clear the point or to conceal it while you go for the capture.

For Perks, bring Flak Jacket and Tactical Mask to render you resistant or immune to incoming explosive spam.

If you're going for a rear point capture, any standard offensively-minded custom classes can work fine as long as you move with your team. However, don't bring an LMG or Sniper for a forward push.

If you're fighting over the center point, consider taking a loadout that includes an Assault Rifle with Grenade Launcher Attachment, Launcher secondary, Scavenger Pro, Warlord Pro, and Hacker Pro or Tactical Mask Pro. This gives you a huge number of explosives, which makes clearing enemies contesting the point or camping in nearby buildings very easy.

You can also clear out a point from a distance with an AR, an LMG, or a Sniper Rifle, but this can be difficult for some points, depending on the map. Consider the terrain involved, and then figure out how best to clear enemy forces from around the point.

DEFENSE

When defending in Domination, set up a perimeter around the point. It should cover all major approach avenues to the point.

You can cover a point at close quarters, but doing so exposes you to risk, and defending a point in Domination is one of the easiest ways to rack up high-end Killstreaks.

You can also cover a point defensively by locking down the only approach routes to it. Use a Camera Spike or Motion Sensor for early warning of enemies following routes you can't watch directly—shut them down before they get close to the point.

Remember that Hacker Pro and Ghost Pro can bypass your Equipment, so keep your ears open for sneaky players, and your eyes open for those using Ninja!

Communication is just as vital on defense as it is on offense. Let your teammates know if you see an enemy you can't hit. If you get taken down, tell your teammates who killed you and from where.

DEFENSIVE LOADOUT TIPS

Setting up C4, Claymores, and Jammers, and waiting at a distance with an AR, LMG, or Sniper Rifle works well for holding a point.

Perks like Scavenger, Hardline, Hardened, Warlord, and Second Chance Pro are useful on defense. They you extra staying power.

You may also want to bring explosives, as they can be handy for quickly taking out enemies who get to the point at the same time.

Nova Gas is particularly useful on defense. With Scavenger, you can replenish your supply to continually bombard a defended point with poisonous smoke. Unless the attackers have Tactical Mask, this makes it almost impossible for them to secure a point safely.

Lone Wolf Tactics

AGGRESSIVE

Even running solo-minded players can do several things to greatly assist their teams. In general, solo captures on point B are difficult. Focus your efforts on two things: flanking enemy defenders and hitting their rear point either to distract or to actually capture the point.

Both roles require playing on the enemy side of the map. You're often outnumbered and have no support. Discretion is the better part of valor if you're holed up partway to the enemy's rear point and you see four of their team running past your hiding position.

To support your offensive push, Lightweight, Marathon, Ninja, Ghost, and Hacker are all very helpful for reaching and then penetrating enemy lines. Depending on the map, you may want to take an SMG or Shotgun because movement speed is paramount. You can also comfortably use an Assault Rifle on some maps.

If you need to pull some defenders away from point B toward A or C, try tapping the point just long enough to trigger the audio warning to the enemy team. Then hightail it to cover and wait for nearby enemy forces to divert to your position. Even better, pull back from the center of the map.

Playing sneaky and backstabbing enemies when they come to investigate works well. If you move fast and stay in cover, you can frustrate the enemy team considerably. Hopefully, this breaks their focus on the center of the map long enough for your team to push up and secure it.

If your team is in a dire situation, or if you're trying to avoid getting locked down on an unfavorable point, try to capture the rear point. This is risky, but it can pay off if you grab the point long enough for your teammates to start spawning around it. The sudden shift in battlefield position can easily lead to a rout of enemies facing the wrong direction when your team rolls in.

DEFENSIVE

Playing smart solo defense can be extremely helpful in Domination, whatever your team is doing. Generally, covering point B is the most important task of any single defender. Get familiar with the turf around the Bravo point and find the best cover and sight lines to protect it.

Assault Rifles, LMGs, and Sniper Rifles are all good choices for defense, as they have the range and power to take down enemy forces that go for the point.

Part of playing defense is simply sitting in one area and waiting for the other team to make a move. On some maps, you need to move between a few defensive positions just to keep an eye on enemy movement.

While you're at it, call out enemies that you spot to your teammates. This is very helpful, as you can't always get a clear shot on every enemy you see.

When you defend B, remember to keep an eye on A or C, whichever of these is your rear point. Canny enemies try to slip past midfield and capture the rear point. Because you rarely see a large enemy push to do this as a group, you can usually handle any stragglers by yourself.

On some maps, it's difficult or impossible to cover both the center and your rear point. In those situations, it's usually better to cover the center. Just be aware that if you lose your rear point for more than a few seconds, the enemy team may begin to spawn there. If that happens, you must usually shift your position quickly or get shot in the back of the head. Grab your equipment and move!

SEARCH AND DESTROY (S&D)

Teams trade offensive and defensive rounds, playing a best of five. The offense starts with a single bomb case, while the defenders must guard two different targets.

Players who die in a round of S&D stay dead.

Either team can win by eliminating the other team completely. The offensive team can win by planting the bomb and guarding it until it detonates. If a defender disarms a planted bomb, or if the time limit expires, the defenders win.

Suggested Custom Classes

THE GRUNT

PRIMARY/SECONDARY	Commando/Python
ATTACHMENTS	Masterkey/Speed Reloader
LETHAL/TACTICAL/EQUIPMENT	Semtext/Willy Pete/C4
PERK 1	Flak Jacket
PERK 2	Sleight of Hand
PERK 3	Hacker
KILLSTREAKS	RC-XD/Care Package/ Sentry Gun

This class supplies you with the explosives you need to attack and defend. Taking the Commando with Masterkey gives you the option to duel in the open or in close quarters.

DOUBLE THREAT

PRIMARY/SECONDARY	G11/M1911
ATTACHMENTS	Variable Zoom/Suppressor
LETHAL/TACTICAL/EQUIPMENT	Semtex/Willy Pete/Camera Spike
PERK 1	Lightweight
PERK 2	Steady Aim
PERK 3	Hacker
KILLSTREAKS	RC-XD/Care Package/Sentry Gun

This package has everything you need to go on the run or pick off enemies from a distance.

Winning in Search and Destroy

Either team has a few ways to win. Killing off the enemy team works, as does planting the bomb (offense) or defusing it once planted (defense). If the attackers fail to plant the bomb or kill the defenders in time, the defense wins.

The offense can force the defenders to come out of hiding by planting the bomb. But defenders also can also kill the bomb carrier and then guard the bomb location, forcing the attackers to assault a known location or risk running out of time.

On offense, going for a quick blitz of the bomb locations is always possible, as is ignoring the bomb locations and simply hunting the defenders.

Because the defenders always start closer to the objectives, it's easier for them to get into favorable positions and watch known approach routes. On the other hand, the attackers don't need to split their forces. Launching a full-team assault on one bomb location can overwhelm the defenders if their forces are split.

On offense, a mix of focus and flexibility serves your team well. Choose which point to assault immediately, and focus your efforts on it. If your assault fails, but one player manages to get the bomb out, you can always retreat. Then, you can either hunt the remaining defenders or plant the bomb at the second location and attempt to guard it until it detonates.

You can also split your team, with one group carrying the bomb and the other acting as a diversion at the second point. Just be sure to communicate the enemy forces you encounter, preferably before the firefighting starts. Once you're dead, you can't communicate with your team for the rest of the round.

Finally, you can also make a concentrated effort to eliminate the defenders. Ignore the bomb locations and avoid the obvious approaches, attempting to flank the enemy team.

Because only a single offensive player can carry the bomb, that player should use a class custom-tailored to plant it, unless your team deliberately goes for kills over plants.

On defense, make an educated guess as to where the offense hits, and set up as quickly as possible. You can put the bulk of your team at the location that's closer to the offense (or the point that gets hit most often), and then leave a single spotter at the other point. If your spotter sees the enemy team moving in force, he can call it out and your team can shift positions.

If you down the bomb carrier, feel free to camp the dropped bomb and wait out the timer. Just make sure you're set up in a safe location with good sight lines to the area. A smart attacker won't run straight for the bomb; he'll try to find any nearby defenders first.

If you don't spot any attackers closing on the bomb locations quickly, check any alternate approaches. The offense may be going for straight combat instead of bomb planting.

Pay very careful attention to HUD indicators that tell you of downed teammates. Knowing where a teammate dies can tell you where his killers are located. Likewise, sound and your minimap are very important.

In Search & Destroy, Equipment and Perk selection is very important. With only a single life per round, stealth, surprise, and information warfare all matter more than they do in other game modes. Choose your loadouts carefully, and be sure to have custom offensive and defensive classes if you play a lot of S&D.

S&D has more flexibility in play style than many other game modes. As a result, there aren't any clear-cut "do this to win" tactics that apply to some other modes. It's also much less forgiving of sloppy play—one mistake, and you have to sit out the round.

Team Tactics

OFFENSE

Before you head out on offense, quickly decide your strategy for the round. This doesn't have to be a lengthy deliberation—just decide if you're going to blitz a specific point, split your team, or rush the defenders.

Once you determine a strategy, execute it as a group. Stay in constant communication. More than any other mode, keeping everyone updated on movement and target positions is critical. You have only one shot at executing the mission.

If you blitz an objective, it's helpful to have everyone use fast-moving classes. Shotgun or SMG builds with Lightweight and Marathon can get you to the site quickly. Smoke and Nova Gas grenades can help cover the bombsite and temporarily block access to the area.

If you can't easily reach at least one bombsite before the defenders do, consider making a more measured push for the objective. Try to arrive at around the same time, but never in a large pack in one location—losing your team to a single explosive isn't fun.

If you split your team, figure out where you're sending the bomb. Have the other team make some noise at the other location to attract attention. Again, stay in contact. You need to know if your decoy team runs into most of the enemies or just one or two.

Finally, if you go after the defenders instead of focusing on the bomb, speed and stealth work best. It's critical to ensure that your opponents can't spot you coming on a Spy Plane or hear you.

If routes to the bombsites are too numerous for enemy defenders to cover, you have a better chance of flanking their team. If there are relatively few approaches, you may have less success trying to circumvent the enemies' "front." There's nothing to stop you from simply engaging in a firefight, but the defenders usually have positional advantage and more time to set up, and that's not a great way to start a battle. Fight unfairly.

OFFENSIVE LOADOUT TIPS

Because stealth and speed are so important on offense, Perks like Lightweight, Ghost, Hacker, Marathon, and Ninja are important.

Flak Jacket and Tactical Mask are both helpful for planting a bomb.

Hacker bears special mention because on many maps, the defenders can get in place to set up Equipment before you can reach the bombsites. You really don't want to walk past their cameras, into their jammed sensor network, and killed by C4 and Claymores. Make sure at least one player runs Hacker to spot these and clear the way.

Bringing your own Jammers is advisable, as you can set them up to disable nearby enemy equipment.

Motion Sensors are somewhat useful if you plant a bomb. You can set one up nearby for early warning of enemies moving in to clear the area.

For Tactical gear, bring Willy Pete smoke grenades, both for covering the bombsite and for providing cover on the approach. Nova Gas can also flush out campers and block routes to the bomb.

Smoke grenades and Decoy grenades can both create a distraction. Drop them down a route you aren't using to attract attention, or use them to try to make nearby defenders move and blow their cover.

DEFENSE

Defenders in Search and Destroy have the marked advantage of starting much closer to the bombsites than the offense.

Prepare your defense plan before the round starts. Make the most of that time to get into position and set up.

You have to cover two different bomb locations and prepare for the possibility that the offense may ignore the bomb locations or try to bait you into going after the wrong one.

Rapid communication is the key to identifying the enemy's plan quickly. Get into position, set up, and then talk to each other about any enemy sightings.

One risky but workable tactic is to abandon traditional defense entirely and hit the enemy team as they move advance. This tactic's main advantage is surprise—the offense rarely expects to get hit out of position, especially if most of your team moves to attack.

Just be very careful. This is an all-or-nothing strategy. One Ghost/Ninja bomb carrier that sneaks past your line can end the match in a hurry, even if you kill his teammates.

If you opt to hold on defense, decide whether to split your defenders evenly or stack on one point, and whether or not to send out a scout.

Rather than send your whole team forward, have one or two players advance as forward scouts. This method bogs down the attackers, who can't be sure how many players are hitting them. It also gives you an early indication of your opponents' strategy for the round.

If they push one direction en masse, you'll get early warning, and your point man may be able to fall back before he gets overwhelmed. Similarly, no enemy action is as telling as a visible push—you can usually assume they're pushing on your secondary bomb location.

When you set up defense around the bombsites, quickly plant your Equipment. Then dig in near cover, preferably with superior elevation and visibility, in that order. Change your position from round to round. When an RPG hits the wall behind you in round two, you'll understand that surprise matters more than a perfect position.

If you split your defenders, maintain communication. You may have to shift players from one spot to the other if one spot gets rushed.

If you focused on one point, either leave one man behind to catch any sneaky plant attempts, or make sure the map is small enough and your team has fast loadouts to help them switch positions quickly.

DEFENSIVE LOADOUT TIPS

Equipment is very important on defense. Literally, every piece of Equipment except possibly Tactical Insertion is useful for defense. Configure your team loadouts so that each player contributes a different piece of gear.

However, don't rely on Equipment too heavily. While it's useful and important, Hacker, Ghost, and offensive Jammers can shut down or bypass your gear.

Speed and stealth are less critical on defense unless you preemptively attack the offensive team. Otherwise, worry more about firepower and survivability.

Scavenger, Hardened, Warlord, Second Chance, and occasionally Flak Jacket and Tactical Mask can all be useful on defense.

Assault Rifles, LMGs, and, depending on the map, Sniper Rifles are excellent choices. Because you have the luxury of time to set up and prepare for attackers, you can often get into position to engage them at long range before they close with the objectives. However, remember that you usually have to shift your weapons down one range band on smaller maps.

Infrared scopes bear special mention. Because good offensive teams often use smoke to conceal their approach or the bombsites, make sure at least one player can pierce the fog and take down enemy targets.

Nova Gas is particularly good on defense, but be wary about relying on it too much, as Tactical Mask can render it useless.

Lone Wolf Tactics

AGGRESSIVE

In general, lone wolf tactics are a bad idea in Search and Destroy, but you can be effective running on your own.

Definitely use a stealthy build if you run alone. You need to hide from your enemy's Spy Planes, Equipment, and ears.

Ghost paired with Hacker or Ninja works well. The main problem with taking Ninja over Hacker is that Motion Sensors can spot you. On the other hand, if you take Hacker, defenders can hear you if you aren't careful. This is a tough choice to make, because the power of each depends on the skill of your opponents. If your opponents aren't using Equipment, switch to your Ninja build.

Bring a Suppressor for your weapon, and you may want to use a Jammer as well. Just be careful, because smart opponents use radar noise to get an approximate lock on your location. You can use this to fake out defenders to some extent; just be aware of the risk of using it if you're behind enemy lines and undetected.

SMGs and ARs both work well for solo operations, Shotguns are usually too short-range to work effectively, though a silenced SPAS can be effective for CQB on some maps. LMGs and Sniper Rifles aren't typically ideal for running solo, though long-range sniping can be effective on a few maps.

DEFENSIVE

Running solo on defense is a bit easier than offense. As long as you actively protect a bomb location or go after the bomb carrier, you're helping your team.

Just be careful about being overly aggressive. While playing the scout or offensively-minded player on defense can be helpful, it's also very easy to get shot by a mass of attackers and contribute nothing to your team.

Bring useful defensive Equipment and set it up before you take up position. You can also serve your team as a roaming player who keeps an eye on both bomb locations, particularly if you take speedy Perks to move between locations.

HEADQUARTERS

Headquarters places your squad in a battle to control randomly chosen areas of the map. Teams fight to capture a single control point and defend it. The first team to the target score wins the match.

Once a headquarters area is captured, defenders do not respawn until the point is "destroyed" by the attackers.

Suggested Custom Classes

HOT DOGS

PRIMARY/SECONDARY	AK74u/M72 LAW	
ATTACHMENTS	Grip	
LETHAL/TACTICAL/EQUIPMENT	Frag/Concussion/Tactical Insertion	
PERK 1	Lightweight	
PERK 2	Steady Aim	
PERK 3	Second Chance	
KILLSTREAKS	RC-XD/Napalm Strike/Attack Dogs	

With firepower and a "second chance," this class can help you control more headquarters than the enemy team.

BIG BOY

PRIMARY/SECONDARY	M60/M72 LAW	
ATTACHMENTS	Grip	
LETHAL/TACTICAL/EQUIPMENT	Semtex/Nova Gas/Motion Sensor	
PERK 1	Flak Jacket	
PERK 2	Steady Aim	
PERK 3	Second Chance	
KILLSTREAKS	Care Package/Chopper Gunner/Gunship	

This kit puts a hurting on anyone who gets in your way. Use the heavy firepower to rip through the walls of any headquarters you encounter.

Winning in Headquarters

Winning in Headquarters requires a good mix of offensive power and defensive strength to establish control of a point and then defend it. Unlike Domination, there's no easy way to trap the enemy team in a spawn location or establish complete control of a map's scoring areas.

The match starts with teams spawning in normal Team Deathmatch locations. After a short delay, the headquarters control point is announced. Then, an icon is placed on your minimap, and a HUD indicator is created to direct you to the location. There are a predefined set of potential control points, but the selection of each one is random.

Almost every control point in a Headquarters map has multiple attack vectors and defensive positions. Your task at the beginning of a match is to approach the first headquarters point and establish control of the area.

In some cases, the Headquarters spawns closer to one team. If you're fortunate enough to spawn closer to an HQ, establish defensive positions as quickly as possible. If you're on the distant team, expect the enemy team to establish control ahead of you. Your assault should be quick but careful and should avoid as many chokepoints as possible.

Once an HQ is captured, the opposing team must assault the position to destroy it. The team holding the point can defend it but cannot respawn until either the enemy team destroys the headquarters, or the time limit for holding a single point expires.

If you're attempting to destroy a captured Headquarters, it's important to be quick but tactical in your assault. A few extra capture points are far less damaging than handing an unrestrained Killstreak assault to the defenders during the next point's capture period. We recommend careful, surgical assaults.

Class choices and Killstreak configurations are far less obvious in a Headquarters match. It's important to balance assault capabilities with static defensive power, as there is no class change when a point goes from being captured to being defended.

Team Tactics

OFFENSE

Offense is the primary role in Headquarters, as most fighting revolves around establishing control of a point. That said, a polarized configuration that favors offensive power over anything else is typically unsuccessful. The distinctions between offense and defense in Headquarters are fleeting.

OFFENSIVE LOADOUT TIPS

As in offensive Domination loadouts, choose a class with Willy Pete (smoke) or Nova Gas grenades in the Tactical Grenade spot. The smoke offers coverage during a capture or destruction, while the Nova Gas weakens any CQB defenders near the point.

For Perks, we again recommend Flak Jacket and Tactical Mask, as explosives and grenades are a certainty when you defend a captured point. Scavenger Pro and Warlord Pro are also nice, as they give you more explosives to help dislodge a stubborn Headquarters defense.

As in most modes, an Assault Rifle treats you well in Headquarters. Taking Warlord Pro allows you to attach a Masterkey and your favorite sight to the Assault Rifle, which helps with room clearing.

If you play on a map with lots of confined areas, such as the buildings on WMD or Cracked, use an SMG to maximize close-quarters lethality. They can usually assault and defend an interior position.

LMGs and Sniper Rifles can be useful if the point in question has some very predictable paths. With less mobility, an LMG is ill suited to the mobile nature of Headquarters combat, but the upside is that the deep magazines can be very useful for stalling an enemy advance.

DEFENSE

Your role in a Headquarters match constantly changes between assault and defense, without the opportunity to change loadouts. Adopting a pure defensive posture prevents you from properly assaulting a point when the Headquarters moves.

Point defense in Headquarters follows many of the general defense guidelines for any other game mode. Perimeter defenses that cover all attack routes around the point are a must. Defending an HQ from inside the room assuredly results in death from grenade spam.

Constant communication about enemy locations is vital in Headquarters. Dying to a flanking attacker removes you from the battlefield and prevents you from properly warning your teammates. Call out all targets as they approach so that if you die, your teammates know what to expect.

DEFENSIVE LOADOUT TIPS

The usual assortment of C4, Claymores, Jammers, and Motion Detectors are useful when you defend an HQ. Don't stress about placement—you have a small amount of time between capturing a point and the next wave of attackers. Put them in general areas of approach and get to your defensive position.

Assault Rifles and SMGs work well for defense and offer the offensive utility necessary for assaulting the next point. Properly positioned, an LMG can deny one entrance to the Headquarters, which can easily translate to a full hold on a point.

Flak Jacket and Tactical Mask provide the explosive protection to survive an onslaught of explosions if you're defending from inside the control point.

Several teammates with Second Chance Pro can revive each other if one gets killed defending a point. With proper timing, your team can reestablish its defensive posture before the next wave of attackers arrives.

Lone Wolf Tactics

AGGRESSIVE

Solo play in Headquarters is difficult, as every player on the map is focused toward the capture objective. It's unlikely that a single player can break through the defenses of another team or hold off attackers while he captures a point.

Offensive mobility Perks such as Lightweight and Marathon are great for penetrating deep into the enemy position quickly. They also let you move from HQ to HQ more quickly when a point capture time elapses. Perks like Ninja, Ghost, and Hacker assist in slipping into enemy territory to wreak havoc in their backfield. We recommend SMGs for speed, but an Assault Rifle can extend your engagement range, a must on some maps to avoid being overrun by the advancing enemy push.

While a point is contested, the aggressive solo player should focus on attacking an exposed enemy flank as they trundle toward the objective. A good solo player who strikes tactically can remove one or two players per spawn wave from the attacking force, enough to swing the capture in favor of his team. As in Domination, use discretion when you attack enemies from exposed flanks, as they outnumber and outgun you in a fair fight.

Once a team captures a point focuses on defense, an aggressive solo player on the attacking team should assault the enemy from any attack routes that the rest of the team isn't using. A well-placed explosive and some lethal CQB can devastate an HQ defense.

Playing aggressively as a solo player while your team defends a capture point is a good way to give your comrades one less defender. Roaming the attack avenues and removing an attacker or two during a wave can be helpful, but assuming a defensive stance is more effective in the end and assists in holding the captured point for the maximum duration.

DEFENSIVE

While an HQ is still contested, there is no effective means to play defensively. However, once your team captures the point, a good solo player can be extremely effective in holding it.

Most HQs provide multiple attack routes for the other team. A coordinated defense is the only way to hold the capture point, so learning to communicate by calling enemy locations and predicting assault strength is paramount.

Defense in Headquarters is hectic and lively, with the full brunt of the enemy team assaulting your position. Prioritize quick movement and lethality over other factors when you choose a loadout for solo defense. An LMG positioned to cover a major attack route can devastate an enemy team and direct their attack to a more defensible position. Assault Rifles and SMGs also provide enough firepower to fend off an attack. Sniper Rifles are rarely useful in Headquarters defense, as the setup time doesn't allow for careful long-range positioning.

Whichever loadout you choose, your only objective is defending the HQ point. Find a good spot, set up some deployables—C4, Claymore, Motion Sensor, Jammers, Cameras—and wait for the enemy team to come to you.

DEMOLITION

Teams trade offense and defense. One bomb, two bombsites, just like Search and Destroy. Unlike S&D, in Demolition, players do respawn, so defenders must repel a continuous wave of offense. Additionally, both sites must be destroyed, and defusing the bomb does not win the round. In fact, you should expect many defusings in close games, so holding out on defense is a constant struggle.

Suggested Custom Classes

HEAVY DUTY

PRIMARY/SECONDARY	RPK/China Lake
ATTACHMENTS	Extended Mag
LETHAL/TACTICAL/EQUIPMENT	Frag/Decoy/Camera Spike
PERK 1	Ghost
PERK 2	Hardened
PERK 3	Second Chance
KILLSTREAKS	Counter Spy Plane/Mortar Team/Rolling Thunder

Take this setup and help your teammates by laying down massive covering fire while staying off the radar.

QUICK AND THE DEAD

PRIMARY/SECONDARY	MP5K/Ballistic Knife
ATTACHMENTS	Suppressor
LETHAL/TACTICAL/EQUIPMENT	Semtex/Decoy/C4
PERK 1	Lightweight
PERK 2	Sleight of Hand
PERK 3	Ninja
KILLSTREAKS	Spy Plane/Care Package/Mortar Team

Run fast and quiet with this kit in your arsenal. Super fast reloads, speed, and silence are great assets in Demolition.

Winning in Demolition

Because you trade offense and defense, you need a plan for each side.

On offense, quickly decide which point to tackle, and push that point hard with your entire team. Because the defenders typically respawn closer to the bombsites, picking the right target and blitzing is important.

You can split your team, but this is usually a bad idea because of the time penalty for dying. You don't want to give the defenders any more time or Killstreaks than necessary.

In Demolition, it's a good idea to go for the more difficult bombsite first. Once one of the two sites goes down, all of the defenders concentrate at the remaining site. If you remove the more difficult plant site first, you make the job of winning the round much easier.

On defense, decide whether to split your forces and which point to cover first. On a few maps, you can give up one point somewhat easily and defend the point that's much harder for the attackers to assault. However, this can be risky.

It's very important to recognize when a position is lost—avoid throwing away lives and time on a hopeless cause. If the attackers plant the bomb and they're set up in cover around the point, fall back and set up your defenses at the remaining point. Feeding the offense Killstreaks just makes your job harder in the match's later stages.

Communication on defense is vital, especially if you're covering both points. Be aware of the enemy team's position at all times. Quickly determine which point they're pushing harder if you need to shift defenders from one location to another. If you go down on a point, let your teammates know how many attackers are still standing and planting.

One last point: save Killstreaks between rounds. Storing up Killstreaks and then unleashing them in concert at the start of a new round can have devastating results. On offense, it can give you a quick win. On defense, it can shut down the offense entirely until they overcome the barrage.

Team Tactics

OFFENSE

Offensive coordination need not be much more complex than picking an initial target. It's important for your team to move as a group to assault and secure the selected target.

Generally, splitting up is a bad idea, because even if a few players plant a bomb, staying in place and guarding it before defenders assault the area en masse is difficult at best.

Even by a single player can go for a "fake" plant at one site. This can draw defenders away from your real target. It can work particularly well if you have a stealth-specialized player plant on the secondary target, and then have the remainder of the team blitz the primary bombsite.

Keep the team apprised of defender sightings at each bombsite, and advise your team's long-range combatants if you spot a sniper or gunner covering an area.

If a push on your primary target isn't working and you're bogging down, you may have to accept the setback and tackle the secondary bombsite. This isn't an ideal situation, but it's better to extend the round with the chance of a win than to give away the whole round without destroying either point.

Be ready to make this call early enough to switch focus. Realizing you can't break the more important site with only a minute left isn't enough time to change targets and take down a guarded plant.

OFFENSIVE LOADOUT TIPS

On larger maps, Tactical Insertions are your lifeblood. In no other mode is a piece of Equipment so important. Your entire team should use Insertions unless you absolutely need a Jammer to shut down enemy Equipment.

Don't try to be sneaky and plant Insertions very close to the bombsites on your initial push. Instead, set them up about halfway from your spawn to the bombsite. This prevents easy discovery of your team's Insertions, and cuts the time needed to apply pressure on the bombsites tremendously.

Do not plant all of your team's Insertions in one area, and be sure to move them around if the enemy team wises up and clears them out. The offensive benefits of spawning closer to the objective far, far outweigh the cost of an occasional double death to an Insertion.

Jammers are also important on offense. Set them up just outside the bombsite to shut down enemy Equipment and weaken enemy intelligence.

Smoke grenades are extremely important in Demolition. Maintain constant smoke screens to obscure sight lines to bombsites and create confusion around the bomb plant area.

Expect to encounter heavy Equipment and explosive defenses, so bring Perks to nullify or weaken their effectiveness, especially if plan to plant the bomb frequently.

Flak Jacket and Tactical Mask are highly advisable for bomb planting. For general purposes, Marathon is very important to get you back to the front quickly.

Hacker is valuable on offense. Expect to run into all type of enemy Equipment. Be sure to have a Hacker on duty near bombsites to call out trouble.

While you can expect to receive painful explosive fire on most maps, on some, you may wish to bring a boomer of your own. If the defenders set up in small rooms, or if a lot of cover and debris is around the bombsites, Grenade Launchers, RPGs, and Lethal Grenades backed up with Scavenger Pro and Warlord Pro can clear them out easily.

On other maps, having a sniper or an LMG gunner hang back to deal with long-range threats may be important. This is especially true if your enemies have a dangerous sniper or long-range fighter suppressing your team when you're trying to plant the bomb.

DEFENSE

Defense in Demolition can be stressful. You must deal with a constant wave of attackers, disarm bomb plants repeatedly, and shuffle your forces between each bombsite in response to enemy pushes.

Your first push should be to establish a defensive perimeter at each site. Set up your Equipment quickly, and then get to cover.

On some maps, you can anticipate which site is more likely to get hit first. Have the bulk of your team waiting there. On other maps, it may not be so clear-cut. Try to set up defenses at both sites, and have teammates ready to switch positions as needed.

When you're forced to make a choice, always focus on the more difficult of the two sites for the attackers to handle. At all costs, hold the point that's furthest from their spawn, has the best cover for you and the least for attackers, or is closest to your own spawn.

On many maps, it can be very important to have a scout sweeper with Hacker and possibly Lightweight and Marathon with a mobile weapon. The sweeper's job is to push out from bombsites and destroy any enemy Tactical Insertions. You can't allow an offensive team to set up Insertions close to the bombsites unopposed. If you do, you're almost guaranteed to be overwhelmed. Their Insertions almost certainly are more ideal spawns than your natural ones!

The scout can also relay useful intel on enemy movements, letting the rest of the defense know which bombsite is about to be hit.

Don't give up a bombsite until the bitter end. But, if the offense gets a plant and has the area tightly locked down, know when to surrender it, and move to reinforce your position at the remaining bombsite. Get new Equipment in place, and set up your team.

If you do your job well, the attackers will have very little time to secure the remaining bombsite. If you hold the tougher point, so much the better—now they have little time, and they have to attack a very difficult point with the whole defensive team in place to stop them.

DEFENSIVE LOADOUT TIPS

Equipment is very important on defense. Even Tactical Insertions may be useful on certain maps. But in general, C4, Claymores, Motion Sensors, and Jammers should be your first priority, with Camera Spikes used on some maps to cover approaches that aren't worth stationing a player.

Use and abuse explosives heavily on defense. Because you know the attackers must hit a fixed point to plant the bomb, AR Grenade Launchers and the RPG, LAW, and China Lake can all be used to good effect, as well as Lethal grenades and Nova Gas. Have at least one player pack a boom build, and have multiple players carry Nova Gas as their secondary.

Unless the entire offensive force takes Flak Jacket and Tactical Mask, either or both of your explosives and Nova Gas prove an easy deterrent to unsupported bomb plants.

Generally, most plants come from having the immediate defenders cleared out of the area, so you may need one or more players with a speedy setup. Select Tactical Insertions, Lightweight, and Marathon to get back to the bombsite quickly. To stall a push, all you have to do is kill the planter, so have at least one player who can always get back to a bombsite rapidly after dying.

Area saturation Killstreaks bear special mention here. The Napalm Strike, Mortar Team, and Rolling Thunder can have lethal results if you place them on a bombsite where the attackers have just pushed.

And one final, amusing tip: Use drop packages of any sort to distract the attackers. Tossing a SAM or Care Package away from a bombsite often coaxes greedy attackers to go after the package instead pursuing the more important goal.

Lone Wolf Tactics

AGGRESSIVE

It's difficult to play as a solo operative in Demolition, but you can be very effective if you're careful. First, a stealthy build that gets behind the enemy lines is ideal in Demolition, because defenders usually focus on accessing and then guarding bombsites.

If you can get past the bombsites and avoid the path of respawned defenders, you can get into position to perform a devastating sweep. Wait for your team to make a push on the site, and then hit the defenders from behind. Clearing out the defense assures an easy plant.

Tactical Insertions are even more valuable in this role than they are for a general offensive push. You can drop an Insertion behind enemy lines without raising suspicion the way your whole team spawning nearby does. Just be careful, as one alert defender with Hacker can ruin your fun.

Running Hardline with Spy Planes and Counter-Spy Planes is a great way to keep your team aware of enemy positions and deny the enemy any intel.

The other option is to avoid a stealthy CQB push, and instead hang back to support your team from afar. On some maps, a Sniper Rifle or an LMG can provide devastating fire support from a distance, and you can rack up significant Killstreaks by doing so. Use a higher-end Killstreak loadout and go for survival. A properly timed Killstreak can tip the balance in your team's favor, and constantly picking off defenders from a distance doesn't hurt either.

DEFENSIVE

Playing a solo operative on defense is tricky. You can go about this a few ways. The first method is to play an aggressive defense. Take Hacker and push out, playing the "scout" role outlined above. Wipe out enemy Tactical Insertions, or wait to kill them as they spawn. Then move to intercept them when they respawn.

Another option is to play as a floating defender, constantly moving between the points and the midfield, intercepting enemies as they attempt to push on either bombsite. This is a very difficult role to play well. You need exceptional situational awareness and map knowledge, or you'll get overwhelmed and gunned down.

Finally, as on offense, on some maps, having a defender who hangs back with an LMG or Sniper Rifle to provide long-range fire support can be very helpful. Again, running high-end Killstreaks is a good idea, as you're exposed to less risk and can usually rack up bigger streaks. If your team seems to be winning a round, save the pain for the next round, and you can convert the round win into a blowout match victory.

CAPTURE THE FLAG (CTF)

Each team must protect a flag at its base. The object is to steal the opposing team's flag from their base and carry it back to your own base. Capturing the opposing team's flag enough times to reach the score limit wins the match. Return your team's dropped flag by touching it. Your flag must be in your base to capture the enemy flag.

Suggested Custom Classes

SHOOTER

PRIMARY/SECONDARY	HS10/CZ75
ATTACHMENTS	Dual Wield/Full Auto Upgrade
LETHAL/TACTICAL/EQUIPMENT	Semtex/Willy Pete/Tactical Insertion
PERK 1	Hardline
PERK 2	Sleight of Hand
PERK 3	Marathon
KILLSTREAKS	Spy Plane/SAM Turret/Gunship

Use this class to protect your flag runner with dual shotguns. Blast those pesky enemies that pop out just as you're about to return a flag.

RUNNING MAN

PRIMARY/SECONDARY	Skorpion/Makarov
ATTACHMENTS	Dual Wield
LETHAL/TACTICAL/EQUIPMENT	Frag/Flashbang/Tactical Insertion
PERK 1	Lightweight
PERK 2	Steady Aim
PERK 3	Marathon
KILLSTREAKS	Spy Plane/Napalm Strike/Mortar Team

Take this class if you plan to be the flag runner. Use the dual Skorpions to eliminate obstacles in your path.

Winning in Capture the Flag

Unlike some other objective modes, CTF does not have discrete offensive and defensive rounds for each team. To play CTF successfully, you need a mix of offense and defense every round.

Divide your team into defense and offense. Generally, two players on defense are sufficient, while you want one or two flag runners. The remaining two players should lean toward offense, trying to clear out defenders but also clearing a path for friendly runners.

You can afford to field a light defense for two reasons. First, the enemy team's offense must cross the map, which means encountering your own offensive team. Second, your defense typically respawns very near the flag if they end up dying.

Team Tactics

OFFENSE

Split your offensive squad into two smaller teams, one for actually running the flag and the other for clearing out flag defenders and covering the midfield, responding to the flag runners' needs as necessary.

You can get away with one flag runner, but it's usually safer to go with two. If one goes down, the other can pick up the slack.

Midfield roamers need to be alert, flexible players who can push aggressively against the defense. They must also warn your defense when enemies are incoming, escort the flag carrier, clear a route for them, and recover your own flag if it's taken.

Your flag runners need stealthy and speedy builds, the better to get in and out as quickly as possible. Engaging the enemy team is not the top priority; grabbing the flag and bringing it home in one piece is. Fight only when necessary, evade whenever possible.

Remember that the flag is likely to be mined with Claymores or C4. Even if you don't have Hacker equipped, you can disable them temporarily with Concussion or Flashbang grenades. Concussion throws more quickly, while Flashbang may blind a nearby defender for you.

Your flag runners are likely to get killed a lot when they go for the flag. This is simply a part of the job. Don't go feeding the defenders, but if you have a choice between caution and a dangerous flag run attempt, make the attempt.

Your whole offense should be coordinated and communicative. It's important to time flag-run attempts when the midfield offense has cleared out enemy defenders. Alternatively, make a flag run with your whole offensive force en masse to overwhelm defenders and get the flag moving.

OFFENSIVE LOADOUT TIPS

Your midfield players should use flexible combat builds. Assault Rifles are ideal on many maps, and they should be paired with Perks like Scavenger, Warlord, Hardened, Hacker, and possibly Marathon. They must respond to an urgent need for a flag runner or flag recovery.

Equip your flag runners with Shotguns or SMGs with Lightweight and Marathon. Speed is paramount over most other considerations. If you have serious problems getting into the enemy position, Ghost and a Suppressor can help.

Flag runners should always carry Tactical Insertions. You want to respawn as close to the enemy base as possible, so you can make many flag run attempts.

Your offense needs at least one player with Hacker and a Jammer to shut down enemy Equipment around the bombsite. Bringing ranged explosives to clear out campers and Equipment can also help. Make sure the flag site is clear of any C4 or Claymores for your flag runners.

Because flag runners are at constant risk, they should run low-level Killstreaks. On the other end of the spectrum, your defense should run higher Killstreaks, as they are in the best position to rack up kills.

DEFENSE

You can mount an adequate CTF defense with just a few players. Because the other team has to run through most of your team just to get a chance at running the flag, and you have the advantage of Equipment and setup time, it's much easier to guard the flag than it is to capture it.

Assuming you have a partner on defense, pick complementary camping spots with good coverage of the major approaches to the flag. On some maps, you may not even need to keep the flag in line of sight, as long as there is no other way for the enemy team to reach it. On other maps, you may be able to set up shop in view of the flag and still watch approaches.

Longer-range weapons are usually preferable on defense, and the Assault Rifle and Sniper Rifle both work well. The LMG is very powerful on defense as well, but the mobility penalty is undesirable here. You may be called on to react quickly to an enemy who downs another defender. Or you many have to venture into midfield to recover a stolen flag, and the LMG's subpar mobility hinders both of those tasks.

Equipment usage is important on defense. Use it to help protect the flag.

Communication is critical, especially if it looks as though your will be taken, or if it *is* taken. Quickly notify your team. If you see where the enemy runner is going, tell your team. If you respond quickly enough, the runner can be intercepted before he even reaches the halfway point.

DEFENSIVE LOADOUT TIPS

All types of Equipment are important on defense, but Claymores and C4 bear special mention. Because you can place them on or near the flag, the enemy team must clear them before they can safely take the flag. The act of doing so alerts you to their presence.

Use Motion Sensors and Camera Spikes to cover approaches to the flag that you can't watch in person.

Scavenger, Hardened, Warlord, Second Chance, and Tactical Mask are all useful on defense. Flak Jacket may be useful depending on how heavily the offensive team is using explosives to flush you out.

Nova Gas is extremely strong on defense. Tossing it on the flag whenever an enemy draws near and then restocking it with Scavenger makes it very difficult for flag runners to get in and out without Tactical Mask. If they do have the mask, they lose Marathon, making them less effective at getting back across the map.

Lone Wolf Tactics

AGGRESSIVE

Solo operatives can be very effective in CTF. You're especially valuable in the midfield role, as long as you communicate well with your team. At the very least, pay close attention flag status and teammate positioning so you can move to intercept a stolen flag or help escort a flag runner.

You can also find success as a flag runner if your build is more suited to speed.

Depending on what you favor, take a class that matches with the role you want to assume. Bring Tactical Insertions and Marathon to go flag running, or take a more all-around combatant build to be more effective as a midfield operative.

DEFENSIVE

Running solo defense in CTF is quite easy, as long as you have a build suited to it. Outside of communication, a defender in CTF essentially *is* a solo player.

Make sure your build is suited to defense, and bring along some high-end Killstreaks if you plan to camp heavily. Or use moderate ones if you occasionally leave the flag area to patrol the midfield.

SABOTAGE

Sabotage is the last of the "bomb" modes. Each team has a single bomb plant site, and a single bomb spawns in the center of the map.

Unlike other modes, there is no offense/defense switch. Instead, both teams must rush to secure the bomb and then forcefully push to plant and secure the site until the bomb detonates. The first team to plant and detonate the bomb wins; defusing does not end the match.

Sabotage is also not "even" in that there is no half-time side swap. Your team may end up on an unfavorable position for the duration of some matches.

Suggested Custom Classes

BLUR

PRIMARY/SECONDARY	PM63/Python	
ATTACHMENTS	Extended Mag/Acog Sight	
LETHAL/TACTICAL/EQUIPMENT	Tomahawk/Decoy/Jammer	
PERK 1	Lightweight	
PERK 2	Steady Aim	
PERK 3	Marathon	
KILLSTREAKS	Counter Spy Plane/Blackbird/Attack Dogs	

You're have to be quick when you pick up the bomb. This class can help you on that score. You can't get rid of the "Kill" arrow, but with this loadout, you can move fast enough to spin enemy heads.

VOYAGER

PRIMARY/SECONDARY	Galil/ASP	
ATTACHMENTS	Reflex Scope & Dual Mag/Dual Wield	
LETHAL/TACTICAL/EQUIPMENT	Semtex/Concussion/Claymore	
PERK 1	Ghost	
PERK 2	Warlord	
PERK 3	Ninja	
KILLSTREAKS	Sentry Gun/Valkyrie Rockets/Rolling Thunder	

Use this package to help clear the way for your bomb runner. Toss your grenades in front of you, and place your Claymores behind you.

Winning in Sabotage

Success in Sabotage depends on applying extreme force at the bombsite long enough to remove all defenders from the area, plant the bomb, and hold the bombsite until the bundle of joy detonates.

Because there is only one bomb and one bombsite to defend, this can be very difficult to pull off successfully.

Make an early push to see if you can end the match immediately. If the defenders put up too much resistance, back off. Instead of pushing, hold back and kill the attackers repeatedly when they try to push with the bomb. Do this until your team accumulates several Killstreaks, but do *not* use them immediately.

Once your team "stores" a set of Killstreaks, make a serious push. Grab the bomb and head for the enemy bombsite. When your bomb carrier is almost in position, call down hellfire and fury on the heads of your enemies. Bring in Attack Helicopters, Chopper Gunners, Attack Dogs, or Gunships. Set up Sentry Guns. Call in all forms of bombardment, Napalm Strikes, Mortar Teams, and Rolling Thunder.

The idea here is to so completely overwhelm the defenders with a sudden mass of Killstreaks that they cannot effectively defend the bombsite, even if they are in position to do so.

There is no half-time mode in Sabotage, so if your team ends up on the more difficult side of the map, you may have a harder time winning outright. If that happens, holing up and accumulating Killstreaks becomes even more important, though the success of your team strongly depends on how defensible your bombsite is.

It's important that your entire team stays flexible in Sabotage. You may be pushing across the map one minute, and then chasing a bomb carrier or defending your bombsite the next.

Team Tactics

OFFENSE

Because Sabotage doesn't have a defense/offense split like some other modes, the distinction between offense and defense is a muddy one.

That said, the general idea is that any time you push to plant the bomb, your team is on "offense." Otherwise, you're on "defense," either camping the dropped bomb or guarding your own bombsite.

Because Sabotage demands flexible play, run a generalist class or be prepared to switch classes when you die and you need to shift battlefield roles.

When you push for an enemy bombsite, clear out the defenders to enable a plant. If the enemy is playing defense at all, simply going for the plant even under the cover of smoke and friendly fire is very difficult, and surviving to defend the planted bomb is unlikely.

Try to attack the bombsite from as many different directions as possible to overwhelm the defenders' ability to respond. On some maps, this simply may not be possible, but when the option is there, take it.

If you don't have the bomb in your possession to plant, you need to secure it, which may involve hunting down the enemy bomb carrier and killing him.

One risky option is to let the enemy team make a push while part of your offense stays in enemy territory to secure the bombsite. If you can clear out the remaining defenders while part of their team pushes with the bomb, you have a good chance of setting up shop around the bombsite and taking out any returning defenders. This relies on the rest of your team to secure the bomb and bring it to the bombsite while undermanned, so it's a difficult feat to pull off consistently.

One last point: If it looks like the enemy team is making no effort to move the bomb, they may be camping it in an effort to generate Killstreaks. Don't feed the enemy team free kills. Group up and make a concentrated push to clear out any nearby enemies, and *then* make a move for the bomb.

In Sabotage, securing the area before you make a move, whether around the bombsite or around the bomb itself, is very important.

OFFENSIVE LOADOUT TIPS

If you're pushing on offense for the enemy bomb plant, Hacker and explosives can be handy to spot enemy Equipment and clear out campers. Scavenger can help you stay loaded with ammunition.

Ghost, Marathon, and Second Chance are all helpful, and if you plan to go for the bomb plant, Flak Jacket and Tactical Mask are almost mandatory. Be sure to bring Smoke and Decoy grenades, as both are useful for covering the bombsite and distracting defenders.

While Jammers are still important on offense, you may also want to bring Motion Sensors and possibly Tactical Insertions. You can set up a temporary defensive position once you secure the bombsite and exploit the ability to control your spawn location.

DEFENSE

"Defense" in Sabotage means one of two things: Either you're actively defending your bombsite against an enemy push with the bomb; or you're camping the bomb itself, playing keep-away with the enemy to rack up Killstreaks in preparation for an offensive push of your own.

The tactics here are slightly more mobile than they are in most other objective modes outside of Headquarters. While you can still set up a traditional defensive perimeter around your bombsite, you are constantly moving around the map when you defend the bomb itself.

As a result, you don't always have the advantage of the best defensive positions. Make the most of what you have if you're stuck in an open firefight around a dropped bomb.

Another option is to hide out with the bomb on the terrain of your choice. This can force the enemy team to engage you on your terms.

If you're defending your bombsite, you can push out and return to "offense" once the area is cleared of attackers and the bomb is in your team's hands.

As a general rule, don't let the bomb stay around your bombsite. Camping the bomb or holding it is fine, but if you do this near your bombsite, you risk losing the bomb and the match very quickly. Losing the bomb near the enemy site or midfield is almost always preferable.

DEFENSIVE LOADOUT TIPS

Because defense is rarely completely static in Sabotage, configuring your loadout can be tricky.

Equipment is still useful, but you need to be ready to pick up and move your gear more often than in most modes. If the "front line" moves because the bomb moves, you have to reposition Motion Sensors, Jammers, Camera Spikes, and possibly explosives as well.

In general, C4 and Claymores are a bit less useful in Sabotage, though they are still effective for defending the bombsite itself.

For Perks, Lightweight, Scavenger, Second Chance, and Tactical Mask can all be useful when you defend an area.

Marathon is still important for defenders, because you may be called to relocate quickly, and running out of breath partway there can cause problems.

Nova Gas is still useful for defending the bombsite or dropped bomb. Pair it with a Lethal grenade of your choice.

Bring an Infrared Scope if the other team uses smoke to cover the bomb and bombsite.

Lone Wolf Tactics

AGGRESSIVE

It's very difficult to help your team with solo-style play in Sabotage. Because planting the bomb successfully often requires the coordinated efforts of multiple players using Killstreaks, running by your lonesome is tough work.

With that in mind, aggressive players in certain roles can assist your team. Take a stealth build with a Suppressor, Ghost, and either Hacker or Ninja to the enemy bombsite. If you can clear the bombsite for your team, you can enable a successful plant.

Another option is to use a build that incorporates Marathon to hunt down the enemy's midfield roamers, including their bomb carrier or bomb campers. Rapid mobility is important, as you have to follow the bomb around the map and dispatch any enemies that try to set up shop around it.

Consider taking Hardline and running a Spy Plane/Counter-Spy Plane setup. With aggressive play, you can rack up a ton of double and triple kills, which keeps your team's radar coverage active and shuts down the enemy's coverage.

The most difficult task of all is planting the bomb solo. It is possible, but it's very rarely successful unless the enemy team has no defensive-minded players at all.

Bring smoke and a Motion Sensor, and try to get the plant while the other team is embroiled in a firefight with your team.

DEFENSIVE

Running defense as a solo operator is easier in Sabotage, simply because you don't have to worry about trying to plant the bomb.

Camping the bomb and clearing out enemies that go for it (or your bombsite) as a solo player is definitely possible. It also provides a chance to rack up high-end Killstreaks that can help your team.

Even if your team isn't actively coordinating, you can still wait for a teammate to call in any high-end Killstreak and then launch your own at the same time. This isn't nearly as devastating as four or more players coordinating their strikes, but it does help.

If you really want to hang back, take a Sniper Rifle or LMG and keep your distance from the bomb at all times. Wax enemy players as they attempt to pick up or move the bomb. By tracking the bomb around the map, you can aid your team by picking off enemy players, keeping the bomb safely away from your bomb point.

HARDCORE OVERVIEW

Hardcore is a special mode that completely removes your HUD elements, including your minimap, reduces player health severely, and disables the Killcam, making it more difficult to find who killed you and from where.

Finally, and most critically, it enables team damage. Because player health is low from the start, it's very easy to kill your teammates accidentally. Check your fire!

One to two hits from any gun tends to be fatal in this mode. With no radar, situational awareness and team communication are absolutely vital.

Because there is no minimap, the utility of various combat gear and Perks changes quite a bit.

WEAPONRY

- Sniper Rifles are extremely dangerous in this mode. A good sniper can be a terror on large maps; communicate if you get sniped.
- The stronger LMGs can kill in one shot from a distance.
- Shotguns are basically instant death at close range; any reasonably on-target shot kills.
- SMGs and ARs retain their basic functionality; they're simply much more deadly.
- Launchers are very dangerous to use around your teammates. Be careful when you fire one.
- Suppressors lose value in Hardcore, as you do not have to worry about a minimap. You do still gain the benefit of reduced noise output. Because players have so little health, the damage falloff penalty of a silencer is reduced.

GRENADES

- Semtex and Frags are almost always lethal, but you must be cautious with their use. Flinging them haphazardly is a good way to kill your teammates.

TACTICAL

- All Tactical grenade types are useful in Hardcore, though Decoy loses some value due to the loss of a radar ping... unless the enemy team has a Spy Plane active.

EQUIPMENT

- Some equipment is devalued in Hardcore due to the loss of the minimap, but Camera Spikes and Claymores remain extremely useful.

PERKS

- Flak Jacket is less valuable, as explosions are still likely to kill you instantly.
- Hacker is quite useful, as it gives you an extra means of locating enemies in Hardcore—players often camp out near their placed Equipment.
- Ninja is extremely important. With no minimap, players are more focused on sight and sound—eliminating your aural signature is key.
- Tactical Mask remains very helpful, partly for its normal effect, and partly because the location indicator on Concussion and Flashbang grenades gives you another means to locate players.

KILLSTREAKS

- Spy Planes are very important. Gaining a radar sweep of the enemy team helps everyone in Hardcore. Information is critical without your HUD or Killcams to aid in locating enemy positions.
- Counter-Spy Planes are also important to nullify enemy intel.
- Napalm Strikes, Mortar Teams, Valkyrie Rockets, and Rolling Thunder are all dangerous to use in Hardcore. Communicate with your team before you call in these bad boys.
- Attack Helicopter and Blackbird remain useful, effective, and safe to use.
- Attack Dogs are safe to use, whereas Chopper Gunner and Gunship require more discretion. Calling out enemy positions while gunning in either chopper is extremely important in Hardcore.

SPECIAL OPS

This section is a reference for critical gameplay mechanics and gameplay advice.

Take the lessons here to heart; they can save your life time and time again.

DAMAGE RULES

Weapons in *Call of Duty: Black Ops* deal static damage every shot. There is no randomness from the guns.

All players have 100 health base; this health regenerates fully a few seconds after taking damage, assuming the player survives the encounter and finds cover.

Most weapons inflict damage within a range of values, and most have *a damage falloff* distance at which the gun begins to drop to its minimum damage. Weapons deal 50% bonus damage if you score a headshot—for most guns, this shaves off one shot needed to kill the target, regardless of distance.

Explosives deal a static damage value, but the amount of damage you receive from one varies based on your distance from the explosion. Each explosive has a different radius of effect, and damage falls off in a linear manner from the center of the blast.

At the center of a blast, only a target with Flak Jacket has a chance of surviving, while at the far edges, explosions are rarely fatal.

DAMAGE VALUES

Most weapons deal from 50 to 20 damage per shot. Sniper Rifles and Light Machine Guns are unique in that they deal a set amount of damage per shot that does *not* decrease at a distance.

DAMAGE FALLOFF

Weapons that deal damage within a range of values inflict maximum damage at close range. From there, damage decreases over distance, down to the weapon's minimum value.

All Assault Rifles except the semi-autos deal 40-30 damage, so they kill in three shots up close, four shots at a distance.

Semiautomatic Assault Rifles deal 50-40 damage. They kill in two shots up close, three at a distance.

Most SMGs have a 40-20 damage range, taking three to five shots to kill.

Sniper Rifles deal 70 damage per shot, and they boast more multipliers for stomach and upper body than other weapons. Sniper Rifles do not lose damage at range.

Light Machine Guns deal 30, 40, or 50 damage per shot regardless of distance. They kill in four, three, or two shots.

Most Pistols have a 40-20 range; three shots up close, five at a distance to kill a normal target.

TIME TO KILL

DAMAGE VALUES

WEAPON		MAX DAMAGE	MIN DAMAGE
SMG			
MP5K		40	20
Skorpion		50	20
MAC11		30	20
AK74U		40	20
UZI		30	20
PM63		40	20
MPL		40	20
Spectre		40	20
Kiparis		40	20
ASSAULT			
M16		40	30
Enfield		40	30
M14		50	40
FAMAS		40	30
GALIL		40	30
AUG		40	30
FN FAL		50	40
AK47		40	30
COMMANDO		40	30
G11		40	30
LMG			
HK21		30	30
RPK		40	40
M60		50	50
STONER 63		40	40
SNIPER			
DRAGUNOV		70	70
WA2000		70	70
L96A1		70	70
PSG1		70	70
PISTOL			
ASP		40	20
1911		40	20
Makarov		40	20
Python		50	30
Python Snub		40	30
CZ75		40	20

A weapon's "Time to Kill" is simply its damage per shot combined with its rate of fire. Because two weapons might have differing rates of fire despite having similar damage statistics, the faster-firing weapon can provide an edge to the person who wields it.

Shotguns and Sniper Rifles have the fastest TTK of any weapon, as they can kill in one shot. Burst Assault Rifles are close behind. Sniper Rifles aren't a great choice for close quarters, but they *can* score one shot kills if you get lucky with an upper body hit.

Dual Wielded SMGs and Pistols are high on the list at close ranges.

SMGs with Rapid Fire have the highest rate of fire, followed by SMGs, then Automatic Assault Rifles, and finally Light Machine Guns.

The tradeoff for better TTK is usually either range or accuracy. Shotguns can't kill anyone at a great distance, Dual Wielded weapons have a very hard time outside close-medium range, and high-fire-rate Automatic weapons are more difficult to use at long distances.

Fast-firing weapons (typically SMGs) often have more pronounced damage falloff values than slower-firing Automatic Assault Rifles.

PENETRATION

Bullets can penetrate surfaces and objects. Bullets that penetrate lose damage as they pass through a physical barrier. The steeper the shot's angle is from head-on, the less damage it inflicts when it passes through.

That is, if a target is immediately behind a wall, the ideal way to "wall" them is to shoot straight through the wall at a perfect, perpendicular, 90-degree angle. If you shoot at an offset angle, the damage reduces further.

When you use the Hardened Perk, all bullets gain a penetration upgrade. This is most noticeable for weapons that have poor or average penetration, such as SMGs, Pistols, and some Assault Rifles.

LMGs and Sniper Rifles have strong penetration to begin with, followed by burst, semiautomatic, and automatic Assault Rifles, then SMGs, Pistols, and finally Shotguns.

SUPPRESSOR REDUCTION

Sniper Rifles lose base damage with a Suppressor equipped, requiring you to land two shots to kill instead of one in the upper body. All other weapons have increased *damage falloff* with a Suppressor equipped.

This does not change damage values for any weapon other than Sniper Rifles. Rather, it simply means that you reach the minimum damage value at a shorter distance from the target than without a silencer equipped.

Suppressors make fighting at long range slightly more difficult, so they are typically best for CQB builds or when stealth is absolutely mandatory at a distance.

Aiming for headshots can compensate for the damage falloff at a distance, as headshots typically reduce the shots needed to kill by one. Otherwise, Suppressors usually require the maximum number of shots to kill at a distance.

HIT MARKERS

Any time you hit an enemy in *Call of Duty: Black Ops*, you receive a "hit marker," a visual marker around your crosshair and a distinctive sound effect that tells you your bullet impacted an enemy target.

These hit markers are very valuable tools, because they also work for secondary grenades (including smoke), explosives, and shots fired through cover and walls.

You can fire through a wall with a high-penetration weapon to detect enemies hiding behind cover. You can use hit markers to track sprinting targets through a wall, and gun them down without even having them in sight. You can use hit markers from explosives to detect or verify the presence of an enemy inside a room or around a corner.

Finally, you can use hit markers to complain bitterly when you score a marker instead of a one-shot kill with a Sniper Rifle...

COMBAT

Always keep the following core combat concepts in mind when you play *Call of Duty: Black Ops* in multiplayer.

Aim Down Sights (ADS)

ADS stands for Aim Down Sights. This means sighting in with your ironsights or scope to fire at your target, as opposed to just shooting from the hip.

The act of ADS-ing takes time, and the speed at which a given weapon allows you to ADS varies.

ADS TIMES

- LMGs and Sniper Rifles are the slowest.
- Assault Rifles are in the middle.
- SMGs and Pistols are the fastest.
- Shotguns ADS fairly quickly, but you rarely need to ADS if you're within Shotgun range.

ADS greatly increases accuracy, reducing the spread of bullets at a distance. Any time you engage at medium range or farther, you should ADS before you shoot.

Movement speed decreases while using ADS. The speed penalty varies by weapon and lines up with the ADS times of the various weapons. SMGs and Pistols let you retain most of your movement speed, while LMGs or Sniper Rifles slow you more significantly.

SLEIGHT OF HAND

The Sleight of Hand Pro Perk cuts the time it takes to ADS nearly in half for almost all weapons, but it does not affect Sniper Rifle scoping time.

Because Shotguns generally do not need to be fired from ADS to be effective, they have an inherent speed advantage in CQB, where you can move and fire from the hip effectively.

SMGs function similarly, because they have a tight hipfire spread and can be used effectively in CQB. Although it does not kill in one shot, a Shotgun can come out on top in close quarters.

Accuracy

Several factors affect your accuracy while firing.

ACCURACY BONUSES

- Using ADS increases accuracy.
- Crouching increases accuracy, and going prone increases accuracy even more.
- Holding your breath with a precision sniper scope increases accuracy.

ACCURACY PENALTIES

- Moving decreases accuracy.
- Jumping imposes a sharp accuracy penalty.
- Holding down the trigger on an automatic weapon decreases accuracy steadily.
- Rapidly firing a semiautomatic weapon decreases accuracy.
- Getting shot jerks or flinches your view, throwing off your aim. The Hardened Pro Perk can reduce this effect.
- Concussion grenade detonations throw off your aim.

When fired from the hip, weapons have different spreads, dependent on weapon class.

HIPFIRE PROFILES

- Pistols, SMGs, and Shotguns have minimal hipfire spread.
- Assault Rifles are in the middle.
- Light Machine Guns and Sniper Rifles have very poor hipfire accuracy.

STEADY AIM

The Steady Aim Perk applies a 0.65 multiplier to hipfire spread base values. This has the effect of bumping a weapon's hipfire spread up one notch, from LMG to AR, or AR to SMG. Submachine Guns, Shotguns, and Pistols become extremely accurate when hipfired with Steady Aim.

An SMG with Steady Aim can kill a target out to a medium distance that would otherwise require ADS-ing.

Using Steady Aim on a Shotgun comes down to personal preference. You gain a tighter pellet spread for close-medium combat in exchange for some close-range ease of use.

Sway

Some weapons have a very slight idle sway, causing your view to move gently around dead center when you ADS. Some Attachments can increase this effect.

Idle sway is most pronounced and obvious when you're looking through a sniper scope without holding your breath, but other weapons *do* have some sway, albeit much less.

You cannot completely nullify a weapon's idle sway; just be aware of it.

MOVEMENT

Movement in *Call of Duty: Black Ops* is extremely important. How well you move around the map can make the difference between life and death, and it's vital that you know when and how to use all the options available to you.

Base Movement Speed

Whichever weapon you have equipped at a given moment determines your base movement speed.

MOVEMENT SPEEDS

- Pistols, SMGs, and Shotguns have the best base movement speed.
- Sniper Rifles and Assault Rifles are next.
- LMGs and Launchers have the slowest movement speed.

Getting shot causes you to "flinch," temporarily slowing your movement speed. The Hardened Pro Perk nearly eliminates this penalty, making it much easier to sprint across open ground to reach cover safely.

LIGHTWEIGHT

The Lightweight Perk gives you a speed multiplier of 1.07, so your equipped weapon's base speed determines its effectiveness.

This means that running with Lightweight and an SMG or Shotgun is still faster than running with an LMG, which gains less of a benefit.

Crouched and Prone

Crouching increases your accuracy, reduces your silhouette at range, and lets you use low cover more effectively.

Crouching reduces your movement speed. You can sprint to get out of a crouch instantly.

Going prone greatly increases your accuracy and flattens your silhouette, reducing your visibility considerably, especially when you're prone in an area of underbrush or other concealment.

Going prone has the downside of facing your head directly toward the enemy. Likewise, be very careful about silhouetting yourself against the skyline if you're prone on a building.

Movement while prone is very slow, and turning while prone may cause your legs to get caught on an object. Be very cautious about using prone if you suspect an enemy may be nearby (unless you're hiding from them in the bushes with Ghost Pro).

MOVEMENT NOISE

As you walk around normally, you make different noises depending on the surface you're moving across (metal is very loud). This noise can give away your position to any nearby enemy. Because you can't run Ninja on every build, you need to know how to control your noise output.

Crouching eliminates movement noise, so if you're in hostile territory or you've located a nearby enemy who's unaware of your presence, move while Crouched to stay quiet.

Prone is also quiet, but the movement is too slow to get into range in most situations.

Crouching and sneaking up on someone can give you the first lethal shot.

THE DROPSHOT

Dropping to prone mid-firefight and continuing to fire at your target can win you some battles. The sudden shift in your target profile may throw off your opponent's aim just long enough for you to score a kill.

This is typically most useful in heads-up, close-medium to medium-range engagements in which both players have spotted each other and have begun firing. It's often a coin toss who wins these fights, but performing a drop shot can occasionally save your life.

The downside is that the sudden stop in your movement makes you an easy target for anyone else who happens to be nearby.

PERK VISIBILITY

All Slot 1 Perks change the physical appearance of your in-game model.

If you take Ghost, you're given a basic form of a ghillie suit customized to match the terrain of the map you're playing. This can be useful for further reducing your visibility in cover.

MOVEMENT VISIBILITY

When you're crouched or standing at a long distance from the enemy, and you're behind cover or in a window, do your best to avoid moving even slightly.

While this makes you an easy shot for anyone who spots you, moving around makes you much easier to spot at a distance.

Even a tiny movement results in a very visible shift of your in-game model, which can be enough to alert an enemy to your presence.

Remember, the human eye picks up movement quickly, and skilled *Call of Duty: Black Ops* players constantly scan common camping areas for movement. Staying in the shadows and immobile is one of the best ways to avoid detection at a distance.

Dive to Prone

New to *Call of Duty: Black Ops* is the ability to perform a swan dive into a prone position while sprinting.

This has several useful applications. When sprinting across open ground, you can dive to cover. This breaks can throw off a distant sniper aiming for your upper body.

While diving, you can rotate 90 degrees to the left or right, so it's possible to dive around a corner and land facing another direction. If you suspect enemies are lying in wait, this can get you into firing position and present an unusual target that may throw off their aim.

Unlike drop-shotting, you cannot fire while diving to prone until you actually land and bring up your weapon again.

Sprint

Sprinting is vital for moving around in *Call of Duty: Black Ops* for several reasons. It allows you to move from cover to cover much more safely, make a sudden dash at an enemy to go for a knife kill, escape pursuit, or reach an objective more quickly.

Sprinting is time-limited, and how long you can sprint depends on your weapon.

SPRINT DURATION

- Pistols, SMGs, and Shotguns have the best sprint times.
- Sniper Rifles are next on the list.
- Assault Rifles are in the middle.
- LMGs and Launchers have the worst sprint times.

Sprinting is both very important and very dangerous.

While sprinting, you're much louder, so you're easier for enemies to hear. Furthermore, you cannot fire your weapon while sprinting, and it takes time to ready your weapon after you finish a sprint.

Always stop sprinting before you enter an area where you expect to encounter opposition. Don't sprint around corners if you're in enemy territory. And don't sprint to close the distance on opponents if they're unaware of your presence, as the noise gives you away.

Ninja can suppress the noise of sprinting, making you more lethal and mobile in enemy territory.

Sprinting is very useful for knife kills. Sprint to close the distance, and stab to end the fight. Charging an enemy who is already aware of you is usually a bad idea, unless you have no other option.

MARATHON

Marathon allows double the normal sprint time, while Marathon Pro allows unlimited sprint.

Marathon is a very useful Perk, but it's also very dangerous, as it encourages bad habits—sprinting around corners is high on the list of ways to get shot.

Marathon is useful for all weapon classes, but it's particularly noticeable with LMGs, which suffer from slow movement and limited sprint times.

Mantle

Mantling is the act of pulling yourself up over low barriers.

You can mantle over any object that is roughly hip high, including debris, barricades, vehicles, windowsills, and more.

It's also possible to sprint, jump, and mantle onto a higher ledge. Spend time exploring where you can use this maneuver to increase your mobility options.

Skilled use of sprinting and mantling in combination can open up your travel through the maps.

Remember that your base movement speed affects your ability to make longer jumps, so using Lightweight with a fast weapon gives you the best opportunity for trick jumps.

Be aware that you put your weapon down while mantling, so you're vulnerable to nearby enemies as you clamber over obstruction in your way.

As a result, mantling into a room through a window is usually a bad idea if you know someone is inside. Find another entrance, or toss a grenade in first!

Climbing

A few maps have ladders or other surfaces that you can climb. While climbing, you're completely exposed and cannot use your weapons. Try to avoid climbing ladders if you suspect enemies are nearby!

EYES AND EARS

Your situational awareness is just as important as your skill using weapons. How rapidly you identify and locate threats can have an enormous impact on your battlefield success.

In a game where combat rarely lasts more than a few seconds, getting the drop on your enemies isn't just a good idea; it's absolutely critical.

You can use several tools to gain an edge on the battlefield, and a few Perks that can have an impact on your battlefield presence.

Going Loud

Firing your weapon is the loudest, most obvious way to give yourself away in *Call of Duty: Black Ops*.

First, the enemy hears the gunfire. Second, they can see the tracer rounds. And third, you appear on the minimap as a red dot while firing.

All of these are bad things.

Be aware when you fire that you're giving away your position and the positions of nearby teammates. If you spot an enemy and have a shot, you should take it, but remember the repercussions of firing.

A Suppressor Attachment eliminates the minimap red dot, and it reduces the sound of firing (though it does not eliminate it). This makes silenced weaponry ideal for operating in close proximity to enemy forces—it gives them less chance of locating your position.

You can use the minimap dot to bait enemy forces. Deliberately fire some shots in one visible location, then move to cover the area—nearby enemies often come to investigate, and you can then finish them off.

Decoy grenades are designed specifically for this purpose, as they generate random gunfire sounds and create a minimap red dot "ping" that is indistinguishable from someone firing their weapon.

Death Markers

When a teammate dies, they leave behind a HUD icon that indicates a dead player. Because you can see these from almost anywhere on a level, they're very quick visual cues that enemies may be near those positions. Use death markers to home in on enemy positions. Even if your team isn't communicating, you can at least still get good intel from their untimely demise!

Minimap

Your minimap is an incredibly powerful tool. Learn to exploit it to maximum advantage.

You can always see the location and facing of nearby teammates. Enemies show up as red dots on the minimap when they fire unsilenced weapons.

Your local minimap only shows the immediate vicinity around you. Hit the Main Menu to see a full map of the level. This is a very important tool. Because you can see the entire map, you can see red dots anywhere on the level. This includes when a Spy Plane is in the air.

Periodically check your full map when you hear distant gunfire. By comparing the positions of your teammates and any death indicators with the positions of red dots, you can often quickly deduce the enemy team's current location.

With practice, a quick glance at the full map tells you exactly where the enemy team is, and whether they're pushing on offense or guarding on defense.

This information is useful for you and your team, and it's especially vital if you're attempting to flank the enemy position.

SPY PLANE SWEEPS AND THE BLACKBIRD

When a Spy Plane flies overhead, it reveals all non Ghost-equipped enemies on the minimap as red dots. These sweeps occur periodically, so the information lags slightly behind real time, especially for fast-moving enemies.

Spy Plane intel is a tremendously powerful tool, but don't get so blinded by watching your minimap that you lose sight of the world around you. When a Spy Plane first comes online, check your full map to verify enemy positions, and then use that information to choose a course of action.

Act on the intel by responding with your own movement, and stay alert to nearby enemies. If enemies are distant, you can refernce the full map periodically to double-check their positions. However, if you're close to an enemy position, keep your eyes in front of you, not on the minimap.

The Blackbird acts as a mega-powerful Spy Plane, fully revealing enemy positions and facings. An active Blackbird is essentially a cheat mode for your entire team. You can track down and execute foes with ease, shooting them through walls, firing explosives into their hidey-holes, and ambushing them when they sprint down alleys or hallways.

COUNTER-SPY PLANE

Because the Counter-Spy Plane shuts down enemy radar entirely, including Spy Planes or the Blackbird, it's a very powerful Killstreak.

Use Counter-Spy Planes just after enemy Spy Planes go in the air, or just before making an offensive push or stealthy entry into enemy territory.

Counter-Spy Planes act as Suppressors for your entire team. The enemy can no longer verify position simply by checking their minimap against gunfire sounds.

While a Counter-Spy Plane is in the air, your enemies are more focused on using their eyes, so exercise caution when you approach an area you know to be defended. The defense is that much more attuned to sight and sound.

One odd quirk of the Counter-Spy Plane: If you have one active, you cannot use the enemy Killcam's full map to check their team's position—their map is jammed! Hardly a reason to avoid using the Counter-Spy Plane, but something to remember.

SUPER KILLCAM SCOUTING

Killcams are normally useful for revealing the position of the enemy who just killed you, which can help you track down a distant camper.

However, one extremely powerful use for the Killcam makes it an incredibly strong informational tool.

If you visit the full map *while in a Killcam*, you can see the enemy's full map. This includes all enemy team locations and their facings.

In essence, this means that any time you die, you can quickly get a picture of the entire enemy team's positions. Because a Killcam's events happened a few seconds in the past, this is just a snapshot of enemy positions, similar to a single Spy Plane sweep.

Use this feature often. It turns a painful death into a useful tool for you and your team.

Using Sound

Sound is your next most important informational tool. You can hear gunfire, Equipment usage, movement, grenade tossing, jumping, mantling, landing, and climbing.

Enemies with Ninja suppress their movement noises, while Ninja Pro suppresses all of their "personal" movement noises.

Enemies with Suppressors reduce but do not eliminate the sound of their weapon fire.

It's very important to use the sounds of the battlefield around you to pinpoint enemy locations.

You can bait an enemy by using sound instead of gunfire, but this is more difficult. Most players respond to minimap red dots and gunfire, but comparatively fewer players are alert to movement sounds. Those who are tend to be better players who are very alert and cautious about pursuing an unknown noise.

When operating in enemy territory, be very careful if you aren't using Ninja. Assume that every enemy you pass is alert to sound. While some players aren't, good players are, and you don't want to risk revealing yourself.

Remember that you can crouch to silence your movement noises, and you can use Suppressed weapons, the Tomahawk, Ballistic Knives, and regular knife stabs to kill quietly.

Don't forget that using a Killstreak can make a distinctive "clicking" sound that cues in nearby enemies on your location, as does throwing grenades.

Using Your Eyes

This seems obvious, but it's important to mention. Constantly scanning the battlefield for threats is important. The faster you can acquire targets, especially concealed ones, the better your odds of survival on the battlefield.

SLEIGHT OF HAND PRO

Sleight of Hand Pro cuts your ADS times in half. This is important for engagements that occur anywhere from close-medium to medium-long range. It helps you fire accurate shots at your target faster than they can. Whoever gets the first hit is likely to win a heads-up firefight, simply due to the flinching and view recoil it imparts.

Sleight of Hand Pro also greatly aids LMGs when you're forced to move around a level, as it reduces the slow ADS they impose.

TARGET AQUISITION

In enemy territory, keep your eyes on the battlefield and not on the minimap.

With practice, you gradually learn the common camping spots on each map. As you move across hostile terrain, stay in cover and constantly scan the most likely enemy locations.

Targets often give themselves away by making slight movements. On their end, it doesn't "feel" like they're moving much if they take a step while crouched. But from your perspective, a silhouette shift in a window, behind some cover, or in some brush that alerts you to their presence.

As you move through an area with known enemy presence, train your weapon on the most likely enemy position and use your eyes to scan for enemies. The less time it takes for you to get your crosshairs on target, the better.

The least favorable encounters are those in which you and your enemy spot each other simultaneously. If this situation occurs and you already have your weapon aimed in the right direction, the odds are in your favor.

THE FATAL FRAME AND OTHER DANGERS

Corners, doorways, and windows are some of the most dangerous areas in the game. Walking through a doorway frames your silhouette and makes you a very easy target for anyone camping inside.

Similarly, windows make a nice target for enemies to watch. Snipers and long-range gunners love picking off players who expose themselves in windows.

Finally, corners and doors are two of the most dangerous terrain elements on any map, and they are especially common on urban maps.

Doors and Windows

To safely clear a door or window, start to the side of the window or doorframe, ADS, and make a smooth rotation from one side of the door or window to the other.

This gives you the maximum visibility to each side, and it alerts you to an enemy off to either side who might not be visible straight through. It also brings them into your sights while you're already ADSed and ready to fire. Meanwhile, they may not be aware of your presence. At worst, this puts you on even ground with someone watching the door or window.

GET OUT OF THE WINDOW

Never stand pressed against a window opening. You can maintain most of the sight lines that you would normally need through a window even if you hang back a few feet or off to the side. Doing so makes you much more difficult to spot.

Only move up to a window to make a shot if you can't get line of sight from a shielded position.

Not only are you an easy target in a window, but your gun pokes through the opening if you stand too close, even if you aren't visible directly. Don't do this!

Corners

When you clear a corner, perform a rotation similar to the one you use with a window or doorway. Step out slightly from your wall, ADS, and make a smooth rotation around the corner, keeping your sights trained on the terrain as it comes into view. Corner-clearing is incredibly important on almost every map. Get into the habit of doing this when you suspect enemies are nearby.

You don't have to clear every corner in this cautious manner, but clearing the dangerous ones often saves your life several times a game.

The slower your ADS time, the more important is to clear corners this way. If you round a corner without being ADS'ed, and an enemy around the bend is looking straight at you, you have little chance to get your sights up and on target.

Accurate hip-fire weapons and fast character classes can get away with moving speedily, but even that is risky if the corner opens to an area where distant players can spot you. Either sprint *past* the corner to cover, or clear the corner.

CORNER CHECKING, PC STYLE

In most areas, gameplay between the PC and console versions of *Call of Duty: Black Ops* is nearly identical. One key difference is that PC players can use lean controls to peek around corners.

This makes corner-clearing and checking for targets from behind cover a bit safer on the PC. Of course, PC users also have to contend with very accurate enemy weapon fire, so there's a tradeoff.

Breaching

Finally, let's discuss passing through doors into rooms, or "breaching." This is a dangerous operation, and disciplined tactics can only reduce the danger, not eliminate it entirely.

The basic problem is this: When you pass through a doorway, especially one that the enemy is likely watching, you make a perfect, easy target.

Worse, because the enemy can hide in the left or right corners nearest to the door, you have no way of knowing which way to aim.

Clearing a doorway gives you line of sight on most of the room, but not all of it. Cautious campers still are difficult to see as you finally move through the opening. However, some precautionary measures can minimize the danger.

First, pick a corner to target. This is a 50/50 shot, but it's still better than running straight through without checking either corner! With practice, you can make this a 60/40 or 70/30 guess, just based on the specific map and the common habits of most players.

TAG TEAM

Of course, it's possible to clear a room by having a point man take one side and a teammate take the other.

Unfortunately, while this tactic seems sound, in practice, it's very dangerous in *Call of Duty: Black Ops*.

First, it requires good coordination. You may be able to count on this with good friends or clan mates, but not with random online players.

Both "breachers" are vulnerable to penetrating bullets, explosives, and weapons that stun or disorient. Furthermore, bunched-up targets near doorways are incredibly tempting targets for any nearby enemy.

If one player enters and gets taken down from a corner, his teammate knows which side of the room to hit. This allows the teammate to finish off the enemy while he reloads. Alternatively, the teammate can use an explosive much more safely than risking both players entering and getting gunned down.

If you're dead-set on clearing a room as a duo, send in one fast sprinting or diving player, and have the second player quickly enter close behind. The first player draws fire while the second one cleans up.

Draw straws for lead man...

Next, you can sprint, sprint and jump, or dive to prone into a room. Having Steady Aim Pro to reduce the sprint recovery is helpful for the first option.

Finally, Explosives!

TACTICAL MASK PRO

This Perk bears special mention when it comes to room clearing.

Tactical Mask Pro gives an "upgraded" hit marker for Concussion or Flashbang grenades. When you score a hit marker with Tactical Mask Pro equipped, you gain a positional indicator that flares on your crosshair, pointing toward the damaged target.

As you clear a room or corner, this information is incredibly valuable. You can enter the area certain of the enemy's position.

You can also use this information to shoot the target through the wall, use an explosive, or tell a teammate with a different angle where the enemy is located. Oh, and Tactical Mask Pro lets you run safely into your own Nova Gas!

Tactical Mask Pro is a useful defensive tool, but it's also a powerful offensive weapon for clearing defended areas.

Pair this with Scavenger and Warlord Pro, and you have an excellent build suited for clearing rooms and corners.

Secondary Tactical Grenades are custom built for clearing rooms. Concussion Grenades and especially Flashbangs are very helpful for clearing a room.

Nova Gas is also great. In smaller rooms, targets hit with Nova Gas must move or the gas kills them!

Frag Grenades, Semtex, and Launchers of all sorts are also very useful for clearing a room. Even if you don't kill the target, you can weaken him or force him to run, making him easy prey.

One warning about Flashbangs in particular: If you toss a Flashbang into an occupied room and get a hitmarker, you have no way of knowing the extent to which a target (or targets) is blinded. You also don't know if the target was already facing the doorway.

Flashbangs don't disrupt aim, so even completely blinded targets can kill someone running through a doorway if they're already lined up.

Nevertheless, Flashbangs are worth using—just be aware of the risks. Whenever you can, toss a grenade in one way and enter via another way. Even better, pick one entry and have a teammate breach with you via an alternate entry.

Using the Killcam

Whenever you get killed in *Call of Duty: Black Ops*, you can watch a replay of your death from the perspective of the player who killed you.

This is a very useful tool. It can help you identify the position of a camper or a sniper. At the very least, you can see what got you into trouble in the first place.

A few points:

- The Killcam shows what happened from the perspective of the other player. Remember, with internet latency, this doesn't always match up with what you saw from your end. If you got killed in a straight one-on-one situation and the Killcam disagrees with what you experienced, chalk it up to lag and exercise the best solution to the problem: avoid those types of coin-flip firefights in the first place.
- You can "hide" the Killcam when you snipe or use a long-range scope by staying zoomed in for a few seconds after a kill. This prevents the player you killed from getting a complete look at your position, unless he quickly checks your map and deduces your location from that.

Killstreaks and Objectives

As you improve your skills in *Call of Duty: Black Ops*, you naturally tend to earn Killstreaks with increasing frequency. This allows yoy to aim for even higher streaks with greater confidence. Some aspects of Killstreaks affect you and your teammates in any objective game mode.

First, and most obviously, you can't earn a Killstreak reward if you die. Too obvious? Not really. Here's the problem: Playing most objective-based modes on offense requires you to take risks. Taking risks is the exact opposite of what you want to do if you're aiming for a Killstreak.

So, here's the rub: You can either contribute in objective modes by racking up kills and laying down high-end Killstreaks, or you can contribute by actually going for the objectives and helping to win the game for your team.

To be clear, both are helpful, but it's very easy to lose a match when most of your team is focused on Killstreaks and, by extension, the omnipresent k/d ratio. If this bugs you too much, either avoid objective modes or only play them with your friends, when you know they'll work together to win.

When you aren't playing with friends but you still want to play objective modes, there are a few things you can do. The first is to drop your Killstreaks down a few notches. The lowly Spy Plane is one of the most useful Killstreaks in the game. Getting a three-kill streak even when you offensively push a Domination point, Headquarters, or Demolition point isn't out of the question.

Another option is to run Hardline in combination with sub-six Killstreaks. This is another way to guarantee contributing streaks to your team, but without worrying about breaking your kill chain because you're trying to run the flag in CTF.

Amp up your Killstreaks if you're playing defense. Some of the higher Killstreaks can directly help your entire team. A well placed Mortar bombardment, Napalm Strike, or Rolling Thunder on an objective can clear the area of enemies long enough for your offense to secure it.

Similarly, the Blackbird is like activating a cheat mode for your team. Good players gain a crushing advantage while it's active. Relatively few players like running the support-oriented Counter-Spy Plane (and it can be shot down), so Blackbird can rarely be stopped once it's active.

If you can coordinate with your teammates, dropping multiple Killstreaks simultaneously is a great way to break a deadlock. It's also a very important part of winning in Sabotage. Stock up on Killstreaks, and then coordinate Spy Planes alongside air and mortar strikes. Call in air support while you bombard a target area, and get your Spy Planes or Blackbirds into the air.

Using Theater Mode

Recorded games are very powerful learning tools. Beyond being incredibly cool for sharing awesome moments with your friends, they can also help you improve your game.

If you played a match where your team was simply dominated, take a look at the replay and figure out what the other team was doing.

This is also useful when you're very new to the game, or if you're arriving late to the party. Watch replays in objective modes to quickly figure out common routes, popular camping spots, and so on. This is all extremely useful information and can easily improve your game.

Fast Leveling

The easiest way to level quickly is to complete as many Challenges as possible while you're playing.

To accomplish this, configure a set of custom classes that feature one of each major weapon group. Constantly cycle through different Lethal, Tactical, Equipment, and Perk choices.

Check your Challenges screen occasionally, and go after whatever Challenges are suitable for the modes you play.

Remember that some Challenges are much easier to tackle in some modes. Challenges that require destroying enemy Equipment are hard to do if the enemy rarely uses Equipment in the modes you play! Similarly, if the Challenge requires many kills, Search & Destroy isn't the place to do it.

Switch out your weapons for new ones as you reach the higher Challenge thresholds for kills and headshots. It's easier to start up with a new weapon and grab the low-hanging fruit than it is to max out each weapon completely.

Due to their differences in game play, some game modes pay out more experience over time. Spend some time in each playlist to learn what your average gain per game is. Then you can decide where to spend most of your time if you're focused on leveling quickly.

RULES OF THE GAME

Finally, one last tactical gift to you. This is a selection of very brief, but very important tips. Pick a few and follow them to the letter when you play online. Without a doubt, they will help.

Short, Controlled Bursts

When you target enemies at medium-long range with an automatic weapon, fire in short bursts. The exact number of shots depends on the weapon. Some can get away with longer sprays, whereas others need to be fired almost one bullet at a time.

You should indulge in full-auto sprays only at short range, where time to kill matters more than accuracy or ammo.

From the Hip

Shotguns and SMGs are designed to be fired from the hip. With Steady Aim, Assault Rifles can pull this off as well.

Factors like the time it takes to ADS, the associated movement penalty, was well as the movement hitch and view recoil from getting hit, mean that the first player to land a shot in CQB usually wins.

Take advantage of weapons with good hipfire spreads to land that first shot, and finish your targets before they can line up accurate shots on you.

With Steady Aim in place, SMGs can hip-fire targets even at medium range. Use their mobility to keep moving as you shoot. This wastes more ammo, but it's better to have less ammo than no health.

There Are Always Two (and Three in Ground War)

Whenever you kill an enemy, always expect his buddy to come around the corner a few seconds later. Don't stand out in the open, and don't sprint into enemy territory immediately. Move from cover to cover.

Why? Because your victim's teammate saw you, or heard you, or saw you on the minimap, or saw his teammate's death icon, or his teammate told him where you were. Odds are, his buddy is going to come looking for you.

And in Ground War, where there are more players on the field, you can often expect more than one extra enemy to show up at the party. Be ready for this.

Press Reload to Spawn Enemy

Learn to exercise reloading discipline. If you use your weapons well, you should never need an entire magazine to take down a target.

Immediately after killing an enemy, resist the urge to reload. First, wait and see if another enemy shows up. If you aren't immediately threatened, or you've moved into good cover, then you can reload.

If you have Sleight of Hand, you can get away with this bad habit more often, but avoid developing the habit in the first place. Sleight of Hand should help you, not make you vulnerable when you aren't using it!

Throw a Grenade to Spawn Enemy

Grenades are useful tools, but using them in close proximity to an enemy position is dangerous. Nearby enemies can hear you throw grenades, and if you happen to be in mid-throw, you can't retaliate with your weapon.

Remember that Decoy and Concussion grenades throw more quickly than any other type. Give preference to Concussion over Flashbangs or Nova Gas for close-quarters grenade use, simply for the speed difference.

Take the Shot

Do you see someone sprinting halfway behind cover, in the distance, through a window and some bushes? Go ahead and take the shot.

You can't improve your long-distance accuracy without wasting some lead. Unless you risk putting yourself or teammates in immediate danger by revealing your position, going for the kill is always worthwhile.

Don't Sprint around Blind Corners

Really. Just don't do it. This applies doubly to players running Marathon Pro who are addicted to sprinting. Once you're near enemy turf, slow down and take corners more carefully.

Slice that Corner

When you have to clear a corner or scan a doorway or window, edge up to it from the side, step out, and round the corner with your weapon in ADS. This isn't necessary for every last corner, door, and window on a map, but if you know (or suspect) enemy presence, slow it down a step and take your time.

Fatal Frame

Be careful about running through doorways blindly. Just like corners, if you suspect enemies are around, use your secondary grenades to check for enemy presence, and scan the room as best as you can from outside.

Smoke the Open Ground

Smoke is an underused tool, even in non-objective modes. Instantly creating dense "visual cover" is very useful. The enemy can spray bullets into the smoke, but without an Infrared scope, they're unlikely to take you down if you sprint.

Sprint through Hotspots

Never walk out in the open for an extended period. Sprint from cover to cover, and if you absolutely must go through an area where many routes intersect, sprint for your life!

The Back Route is the Best Route

When you assault an enemy position, the longer route that takes you away from the faster frontal route is always preferable.

Take your pick: 30 seconds of running and killing half the enemy team from behind; or 15 seconds of running, killing one enemy, and then dying, only to run another 15 seconds to get back.

Controlling Enemy Focus

You can control enemy attention. Use gunfire, explosives, Decoy Grenades, and Killstreak package drops to distract the enemy team into focusing on an area of your choice.

Coordinate with your team to hit your foes from behind while they're distracted, and you can inflict heavy losses with a minimal investment in sneaky subterfuge.

The Fine Art of Walling

Shooting targets through walls takes some practice. Start by learning the levels, and then shoot at targets when they duck behind cover. Search for enemies in common camping spots by shooting through the wall before you even see anyone.

If you want to practice this extensively, bring Hardened or an LMG with Extended Mags and burn through a few thousand rounds. Taking down enemies through walls is a very useful skill to acquire.

Reload Out of Sight, Out of Mind

When you have to reload, duck behind cover, quickly crouch, and scan the area while you reload. When you're quiet, motionless, and in cover, you're nearly invisible.

Look Left! (Killing the Herd)

If you happen to be in cover when you see a fresh enemy spawn start to run past you to the right, wait.

There's no worse feeling than swinging out to light up three enemies that just respawned, only to discover that the fourth one is behind you.

Control your bloodthirst for just a moment and check the direction from which the team originated. If the coast is clear for just a moment, you're good to go—engage from the rear and mop them up.

Hey, He Found My Claymore!

Well-placed Claymores are very effective for protecting objectives, chokepoints, and guarding your back. Even if the enemy destroys your Claymore, the explosion alerts you of enemy presence.

Plant Claymores with the front facing the direction you expect enemies to be moving, not the direction from which they approach. If you place it at a door, set it off to the side, facing inward, not outward. If you place it in a hall, face the dangerous part away from the enemy team's direction of travel. They run past and eat the explosion in the rear.

Disable that Gear

Equipment is powerful and useful in many game modes. You can disable Equipment with Ghost Pro, Hacker Pro, Jammer, and explosives.

You can destroy all Equipment by shooting it, and Hardened Pro ups your damage against placed items.

Concussion and Flashbang grenades temporarily disable Equipment—even friendly gear, so be careful!

Danger Senses, Tingling

If you're in an open area with multiple routes to your position and multiple camping spots with lines of sight, the hair on the back of your neck should be standing up.

Don't expose yourself more than absolutely necessary. Stay in cover and stay safe.

Monster Kill

Guided Killstreaks are much, much more effective when you know where to guide them!

Save a Spy Plane or wait for a friendly Spy Plane to come online before you use these streaks, unless you know where most of the enemy team is located.

Psychic. Or a Hacker. He's Definitely Cheating.

There are many ways to find enemies:

- **Hear them:** movement, sprinting, climbing, jumping, mantling, reloading, firing, using a Killstreak, placing Equipment, planting a bomb, tripping a Claymore, objective audio alerts.
- **See them:** long-distance scopes, Infrared scopes, tracers, tossed grenades, launched explosives, visible Equipment, care package in the open, objective HUD alerts.
- **Detect them:** minimap red dots, Spy Planes, Motion Sensors, Camera Spikes, Hacker, Killcams, Main Menu full map, friendly players firing at an area.
- Blackbird *is* cheating.

Respawn Behavior

Learn how the team respawn locations work in each mode and on each map. Knowing where the enemy respawns is a powerful advantage.

The Right Tool for the Job

Remember the range bands:

- Sniper Rifles and LMGs for long-distance work.
- Assault Rifles for medium-range combat.
- SMGs for close-range combat.
- Shotguns for ultra-close encounters.

RELOADING

Reloading your weapon is a simple and common task, but it's an important one.

The Sleight of Hand Perk cuts a weapon's reload time in half, reducing your window of vulnerability. You're vulnerable while reloading, but you can cancel a reload in two ways: either by sprinting or by switching weapons.

Sprinting is not the safest way to re-ready a weapon, but you can sprint away in the middle of a reload to reach safety if you're surprised.

On the other hand, switching weapons is very useful. If you have a Pistol secondary, or you have the Scout Pro Perk, you can switch to your second weapon extremely quickly, much faster than reloading your primary weapon.

Another option is "double switching." By tapping the Switch Weapon button twice, you quickly switch away from and back to your current weapon, canceling the reload animation and readying your weapon again. This is often faster than reloading your weapon fully, especially if it has a slow reload animation.

RELOAD QUIRKS

All weapons have three reload statistics:

- **The time it takes to reload a partially spent magazine.**
- **The time it takes to reload a fully empty magazine.**
- **The time it takes for the ammo in a magazine to actually become "active."**

Partial reloads are faster than empty-mag reloads. If you empty a magazine fully, you have to chamber a round from the magazine by racking the slide on a pistol or pulling the charging handle or bolt.

For either type of reload, the time before the ammo actually becomes available for use is not always the same as the weapon's reload—in many cases, it's faster.

This is important, because it means you can sprint or double-switch, and your weapon is fully reloaded. In essence, you can cut the reload time for your weapon with practice.

Because these values are different for every gun, experiment to see when this can be helpful to you.

With Scout Pro, double-switching to reload some weapons can be effective. But for all weapons, sprint-cancelling a reload after the ammo has refilled can save you some time on the battlefield. Reload, wait for the ammo to fill, and then sprint to cancel the animation.

WEAPON SWITCHING

Weapon switch times are not the same for all weapons. Agile weapons like Pistols come up more quickly than very slow weapons like LMGs or Sniper Rifles.

The time it takes to fully switch weapons is the combination of your current weapon's "put-down" time and the selected weapon's "equip" time.

Scout Pro cuts the switch times in half, allowing you to switch to weapons other than a Pistol much more quickly, or to bring up a Pistol almost instantly.

Finally, remember that it's often faster to switch to a Pistol secondary than it is to reload your primary.

MELEE

All soldiers possess a lethal combat knife that can perform one-hit kills on enemies at short range.

Performing a melee strike causes you to lunge forward slightly. If your target is in range and lined up, you lunge and stab, killing the enemy instantly.

Knife kills are especially useful because they are silent and nearly instant.

If you round a corner into an enemy at pointblank range, and he fires while you stab, you may come out damaged but standing.

Knifing enemy campers in the back is always helpful, as it takes them down with a reduced chance of alerting nearby teammates. However, if they are alert, they can still hear you attack or spot the death indicator on the HUD.

It's also possible to sprint and stab a target, though attempting this when the enemy has eyes on you is a good way to get shot. Faster weapons (SMGs, Shotguns, Pistols) and the Lightweight and Marathon Perks all make for more dangerous melee strikes.

Hit or miss, there is a delay before you can perform a second melee strike. The Steady Aim Pro Perk cuts this recovery time in half, making it ideal for Shotgun or SMG CQB builds by giving you another close-range advantage.

Using melee strikes should be second nature. If they aren't, spend some time practicing!

LAST WORDS

And that's everything! You now have information on every aspect of the game, from creating classes, to the maps, the modes, and the gameplay mechanics that drive the game.

Use this information to improve your game, explore all the game modes, play with all the weapons, and experiment with wacky custom classes.

Bring some friends, play with a party, enjoy custom games, smack some bots in Combat Training, or shoot some zombies.

Winning is great, and topping the scoreboards is cool, but enjoying yourself is the most important part of the game.

Have fun!

REFERENCE MATERIAL

This chapter functions as a quick reference for custom class items, and it provides a few other charts and tables you may find helpful.

BUILD A CLASS

1 **Determine the purpose of the class.** Offense? Defense? Flag running? Point capture? Long-range combat? CQB?

2 **Pick a primary weapon.** Match the weapon's range band with the size of the map, the needs of the mode, and your intended role.

- **Sniper Rifles and LMGs:** Long-range, point coverage.
- **Assault Rifles:** Medium-range, all purpose.
- **SMGs:** Close quarters, fast movement.
- **Shotguns:** Ultra-close-range, one-shot kills, and fast movement.

3 **Pick a secondary weapon.** Compliment your primary weapon, give yourself another option in firefights.

- **Pistols:** Useful backup weapon for Sniper Rifles or LMGs; can be helpful if you run low on ammo in a firefight.
- **Launchers:** Dig out campers, guard objectives, and take down groups of enemies or equipment.
- **Special:** Specialist gear for special purposes. Use Ballistic Knives when stealth is required and you want a quicker kill than a suppressed pistol. Use the Crossbow for longer-range explosive power.

4 **Choose Lethal Grenades.** Take Frag or Semtex based on the distance you expect to engage. Choose Frag for longer distances, Semtex for shorter ones. Use Tomahawk if stealth is required or if you want a weapon to protect yourself while reloading or sprinting.

5 **Choose Tactical Grenades.** Select these based on the game mode and your desired role.

- **Willy Pete:** Create cover on objectives or in open terrain, utilize Infrared scopes.
- **Nova Gas:** Cover objectives, clear campers out of small rooms, block chokepoints.
- **Flashbang:** Clear rooms, disorient enemies in the open.
- **Concussion:** Throws quickly and stuns enemies in the open.
- **Decoy:** Throws quickly and creates distractions.

6 **Take Equipment.** Bring along Equipment that matches your intended role.

- **C4:** Cover objectives, block chokepoints, use as an extra explosive. Remember that C4 requires your attention to be effective and is usually more powerful on defense. But it can be used as a short-range '"grenade"' to clear rooms if necessary.
- **Claymore:** Block chokepoints, cover objectives. Unlike C4, the Claymore doesn't require your attention, so it can be used on offense or defense. Also useful for guarding your back when camping.
- **Camera Spike:** Monitor a route that you can't watch in person. Create visual '"tripwires"' to spot enemy forces. Most useful on defense, even more so when you communicate with your team effectively. Can protect your back when camping.
- **Jammer:** Important on offense and defense. Confuse enemy forces and prevent their equipment from working. Critical for disabling equipment near an objective on offense, and very helpful for protecting an objective on defense.
- **Motion Sensor:** Gain immediate intel on enemy movement within a limited area. Use this to watch a chokepoint or guard your back while camping. Very effective on defense.
- **Tactical Insertion:** Vital on offense in certain objective modes, very important on larger maps. Can be useful in other modes where controlling your spawn location is important.

7 **Pick your Perks.** Carefully consider what role you want to play on the battlefield, and match your Perks to that task.

- **Perk Slot 1:** Powerful Perks that influence your battlefield role. Many combine well with choices in Perk Slot 3 to increase in power.
- **Perk Slot 2:** General-purpose Perks that increase your effectiveness in direct combat. Match this choice with your weapon and your personal preferences.
- **Perk Slot 3:** Very important support Perks that aid in your battlefield role. Pair them carefully with Perk Slot 1 choices.

8 **Go forth and kick ass.**

CREATE A CLASS UNLOCKS

Weapons in *Call of Duty: Black Ops* are the only Create a Class items that are level restricted. Like all other items in the game, weapons require CODPoints to purchase, even once they're unlocked.

Buying all of the weapons in a weapon class unlocks the final "'Classified'" weapon for that weapon group. These weapons are not necessarily more powerful; they are simply rare or otherwise unusual choices.

ASSAULT RIFLES

ASSAULT RIFLE	LEVEL UNLOCKED	COST
M16	Immediately	0
Enfield	5	2000
M14	9	2000
Famas	14	2000
Galil	20	2000
AUG	26	2000
FN FAL	32	2000
AK47	38	2000
Commando	44	2000
G11	Classified	2000

SUBMACHINE GUNS

SMG	LEVEL UNLOCKED	COST
MP5K	Immediately	0
Skorpion	7	2000
MAC11	11	2000
AK74u	17	2000
Uzi	23	2000
PM63	29	2000
MPL	35	2000
Spectre	41	2000
Kiparis	Classified	2000

LIGHT MACHINEGUNS

LMG	LEVEL UNLOCKED	COST
HK21	Immediately	0
RPK	6	2000
M60	21	2000
Stoner63	Classified	2000

SNIPER RIFLES

SNIPER RIFLE	LEVEL UNLOCKED	COST
Dragunov	Immediately	0
WA2000	10	2000
L96A	27	2000
PSG1	Classified	2000

SHOTGUNS

SHOTGUN	LEVEL UNLOCKED	COST
Olympia	Immediately	0
Stakeout	8	2000
SPAS	24	2000
HS10	Classified	2000

PISTOLS

PISTOL	LEVEL UNLOCKED	COST
ASP	Immediately	0
M1911	2	1500
Makarov	4	1500
Python	18	1500
CZ75	Classified	1500

LAUNCHERS

LAUNCHER	LEVEL UNLOCKED	COST
M72 LAW	Immediately	0
RPG	12	2000
Strela-3	30	2000
China Lake	Classified	2000

SPECIAL

SPECIAL	LEVEL UNLOCKED	COST
Ballistic Knife	15	1500
Crossbow	33	2000

LETHAL

LETHAL	COST	EFFECT
Frag	0	A thrown hand grenade that can be primed before throwing to detonate early or in midair. Bounces and rolls. Detonates 3.5 seconds after pulling the pin. Can be "cooked" by holding the throw button. Crosshair pulses once each second while held.
Semtex	2000	A thrown sticky grenade with a fixed timer. Sticks to players or surfaces on impact. Detonates two seconds after being thrown. Throw can be cancelled by switching weapons. Friendly Semtex shows a blinking green light, hostile shows a red light.
Tomahawk	2000	A thrown Tomahawk! Instantly lethal, can be thrown while reloading or out of a sprint. Can be retrieved. Throw can be cancelled by weapon switching if held.

TACTICAL

TACTICAL		COST	EFFECT
Willy Pete		0	Creates a cloud of smoke. Smoke can be penetrated with an Infrared Scope. Impact causes very brief stun and minimal damage. Tactical Mask negates stun. Detonates one second after being thrown, must hit the ground to detonate. Smokescreen lasts 12 seconds. Causes a Hit Marker if it hits a player.
Nova Gas		1500	Creates a cloud of poisonous smoke. Damages, disorients, and slows targets. Nullified by Tactical Mask Pro. Detonates one second after being thrown. Gas lasts eight seconds.
Flashbang		1500	Blinds targets in the area (including yourself). Degree of blindness depends on proximity and facing. Nullified by Tactical Mask. Detonates 1.5 seconds after being thrown. Can be detonated midair. Disables Equipment and turrets.
Concussion		1500	Stuns targets near the blast zone. Nullified by Tactical Mask. Throws quickly. Detonates one second after being thrown, must hit the ground to detonate. Disables Equipment and turrets.
Decoy		1500	Creates a red ping on the minimap and generates random gunfire noises. Detonates immediately. Decoy lasts for 30 seconds.

EQUIPMENT

EQUIPMENT		COST	EFFECT
Camera Spike		2000	Places a camera that supplants your minimap with the camera view. Press your Equipment button to cycle between camera and minimap views. Ghost Pro enemies do not appear as bright white in camera view.
C4		2000	Places a sticky explosive that can be detonated manually or by other explosions or gunfire. Double-tap reload to quick detonate, or press Equipment button to use detonator manually.
Tactical Insertion		2500	Places a glowing Tactical Insertion that sets your respawn location. Insertions can be destroyed by moving on top of them or detonated with explosives. Can be cancelled while in a Killcam.
Jammer		2500	Places a radar Jammer that shuts down enemy Equipment in its radius and obscures enemy minimaps. The effect is greater the closer the player is to the Jammer. Maximum effective radius is about 100 feet.
Motion Sensor		5000	Places a Motion Sensor that detects enemy movement in a small radius. Can be nullified by Hacker Pro. Effective to about a 60-foot radius.
Claymore		5000	Places a Claymore that detonates if an enemy passes in its frontal arc. Can be destroyed with explosives or gunfire. Frontal arc is about 70 degrees, triggers on targets within 2-3 feet. Can be tripped and evaded with fast footwork.

PERK 1

PERK		COST	EFFECT	PRO EFFECT
Lightweight		2000	Move faster.	No Fall Damage.
Scavenger		2000	Pick up ammo from fallen enemies and replenish Lethal grenades.	Start with extra mags, replenish Tactical grenades.
Ghost		2000	Undetectable by Spy Plane and Blackbird.	Undetectable by Aircraft, Dogs, IR, and Sentries. No red name or crosshair when targeted.
Flak Jacket		2000	Reduces Explosive Damage.	Immune to Fire Damage, can throw back Frag Grenades safely.
Hardline		2000	Killstreaks require one fewer kill.	Can change the contents of a Care Package.
Pro Upgrades		3000		

PERK 2

PERK		COST	EFFECT	PRO EFFECT
Hardened		2000	Increased bullet penetration.	Increased damage to aircraft and turrets, reduced flinch and recoil when shot.
Scout		2000	Hold breath longer.	Faster weapon switching.
Steady Aim		2000	Increased hip-fire accuracy.	Quicker aiming after sprinting, quicker recovery from knife lunges.
Sleight of Hand		2000	Faster reloading.	Faster ADS with non-scoped weapons.
Warlord		2000	Warlord.	Equip two Attachments on primary weapon.
Pro Upgrades		3000		

PERK 3

PERK		COST	EFFECT	PRO EFFECT
Marathon		2000	Longer sprint.	Unlimited sprint.
Ninja		2000	Silent movement.	Completely silent, and enemies are louder.
Second Chance		2000	Pull out your pistol before dying.	Survive longer and teammates can revive you.
Hacker		2000	Detect enemy Equipment and explosives.	Ability to sabotage enemy Equipment, turrets, and crates. Invisible to Motion Sensors.
Tactical Mask		2000	Tactical Mask.	Reduces the effect of Flash and Concussion grenades.
Pro Upgrades		3000		

ATTACHMENTS

SUBMACHINE GUN ATTACHMENTS

ATTACHMENT		COST	EFFECT
Extended Mag		1000	Increases magazine size by roughly 50%
Dual Mag		1000	Greatly speeds every second reload
ACOG Sight		1000	Long-range scope, slower ADS
Red Dot Sight		1000	Medium-range sight
Reflex		1000	Medium-range sight
Grip		1000	Reduces recoil
Grenade Launcher		3000	Launches a non-contact fuse grenade
Rapid Fire		3000	Increases rate of fire
Suppressor		2000	Removes minimap red dot, reduces sound, increases damage falloff
Dual Wield		1000	Doubles rate of fire, greatly decreases accuracy, cannot ADS

ASSAULT RIFLE ATTACHMENTS

ATTACHMENT		COST	EFFECT
Extended Mag		1000	Increases magazine size by roughly 50%
Dual Mag		1000	Greatly speeds every second reload
ACOG Sight		1000	Long-range scope, slower ADS
Red Dot Sight		1000	Medium-range sight
Reflex		1000	Medium-range sight
Grip		1000	Reduces recoil
Masterkey		1000	Adds an underslung shotgun
Flamethrower		1000	Adds an underslung flamethrower
Infrared Scope		2000	Precision scope that highlights enemy targets in white, can pierce smoke clouds
Grenade Launcher		3000	Launches a contact fuse grenade
Suppressor		2000	Removes minimap red dot, reduces sound, increases damage falloff

G11 ATTACHMENTS

ATTACHMENT		COST	EFFECT
Low Power Scope		2000	Precision scope, adds sway
Variable Zoom		2000	Precision scope, multiple levels of zoom

SHOTGUN ATTACHMENTS

ATTACHMENT		COST	EFFECT
Stakeout Grip		1000	Reduces recoil
SPAS Suppressor		2000	Removes minimap red dot, reduces sound, increases damage falloff
HS10 Dual Wield		1000	Doubles rate of fire, greatly decreases accuracy, cannot ADS

LIGHT MACHINEGUN ATTACHMENTS

ATTACHMENT		COST	EFFECT
Extended Mag		1000	Increases magazine size by roughly 50%
Dual Mag		1000	Greatly speeds every second reload
ACOG Sight		1000	Long-range scope, slower ADS
Red Dot Sight		1000	Medium-range sight
Reflex		1000	Medium-range sight
Grip		1000	Reduces recoil
Infrared Scope		2000	Precision scope that highlights enemy targets in white, can pierce smoke clouds

SNIPER RIFLE ATTACHMENTS

ATTACHMENT		COST	EFFECT
Extended Mag		1000	Increases magazine size by roughly 50%
ACOG Sight		1000	Long-range scope
Infrared Scope		2000	Precision scope that highlights enemy targets in white, can pierce smoke clouds
Suppressor		2000	Removes minimap red dot, reduces sound, reduces damage
Variable Zoom		2000	Precision scope, multiple levels of zoom

PISTOL ATTACHMENTS

ATTACHMENT		COST	EFFECT
Upgraded Iron Sights		250	Adds tritium highlights to Pistol ironsights
Extended Mag		1000	Increases magazine size by roughly 50%
Suppressor		2000	Removes minimap red dot, reduces sound, increases damage falloff
Dual Wield		1000	Doubles rate of fire, greatly decreases accuracy, cannot ADS
Python ACOG Sight		1000	Long-range scope, slower ADS
Python Snub Nose		500	Reduces Python damage, reduces Python recoil
Python Speed Reloader		1000	Reloads Python fully in one animation
CZ75 Full Auto Upgrade		2000	Converts CZ75 to a fully automatic machine-pistol

KILLSTREAKS

KILLSTREAK	COST	KILLS REQUIRED	EFFECT
Spy Plane	Free	3	Displays enemy locations on minimap
RC-XD	1200	3	Remote-controlled explosive RC car
Counter-Spy Plane	1600	4	Completely disables enemy minimap
SAM Turret	1600	4	Airdrops a placeable SAM turret that destroys enemy air support
Care Package	Free	5	Airdrops a random Killstreak reward or ammo crate
Napalm Strike	2400	5	Targeted Napalm airstrike
Sentry Gun	3200	6	Airdrops a placeable Sentry Gun
Mortar Team	3200	6	Target three locations to bombard with artillery support
Attack Helicopter	Free	7	Calls in helicopter air support
Valkyrie Rockets	4000	7	Airdrops a Valkyrie launcher with two remote-controlled missiles
Blackbird	4500	8	Displays enemy locations and movement on the minimap, cannot be shot down
Rolling Thunder	4500	8	Targeted massive-bombing airstrike
Chopper Gunner	5000	9	Take control of a high-powered Gatling gun on an orbiting helicopter
Attack Dogs	6000	11	Call in attack dogs that hunt down and eliminate enemy forces
Gunship	6000	11	Take full control of an attack helicopter armed with minigun and rockets
Death Machine	Special	Special	Rarely appears in Care Packages or Hardline Pro switches, grants you a Gatling gun
Grim Reaper	Special	Special	Rarely appears in Care Packages or Hardline Pro switches, grants you a one-use quad-barrel Rocket Launcher

RANK REWARDS AND SPECIAL UNLOCKS

RANK REWARDS

PLAYER RANK	UNLOCKS
4	Create a Class
5	Contracts
6	Clan Tag
8	Game Mode Challenges
10	Killstreaks, Killstreak Challenges, Playercard Emblems
13	Combat Record
15	Medal Challenges
16	Gun Emblems
19	Gun Tag
20	Elite Challenges
22	Camo
25	Custom Reticules
28	Custom Lenses
30	Final Challenges
31	Facepaint
50	Prestige Mode
Prestige 1	Prestige Leaderboard, Custom Class 6
Prestige 3	Custom Class 7
Prestige 5	Custom Class 8
Prestige 7	Custom Class 9
Prestige 9	Custom Class 10
Prestige 11	Face Tattoos
Prestige 13	Clan Tag Colors
Prestige 14	Golden Camo
Prestige 15	Prestige Playlists

SPECIAL UNLOCKS

SPECIAL UNLOCK	COST
Facepaint	500
Emblems	100
Playercard Backgrounds	500
Emblem Layers	100, 200, 300, 400, 1000, 1500 2500, 5000, 5500, 6000, 7000, 8000
Gun Camo	3500
Reticules	500
Lenses	500
Gun Tag Application	1000
Gun Camo Application	1000
Prestige Leaderboards	50000
Clan Tag Colors	250

ATTACHMENT AVAILABILITY

Note that certain Attachments are incompatible when using Warlord.

A weapon can use only one modified magazine and one sight.

Rapid Fire and Dual Wield are incompatible with modified magazines.

Weapon Attachments (Grenade Launcher, Masterkey, Flamethrower) cannot be combined with other Attachments.

		Extended Mag	Dual Mag	ACOG Sight	Red Dot Sight	Reflex	Grip	Masterkey	Flamethrower	Infrared Scope	Grenade Launcher	Suppressor	Variable Zoom	Dual Wield	Upgraded Iron Sights	Snub Nose	Speed Reloader	Full Auto Upgrade
ASSAULT RIFLE	M16	X	X	X	X	X		X	X	X	X	X						
	Enfield	X	X	X	X	X		X	X	X	X	X						
	M14	X	X	X	X	X	X	X	X	X	X	X						
	Famas	X	X	X	X	X		X	X	X	X	X						
	Galil	X	X	X	X	X		X	X	X	X	X						
	AUG	X	X	X	X	X		X	X	X	X	X						
	FN FAL	X	X	X	X	X		X	X	X	X	X						
	AK47	X	X	X	X	X		X	X	X	X	X						
	Commando	X	X	X	X	X		X	X	X	X	X						
	G11																	
SUBMACHINE GUN	MP5K	X		X	X	X			X	X								
	Skorpion	X					X		X	X	X							
	MAC11	X			X	X	X		X	X	X							
	AK74u	X	X	X	X	X	X	X	X	X								
	Uzi	X		X	X	X	X		X	X								
	PM63	X					X		X		X							
	MPL		X	X	X	X	X		X	X								
	Spectre	X		X	X	X	X		X	X								
	Kiparis	X		X	X	X	X		X	X	X							
LIGHT MACHINE GUN	HK21	X		X	X	X				X								
	RPK	X	X	X	X	X				X								
	M60	X		X	X	X	X			X								
	Stoner63	X		X	X	X				X								

Category	Weapon	Extended Mag	Dual Mag	ACOG Sight	Red Dot Sight	Reflex	Grip	Masterkey	Flamethrower	Infrared Scope	Grenade Launcher	Suppressor	Variable Zoom	Dual Wield	Upgraded Iron Sights	Snub Nose	Speed Reloader	Full Auto Upgrade
SNIPER RIFLE	Dragunov	X		X						X		X	X					
	WA2000	X		X						X		X	X					
	L96A	X		X						X		X	X					
	PSG1	X		X						X		X	X					
SHOTGUN	Olympia																	
	Stakeout						X											
	SPAS											X						
	HS10													X				
PISTOL	ASP													X				
	M1911	X										X		X	X			
	Makarov	X										X		X	X			
	Python			X										X		X	X	
	CZ75	X										X		X	X			X

CHALLENGES

Challenges are special tasks that you can complete in any game to earn Experience (XP) and CODPoints.

Some Challenges are simple, merely requiring you to earn kills or headshots with a specific weapon. Others may require you to win a specific objective mode, or to pull off a crazy stunt like killing someone through a wall with an explosive.

New Challenge groups are unlocked as you gain Ranks.

You can reference all available Challenges while in-game at any time via your Playercard.

CONTRACTS

Contracts are special types of Challenges that come in three different categories: Kills and Killstreaks, Game Modes, and finally a catchall category that includes Grenades, Secondary Weapons, Headshots, and others.

Contracts differ from Challenges in that you must specifically select a Contract from each category to pursue, *and* they cost CODPoints to activate.

The benefit? Complete the Contract and earn more cash! The tough part? Contracts are time-limited. Once accepted, you must complete the Contract within the time limit, or you fail and lose your money.

Once accepted, you cannot accept a new Contract in the same category until the timer refreshes, so choose carefully!

Contracts are a good way to earn extra cash, and they encourage you to try new weapons and tactics. They're also a great way to test yourself. As you grow in experience and skill, you can tackle Contracts that might have seemed impossible when you began playing.

The following tables provide just a few examples of the available Contracts. The Contracts available at any given time change, so check back frequently.

CATEGORY 1 EXAMPLES

CONTRACT	DESCRIPTION	BUY IN	REWARD	TIME LIMIT
Contract Killer	Earn 15 kills	25	100 CP	40m
MP5k Cruelty	Earn 25 kills with the MP5k	50	250 CP	40m
Combat Gunsight	Earn 25 kills using the ACOG	50	250 CP	40m
Emperor of the SMG	Get 8 kills using an SMG without dying	150	1100 XP, 1100 CP	40m
Devil from the Heavens	Earn the Gunship Killstreak	250	2500 XP, 2500 CP	40m

CATEGORY 2 EXAMPLES

CONTRACT	DESCRIPTION	BUY IN	REWARD	TIME LIMIT
Cold Efficiency	Finish a match with more kills than deaths	25	100 CP	40m
CTF Beast	Win four CTF matches	100	600 XP, 600 CP	60m
S&D Ripper	Finish an S&D match with twice as many kills as deaths	100	500 XP, 500 CP	40m
FFA Massacre	Get 24 kills in one FFA match	150	1000 XP, 1000 CP	40m
Demolition Colossus	Finish two Demo matches with the highest score	250	4000 XP, 4000 CP	60m

CATEGORY 3 EXAMPLES

CONTRACT	DESCRIPTION	BUY IN	REWARD	TIME LIMIT
Weapon Versatility	Get three kills using any Pistol, Launcher, or Special weapon	25	100 CP	40m
Fragged	Kill seven enemies with Frag Grenades	50	250 CP	40m
Shotgun Shock	Get two kills in one life with the Masterkey	100	400 XP, 400 CP	40m
AK74u Master	Get six headshots with the AK74u	100	600 XP, 600 CP	40m
Brains on Walls	Get 16 headshots with LMGs	250	2500 XP, 2500 CP	40m

WEAPON MAGAZINE SIZES

The following table functions as a quick reference for all weapons in the game, with or without Extended Magazines.

SMG		BASE MAG SIZE	EXT MAG SIZE
MP5K		30	45
Skorpion		20	30
MAC11		20	30
AK74u		30	45
Uzi		32	48
PM63		20	30
MPL		32	N/A
Spectre		30	45
Kiparis		20	30

ASSAULT RIFLE		BASE MAG SIZE	EXT MAG SIZE
M16		30	45
Enfield		30	45
M14		20	30
Famas		30	45
Galil		35	50
AUG		30	45
FN FAL		20	30
AK47		30	45
Commando		30	45
G11		30	45

LMG		BASE MAG SIZE	EXT MAG SIZE
HK21		30	80
RPK		40	75
M60		100	200
Stoner63		30	100

SNIPER RIFLE		BASE MAG SIZE	EXT MAG SIZE
Dragunov		10	15
WA2000		6	12
L96A		5	10
PSG1		5	10

PISTOL		BASE MAG SIZE	EXT MAG SIZE
ASP		7	N/A
M1911		7	14
Makarov		8	12
Python		6	N/A
CZ75		12	18

CALL OF DUTY BLACK OPS

Written by Thom Denick, Phillip Marcus, and the Sea Snipers

DK/BradyGames, a division of Penguin Group (USA) Inc.
800 East 96th Street, 3rd Floor
Indianapolis, IN 46240

ISBN-10: 0-7440-1272-4

ISBN-13: 978-0-7440-1272-9

Printing Code: The rightmost double-digit number is the year of the book's printing; the rightmost single-digit number is the number of the book's printing. For example, 10-1 shows that the first printing of the book occurred in 2010.

13 12 11 10 4 3 2 1

Printed in the USA.

BradyGAMES Staff

Global Strategy Guide Publisher
Mike Degler

Digital and Trade Category Publisher
Brian Saliba

Editor-In-Chief
H. Leigh Davis

Operations Manager
Stacey Beheler

Credits

Title Manager
Tim Fitzpatrick

Sr. Development Editor
Chris Hausermann

Book Designer
Dan Caparo

Production Designer
Tracy Wehmeyer

Acknowledgments

BradyGAMES sincerely thanks everyone at Activision and Treyarch for their exceptional support throughout this project and their generous hospitality at their studios. Very special thanks to Letam Biira, Daniel Shaffer, Joel Taubel, Kap Kang, Jason Harris, Jay Puryear, David Vonderhaar, Aaron Eady, and Leif Johansen for all your help in creating this guide and making it the best it can be—we truly appreciate it!

Thom Denick: I would like to thank Erik Melen and Vince Sinatra for answering questions about Achievements and the Campaign, and for being helpful resources throughout writing this guide. Additionally, special thanks to Micheal Clarke, Tom Chua, and Frank So, who are the Activision experts on Zombies and gave me some good tips—they can get much further than I can! Thanks as well to Glenn Vistante for providing Zork help.

Also, thanks to my Zombies co-op team: Paul Williams, T'Challa Jackson, and Derrick L. Davis.

The Single-Player guide is dedicated to Ji Young Hwang, who was extremely supportive, patient, and helpful.

Phillip Marcus: I've been a fan of Call of Duty multiplayer for a long time, so having a chance to take my pen to helping thousands of Call of Duty fans was an honor and a pleasure.

Thanks go to Rich Hunsinger and the Sea Snipers for their awesome maps and multiplayer advice. I also have to thank Jason Fox, with whom I was up late every night for many months playing Call of Duty online. Last, and most definitely not least, my wonderful girlfriend Daphne, who helped me through a very rough patch when I came down with a nasty illness while writing this guide—I love you!

At Treyarch, thanks to Jay Puryear for welcoming us into their offices and getting us set up; Tristen Sakurada for answering my random queries about multiplayer details; and both Brent Toda and Kevin Worrel, who went out of their way to get needed map materials into Rich's capable hands. Everyone at Treyarch who helped in matters large or small, your contributions are appreciated!

Finally, a very special thanks to the Evilgamer fans out there—you guys are awesome!

Jason Fox: Thanks again to Phil and the Brady team for getting me involved with another *Call of Duty* guide. The guidance within was fueled by Mr. Goodbar and the history of a particularly worldly grandfather. Big thanks to Tristen Sakurada for answering our endless questions. Lastly, another huge thanks to my wife Lindsey and son Jake for tolerating my absence and generally understanding my addiction to gaming.

Rich Hunsinger: Thanks to [SS]Snakebite, a.k.a. Dale Pittman, and [SS]Hobo, a.k.a. Jamison Carroll, for their time, attention to detail, and hard work throughout this project as part of the Sea Snipers Tactical Research And Development Team.

[SS]Rator, a.k.a. Rich Hunsinger

[SS]Snakebite, a.k.a. Dale Pittman

[SS]Hobo, a.k.a. Jamison Carroll

We would like to thank Jay Puryear, Brent Toda, and Kevin Worrel for their hospitality and help while hosting us at Treyarch.

Special thanks to Phil Marcus, Jason Fox, and Thom Denick for their dedication and hard work on this guide.

Extra special thanks to my beautiful wife Kate. She continues to make sure I am well fed and have everything I need to do my job. I love you, baby girl!

THE SEA SNIPERS ARE:

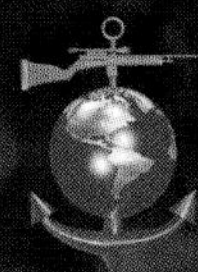

[SS]Bassani
[SS]Chief
[SS]Grunt
[SS]Hobo
[SS]Midnight
[SS]Raiden
[SS]Rator
[SS]Sabotage
[SS]Shooter
[SS]Showstoper
[SS]Snakebite
[SS]SportoFu
[SS]Switters
[SS]Wally